Wales in an Age of Change, 1815-1918

Acknowledgments

This book was commissioned by the Qualifications, Curriculum and Assessment Authority for Wales and is published with their financial support.
Copyright: ACCAC
Editor: Eirlys Roberts
Illustrator: Enfys Beynon Jenkins
Picture Researcher : Gwenda Lloyd Wallace
Printers: Gwasg Gomer
ISBN: 1 85644 769 4

The publisher would like to thank the following for permission to reproduce illustrations in this volume:
Front cover: National Library of Wales (Wales depicted as Owain Glyndŵr, printed by Vincent Brooks, Day and Son, London)

An Introduction to Nineteenth-Century British History 1800-1914, Michael Lynch, reproduced by permission of Hodder and Stoughton Educational Limited p. 42, 43(t), 45(t,c), 51, 58; Hughes and Son p. 48, 49, 96; Department of Industry, National Museum of Wales p. 55(t) (76.35); Mary Evans Picture Library p. 55(b), 60; © Copyright The British Museum p. 61, 273; *Some Aspects of the Spatial Structure of Two Glamorgan Towns in the Nineteenth Century,* Harold Carter and S. Wheatley, *The Welsh History Review*, 1978, University of Wales Press p. 73; Rex Features p. 83; NWP132619 Chartists Attack on the Westgate Hotel, Newport, November 4th 1840, 1893 (litho) by James Flewitt Mullock (1818-92), Newport Museum and Art Gallery/Bridgeman Art Library p. 87; Hulton Archive p. 94, 153, 156(t), 298; The Open University/*Wales 1880-1914*, ed. Trevor Herbert and Gareth Elwyn Jones, University of Wales Press, 1988 p. 98, 99, 104, 105, 203; Museum of Welsh Life p. 102; The Illustrated London News Picture Library p. 113, 356; © David Jones 1989. Reprinted from *Rebecca's Children: A Study of Rural Society, Crime and Protest* by David Jones (1989), by permission of Oxford University Press p. 114, 116, 170; Carmarthenshire Record Office p. 115; Public Record Office p. 119 (HO45/265), 120 (HO52/6); by permission of The British Library p. 125 (LD.22); © Punch Ltd. p. 140, 161, 193, 293; National Library of Wales p. 141 (JHD XI 101), 176, 196, 207, 208, 229, 240, 241, 248, 254 (Folio 189), 324(b, l and r), 326, 327; *A History of Wales* (p. 370) by John Davies (Allen Lane 1993, first published in Welsh, under the title *Hanes Cymru* by Allen Lane The Penguin Press 1990) Copyright © John Davies, 1990, 1993 p.152; BL 22499 *'Just Starve Us. Tell Ah! Tell Us, Can Aught be Worse? Than Hungry Maw and Empty Purse! Mercy Show and Pity Us. Great Overseer'* (print) by Isaac Robert Cruikshank (1789-1856). British Library, London, UK/Bridgeman Art Library p. 156(b); Glamorgan Record Office p. 167; *Crime and Punishment* by Roger Whiting, Her Majesty's Stationery Office/reproduced by kind permission of Ordnance Survey © Crown Copyright NC/01/026, 1986 p. 172; Denbighshire Record Office p. 197; *The Western Mail and South Wales Echo Limited* p. 209, 324(t); *Wales 1880-1914*, ed. Trevor Herbert and Gareth Elwyn Jones, University of Wales Press, 1988 p. 220; Gwynedd Archives Service p. 318; C. Batstone/South Wales Coalfield Collection, University of Wales Swansea (PHO/DIS/25) p. 323; South Wales Miners' Library, University of Wales Swansea p. 328

We wish to thank the team who have been involved with this project: Professor Gareth Elwyn Jones of Swansea University, Vaughan Davies, Gareth Holt, Paul Nolan, Dylan Rees.

Every effort has been made to trace and acknowledge ownership of copyright. The Publisher would be glad to make suitable arrangements with any copyright holders with whom it has not been possible to make contact.

Wales in an Age of Change, 1815-1918

Roger Turvey

I

II

III

IV

V

VI

VII

VIII

IX

X

1

Contents

I
II
III
IV
V
VI
VII
VIII
IX
X

Chapter III
Rural Change and Popular Protest, c. 1830-95
  1. Change
      a) Agrarian Life and Economy
      b) Migration
      c) The Land Question
  2. Protest
      a) Rebecca
      b) The Tithe Wars

Chapter IV
Social Reform and Social Issues
  1. Health
      a) Contemporary Attitudes
      b) Problems in Public Health: Cause and Consequence
      c) Remedy through Reform
  2. Poverty
      a) Attitudes to the Poor and the Treatment of Poverty
      b) Penury and Policy: The Poor Law Amendment Act 1834
      c) Booth and Rowntree
      d) The Liberal Government Welfare Reforms, 1906-14
  3. Crime
      a) Definition
      b) Causes and Nature of Crime
      c) Law and Order
      d) Punishment of Crime

Chapter V
Education and Religion
  1. Education
      a) Schools, Schooling and Scholars before 1847
      b) The Report of the [Blue Books] on the State of Education in Wales, 1847
      c) Education, Educators and the Educated after 1847
  2. Religion
      a) The Religious Census of 1851
      b) Aspects of Popular Belief: Revivals and Revivalism
      c) The 1904-5 Revival
      d) 'A Nation of Nonconformists'?

I
II
III
IV
V
VI
VII
VIII
IX
X

I
II
III
IV
V
VI
VII
VIII
IX
X

I

II

III

IV

V

VI

VII

VIII

IX

X

Preface

1815 to 1918 is one of the most eventful and crucial periods in Welsh history. To do it justice one must examine the main industrial, social, political, religious and cultural developments of this truly dynamic era. However, no history of a century so full and complex as the nineteenth can be completed satisfactorily within the space of a comparatively short volume. Therefore, a book such as this presents an author with a challenge, for in the selection and delineation of the main events and key issues it is almost inevitable that there will be some disagreement over what constitutes main events and key issues. Moreover, in describing those events and in discussing the issues it may be that some have been over-simplified while others have been too heavily pruned, but be assured that the aim throughout has been to provide a concise, readable, source-rich and stimulating introduction to the major themes of nineteenth and early twentieth century Welsh history. Whether this has been achieved is for the readers, and their teachers, to decide since this book has been written specifically for the needs of students studying the subject at AS and A level.

I wish to take this opportunity to thank Glyn Saunders Jones, Director of the Centre for Educational Studies, University of Wales, Aberystwyth, for commissioning me to write this book and for allowing me the freedom to do what I think I do best. I should also like to thank my editor Eirlys Roberts for her unfailing help and support, but especially for her sympathetic understanding of the practical difficulties of putting such a book together when the AS/A courses for which it was designed did not then exist.

Finally, I should like to acknowledge the great debt I owe to the works and ideas of those historians, some of whom are sadly no longer with us, who have so professionally ploughed the field of nineteenth and early twentieth-century Welsh history before me. David V.J. Jones, Gareth Elwyn Jones, Ieuan Gwynedd Jones, Kenneth Morgan, Gwyn A. Williams, John Davies, David Egan, Gareth Evans and David Howell are foremost among those on whose great works I have relied. If this book has any merit it is due almost entirely to them, if it has any weaknesses this is due entirely to me! If the book fulfils its aim in helping students to become certificated, and in the process better historians, then I am sure we will all be well satisfied.

List of Maps, Figures and Tables

List of Maps

List of Figures

I
II
III
IV
V
VI
VII
VIII
IX
X

I

II

III

IV

V

VI

VII

VIII

IX

X

List of Tables

I
II
III
IV
V
VI
VII
VIII
IX
X

I
II
III
IV
V
VI
VII
VIII
IX
X

Approach to Study

1. General

This book is a history of Wales between 1815 and 1918. It is, however, not an entirely conventional history of Wales, for though it is set out chronologically it is not, and was never intended to be, a comprehensive history of Wales. It is designed to give those students starting out on the study of nineteenth and early twentieth-century Wales an accessible and thought-provoking introduction to the subject. As such, it should be used in conjunction with other recommended texts the titles of which are referred to in the suggested further reading sections at the end of every chapter. Besides providing core historical information, the aim of the book is to encourage students to read, think, research and work for themselves. It is therefore, also a workbook containing documents, activities and advice all of which have been designed to meet the demands of the new AS and A level courses currently being offered for examination by the WJEC.

1. The following chart shows the courses and the recommended schemes of assessment which are covered, either in full or in part, by the chapters in this book:

Period Study 3

Aspects of the History of Wales and England, c. 1815-1914

Module	Chapter	Assessment
HI1	Chapter 4	Structured Questions
HI2	Chapters 2, 4, 6, 8	Open-Ended Essays (Historical Interpretation)
HI4	Chapters 6, 7, 8, 9	Open-Ended Essays
HI6	Chapters 1, 2, 4, 6, 7, 8, 9	Open-Ended Essays (Synoptic)

Period Study 4

Aspects of the History of Wales and England, c. 1880-1980

Module	Chapter	Assessment
HI1	Chapters 8, 10	Structured Questions
HI6	Chapters 1, 8, 9, 10	Open-Ended Essays (Synoptic)

I

II

III

IV

V

VI

VII

VIII

IX

X

In-Depth Study 3

Reform and Protest in Wales and England, c. 1830-48

Module	Chapter	Assessment
HI3	Chapters, 2, 3, 4	Single and Multi-Source Document Questions
HI5	Chapter 3	Extended Writing (Evidence-Based Coursework)
HI6	Chapters 1, 2, 3	Open-Ended Essays (Synoptic)

In-Depth Study 4

Change and Conflict in Wales, c. 1900-14

Module	Chapter	Assessment
HI3	Chapters 5, 6, 8, 9	Single and Multi-Source Document Questions
HI5	Chapter 9	Extended Writing (Evidence-Based Coursework)
HI6	Chapters 1, 8, 9	Open-Ended Essays (Synoptic)

2. Key Issues and Key Skills

This book has been written with two basic principles in mind, namely, key issues and key skills (both historical and general).

The key issues are intended to cover the most significant events and themes of the period and the most important ideas, concepts and questions relating to the subject. In this way they should help

- (i) to focus attention on the main elements contained within each chapter
- (ii) to promote knowledge
- (iii) to test understanding
- (iv) to stimulate debate
- (v) to provide a framework for effective and structured note making.

The acquisition and practice of Historical Skills (HS) is the key to success in AS and A level history. These key historical skills include

- (i) acquiring sound factual knowledge
- (ii) source analysis

(iii) evaluating evidence and drawing conclusions
(iv) understanding the nature of historical interpretations
(v) understanding the nature of concepts like change and continuity associated with specific topics and themes over a long period of time, and the causes and consequences of historical events
(vi) personal research and independent study
(vii) the ability to communicate verbally and, more importantly, in writing.

The acquisition and practice of historical skills will help to broaden and develop wider Key Skills (KS) so as to enable AS and A level candidates to demonstrate their ability to fulfil aspects of each of the following

(i) communication
(ii) information technology
(iii) problem solving
(iv) working with others
(v) improving own learning and performance

3. Study Guide for Students

The study guides in this book are entitled **Advice and Activities** and they appear at the end of every chapter. They have been designed to offer brief but practical advice followed by a range of activities which should add to your experience of AS/A level history.

Advice and Activities

At the end of each chapter you will find a variety of activities followed by practical advice, which have been incorporated to further and enrich your studies. The activities have been broadly divided into two sections:

(i) general – reading, research, debate/discussion and source work – covering every chapter and providing opportunities to develop Key Skills;
(ii) examination specific – structured questions, source questions and essays – according to the scheme of assessment recommended in the syllabus and providing opportunities to develop Historical Skills.

I
II
III
IV
V
VI
VII
VIII
IX
X

(i) General

Reading and Research

This is designed to extend the range and depth of your knowledge and understanding and is aimed primarily at those who intend to follow the full Advanced Level (A2) course and who wish to study independently or for preparation for assignments and/or coursework. This should prove useful in helping you to improve your own learning and performance **(KS v)**. At some stage you will likely be required to use the internet and other finding-aids like encarta to aid your research, the results of which could be word processed for submission to your teacher. This should help you demonstrate your competence in information technology **(KS ii)**.

Issues for Debate and/or Discussion

Debate and discussion lies at the heart of good history and you should take every opportunity to practise your historical and key skills by confronting significant issues and problems. This section should help you to think clearly, to plan an argument and to form and express your opinions. This should prove useful in helping you to demonstrate your competence in communication (KS i) and problem solving (KS iii) and could provide opportunities for working with others (KS iv).

(ii) Examination Specific

AS Questions
Structured Questions. (Period Study HI 1)

You will be asked to answer two-part structured questions:

- (i)   The first part of the question will target historical knowledge and understanding – e.g. Explain briefly ...
- (ii) The second part will target historical evaluation and analysis – e.g. To what extent ...? / How far ...?

Open-ended essays (Period Study HI 2)

The questions on this paper will ask you to comment on the validity of one interpretation of a topic you have studied as part of your course. You will be expected to evaluate the interpretation and to construct a coherent argument using your own knowledge both of the topic and of the ways in which it has been interpreted.

Single and Multi-source Document Questions (HI 3)

There are two parts to this paper. In Part A, you will be asked to comment on a single source in three stages. You will be asked

1. to explain the meaning of one phrase from the source;
2. to infer information from the whole source and
3. to assess its strengths and limitations as a source for the topic under consideration.

In Part B you will be given a number of sources to study. Again, there are three parts to the question. You will be asked

1. to compare the content of two of the sources;
2. to compare the reliability of another two;
3. to evaluate the strengths and limitations of all the sources taken together.

A2 Questions

Open-ended essay (Period Study HI 4)

You will be asked to write an essay in response to a general question on a topic you have studied as part of this module. You will be expected to construct a coherent argument to evaluate the opinion expressed in the question.

Assignment (In-Depth Study HI 5)

This unit may be externally or internally assessed. You will be assessed on your knowledge and understanding of a range of sources (between 10 and 15). These will include at least two contrasting historical interpretations, and you will be required to write at length (between three and four thousand words for the internally assessed coursework and for three hours for the externally assessed assignment). You will be expected to consider a range of sources and examine a range of historical interpretations, and to draw reasoned conclusions from them.

Synoptic essay (Period Study HI 6)

Unit 6 is in two parts, one addressing the work you have done as part of your Period Study, the other work you have done as part of your In-Depth Study. In the question on the Period Study, you will be asked to comment on the historian's interpretation of events and developments in the period

I

II

III

IV

V

VI

VII

VIII

IX

X

you have studied. You will be expected to construct a coherent and consistently evaluative synoptic argument, drawing together developments from the entire period you have studied, and from a range of different perspectives, as appropriate.

Synoptic essay (In-Depth Study HI 6)

You will be asked to analyse and evaluate two differing interpretations of events and topics, demonstrating in your answer a synoptic overview of the entire period you have studied from a range of appropriate perspectives.

General Issues

Source questions

In those chapters where the Examining the Evidence sections have been included you will be given an opportunity to Question the Evidence. You might even wish to ask your own questions or, more likely, your teacher will set his/her questions. As you study the Examining the Evidence sections you should do so with a critical eye and never take anything for granted. Check that you understand what each source is saying. Look for the information to be gained from each source, by inference or by deduction, and as you do this, evaluate the source against what you already know.

Essay questions

A key feature of AS/A level history is of course the essay. Mastering the art of essay writing is an essential skill which will take time and effort to learn. The key to success is practice. The lists of essay questions are there for you to practise but they are also useful as guides as to what the key historical issues are for each topic you study. They also provide you with a rough and ready guide to what examiners are looking for and what they are likely to ask in examinations.

The structured essay questions for HI 1 help you to construct your response. The essay questions for the other units are all open-ended, but at both AS and A2 you will be expected to construct arguments and to analyse and evaluate opinions and interpretations. Keep your focus on the questions likely to be asked: "How valid is this interpretation ...? To what extent ...? How far ...?"

These questions do not ask for description or narrative; they ask you to deploy your knowledge and understanding effectively to answer the question.

I

II

III

IV

V

VI

VII

VIII

IX

X

I

II

III

IV

V

VI

VII

VIII

IX

X

Map 1
Counties and Towns of Wales, 1815-1918

Chapter I
Introduction: An Overview of Wales, 1815-1918

1. Industrialisation, Change and Popular Protest

■ **Key Issue:**
In what ways and to what extent did the changes caused by industrialisation affect the people of Wales?

Until the mid- to late eighteenth century the vast majority of Welsh people lived, worked and earned their living on the land. Their lives were dominated by the rhythms of the seasons, by the harvest, village life and rural custom.

The story of Wales during the nineteenth century is one of transition and change. As industry rose in importance agriculture declined, populations moved, villages became towns and, after 1905, some towns grew into cities.

• Industrialisation

South east Wales had been among the first areas in Britain to experience the industrial revolution. The iron and coal industries were the first to be developed, soon to be followed by other heavy industries such as slate, tinplate and copper.

• Urbanisation

The bulk of the workforce were native Welshmen drawn to the valleys of the south-east and lowland plains of the north-east from the rural heartland of the mid, north and west. Between 1860 and 1910 over 320,000 people migrated into the coalfields of south Wales from the Welsh countryside. This

I

II

III

IV

V

VI

VII

VIII

IX

X

in turn led to the rapid urbanisation of the south Wales valleys which managed with some difficulty to keep pace with the massive growth in population.

• **Transport and Communications**

There was a similar revolution in transport and communications. Although the road network was improved the chief means of transporting industrial goods was by rail and sea.

• **Tension and Violence**

In the face of such massive economic and social change there was inevitably tension and sometimes violence. The largely localised and small-scale demonstrations (mainly food riots) and other disturbances of the previous century gave way to large-scale riots, such as at Merthyr in 1831, and mass protest movements like Chartism.

Rural Wales was every bit as 'violent' as urban Wales, indeed, the differences between rural, urban and industrial Wales in the nineteenth century were not as sharp and clear cut as they are sometimes presented. The urban Chartist and rural Rebeccaite did not exist on different planets, they co-existed and sometimes co-operated, some Rebeccaites were also Chartists and vice-versa.

2. Rural Change and Popular Protest

■ **Key Issue:**
What was the nature of change in the countryside and to what extent did it contribute to rural discontent and popular protest?

• **Depopulation**

The development of towns such as Merthyr Tydfil, Cardiff, Pontypridd, Wrexham and Swansea and the opportunities afforded by industrial employment persuaded many to leave the countryside in search of a different, if not entirely better, life. In 1800 around 54% of the population of

England and Wales had lived and worked in the countryside but by 1911 this had fallen to just 20%.

This led to rural depopulation which in time had a marked effect upon the culture and language of the people of Wales.

- **Depression**

Despite the advent of greater mechanisation in the agricultural industry by 1914 Britain was importing over 50% of its food, including around 75% of its grain to make bread.

- **Oppression and Violence**

The oppression of those in ownership and authority led to the formation of secret movements and violent protests, such as the Swing Riots (1830-31) in Kent and south-east England and Rebecca Riots (1839-44) in south-west Wales. In Wales, the Rebecca Rioters and Tithe Agitators sought to make known to the local authorities and national government their deep-seated discontent by refusing payments of tolls and tithes, destroying toll-gates and workhouses and generally causing mayhem until their grievances were dealt with.

3. Social Reform and Social Issues

■ **Key Issue:**
To what extent was there a demand and need for social reform in the period 1815-1918?

In the period between the last decades of the eighteenth century to the early years of the twentieth, it can fairly be said that Wales moved from an 'Age of Enlightenment' to an 'Age of Reform'. The ideas, hopes and ambitions of the people of one age were realised by the people of another.

- **Demand for Reform**

The social reforms envisaged by the great eighteenth-century utilitarian (belief in being useful) and social philosopher Jeremy Bentham (d. 1832)

I

II

III

IV

V

VI

VII

VIII

IX

X

were realised by a new generation of radical thinkers like Edwin Chadwick. Benthamite theories of utilitarianism – the belief that policy and legislation should have a moral edge which strives to achieve the greatest good of the greatest number – was a powerful legacy which influenced governments for much of the nineteenth century.

It was a period of social experimentation in which theory was put into practice though the results were not always those envisaged or expected. This was due, in part, to contemporary ignorance of social issues for which reforms were attempted by those who did not really understand either the issues or the problems. This was especially true in matters connected with health and poverty where those responsible for reforms in both generally enjoyed much the better of the one without ever really experiencing the debilitating effects of the other.

- **Considerations:**

    - **Health**

Public health became a matter for government intervention during the nineteenth century partly on account of the devastating cholera epidemics whose virulence paid little heed of social class. Intervention was based largely on theories about the links between health, clean water supplies and adequate sanitation and for much of the century the health problem was regarded as almost exclusively an urban one.

After 1840 governments were able to identify and analyse significant trends in population because of
- the systematic collection of statistics through decennial Census after 1801,
- the compulsory registration of births, deaths and marriages after 1837
- the widening of the data-collection role of the Registrar-General's Office. One of the most sensitive indicators of a nation's health was the infant mortality rate which recorded the death rate of children under a year old.

- **Crime**

It was during the nineteenth century that crime was first identified as a major social problem – crimes were largely caused by desperate poverty and the threat of starvation – which required urgent remedy. Consequently, the period witnessed
  - the origins of criminology as a scientific discipline,
  - the introduction of local and later national crime statistics.

It was a century of change which embraced the idea of
  - professional police forces
  - the humanisation of the criminal code
  - the greater use of prisons as a form of punishment which were themselves reformed to bring them into line with proposals put forward by the Howard Association and Prison Reform League.

4. Religion and Education

■ **Key Issue:**

To what extent had attitudes to, and the provision of, education changed between 1815 and 1918? How religious were the Welsh and how affected were they by religious change?

- **Religion**

The Church of England or Anglican Church may have been the religion of the state but in Wales it was not universally popular. It was seen by many as the religion of the middle and wealthy classes – the landowner, the mine and factory owner – and, with some exceptions, its services were conducted mainly in English.

In the 1851 Religious Census it was found that only 9% of people who attended a place of worship went to Anglican churches while 87% went to Nonconformist chapels. The Census also found that only a third of the population bothered to attend either church or chapel, religious observance it seems was in decline.

I

II

III

IV

V

VI

VII

VIII

IX

X

I

II

III

IV

V

VI

VII

VIII

IX

X

Nonconformity was generally popular because it brought religion to the people in an exciting way and in a language they could understand. Sometimes the spirit of enthusiasm caused religious revivals like the one that occurred in 1904-5 led by Evan Roberts. As a result of this revival it has been suggested that by 1907 the numbers attending both church and chapel were higher than they had ever been in Wales.

• Religion and Education

The nineteenth century witnessed an explosion of interest in education much of which was inspired by religion. Church and charity schools had gone some way to providing the masses with an education.

• The State and Education

Inspired by the thinking of the philosophers Bentham and John Stuart Mill, Radicals too entered the debate on education. In their view education was a privilege that should be available to all, but this would require state intervention.

The two main questions that politicians had difficulty in answering were:
  (i)   To what extent ought the poor to be educated, assuming that they should be? and
  (ii) What form of provision was needed to effect it, a national or a voluntary system?

It took government fully seventy years before they were ready to answer both and with Forster's Education Act of 1870 they did.

Having mastered the ability to read, the newly-literate turned to secular reading matter which in turn opened up their eyes, and minds, to a wider world. This was an increasingly English world into which, by means of largely free education, the Welsh were slowly absorbed. The old way of life was evolving into the new.

5. Culture, Language and the 'National Revival'

■ Key Issue:

What was the nature of Welsh culture in the nineteenth century and what part did the Welsh language play in the so-called 'National Revival' in Wales?

Culture may be defined as the arts, customs and other manifestations of human intellectual achievement which, when regarded collectively, might be said to define a people and a nation also.

• The Welsh Language

One of the most important elements determining the cultural identity of a nation is its language. The Welsh language has an ancient pedigree and through its use generations of Welsh people have expressed themselves in verse, prose, music, law and religion. This historical and cultural heritage served to preserve in the Welsh a sense of identity.

During the nineteenth century the language came to represent the chief difference between the Welsh and their English neighbours and it was this gradual awareness of themselves as a people as distinct from either the English, Scots or Irish which came to symbolise and gave expression to a growing sense of nationalism. It is this factor in Welsh life that historians refer to as the so-called 'National Revival' or 'National Awakening'

• The Culture

Although nineteenth-century Wales was nowhere near the multi-cultural society it is today, it was a country of broadly three cultures –
  (i)   the 'Welsh' [native Welsh speakers]
  (ii) 'Anglo-Welsh' [native non-Welsh speakers]
  (iii) the immigrant foreigners who spoke only English –
        one or more of which may not have been touched or included in the so-called 'national revival'.

The nineteenth century witnessed the seeding and growth of a new or alternative culture, an Anglo-Welsh culture, if you will, which, by the early

I

II

III

IV

V

VI

VII

VIII

IX

X

decades of the following century, accounted for over half the population of Wales.

At the end of the nineteenth century half the population of Wales was still Welsh-speaking which enabled them, if they desired, to be a part of the cultural tradition that had for generations been based primarily on language, its associated literature both secular and religious, the Sunday School and chapel.

6. Nationalism and Nationalist Movements

■ **Key Issue:**
What were the key features of Welsh nationalism and what factors promoted its growth in the period 1850-1914?

To the outsider, the visitor, the settler and the merely curious, the Welsh were regarded as Welsh-speaking, hymn-singing, poetry and music loving religious zealots of the Nonconformist kind. This was how their culture was defined. It was this almost wholly false or patronising impression of the Welsh which contributed to the shock at having to witness the Rebecca riots and Chartist uprisings.

• **Nationalism**

In common with the rest of Europe the Welsh experienced a surge of interest in nationalism which showed itself most clearly in religion (e.g. Nonconformity), culture (e.g. Eisteddfod), sport (e.g. Rugby) and politics (e.g. Cymru Fydd).

- • Formed in the mid-1880s Cymru Fydd hoped to inspire a cultural and political revolution which might culminate in home rule. Unfortunately, it failed.
- • The reason for the movement's dissolution was the 'deep divisions between the commercial, rich, cosmopolitan southern seaboard and the rest of Wales'.

Welsh separatism or political nationalism was either too weak or too narrow to sustain a movement which aimed at a marriage of the two.

7. Politics and Political Issues

■ Key Issue:

How had politics and the political system changed during the period 1815-1918 and to what extent had people achieved more say in government?

At the beginning of the nineteenth century politics and political power was the privilege and preserve of the rich, by its end almost the entire adult male population had been enfranchised and the rich were forced to share their political power.

- ### • Origins of change – the reasons:

  - the social and economic distress of the early part of the century
  - the religious grievances of Nonconformists which in Wales gave rise to political radicalism.
  - working-class radicalism born of economic distress and social deprivation.

Rioting, such as occurred at Merthyr in 1831, may have been the traditional release valve for social discontent but during the nineteenth century it became ever more politicised.

- ### • Leaders

The Reform crisis prior to 1832 was something of a turning point for it witnessed the emergence of working-class political leaders who were inspired less by native Nonconformity and more by English radicalism led by the likes of Henry 'Orator' Hunt (d. 1835), William Cobbett (d. 1835), Jospeh Hume (d. 1855) and Richard Cobden (d. 1865).

- ### • Reform

For much of the rest of the century the main political issue was reform and only after a series of Parliamentary Reform Acts – 1832, 1867 and 1884 together with the Ballot Act of 1872 – was the issue largely resolved. As a result of these acts the political initiative gradually slipped from the grasp of the rich – the aristocracy in the House of Lords and the landowning landlords in the House of Commons – into the hands of the middle class who secured the votes of the newly-enfranchised poor and working-class.

I

II

III

IV

V

VI

VII

VIII

IX

X

• The Liberal Party

The ascendancy of the Liberal Party in Wales was a truly remarkable phenomenon for not only did it brush aside the challenge posed by the rival Conservative Party, its Welsh representatives in Parliament formed themselves, for a short time, into a loosely-knit 'Welsh Party' which claimed to represent the people of Wales.

• The Labour Movement

By the beginning of the twentieth century the Liberals came under increasing pressure from the new Labour movement which at first it embraced but was soon to reject. The Labour Party announced its arrival on the political scene with the election in 1900 of Keir Hardie for the radical stronghold of Merthyr Tydfil.

Despite their electoral success and rapid growth the thirty years before the outbreak of war in 1914 was dominated not by Labour but by Liberalism and the two outstanding issues yet to be resolved were Disestablishment of the Church in Wales and Home Rule.

8. Social and Industrial Discontent

■ Key Issue:
What was the cause and nature of the conflict between workers and employers in the two decades before the outbreak of war?

• Workers and Employers

The nation's wealth was not evenly distributed and conflict between the haves and have-nots was the social consequence of industrialisation and economic growth.

The haves included the industrialists who were exceptional captains of industry and shrewd businessmen but who seemed incapable or unwilling to understand those whom they employed and commanded.

The have-nots were the workers and their families upon whose hard work, in harrowing conditions, the wealth of the industrialists and of the nation rested. They sacrificed their health for occasional prosperity and regular redundancy but without the means to redress their grievances.

• Reasons for Discontent

In the two decades before the outbreak of war Britain was hit by a wave of bitter strikes and armed clashes that at times all but crippled British industry and the country's economy.

The reasons for discontent were:
- the often arrogant and indifferent attitude of many employers towards their workforce,
- the rise in unemployment which was due largely to foreign competition.

To become more competitive and to combat rising costs in industrial production British employers decided it was easier to cut jobs rather than invest in new technology. Some employers were accused of cutting safety standards – ensuring profits, not considering the lives of their employees.

• Disturbances

The increasing militancy of the trades unions was matched by the obstinacy of employers who turned to central government in order to resolve what they characterised as workers' uprisings organised and led by political agitators. The deployment of troops in these industrial 'hot spots', such as at Tonypandy and Llanelli, came to loom large in industrial relations in pre-war Wales.

9. War and the Impact of War, 1914-18

■ Key Issue:

How significant an event for Wales was the First World War?

• Significance of the War

The Great War, the first truly global war in human history, was an event of massive significance:

- it involved and killed more men, women and children from more countries,
- it introduced and developed new technology,
- it impacted on the world's and the individual nation's economy like no war ever before
- it changed attitudes and traditional patterns of life.
- The illusion of heroic combat gave way to the reality of mud and machine guns, death and destruction the horror of which was more graphically represented than previously through the cinema newsreel.

• Military Service

On the eve of war the Welsh population stood at approximately 2,350,000, of whom nearly 400,000 were men of military age, i.e. between 18 and 40. During the war the number of men who enlisted or were conscripted from Wales was around 280,000, which means that just over 70% of this age group was recruited into the armed forces.

Effects:

- enlistment and conscription impacted on the world of work and on family life. The lives and the attitudes of those who returned from the front would be changed forever.
- equally, those who received the returned back into their lives, their homes, their families and their places of work were affected, if only because they were ignorant of the horror the soldiers had endured and misunderstood the change wrought in their characters and personalities.

- the impact of war on the Welsh economy was significant – patterns of work changed, household income was affected while thousands of women were recruited to work in the factories and on the farms. At the war's end Welsh industry was no longer the dominant force it had been before 1914: trade had been disrupted, markets had been lost and the balance between imports and exports dipped more in favour of one than the other.

- Religion. The war had shattered the belief of many in the existence of God while others, desperately searching for answers to make sense of the carnage, sought out God in church and chapel.

- Welsh culture. Welsh poetry and literature reacted to and reflected on the war in a variety of works by the likes of the playwright and war survivor Saunders Lewis and the poet and war casualty, Hedd Wyn.

- most significantly of all, perhaps, was the liberation of women. Despite an active and increasingly militant campaign, the pre-war suffragette movement had failed to secure the vote for women. The war changed this. The contribution of women to the war effort was recognised and their demand to be represented in Parliament was partially granted in 1918 – to women over 30.

I

II

III

IV

V

VI

VII

VIII

IX

X

Table 1

Timechart/Chronology of Major Events, 1815-1914

	1815	End of Napoleonic Wars. Corn Law introduced.
Ironworkers strike in south Wales and riots at Merthyr Tydfil.	**1816**	
Riots at Carmarthen during food shortages.	**1818**	
	1819	Peterloo 'massacre'.
Colliers' strike in Monmouthshire. First appearance of Scotch Cattle.	**1822**	
	1824	Repeal of the Combination Act which had forbidden trade unions.
Dispute at Penrhyn Quarries.	**1825**	
Repeal of Test and Corporations Act which had disqualified Nonconformists.	**1828**	
	1829	Peel's Metropolitan Police Act in Britain.
First cholera epidemic in Wales. Reform 'crisis'. Merthyr Rising followed by hanging of Dic Penderyn.	**1831**	Lord John Russell introduces first Reform Bill – resigns after its defeat.
Parliamentary Reform Act passed. Religious revival.	**1832**	First Reform Act.
Poor law Amendment Act.	**1834**	
Arrest and trial of Scotch Cattle.	**1835**	
Tithe Commutation Act.	**1836**	
First Working Men's Association formed at Carmarthen.	**1837**	Queen Victoria succeeds to the throne.
Publication of People's Charter.	**1838**	Anti-corn Law League founded.

Chartist disturbances at Llanidloes. Chartist march on Newport. First Rebecca attacks.	**1839**	Chartist riots in Birmingham.
Renewal of Rebecca attacks. Chartist revival and strike in south Wales.	**1842**	
Rebecca at its height.	**1843**	
Formation of Liberation Society. Turnpike Trusts Act – reform.	**1844**	
	1846	Repeal of the Corn Laws.
Commission on Education in Wales ('Blue Books'). Cholera epidemic.	**1847**	
Public Health Act allows Local Boards of Health to be created.	**1848**	Third of Chartist petitions presented to Parliament. Year of revolutions in Europe.
Religious revival.	**1849**	
Census of Religious Worship.	**1851**	
Chartist revival.	**1853**	
	1854-6	Crimean War.
	1855	Tax on newspapers repealed.
Law makes it compulsory for all counties and boroughs to have police force.	**1856**	
Political evictions in Merionethshire following General Election. Religious revival. *Baner ac Amserau Cymru* started by Thomas Gee.	**1859**	
National Reform Union formed to campaign for household suffrage.	**1864**	
First attempt to form trade union at Penrhyn Quarry.	**1865**	Irish Church Act disestablished the 'Anglican' church in Ireland.

I

II

III

IV

V

VI

VII

VIII

IX

X

I

II

III

IV

V

VI

VII

VIII

IX

X

National Reform League founded to campaign for manhood suffrage and secret ballot.	**1866**	
Second Reform Act enfranchises working-class householders in towns.	**1867**	
Liberal victories in Wales in General Election.	**1868**	National Federation of trade unions starts meeting annually.
	1870	Forster's Education Act.
Ballot Act introduces secret ballot.	**1872**	
	1874-6	Major social reforms by Disraeli's government.
North Wales Quarrymen's Union formed.	**1874**	
	1875	Public Health Act.
	1879	Zulu War. Irish National Land League founded.
Liberals – 29 out of 33 seats. Welsh Rugby Union founded. Creation of National Eisteddfod Association.	**1880**	General Election – Gladstone Prime Minister. Education Act – education compulsory for 5-10 year olds.
Sunday Closing (Wales) Act. Report of Aberdare Committee on Education.	**1881**	
Reform Act enfranchises working-class householders in countryside.	**1884**	Parliamentary Reform Act.
Liberals – 30 out of 34 seats.	**1885**	Redistribution Act. General Election (Nov).
Welsh Land League formed. Liberals – 25 out of 36 seats. Beginning of the 'Tithe War'.	**1886**	Irish Home Rule Bill. General Election (July) – Marquess of Salisbury Prime Minister.
Creation of Liberal Federations of North and South Wales.	**1886/7**	

	1888	Local Government Act creates County Councils.
Welsh Intermediate Education Act. Barry Docks opened.	**1889**	
Lloyd George becomes MP for Caernarfon Boroughs.	**1890**	
Tithe Rent Charge Act. O.M. Edwards founds *Cymru* (magazine).	**1891**	
Liberals – 31 out of 34 seats. Cymru Fydd launched.	**1892**	General Election (July) – Gladstone Prime Minister.
Charter for University of Wales.	**1893**	
Royal Commission on Land. Explosion at Cilfynydd colliery killed 250.	**1894**	Tom Ellis becomes Liberal Chief Whip. Earl of Rosebery Prime Minister.
Effective end of Cymru Fydd. Report of Royal Commission on Land.	**1896**	
Creation of Central Welsh Board. Six months stoppage in coal industry. Founding of South Wales Miners' Federation.	**1898**	
Death of Tom Ellis.	**1899**	Outbreak of Boer War.
Liberals - 28 out of 34 seats. Keir Hardie elected ILP MP for Merthyr. Penrhyn Quarry dispute starts.	**1900**	General Election (October) – Salisbury Prime Minister. Taff Vale railway dispute.
'Welsh Revolt'.	**1902**	
Start of religious revival (Evan Roberts).	**1904**	
Wales defeat All Blacks in Cardiff. Cardiff achieves 'city' status.	**1905**	Lloyd George President of Board of Trade.
Liberals – 33 out of 34 seats.	**1906**	General Election – Campbell-Bannerman Prime Minister.
Creation of Welsh Department of Board of Education.	**1907**	

I

II

III

IV

V

VI

VII

VIII

IX

X

I

II

III

IV

V

VI

VII

VIII

IX

X

	1908	Miners' Federation of Great Britain affiliates to Labour Party. H.H.Asquith becomes Prime Minister.
National Library of Wales founded.	**1909**	
Cambrian Colliery dispute. Tonypandy riots.	**1910**	Lloyd George's 'People's Budget' Campaign.
Investiture of Prince of Wales. Two railway-men shot dead by troops in Llanelli.	**1911**	Lloyd George's National Health Insurance Act. National Railway Strike.
Establishment of Welsh Council of Agriculture. Welsh Commission for National Health Insurance Act. *Miners' Next Step* published.	**1912**	
Senghennydd colliery disaster, 439 killed.	**1913**	
Welsh Church Act – Disestablishment.	**1914**	Outbreak of First World War (August).
South Wales Miners' strike.	**1915**	
	1916	Battle of the Somme. Conscription introduced. Lloyd George becomes Prime Minister.
Hedd Wyn killed.	**1917**	Lloyd George wins election.
	1918	First World War ends (November).

Advice

Starting Out

Each chapter aims to provide you with useful background information which, if you have no prior knowledge of the period, should serve you well as a starting point. Take note of the key issues and have them in mind when you read each section. Make good use of the chronological table by referring back to it regularly, you might even wish to add to it by drawing up your own. If you are near the beginning of your course you should make a point of writing down the meaning of any terms that you have not met before. This is a good habit which should be repeated for every chapter you read. The same advice applies to the meanings of words you are not sure of or have not come across before. A dictionary is an essential tool so get into the habit of having one near you at all times and use it.

You may wish to broaden your understanding of the period. If so, then you must be selective in your choice of reading which should be limited to general histories such as those listed below in the section headed Suggested Further Reading.

Reading

Reading is a skill that needs regular practice and, since it is an essential part of AS/A level History, reading effectively is vital for success. How you read will depend on why you are reading.

You read (i) to acquire knowledge (ii) for information (iii) to gain understanding. Reading can also help you expand your vocabulary and improve your written style. Reading books by different authors can (i) give you ideas on how you might vary your approach to written tasks set by your teacher (ii) provide you with a balanced view of a topic (iii) enable you to form your own opinions.

There are a variety of skills which you might employ to make your reading effective, lively and enjoyable.

   (i) scanning – if you are looking for a particular person (Edwin Chadwick), institution/organisation (Cymru Fydd) or event (Merthyr Riot) scan the index. If you are seeking information on a broader issue such as trade unionism or nationalism scan the contents page. As you scan take care to note down the page references on a separate piece of paper, don't try to memorise them.

I

II

III

IV

V

VI

VII

VIII

IX

X

I

II

III

IV

V

VI

VII

VIII

IX

X

(ii) skimming – if you wish to find the key points in a chapter read the first and/or second sentence of each paragraph that makes up that chapter. Writers of history aim to inform and the most effective way of doing this is to express as clearly as possible each key point or idea at the beginning of their paragraphs. Thereafter the writer goes on to explain, develop and illustrate the opening point or idea.

(iii) reading – if you need to acquire a depth of knowledge and/or broader understanding of a topic then you will need to read in detail. You need not read the whole book but only those chapters and/or sub-sections which are relevant and essential to your needs. To get the most out of your reading (i) have a reason, purpose or aim in mind before you begin reading the chapter or sub-section (ii) read the content in one sitting (iii) take a break and then go back to the chapter with a pen and paper to note down key points or ideas. Try always to vary your reading routine, make it interesting and fun.

Making Notes

You may wish or be requested to make notes on the different sections within this and the other chapters in this book. Before you do so it is important that you know why you are making notes and what use you intend to make of them. Arguably, there are three main reasons for making notes:

(i) to aid concentration

(ii) to help clarify and aid understanding

(iii) to have a record for future use such as an aid to revision or help in gathering material for writing essays.

Making notes is a skill that will require practice and it will involve you in active reading so you should have a pen and paper with you. What you write will depend on what you want:

• to make a list of key words and phrases or simply

• to list the meanings of words

• to question what you have read either by writing the questions down as they occur so as to answer them yourself later or, more likely, to ask your teacher to explain them. Or,

• you may want something more comprehensive such as a framework for ideas or a record of the main points and arguments.

This will require a more structured approach to your note-making and there are three main ways of doing this:

(i) summary notes – summarising the main points by writing them out in complete sentences and paragraphs. This will give you a condensed version or précis of the original.

(ii) skeleton plan or outline – this will usually consist of a brief list of words and phrases which can act as a trigger for memorising the key points of a chapter.

(iii) summary diagram – this might consist of questions or brief explanations laid out in a spider or other form of diagram usually revolving around central title or issue.

Of course, do not forget the key issues, your answers to them might well provide you with the summary of the chapter you need.

Research

You are likely to be asked to undertake some research or independent study during the course of your studies. If so, you must be prepared, focused and organised. Research begins with reading: scanning the bibliography, selecting the book or article, and skimming the content until you are confident you know why you want to read that particular publication. What you read will depend on what you expect or what is expected of you by your teacher and by the demands of your syllabus. You will not be expected to read every book and article listed in the Suggested Further Reading Sections, you simply will not have the time. Therefore, you must make critical decisions on what you need to read or what is recommended for you by your teacher.

One of the best ways to approach new topics or subjects is by using historical dictionaries which offer quick and easy references to key people, events and institutions. The following reference books can be found in most town or school libraries and should prove invaluable for your studies.

Dictionary of British History

Dictionary of Labour Biography

Dictionary of National Biography

Dictionary of Welsh Biography

The Oxford Companion to British History

The following work of reference provides the most recent and comprehensive list of important publications on the history of Wales. Check the entries carefully and be selective in your choice of reading.

P.H. Jones (ed.), *A Bibliography of the History of Wales* (Cardiff, 1989, microfiche edn.).

Don't forget to use the latest study guides and make use of the Internet!

I

II

III

IV

V

VI

VII

VIII

IX

X

For the most efficient ways of surveying nineteenth-century English history look up the latest study guides such as those published by Letts: D. Weigall & Michael Murphy, *Modern History A Level Course Companion* (Letts Study Aids) and Longman: E. Townley, *A level and AS Level Modern History* (Longman Revise Guides).

Preparing for Examinations

Here are some helpful hints.

(i) Needless to say revision remains at the heart of examination success but AS/A Level History is more than simply learning about what happened, it is about why and how things happened. Therefore, knowing your work will not be enough you must use what you know since knowledge alone often results in narrative/descriptive answers. Remember, you will never be asked just to describe what happened. Using the historical skills you have learnt will help you argue, debate and question issues which will make for a more comprehensive and relevant answer. Your revision must reflect this approach so you should aim to interrogate the information rather than just learn the information itself.

(ii) Know your syllabus and the number and structure of your examination papers. By all means use study guides but make sure you look at and use the past papers of your particular examination syllabus. Knowing what to expect before you go into the examination room will give you confidence and help banish your fear of the 'unknown'. Plan the way you intend to tackle the examination before you go in. Be clear about the choice of questions on offer and always aim to answer your best/strongest first and leave the worst/weakest until last.

(iii) Look at past mark schemes as well as past papers.

(iv) In the examination itself, stay calm, skim-read the whole paper and choose your questions carefully. Read the questions carefully, note down the key words and be aware of any dates. Make a brief written plan before you answer each question and pace yourself as you write. Remember, quality not quantity.

(v) Remember what the target of each question is, and focus on that in your answer. You will not gain marks for detailed evaluation if the question asks for a brief explanation, but neither will you gain marks for a long description when the question asks for analysis and evaluation.

Chapter II
Industrialisation, Change and Popular Protest

1. Industrialisation and Change

■ **Key Issue:**
To what extent did nineteenth-century Wales experience an industrial and urban revolution?

a) The Main Industries

In order of size, wealth, employment and economic importance, the main industries in nineteenth-century Wales were coal, iron (and related metallurgical industries), slate and wool. Their location and development did much to change Wales for in consequence of their existence:

(i) a large percentage of the population moved and the resulting migration led to rural depopulation

(ii) many people found new working opportunities so that the traditional pattern of work and skills changed

(iii) people exchanged a rural for an industrial lifestyle which led to massive urban growth in south-east Wales

(iv) emigration, immigration and migration affected the cultural development of Wales which contributed to an overall decline in the Welsh language.

I
II
III
IV
V
VI
VII
VIII
IX
X

I

II

III

IV

V

VI

VII

VIII

IX

X

Map 2

Industrial Wales by 1885

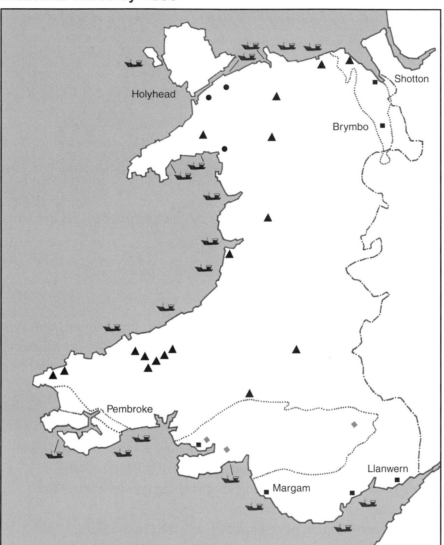

What were the key statistical features of Welsh and British industry?

Listed in order of size and economic importance, the following industries were dominant in Wales:

  (i) Coal

 (ii) Iron and steel

(iii) Copper, Zinc, Tinplate and other metals

 (iv) Slate

  (v) Wool

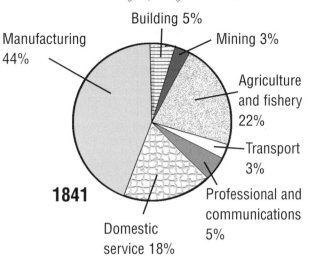

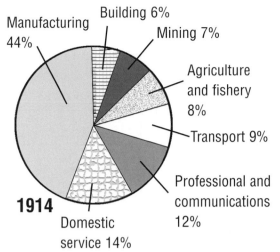

Fig. 1
Pie charts showing the occupations of British workers in 1841 and 1914

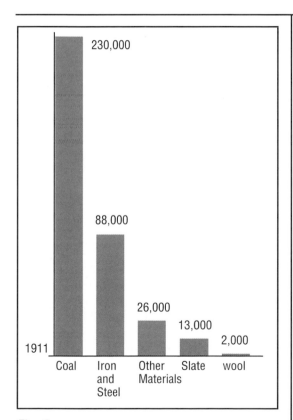

Fig. 2
Graph showing the numbers employed in Welsh industry (1911)

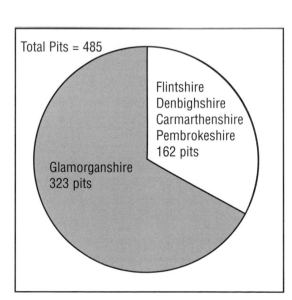

Fig. 3
Pie chart showing number and distribution of coal mines in Wales (1911)

I

II

III

IV

V

VI

VII

VIII

IX

X

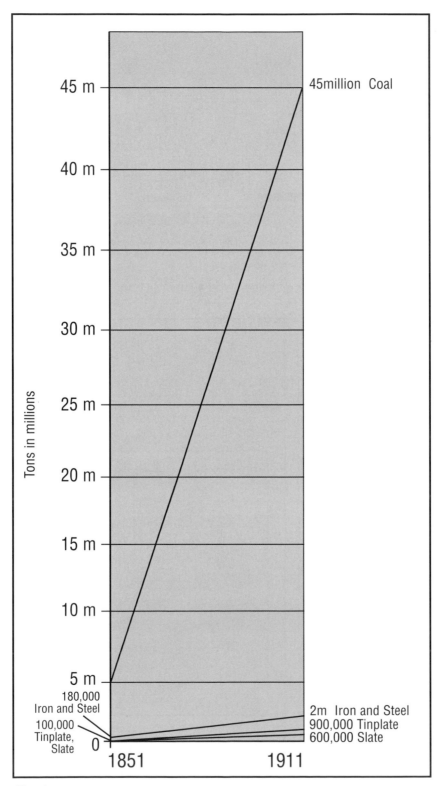

45million Coal

2m Iron and Steel
900,000 Tinplate
600,000 Slate

180,000 Iron and Steel

100,000 Tinplate, Slate

Tons in millions

45 m
40 m
35 m
30 m
25 m
20 m
15 m
10 m
5 m
0

1851   1911

Fig. 4
Graph showing industrial production in Wales (1851-1911)

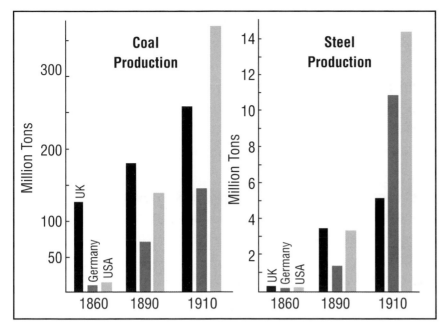

Fig. 5
Graphs showing
British, American
and German coal
and steel production
1860-1910

Fig. 6
Graph showing
Britain's share of
world trade (1800-
1918)

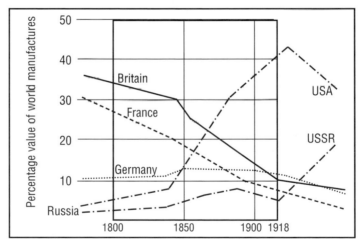

Fig. 7
Coal exports from major Welsh Ports in 1875

Milford	Llanelli	Swansea	Cardiff	Newport
↓	↓	↓	↓	↓
47,000 tonnes	283,000 tonnes	770,000 tonnes	3,578,000 tonnes	1,028,000 tonnes
↓	↓	↓	↓	↓

I

II

III

IV

V

VI

VII

VIII

IX

X

I

II

III

IV

V

VI

VII

VIII

IX

X

Who were the key players in the development of Welsh industry?

These were known collectively as the 'Captains of Industry', men who, by their skill, energy and wealth, had revolutionised their respective industries. However, by their very nature these were hard men driven by single-minded ambition and they did not always prove to be kind men or at least men who understood or sympathised with their workers.

(i) The Coal Kings

- Walter Coffin was among the earliest. He was possibly the first to see the potential benefits of breaking free from the control of the ironmasters of south Wales to become an industrialist of independent means.
- David Davies – a man of considerable energy who promoted and developed the independence of the coal industry which by his time had overtaken the iron industry in importance.
- David Alfred Thomas (later Baron Rhondda), arguably, the most powerful of them all, whose determination to become the most successful industrialist in south Wales led him to establish, in 1908, the Cambrian Coal Combine, a company worth £2 million. However, he was not popular and was accused of profiteering by the unions who resented his refusal to discuss pay and conditions for his workers which by 1910 numbered some 12,000. His company's decision to sack 900 miners in the Rhondda, a recurring feature of his management style, was partly responsible for the riots that followed in Tonypandy. As a businessman Thomas was highly successful and by the beginning of the Great War he was among the richest and most influential of the industrial 'kings' of Wales.

(ii) The Iron Masters

The iron masters were the first to develop and dominate Welsh heavy industry. The iron industry was dominated not so much by individuals but by family dynasties. The Crawshays, Guests, Wilkinsons and Bacons were well known to their considerable workforce and beyond, for it was largely as a result of their efforts that Merthyr Tydfil became established as the largest town in Wales and among the most powerful in Britain. However, this was a mixed blessing for the likes of William and Richard Crawshay, John Guest, Isaac Wilkinson and Anthony

Bacon who ruled with a rod of iron and did little to improve the slum conditions endured by the majority of their workforce. It was weak leadership and conflicting signals from the pro-radical William Crawshay II which partly contributed to the outbreak of the Merthyr Rising in 1831. The swing between the benevolent paternalism of the son and brutal suppression of the father (William Crawshay I) confused and angered the working masses of Merthyr many of whom, encouraged by radicals and influenced by trade unionism, came to hate the masters and everything they stood for.

(iii) The Slate Magnates

The premier slate magnate of north Wales was undoubtedly the Pennant (from 1841 the Douglas-Pennant) family of Penrhyn. Unlike most of the industrialists of south Wales, the Pennants (described by Gwyn A. Williams as 'a bunch of Liverpool merchants' though they had acquired the title of Barons Penrhyn!) were first and foremost landowners and landlords of vast rural estates in north-west Wales. They were generous landlords who treated their rural workforce well but they rarely saw eye to eye with the quarrymen who worked in their rapidly developing slate quarries. To maximise profits the Pennants were determined to cut across traditional patterns of work so they attempted to do away with the difference between skilled and unskilled labour, sub-contracted work, forbade the formation of trade unions and were prepared to employ blackleg labour if their workers complained. The result was one of the longest and bitterest disputes in the history of industrial Wales.

What were the key features of transport and communications?

In order for an 'industrial revolution' to occur a 'revolution' in transport had to happen as well. Without sound communications the industrial products of the mines, quarries, foundries and mills could not be transported to their markets or exported in trade. Economic necessity was the driving force behind the transport revolution and in a period spanning two centuries three transportation systems were developed – roads, canals and railways. Their construction and repair created thousands of jobs for native and migrant workers which in turn, added to the industrialisation of Wales.

I

II

III

IV

V

VI

VII

VIII

IX

X

47

I

II

III

IV

V

VI

VII

VIII

IX

X

(i) Roads

> What am I to say of the roads in this country! The turnpike! as they have the occasion to call them and the hardiness to make one pay for. From Chepstow to the half-way house between Newport and Cardiff, they contain mere rocky lanes, full of hugeous stones as big as one's horse, and abominable holes. The first six miles from Newport, they were so detesable and without direction-posts or milestones, that I could not well persuade myself I was on the turnpike, but had mistook the road!

Farmer, journalist and foremost writer on and popularizer of the 'Agricultural Revolution', Arthur Young was left deeply unimpressed by the roads he found on visiting Wales. His experience was such that he vowed never again to visit the country. What Young had described in 1768 was to be echoed by later travellers for much of the next century. To make matters worse the care, repair and running of these roads was eventually to lead to conflict and riots in south-west Wales.

Map 3

The Road Network in Wales (by 1850)

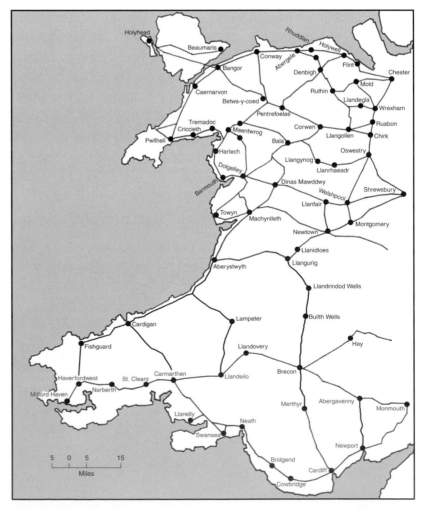

(ii) Canals

Although the canals of Wales were never as extensive or as important as those of England they did experience a golden age between 1760 and 1819 when industrialists were seeking to cut costs and by-pass the shoddy and expensive road system.

Map 4

The Welsh Canal Network (1766-1819)

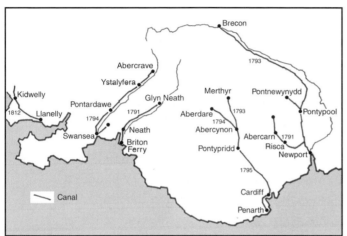

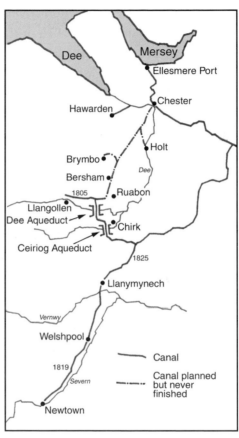

(iii) Railways

> In the year 1791 there was not ... one yard of iron rail-road in South Wales: in September 1811 the completed rail-roads, connected with canals, collieries, iron and copper works, in the counties of Monmouth, Glamorgan and Carmarthen, amounted to nearly 150 miles.

To contemporaries like the north-Wales cleric, poet and *eisteddfodwr* Walter Davies (Gwallter Mechain), the rapid development of rail transport and industrial expansion was nothing short of miraculous. If he was impressed by these early railroads, which were nothing more than tramways along which wagons were drawn by horses, one can but imagine

I

II

III

IV

V

VI

VII

VIII

IX

X

his wonder at the development, some thirty years later, of the railway. By the time of his death at the advanced age of 88 in 1849, he had witnessed the ultimate in transportation technology for the railway was surely the true revolution in transport. It is perhaps fitting that the very first steam locomotive 'Trevethick's High Steam Tram Engine' was built and trialled at the centre of Welsh iron-making at Merthyr. By 1839 railway construction had commenced in Wales and almost from the beginning of its development the country was gripped by 'railway mania'. Among the first lines to be completed was the Taff Vale Railway (1841) which connected the iron foundries of Merthyr with the port facilities of Cardiff. The easier transport and increased export of iron and steel benefited the foundries at Merthyr which also provided the rails upon which the goods were carried.

Railway entrepreneurs included the coal-king David Davies who not only built Barry docks but drove the railway into the heart of Wales, including his own home village of Llandinam, in the belief that it would result in a flowering of Welsh manufacturing industry. However, contrary to Davies' belief, the building of railways had a quite different effect on Wales for not only did it result in a flood of visitors from across the border, it widened the horizons of Welsh people also. By the 1880s even some of the remoter parts of Wales had their railway stations the effect of which was massive social and cultural change. One notable casualty of this process of change was the Welsh language which was put under tremendous pressure by the close proximity to and influence of English people, speech and way of life.

Some historians are even prepared to go as far as to say that what centuries of government from London had failed to do to change the language and culture of Wales the railways did in a few short decades. As in the case of canals, the construction of railways created employment opportunities the majority of which were taken up by non-Welsh speaking migrant workers.

Map 5

The Development of the Rail Network (1825-1914)

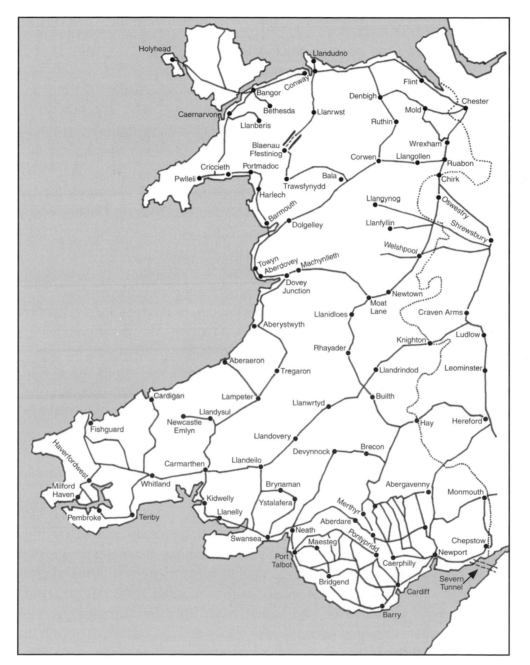

I
II
III
IV
V
VI
VII
VIII
IX
X

b) Industrial Life, Working Conditions and Factory Reform

Industrialisation was advantageous in the long term, but by no means a blessing for all who lived through it. Life for the industrial worker was hard:

- 12 to 14 hour days,
- variable pay and insecure employment,
- lack of safety measures or sickness benefit,
- slum housing, poor sanitation and polluted drinking water.

Although these horrific conditions did not apply to all workers, even among contemporaries the general consensus of opinion was that the lot of the mine and factory worker was far from satisfactory. Of course, this opinion was held most strongly by those calling on the government for reform, men like Robert Owen, Michael Sadler and Richard Oastler who shared a belief in the principles of humanitarianism i.e. a concern for the relief of human suffering. They were disturbed by the grim working conditions which industrialisation had brought and though they tried to improve the lot of their workers (Owen and Sadler were themselves factory-owners) they realised that more needed to be done for workers across Britain which is why they advocated factory reform. Among the most passionate and effective supporters of factory reform was Ashley Cooper (d. 1885) (or Lord Ashley until he inherited his father's title of Earl of Shaftesbury in 1851). In a political career spanning some sixty years, he promoted a succession of reform measures e.g. the Ten Hour Bill; the 1842 Mines Act; reform of the lunacy laws; abolition of child chimney-sweeping; public health and slum housing; the plight of agricultural labourers; training for destitute children (Shaftesbury homes); but perhaps most important of all, the 1833 Factory Reform Act.

Owen and Sadler's humanitarianism was not generally shared by their fellow mine and factory owners who seemed to have little sympathy for the plight of their workforce and who tended to judge matters in terms of profit and loss. In their defence it must be remembered that they too were overwhelmed by the scale and rapidity with which industrialisation took effect in Britain and they were often at a loss on how best to deal with the bewildering variety of problems associated with an ever expanding workforce. For example, they built to house their workforce, building too quickly and too cheaply perhaps, but the slums that were created were often as much the fault of those who lived in them as of those who let them out on rent. Very often even the workers themselves were opposed to factory reform, particularly when it involved restrictions and regulations placed on working women and children. Many families had become dependent on the earnings of wives, sons and daughters which meant they could ill-afford to lose the income. This very point was used by some employers to argue the case against factory reform. Since Parliament was the only body capable of legislating and enforcing new regulations it was here that the issue of factory reform would be won or lost.

In order to debate the issue evidence had to be gathered which took the form of written reports and visual representations. As the following extracts show, the plight of children especially caught the attention of MPs and much is revealed in them about the attitudes of contemporaries.

Examining the evidence

A

Mr. [blank] remarked that nothing could be so beneficial to a country as manufacturers. 'You see these children, Sir,' said he, 'In most parts of England poor children are a burden to the parish; here the parish is rid of all expense; they get their bread almost as soon as they can run about, and by the
5   time they are seven or eight years old bring in money. There is no idleness among us; they come at five in the morning; they leave work at six, and another set relieves them for the night; the wheels never stand still.' I was looking while he spoke, at the dexterity with which the fingers of these little creatures were playing with the machinery.

[The poet Robert Southey interviewing a cotton mill owner in *Espriella's Letters from England* (1809)]

I
II
III
IV
V
VI
VII
VIII
IX
X

B

The cruelties which are inflicted personally upon the little children not to
mention the immensely long hours which they are subject to work, are such
as I am very sure would disgrace a West Indian plantation ... I know many
cases of poor young creatures who have worked in factories ... worn down by
the system ... who, after living all their lives in this slavery ... are kept in   5
poor-houses, not by the masters for whom they have worked, as would be the
case if they were negro slaves, but by other people ...

[Evidence of Richard Oastler from *Report of the Committee on the Bill to
regulate the labour of children in the mills and factories ...* (1832)]

C

Factory Labour is ... less irksome than that of the weaver, less arduous than
that of the smith, less prejudicial to the lungs, the spine and the limbs than
those of the shoemaker and the tailor ... The only thing which makes factory
labour trying even to delicate children is that they are confined for long hours
and deprived of fresh air; this makes them pale, and reduces their figure, but
it rarely brings on disease.

[Edward Baines, a Leeds businessman, newspaper proprietor and author of
History of the Cotton manufacture in Great Britain (1835)]

D

Q. At what time in the morning, in the busy time, did these girls go to the
    mills?
A. In the busy time, for about six weeks, they have gone at 3 o'clock in the
    morning and ended at 10, or nearly half past at night.
Q. What was the wage in the short hours?   5
A. Three shillings a week each (15p).
Q. When they wrought those very long hours what did they get?
A. Three shillings and sevenpence halfpenny (18p).

[Interview with a child worker in *Report of Committee on Factory Child
Labour* (1831)]

In the days before adequate photographs, drawings such as those below
were the only way of conveying the reality of the conditions being discussed
in Parliament by MPs.

E

Fig. 8: Iron works at Abersychan

F

Fig. 9.

Contemporary illustration of Lord Ashley (Shaftesbury) seeing for himself the working conditions of children

I

II

III

IV

V

VI

VII

VIII

IX

X

Table 2

Principal Acts of Parliament Concerning Factory Reform

1819	Peel sponsored Factory Act	• prohibited the employment of children under 9 • children aged between 9 and 12 to work no more than a 12 hour day.
1833	Ashley's Factory Act	• children under 9 not to be employed in textile factories • children aged between 9 and 12 to work no more than nine hours a day • children aged between 13 and 18 to work no more than a 12 hour day.
1842	Mines Act	• abolished female labour • boys under 10 banned from working underground • inspectors to be appointed to enforce regulations.
1844	Ashley's Factory Act	• children under 13 to work no more than a six hour day • females and young persons under 18 not to work more than 12 hours.
1847	Fielden's Factory Act	• established the 10 hour day for female and young male workers.
1850	Grey's Factory Act	• gave factory inspectors greater powers.
1864	'Climbing Boys Act'	• prohibited chimney sweeps to use children under 16.
1878	Consolidating Act	• regulated all factory inspection under one set of rules.

c) Urbanisation

Every colliery creates its own small town of 6,000 or 7,000 inhabitants; and where the workers are well paid the whole character of the town is different. In South Wales and Monmouthshire, in those towns where wages are high, there is always a large Workmen's Institute with a fine hall, occupying a commanding position.

In his book *The British Coal Trade* (1915), H.S. Jevons captures the essence of what industrialisation meant to some parts of Wales. Industrial Wales witnessed the mushroom growth of new towns and new communities but the pace and nature of that change was not uniform. While some areas experienced the effects of urban growth others remained relatively rural and unspoilt. The nature of these industrial towns varied also. In the wealthier and healthier open coastal plains there was a greater opportunity for planning and proper regulation (though this did not always happen). But in the upland regions housebuilding and the physical limitations of narrow valleys often led to squalid, dangerous and overcrowded conditions. Only the well-to-do could afford to buy the best land and build the best houses. These were usually situated apart from the packed urban sprawl in which the less fortunate were condemned to live.

Beginning, in the words of I.G. Jones, as 'condensations of people', community life in these 'industrial colonies' was lively and with no little variety. Public buildings such as libraries, workmen's institutes, churches, chapels, schools, community and town halls soon followed their foundation. Pubs and drinking clubs also witnessed a mushroom growth but were followed by Nonconformist-sponsored temperance societies determined to root out the demon drink, and its associated evils. The unregulated and hastily-built dwellings quickly turned into slums in which open sewers lay side by side with water pumps intended for drinking. Brothels and gambling dens too found a place in these industrial towns each of which could lay claim to a thriving underworld of crime. 'The very names of Merthyr Tydfil and Newport were', in the opinion of David Jones, 'synonymous with violence, drunken behaviour and petty theft.' In fact, he argues that 'The most industrialised of the Welsh counties were notorious in Britain for the sharp rise in their criminal statistics'. Crime ridden and unhealthy in places they may have been but these towns became important commercial centres with shops, markets and other vital business premises.

I
II
III
IV
V
VI
VII
VIII
IX
X

57

I

II

III

IV

V

VI

VII

VIII

IX

X

The development of the railway promoted their growth and linked them together more effectively and efficiently while the port-towns established themselves as centres of European and world trade. Gradually, the influx of a culturally-diverse population, the effects of the creation of wealth and the influence of government regulation transformed some of these towns into large, attractive, well-built and self-governing municipalities. Cardiff especially witnessed unprecedented growth which, as a direct result of trade, money, industry and immigration, changed into the largest urban centre in Wales. In 1905 Cardiff became the capital city of Wales and within its boundaries were built an university, sports stadia, fine Baroque buildings such as the city hall and the national museum. By 1914 the city could also boast a fine park, Cathays, located at its centre. Cardiff was built on the wealth and opportunities brought by coal which by 1913 had become king of the Welsh industrial economy.

Map 6

Population Growth and Urban Development in Britain (1801-1901)

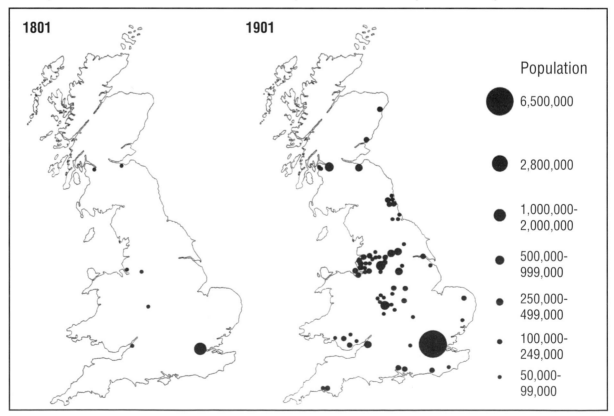

According to the Census of 1861 about one-third of the population of Wales were estimated to be urban which means that for the purposes of local government statistics they were classed as living in towns, parliamentary boroughs or districts. This population growth can be illustrated by a selection of statistics (Calculated from Census Returns: 1801-1901) for both Welsh industrial towns and districts.

Table 3

Growth of selected Welsh industrial towns and districts (1801-1901)

District	1801	1851
Tredegar/Uchlawrcoed	513	15,424
Blackwood/Mynydd Islwyn	1,846	8,633
Town	**1851**	**1901**
Cardiff	18,351	164,333
Merthyr Tydfil	46,378	69,228
Newport	19,323	67,270
Swansea	21,533	94,537

By 1911 two in every three Welshmen and women were town dwellers so that Wales became the first country in the world in which more people lived in urban rather than in rural districts. Neil Evans is surely right to claim that 'By the end of the nineteenth century industry, not land, was the pulse of Wales'.

2. Protest

■ **Key Issue:**
'A nation racked by riot and revolution'. How apt is this description of Wales between 1815 and 1885?

The period after the end of the Napoleonic War in 1815 proved to be a turbulent time in Wales. The country was racked by popular protest due to widespread discontent over various social, economic and political

I
II
III
IV
V
VI
VII
VIII
IX
X

59

grievances. Nor was this peculiar to Wales, in England too there were demonstrations, protests and riots chiefly over the price and, in some areas, the lack of basic foodstuffs. The cities of London and Manchester witnessed some of the worst disturbances, for example:

(i) the Spa Fields Riots of 1816 – a crowd of workers had gathered for a political meeting and to hear a leading radical, Henry Hunt (nicknamed the 'Orator') speak to them on parliamentary reform. Some in the crowd became too agitated and following the looting of nearby shops and march on the city they were scattered by the forces of the Lord Mayor.

(ii) the 'March of the Blanketeers' in 1817 – a group of Manchester cotton workers planned to march to London where they hoped to present a petition to the government, but before they could do so their leaders were arrested and the marchers dispersed.

(iii) the St. Peter's Fields Riots of 1819 – fearing the size of the crowd being addressed by Henry Hunt in Manchester on the benefits of parliamentary and social reform, the magistrates took the drastic step of reading the Riot Act to disperse them. When they did not, a troop of cavalry was ordered to charge them killing eleven and injuring over 200. This became known as the Peterloo Massacre. Hunt's speeches were later translated into Welsh and circulated in Wales.

Fig. 10
A contemporary cartoon depicting the Peterloo Massacre (1819).
The commanding officer is shouting 'Down with 'em! chop 'em down my brave boys. Give them no quarter'

Fig. 11
Contemporary cartoon pouring scorn on the Corn Law

The landowners in Parliament passed the Corn Laws to maintain a high price for corn and high incomes for themselves. The Corn Laws were highly unpopular and were a frequent target of the mob and a popular slogan for the rioter.

In Wales too the Riot Act of 1716 was used – Merthyr in 1831, Newport in 1839, Carmarthen and Pontarddulais in 1843 – to disperse large crowds because once read the magistrates were empowered to use whatever force they thought necessary to end the gathering. Below is an extract from the Act:

> Our Sovereign Lord the King (Lady the Queen) chargeth and commandeth all persons being assembled immediately to disperse themselves, and peaceably to depart to their habitation or to their lawful business, upon pains contained in the Act made ... for preventing tumultuous and riotous assemblies. God Save the King /(Queen).

I
II
III
IV
V
VI
VII
VIII
IX
X

Following the French Revolution of 1789, which in turn led to the overthrow and execution of the king, most western European governments, Britain included, were fearful of the same happening in their country hence the use of suppression to put down protests and demonstrations and repression to destroy workers clubs, reform leagues and trade unions. Economic depression, social injustice, political exclusion, poverty and periodic famines made worse an already volatile situation.

The formation of the National Union of the Working Classes in the 1820s shows that the working masses were slowly being organised and mobilised. Whereas the growing power and strength of the working class was feared by those in authority, mainly the propertied classes, it was celebrated elsewhere most notably by Nonconformist radicals. During the Rebecca Riots the Baptist periodical *Seren Gomer* tried to show that the power of the ordinary people had changed history and that the rioting Welsh folk of south-west Wales were only continuing this tradition – 'Beca is the country ... it was Beca who obtained the Charter from King John (1215), who severed the head of Charles I (1649) and who won the Independence of America (1776); Beca executed Louis XIV (1793), Beca won the Reform Bill' (1832). The attitude and atmosphere of the time can best be summed up by the slogan adopted on behalf of the working classes in 1838 by the Rev. David Rees, editor of the Independent periodical *Y Diwygiwr, 'Cynhyrfer! Cynhyrfer! Cynhyrfer!'* ('Agitate! Agitate! Agitate!').

a) Working-Class Consciousness

> The extent to which Britain was a class society during the period of the industrial revolution has long been a matter of debate amongst historians. By the 1840s there was a general acceptance that a working class had emerged, with its own values and ambitions. In a number of regions this class consciousness reached such an intensity that the authorities were seriously alarmed.
>
> [David J.V. Jones, 'Scotch Cattle and Chartism', in *People and Protest: Wales 1815-80* (1988)]

One of those areas of Britain in which 'class consciousness' had developed early and had reached an 'intensity' was in Wales, or more particularly, and in the opinion of at least two historians, Merthyr Tydfil.

When the Welsh working class is conjoined to Merthyr the noun is 'birth' and the adjective 'first'. What occurred in Merthyr even before the 1840s can only really be comprehended through such metaphor.

[David Smith, *Wales! Wales?* (1984)]

Professor Smith's opinion is supported by the Merthyr-born historian Gwyn A. Williams who believed that it was the working-class rebellion in Merthyr in 1831 which gave birth to the notion of a 'working class' in Wales. On the other hand, it might be argued that it was the fact that the 'working-class' were more than simply a notion which gave rise to the rebellion in Merthyr! The rioters at Merthyr were, after all, like-minded men who had come together and organised themselves if only to protest. To feed the insatiable demand for labour in the rapidly expanding iron foundries and coal mines migrant workers from across Wales and the western counties of England flocked to Merthyr. Thrown together by circumstance in a hastily built and ever expanding town their numbers soared and so did their sense of brotherhood, forged as it was in the face of a shared adversity. The Merthyr migrants shared also a set of working-class values –

- fair wages
- reasonable working conditions and hours of work
- equitable treatment by their employers.

They suffered a similar set of working-class problems –

- insensitive employers
- harsh working conditions
- poor pay and job insecurity.

They were, in addition, poorly housed, suffered ill-health and had no means to better their lot either by the ballot box or by peaceful demonstration.

The working population of Merthyr were ripe for action and ready to be inspired or inflamed by the persuasive speeches of political agitators and union organisers. The resulting riot in 1831 gave Merthyr, and Wales, its first working-class martyr in Richard Lewis or Dic Penderyn, an innocent man hanged for a crime he did not commit. In such circumstances, possibly before but certainly after 1831, it was perhaps inevitable that a working-class 'consciousness', 'awareness' or 'togetherness' developed in a town like Merthyr. This is not to suggest that a working-class consciousness did not begin elsewhere in Wales (though to prove the occurrence, let alone the

I

II

III

IV

V

VI

VII

VIII

IX

X

I

II

III

IV

V

VI

VII

VIII

IX

X

existence, of something as vague and abstract as consciousness is almost impossible) only that the necessary ingredients – industrialisation, urbanisation, population, confrontation, deprivation and demonstration – for such development existed in abundance in Merthyr. So too does the source material on which historians can draw to analyse patterns of change, and behaviour, in this corner of industrial Wales. In the final analysis, all that can be said with confidence is that the first half of the nineteenth century witnessed a growing awareness among the workers of Wales that they formed or belonged to a class of people who had much in common whether they were from Merthyr or Mountain Ash, Bethesda or Bagillt. The chapel, the Chartist, the union and Friendly Society, the workman's institute, and the age-old rural customs brought with and adapted by the migrant worker, all helped to frame a unique working-class culture in Wales.

b) Trade Unionism

The origin of modern trade unionism lay in the eighteenth century when workers joined together either in combinations to protect themselves from unscrupulous employers or in friendly societies which aimed to provide relief and benefits during times of economic hardship or at times of death, old age and sickness. Fearful of workers' unrest and worried by possible revolution, combinations were outlawed by successive Parliaments culminating in the Combination Acts of 1799-1800. Although these Acts were intended to simplify and speed up the prosecution of workers found guilty of union activity, they failed to crush combinations which continued to operate in secret. Following the repeal of the Combination Acts in 1824 and the legalising of unions in 1825 there was a massive upsurge in union activity and a number of unions were established though the vast majority tended to be local, small and often poorly organised. Despite the change in the law employers, many of whom sat or had influence in Parliament, remained hostile to the idea of trade unionism and when in 1834, six agricultural labourers from the village of Tolpuddle in Dorset formed a trade union, they were promptly arrested, tried and sentenced to seven years' transportation under an Act of 1797 forbidding 'unlawful oaths'.

This worried the newly-founded Grand National Consolidated Trade Union (1834), formed to co-ordinate the activities of the various unions across the country, which tried but failed to protect the Tolpuddle Martyrs from prosecution. Within a year of its foundation and despite a membership of nearly 500,000 workers, the organisation folded blaming a chronic lack of funding (exacerbated by the corruption of its treasurer) for its demise. Funding and organisation would remain at the root of the problems associated with trade union activity for much of the century. Another problem that tended to damage trade unionism was the fact that its leaders often failed, deliberately in some cases, to distinguish between 'trade' and 'politics'. In other words, instead of looking after and promoting the interests of workmen, they were used as pawns in political battles with local authorities and national governments.

In spite of the problems workers continued to form unions and in this they were assisted in part
  (i) by the Chartist movement which spread the trade unionist message by urging workers on with the slogan 'Organise! Organise! Organise!' as printed in the *English Chartist Circular* (1841) and in *The Northern Star* (1850);
 (ii) by a revival in trade after 1842 which tended to make more relaxed the attitude of employers and also increased union subscriptions due to the upturn in employment levels.

The following unions were founded:
- In 1841 The Miners' Association of Great Britain and Ireland – though it did much to further the rights of its members it was found wanting during the long strike and trade depression of 1847-48.
- The National Association of United Trades for the Protection of Labour (1845-1859) – another short-lived organisation which tried to heal the rift between employer and employee by taking care, as stated in its founding charter, 'to keep trade matters and politics as distinct as circumstances will justify'
- The Amalgamated Society of Engineers (1851) – the first union to successfully organise itself, and even in defeat during a trade dispute to survive and gain strength from the experience. It had a membership of 11,000, an annual income of £24,000 and it was well organised with rules which forbad the usual secrecy that had surrounded union activity. The ASE set an example for other unions to follow.
- By the 1860s unions were becoming better organised though they still had to contend both with the hostility of employers and the often misguided political activism of their own leadership.

I
II
III
IV
V
VI
VII
VIII
IX
X

I

II

III

IV

V

VI

VII

VIII

IX

X

In Wales, trade unionism was slow to take off. Although workers had for some time organised themselves into 'pressure' groups during trade depressions and disputes, they lacked a cohesive organisation, were short-lived and were sometimes violent. More successful were the Friendly Societies which were associations of workers who combined for the purpose of providing insurance benefits of various kinds. One of the most popular of the Friendly Societies was The Independent Order of Oddfellows which by 1835, had established 35 branches in Wales. Although never intended to become involved in overtly political action, it was perhaps inevitable that they would be drawn into responding to such issues as conditions and hours of work and wage levels.

Consequently, some Friendly Societies provided the basis and the means whereby a trade union might develop. Indeed, the first evidence of formal trade-unionism in Wales occurred in Bagillt in Flintshire in 1830 when the Friendly Associated Coal Miners Union was founded. It was widely believed at the time that unionists were behind serious rioting in neighbouring Denbighshire in 1830-31. Whether they were or not mattered little to local employers who took decisive action against them and within months of being established they were destroyed.

It was not long before unions were founded elsewhere in Wales with the first being in Merthyr in 1831, though here it was as a reaction to the injustice of the hanging of Dic Penderyn, a miner who was found guilty of rioting and wounding with intent to endanger life. To the authorities and employers in south Wales, unionism was as dangerous, perhaps more so, than rebellion! The ironmasters and mine-owners of Merthyr issued their workforce with an ultimatum, trade unionism or employment – 4,000 workers chose the union and were promptly dismissed. Unemployment, hunger, disillusionment and pressure applied by local authorities and employers alike conspired to kill off the union and it ceased to exist within months of being founded. Even sympathetic ironmasters, like Jospeph Tregelles Price of Neath, worked hard to persuade their workers to rid themselves of their union clubs. In Neath at least they were dissolved by agreement rather than by force. Elsewhere however, force was the order of the day: in June 1834 a meeting of magistrates and employers in the south Wales iron and coal industries 'Resolved unanimously, ... not to employ hereafter any man who is engaged in any Trades Union Society or in any other association not sanctioned by law, and that every Proprietor of Works will issue notice ... to that effect ...'.

Thereafter, and until the 1870s, trade unionism in Wales was, in the opinion of Ryland Wallace, 'essentially short-lived, local and tenuous, usually confined to times of crisis and often enforced by violence and intimidation'. Added to this was the opposition of Nonconformists who were appalled by the secrecy and oath-taking activities of early trade unionists. As late as 1867 Thomas Rees, an Independent minister from Penpontbren, Llanfynydd in Carmarthenshire and one-time collier at Llwydcoed, Aberdare, denounced trade unions as, among other things, an English device which sought to lead astray honest God-fearing Welshmen! His attitude, and those of many other Nonconformists of other denominations, is captured in the following published extract from his book, *Miscellaneous Papers on Subjects Relating to Wales.*

One very prominent fault of our working men is their readiness to allow themselves to be made the dupes of cunning and designing men. several instances of this have occurred in the counties of Monmouth and Glamorgan within the last thirty-five years. About the year 1833, a cunning Welshman
5   named Twist, who pretended to be a most sincere friend of the working classes, visited Merthyr and other places on the Hills, where he induced thousands of the people to form themselves into a kind of Workingmen's Union for the professed purposes of defending their rights against the tyranny of the masters, and raise the price of labour by refusing to instruct any
10   workmen from the agricultural districts in mining operations. The designing originator of the Union gained his object by securing to himself large sums of money from his dupes, but his plausible scheme led to nothing better than the horrid nocturnal doings of the Scotch cattle, and a series of ruinous strikes which brought hundreds of families to the brink of starvation. The Chartist
15   movement of the year 1839 originated in a similar manner. A number of mob orators came down from England, who, by their thundering declamation against the oppression and injustice of the aristocracy, and fair promises of a perfect earthly paradise to the working classes as soon as the points of the charter would become the law of the land, soon gathered around their standard
20   hundreds of confident expectations of the best things on earth.
But, in the course of a few months all their high expectations ended in a disgraceful riot, poverty, inprisonment, and death.

Without meaning to, the Rev. Rees had pinpointed the reason why workers, frustrated at the failure of unions, Chartism and other forms of peaceful demonstration, turned increasingly to more violent methods of protest to better their lot. Riot, insurrection, destruction and violent intimidation

I

II

III

IV

V

VI

VII

VIII

IX

X

featured heavily in the history of industrial, and to some extent rural west and mid-Wales, in the thirty years after 1815.

c) Scotch Cattle

'Scotching', said an anonymous writer in 1867, 'was a means employed by the ignorant and dissatisfied workman to coerce his fellow-labourer and to prevent him working otherwise than according to the united decree, determined at meetings held for that purpose'. Writing under the pseudonym 'Ignotus', the author of *The Last Thirty Years in a Mining District* might have been describing the activities of an early trade union except for the fact that the Scotch Cattle (*Teirw Scotch*), to which he was referring, were almost unique and quite unlike most 'unions' of the time. They were a secret organisation which used the tactics of terror, against employer and employee alike, to achieve their aims. The earliest reliable reference to the existence of a Scotch Cattle-style organisation occurs in December 1816 when the following notice was found at the Tredegar ironworks:

> **Take Notice**
> The Poor Workmen of Tredega to prepare yourself with Musquets, Pistols, Pikes, Spears and all kinds of Weapons to join the Nation and put down like torrent all Kings, Regents, Tyrants, of all description and banish out of the Country, every Traitor to this Common Cause and to Bewry famine and distress in the same grave.

According to historian David Jones, 'For almost a generation the "Cattle" ... held the allegiance of the south Wales colliers in a way which was the envy and horror of employers, chapel, union, and friendly society'. Who and what were they and from where did they come? are just some of the questions historians ask about the Scotch Cattle.

The Scotch Cattle originated in the midlands and uplands of Gwent and the eastern-most part of the county of Glamorgan in a region described by government commissioners, who were investigating the social conditions in south Wales in the 1840s, as the 'Black Domain'. The movement grew out of post-war distress and economic depression and its members were drawn from the thousands of ironworkers and colliers who, for the most part, lived in wretched conditions in dirty smoke-filled valleys with their diseased and poverty-stricken families. Denied union representation, wage-bargaining, secure employment or the means for seeking redress of their grievances, desperate men turned first to self-help groups before their failure, due to a lack of means, forced them to take industrial action. 'Collective bargaining by riot' was the characteristic feature of the strikes of 1816, 1818 and 1819 so that by the time the Scotch Cattle appeared, sometime during the long strike of 1822, there was already a tradition of militancy in the area. The true origins of the Scotch Cattle are shrouded in mystery but it seems the movement got its name because its members dressed up in animal skins, partly to disguise themselves, and partly to intimidate their victims. These 'victims' ranged from employers to managers, agents, landlords, bailiffs, outsiders and, during periods of strike action, blacklegs. In short, almost anyone could find themselves subject to 'the Scotch Law' once the movement had identified a potential target. It is clear that the movement's origins could be found in rural custom which were brought to the urban-industrial districts by migrant labourers who adapted them to their new surroundings. One of the most popular customs of rural west Wales was known as the *ceffyl pren* or 'wooden horse' in which the community imposed its will on those it felt deserved public punishment or humiliation.

The Scotch Cattle had no single leader and nor, it seems, was it a single coherent organisation, yet it operated as if it were and it did so with remarkable speed and efficiency. It was made up of local cells of various sizes which might act independently of each other or in unison. Communication between them was not a problem and nor did it fear leaks or informers. It met in secret at night during which meetings it drafted warning letters which were then delivered to whatever (company) or whoever (individual[s]) was the target. An example is instanced below.

> **To all Colliers, Traitors, Turncoats and others**
> We hereby warn you the second and last time. We are determined to draw the hearts out of all the men above named, and fix two of the hearts upon the horns of the Bull; so that everyone may see what is the fate of every traitor – and we know them all. So we testify with our blood.
>
> Hoarfrost Castle
> April 12th 1832.

I

II

III

IV

V

VI

VII

VIII

IX

X

I
II
III
IV
V
VI
VII
VIII
IX
X

Issued during a strike at the Clydach ironworks in October 1832, the letter, written in blood-red ink for added effect, caused the entire workforce to walk out, and what is more, to stay out. The old tried and tested tactics of starving striking workers into submission and back to work failed in the face of such effective intimidation. If the 'warning letter' failed, the Cattle began a campaign of vandalism by damaging company property such as engines and machines. For those who continued to stand up to the Cattle another method of attack was adopted, the 'midnight visit'. This involved groups of disguised workers (dressed in such things as cattle skins, women's clothes or just wearing handkerchiefs) venting their anger on individuals or families in their homes or on workers in their place of work. During these attacks, which could last anything from a few minutes to an hour or more, property was damaged or destroyed and people beaten. One of the largest demonstrations of power by the Cattle occurred in April 1832 when nearly 300 men terrorised the village of Trelyn where they smashed in the windows of near a hundred houses, discharged their weapons in the air and posted up notices, in English and Welsh, warning the colliers from returning to the local mine. In this instance the reason for the Cattle's boycott of the mine was due to the owner's policy of undercutting locally agreed wage levels so that men who accepted this reduction in their hourly rates of pay, known as working 'under price', were regarded as traitors. Their action might, and did, contribute to driving down rates of pay, making more difficult the task of those workers who hoped to stop the practice by striking. In his book *The History of the Iron, Steel, Tinplate, and Other Trades of Wales* (1903), Charles Wilkins asked an eye-witness to recount his experience of and opinion on the Cattle:

> I was but young then, but the very mention of the likelihood that the Scotch Cattle were coming that night put me into a fever. The Scotch cattle were bands of men enrolled privately in most of the ironwork towns, with the object first of restricting the output of minerals, and thereby keeping up prices of iron and wages of miners. One of the laws was that no stranger should be   5
> taught mining ... At all events, nothing should be done without the sanction of the Society ... The means adopted for carrying out the rules of the Society were principally personal violence.

Employers and magistrates hit back by issuing instructions 'that they will not at any time hereafter employ any persons who may be found to assist in or give countenance to the outrages committed against the persons or property of their workmen by miscreants who assemble at night under the denomination of Scotch Cattle'. Troops and police were frequently deployed within the Black Domain but their effectiveness was limited as much by the skill of the Cattle in avoiding either detection or capture, as in the reluctance of the locals to offer either aid or intelligence. One of the most determined enemies of the Cattle was the pro-Tory newspaper, the *Merthyr Guardian* which not only reported on the movement's activities but regularly published editorials attacking it. The edition of 14 June 1834 expressed its frustration thus:

> The way-faring traveller passes the scene of outrages often bordering on murder, in silence and fear; no sound escapes his pale lips, no gesture indicates the tragedy of which he is witness; for all that he sees is a living proof, that from Dowlais to Abergavenny, TO HIM THERE IS NO LAW.

The tide turned against the movement in 1835 when victims began giving evidence against those men whom they either knew or suspected of Cattle activity. In the Monmouthshire Assizes three of the Cattle were sentenced to death but while two had their sentences commuted to transportation for life, the third, a thirty-two year old miner named Edward Morgan, was hanged at Monmouth jail. Unfortunately for him, the authorities decided that he should pay the penalty for having been involved in a previous 'midnight visit' in which the wife of the intended victim, Joan Thomas, had been unintentionally shot, as a result of which wounds she later died. Thereafter, the movement gradually withered away, and although this was due as much to the spread and popularity of Chartism as to the repressive measures taken by the authorities, there is no doubt that the adverse publicity attaching to the case of Edward Morgan's fate too had had an impact. It served as a warning to others of what awaited them if they continued to support a 'terrorist' organisation. The report for the 11 April 1835 on the execution of Edward Morgan in the *Monmouthshire Merlin* might be said to mark the end of the terror of the Scotch Cattle.

> On Monday last, the awful and revolting scene of an execution, which has been, fortunately, of such rare occurrence for years at Monmouth, was witnessed, at the front of our county gaol, by from three to four thousand spectators. Edward Morgan, found guilty ... contrary to the expectations of a crowded court, of the murder of Joan Thomas, at the parish of Bedwellty, in a Scotch Cattle riot, received the last sentence of the law in a state of pitiable

5

I

II

III

IV

V

VI

VII

VIII

IX

X

agitation ... Morgan made a confession ... He admitted being present with the gang of rioters on the night of the attack on Thomas Thomas' house, but declared that they induced him by threats to join them; he did not fire the gun by which Joan Thomas was killed, being about twenty yards away from the person who so fired, which he said was done without any intention of murder ... He hoped that his ruin would be useful in teaching bad men to shun those combinations which brought him to an ignominious death, and that content would be restored amongst the working classes.

10

3. The Merthyr Rising

■ Key Issue:

In what ways was the Merthyr 'Rising' a landmark in the growth of the Welsh working class movement?

The Merthyr Rising in 1831 (and it was a rising rather than a riot) was the most ferocious and bloody event in the history of industrial Britain.

[John Davies, *A History of Wales* (1993)].

Beginning 31 May 1831, and for the next seven days, Merthyr was the scene of violence, protests and demonstrations the scale of which had never before been seen in Wales. This 'bloody event' was provoked by the attempted seizure of the possessions of a local miner Lewis Lewis by bailiffs acting on the orders of the clerk of the Court of Requests. Established in 1809 to deal with debtors who were either unwilling or unable to satisfy their debts, the bailiffs of the Court were empowered to enter the homes of debtors and confiscate or seize their property which would then be sold to settle the outstanding sums of money. Needless to say, neither the Court nor its officers were very popular and in this particular instance Lewis' neighbours rallied round and defied the bailiffs eventually forcing them to withdraw. With the backing of the town's magistrate, J.B. Bruce, the bailiffs returned and attempted to carry out their instructions whereby a compromise was reached and Lewis gave up some of his possessions. However, events had taken a turn for the worse for as news, and no doubt rumour, of the incident spread an angry crowd gathered and, ready for any excuse to vent their frustrations, they determined to recover for Lewis his 'lost' possessions and punish the hapless bailiffs. Over the next few days, the ever increasing crowds, which contemporaries estimated to have been anywhere between 2,000 and 10,000 at any one time, took their revenge in an orgy of violence and destruction. Unpopular local shopkeepers were either threatened or 'roughed up' and their shops ransacked, the homes of those bailiffs employed by the Court of Requests were attacked and the men beaten as were the hated money-lenders, and one in particular, Thomas Lewis, who was accused of cheating and bullying his 'clients'.

Fig. 12
A Plan of the centre of Industrial Merthyr. Based on the Tithe Survey of 1850

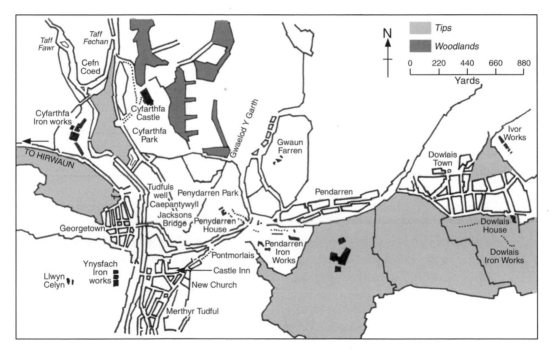

Unsurprisingly, the chief target was the Court of Requests which was stormed by a mob, vandalised and much of its voluminous paperwork burnt. The home and person of the clerk of the Court, Jospeh Coffin, was next attacked and is described below by an eye-witness:

> They ... demanded the books of the court, which, with all the other books in the house, were given them, and burnt in the street; the rioters then broke into the house, and dragged out, and burnt, every particle of furniture belonging to Mr. Coffin, and left the house a complete wreck.

I

II

III

IV

V

VI

VII

VIII

IX

X

I

II

III

IV

V

VI

VII

VIII

IX

X

In the worsening situation, Bruce, the magistrate, swore-in a number of special constables but realising that they would not be able to cope he enlisted the help of local ironmasters, William Crawshay, J.J. Guest and Anthony Hill, and for whom many in the crowd worked, and attempted to mediate with the leaders of the mob. However, buoyed up by their success the crowd had became ever more daring and reluctant to compromise with those whom they blamed for their discontent. Besieged by the crowd in the Castle Inn, and fearing that it was probably only a matter of time before the grand homes of the local ironmasters were targeted, Bruce and his companions sent for military aid citing the complete breakdown of law and order in the town as the reason for his request. Within a day of his request less than a hundred well-armed and well-trained regular troops of the 93rd Foot, a Highland Regiment, arrived from Brecon to accomplish their brief which was to restore order by any means at their disposal. Angered by this turn of events the crowd's hostility towards the soldiers was evident from the moment they took up their position in and around the Castle Inn. Their failure to disperse once the Riot Act had been read, in both English and Welsh, led to some confusion and in the tense atmosphere shots were fired as some of the crowd tried to enter the inn. The incident was described by William Crawshay.

> The most terrific fight ensued ... the soldiers were nearly overcome; the major and many of his men were wounded and knocked down by bludgeons, and stabbed by the bayonets taken from them ... The soldiers who had been placed in the windows fired on the mob in the street. Three were killed dead upon the spot at the first fire ... after the most determined and resolute fighting, on both sides, for a quarter of an hour, the few brave Highlanders ... succeeded in putting the rioters to flight ... major Falls was most severely cut about the head, and was covered with blood; two of the Highlanders were carried in nearly lifeless, with contusions of the brain; and the streets and house were deluged with blood, from the dreadful wounds in the head given by the bludgeons of the mob to the soldiers ...   10

Naturally, Crawshay's sympathies lay with the soldiers, of whom six had been injured. This contrasts with the disdain with which he treated the 'rioters', of whom perhaps 22 had been killed and as many as sixty injured. In spite of the 'battle' at the Castle Inn, crowds of workers continued to harass both the town and the troops, for example, wagon loads of ammunition and supplies destined for the troops at Merthyr, were waylaid and destroyed. When news and rumour of the incident at the Castle Inn spread large numbers of disgruntled workers from nearby towns began marching to support their brethren at Merthyr. To counter this alarming development a further force of regular and irregular troops amounting to nearly 400 men confronted the marchers who numbered some 15,000. After the reading of the Riot Act and a threat to fire into the crowd, the marchers dispersed to be followed a day later by the end of the rising in Merthyr.

It has been estimated that only between 300 and 400 of the thousands involved in the rising were armed and that they had no plan beyond the redress of their local grievances. Nevertheless, the government reacted as if it were a full scale revolution and, fearful of the example spreading to other industrial towns, they determined to stamp it out. Troop numbers were increased and they were quartered in and around the town for several months after the rising. The twenty or so ringleaders were rounded up and charged with various crimes ranging from inciting the riot, destruction of property, assault and, more seriously, wounding with intent to endanger the lives of the soldiers. Whereas a majority of those found guilty were sentenced to transportation, Lewis Lewis and Richard Lewis, alias Dic Penderyn, were sentenced to hang. A storm of protest erupted over the sentences particularly as Richard Lewis claimed, and was generally thought, to be innocent of his crime of wounding Highlander Donald Black. Petitions were sent to the Home Secretary in London but to no avail, Richard Lewis would hang and sentence was carried out at Cardiff prison on 13 August 1831. That a miscarriage of justice had occurred was confirmed in 1874 when a man by the name of Ieuan Parker confessed on his death-bed that he was the one guilty of the crime for which Lewis was hanged. Ironically, Lewis Lewis, who was indeed involved in the rising, had his sentence commuted to transportation for life.

There is no doubt that the rising in Merthyr was serious and though it was nowhere near the 'continental-style revolution' feared by the government, it shook the authorities. It is equally evident that the incident involving Lewis Lewis was not the primary reason for the rising, it was merely the spark that ignited the violence. What had caused weeks of simmering discontent to suddenly erupt into violence? A number of reasons are put forward by historians to explain the Merthyr Rising, the most important of which are listed here:

I

II

III

IV

V

VI

VII

VIII

IX

X

I

II

III

IV

V

VI

VII

VIII

IX

X

Causes of the Merthyr Rising

* Ironmasters – separated physically (by their estates), socially (by their class), economically (by their wealth) and emotionally (by their attitude and lifestyle) from their workforce, the ironmasters understood little, and cared even less about, the daily hardships facing their employees. Their concern was with business, the financial market, trade, profit and loss. The brute insensitivity of some of the ironmasters is amply demonstrated by William Crawshay's decision not only to impose a wage cut on his entire workforce but in sacking also 84 skilled men to save money. Cutting costs during a trade depression might have made good business sense but to the workers and their families, often living at subsistence level, it was catastrophic. Moreover, it was the way in which wage cuts were introduced and men sacked which fuelled the workers' resentment particularly in view of the employers' intransigence on wage advances and refusal to recognise either wage bargaining or union representation. Reporting on the relationship between employer and employee H.S. Tremenheere, a government inspector sent to Wales in the aftermath of the Newport Rising, saw little change to what it had been in Merthyr a decade earlier:

> Except in a few of the works the relations between employers and employed was of the worst description. Next to nothing was done for the comfort and convenience of life among the work-people ... Nearly the whole body of employers acted on [the] theory that the masters had no responsibility beyond paying the men their wages; everything else that they wanted the men had to do for themselves ...

In the aftermath of the the rising *The Observer* newspaper put the blame for the events at Merthyr squarely on the shoulders of Crawshay whom they accused, on the one hand, of encouraging radical ideas and yet, on the other, of tyranny! His angry response was published in a pamphlet entitled *The Late Riots at Merthyr Tydfil* (1831) in which he refuted the allegations and blamed outside agitators and trade unionists for the troubles. In fairness to Crawshay, he simply had no concept of what life was like in the slum areas of Merthyr and had he been aware of the conditions it is as likely that he, like many of his class in a era of temperance and self-help, would have blamed the people for their awful surroundings.

* Working conditions – iron and coal were the primary industries of Merthyr in which over 13,000 men, women and children, some as young as seven, were employed. These are hazardous industries even with proper safety procedures and equipment but when they lack either they are positively dangerous. Unfortunately, both industries were run by men who were generally heedless of minimum safety regulations due principally to the costs involved. Workers were expected to work up to 12 or 14 hours a day possibly seven days a week with only Christmas and Good Friday to look forward to as a break. Accidents were frequent as were deaths, but time off work due to injury or illness went unpaid. The apparent insensitivity of their managers and employers alienated an already disgruntled workforce which was further embittered when wage cuts were imposed without either consultation or representation. The often brutal and tyrannical working regime was a constant source of resentment even for men who might themselves be regarded as rough and used to the harsh realities of heavy industrial work. Although there were humane employers who tried to improve working conditions their efforts were often too little and too late. Some, like Jospeh Tregelles Price, an ironmaster from Neath, were openly sympathetic with the plight of iron workers, Price himself led a campaign calling for Lewis Lewis and Richard Lewis to be reprieved from their death sentences. However, their good work was undone by the bloody-mindedness of their colleagues who, like John Guest and William Crawshay, could not see what they were doing wrong. The more resentful the workers became the more open they were to the persuasive arguments of trade unionists and political agitators.

* Unionism – trade unionism was discouraged by many employers because they were worried about its effects on the attitude and actions of their workers. They tended to come down hard on those who were involved in or merely suspected of trade union activity which often served to engender sympathy among disgruntled workers. Although often unheeded in times of prosperity, the message of trade unionism was particularly attractive during times of economic depression and it is suspected that during the winter months of 1830-31 the Colliers Union of the newly-formed National Association of the Protection of Labour had sent its organisers into south Wales. Certainly, if the testimony of John Petherick is to be believed (he was an agent of the Penydarren Ironworks in Merthyr) an unknown unionist organiser had already addressed a meeting of workers in the town

I
II
III
IV
V
VI
VII
VIII
IX
X

at which he advised them 'to refrain from working any longer'. On hearing this news Crawshay's attitude, unlike that of his fellow ironmasters, was surprisingly ambivalent, he was prepared to tolerate the existence of a union so long as it posed no threat to his power. Workers were encouraged by these union organisers to see strike action as a valuable and powerful weapon in the 'fight' with their employers. It is significant that on 30 May, a day before the beginning of the strife, a mass-meeting attended by over 4,000 workers had taken place on high ground outside the town. Its purpose had been to discuss the recent demonstration, held earlier that month, in favour of the reform of Parliament, although it is not certainly known, it is possible that union activists may have been responsible for organising the gathering. It is noteworthy that after the rising an union was set up in Merthyr and many hundreds of workers signed up but they were sacked and, through the influence of the ironmasters, denied poor relief.

* The Truck System, Housing and Public Health – As if pay, hours and working conditions were not enough of a burden to worry about, the average Merthyr worker had to contend with three further 'evils' of working-class life.

- **The truck system** added to their list of complaints because they were company-run shops and since some workers were paid in company tokens or coins (truck), which could only be exchanged for goods at these shops (Tommy shops), they were subject to the pricing policies of their employers. Needless to say, profit margins were uppermost in the minds of these shop owners and the price increases reflected this, their customers had no choice but to accept the situation and pay the prices demanded. Attitudes however were changing and among the first to abolish the truck system was William Crawshay but his example was not followed by his colleagues.

- **Houses**
  - hastily and shoddily built
  - sanitation was primitive or non-existent
  - clean water was rare
  - space was at a premium therefore no account was taken of the size of the family to be housed
  - rent demanded was far in excess of that one might expect for such poor dwellings.

- eviction for non-payment of rent was common as was the confiscation of property by the Court of Requests for non-payment of debts.

- **Health**
  - disease was rife and epidemics were a fact of life in such slum conditions
  - the town could sport the highest death rate in the country
  - workers lost pay from being off work
  - if the absences continued they might eventually be made redundant.

Unsurprisingly, the squalid conditions were not only a breeding ground for germs but for agitators also, especially when the magnificent homes, such as Cyfarthfa Castle, and opulent lifestyle of the ironmasters was so visible to the wretched beings at the other end of the economic spectrum.

*Radicalism – unsurprisingly perhaps Merthyr was a centre of radicalism and had been since the end of the eighteenth century. The nature of this radicalism was two-fold, working-class radicalism and middle-class radicalism, and though they had some things in common like political reform, they sometimes differed when it came to the issues of working conditions, pay and especially trade unionism. Their views differed also in regard to how they were to achieve their aims, the working-class radicals were increasingly for violent revolution while the middle-class favoured peaceful reform. On one issue they were united, the reform of Parliament and it was this issue which was uppermost in the minds of Merthyr's radicals in the eighteen months preceding the rising. In spite of a population in excess of 30,000 Merthyr had no M.P. to represent its interests and this oversight became the issue which not only united the radicals but the ironmasters also (particularly William Crawshay who stirred up the radicals in support of parliamentary reform) for they too wished to have a voice, preferably one of their own, in Parliament to represent their interests.

The founding of political and philosophical clubs was actively encouraged as were those founded at an earlier time, like the Cyfarthfa Philosophical Society (1806), when such things were generally not welcome. The radicals, workers and middle classes of Merthyr responded enthusiastically to the call to 'Register! Register! Register!' It was to take until 1832 before the Reform Act was passed and although Merthyr gained representation and the franchise was widened it remained the restricted privilege of a few. By

I

II

III

IV

V

VI

VII

VIII

IX

X

May 1831 it was becoming clear to an impatient population that reform would not come easily or quickly which again may have prompted them into violent action. It was in the aftermath of a reform mass-meeting that the troubles began.

*Trade depression and unemployment – There was little job security and although the skilled iron and coal workers were, generally speaking, well paid, this counted for nothing when they were subjected to frequent wage fluctuations or worse, redundancy, during periods of economic depression. During such times the fear of unemployment drove men to contemplate action they would not normally consider but the spectre of the workhouse and the hardships that, and other forms of poor relief, entailed was forever in the back of their minds. There was a general belief that the employers were not doing enough to ease the hardships facing either the industry or its workforce. Nor it seems was the government overly keen to involve itself in the affairs of the iron and coal industry yet they were prepared to support the Corn Laws which contributed to keeping the price of bread artificially high. Without a voice in Parliament, the disillusioned and disgruntled of Merthyr knew they were unlikely ever to persuade the government to change its policies. Practical action was the only alternative to inertia so the workers took to the streets.

4. Chartists and Chartism

■ **Key Issue:**
To what extent were the aims and actions of the Chartists revolutionary and far-reaching?

What was Chartism and who were the leading Chartists?

Working-class consciousness allied with middle-class radicalism gave rise to two pre-Chartist movements The London Working Men's Association (1836) and The Birmingham Political Union (1837). When these groups united to form The National Charter Association in 1838 a workers political movement was born.

However, the Chartist movement was never a cohesive whole but a collective body of different and often conflicting groups which, put simply, can be broken down into those Chartists who believed in 'Moral Force' and those who subscribed to 'Physical Force' as a means to achieving their aims. The 'Moral Force' Chartists were led by William Lovett, Francis Place and John Roebuck, nicknamed 'Tear 'Em' for his fierce attacks on wealth and privilege. The leading 'Physical Force' Chartists were Feargus O'Connor, Henry Vincent, Henry Hetherington and John Watson. O'Connor was by the far the most active, charismatic and powerful of the Chartist leaders and his ownership of the leading Chartist newspaper *The Northern Star*, ensured that it was his views and ideas that received maximum publicity in the press.

What were the Chartists demanding?

In 1838 The National Charter Association issued the following demands in a six point People's Charter:
1. Universal (manhood) suffrage – i.e. the vote for every man over the age of 21 who was of sound mind and good character.
2. Secret Ballot – to protect voters from possible victimisation.
3. Abolition of the property qualification for M.P.s – to enable constituents to return men of their choice without any regard of their financial status.
4. Payment of M.P.s – to enable working men to serve their term in Parliament without fear of debt or other financial disadvantage.
5. Equal electoral districts – to ensure fair representation for a roughly equal number of voters per constituency.
6. Annual Parliaments – to prevent bribery and the possible betrayal of electors by their representatives.

To whom were the Chartists addressing their demands and how successful were they?

The answer to the first part of the question, quite simply, was Parliament. They hoped to persuade their political leaders to adopt and make law the six points of the People's Charter.

How successful were they?

A petition was organised and signed by some 1:28 million people but it was rejected by Parliament. 'They might as well petition the Rock of Gibraltar as the House of Commons' was the pessimistic opinion expressed by David John, a correspondent for the *Northern Star*. Nothing daunted, the 'Moral Force' movement persisted, and in May 1842 a second petition containing 3.3 million signatures (48,000 of which were Welsh and of whom 22,000 came from Merthyr), was presented to Parliament only to be rejected, 'a folly and wicknedness' according to the *Cardiff and Merthyr Guardian* (14 May 1842), by 287 votes to 49.

An attempt by the 'Physical Force' movement to put pressure on the ruling élite to accept their demands by organising a national strike in August 1839 failed. Thereafter, the movement's existence and impact reflected the cycle of economic booms and slumps. For example, between 1839 and 1852 Chartist activity reached its height on only three occasions, during

  (i) the winter of 1839 due to the effects of the severe trade depression;

 (ii) the summer of 1842 on account of wage reductions and mass unemployment in the mills and factories of the north and midlands of England;

(iii) the spring of 1848 following a winter of economic recession and on being inspired by the mini-revolutions sweeping across Europe.

On the other hand, during prosperous periods Chartist membership and support dropped markedly, though it must be stressed that in some areas of the country local Chartist branches bucked the national trend remaining strong, vibrant and active until well into the 1850s. Nevertheless, in the final analysis, Chartism was a failure, mainly, because it failed to achieve the six points. (Certainly, the last point was quite unrealistic.)

What was the nature of Chartism in Wales and how successful was it?

Chartism was a largely urban protest movement of industrial Wales which campaigned for greater political power for working people. Its earliest champion in Wales, Hugh Williams (d. 1874), was a solicitor who came originally from near Machynlleth but who had trained and practised law in London before establishing a law firm in Carmarthen. Motivated by a sense of duty to improve the lot of the working man and influenced by leading London radicals, many of whom he counted among his friends, in April 1837 Williams established a branch of the Working Men's Association in

Carmarthen. This, the earliest 'branch' of Chartism in Wales, was inspired by his friendship with two of the leading Chartists in England and principal authors (along with ten others) of the People's Charter, Hetherington and Watson. The early success of the movement in Wales can be gauged by the fact that over 4,000 people turned up at a meeting in Carmarthen in January 1839 to elect Williams their representative on the Chartist National Convention in London. The purpose of the Convention was to unite the different and rival Chartist groups and to decide on what action to take to persuade Parliament to accept their demands. Chartism soon spread and by the summer of 1839, 34 Working Men's Associations had been founded in the county of Glamorgan alone with the branch at Merthyr Tydfil the most radical of all. It has been estimated that by December 1839, some 25,000 people from across south Wales, many of whom came from the coalfield districts, had enrolled at local Chartist branches.

Fig. 13
A contemporary illustration of a Chartist meeting

I

II

III

IV

V

VI

VII

VIII

IX

X

Mid-Wales too took to the Chartist movement especially in the woollen towns of Montgomeryshire where Political Unions (the equivalent of Working Men's Associations) were established in Newtown (April 1837), Llanidloes and Welshpool. Here too a representative of the mill-workers of Montgomeryshire, Charles Jones of Welshpool, was elected to attend the Chartist National Convention in London. However, the failure of 'Moral Force' (the petition) in March 1839 led to the widespread adoption of 'Physical Force' as a means to achieve results. The Chartists of mid-Wales were stirred to action by Henry Hetherington who made a tour of the principal woollen towns advising the mill-workers '... to procure themselves firearms for the purpose of self-defence'.

According to the Llanidloes-born teacher, historian and author of *Brief Account of the Chartist Outbreak at Llanidloes* (1867), Edward Hamer, 'This ... took the local leaders by surprise, for they never intended resorting to such extreme measures ... In spite of this [Hetherington's] motion was warmly supported by the younger fanatics and carried'.

In expectation of trouble the local magistrate swore in some 300 special constables and requested the Home Office in London to send a team of Metropolitan Police officers to lead them, three of whom duly arrived! Unfortunately, it was the arrival of the three London Police Officers, combined with rumour and excited expectation, that caused the mini-riot that followed in the town. Panic-stricken magistrates exaggerated the scale of the disorder and begged the Home Office to send troops to restore peace to the town. With their arrival the 'rioters', many of whom were not even Chartists, dispersed and, despite the lack of disorder in the town, the authorities nonetheless took action against the supposed ringleaders. 32 local Chartists were rounded up and charged with various crimes ranging from riot and assault to 'training and drilling to use arms'. Among those charged with riot was Charles Powell, the chairman of the Llanidloes branch of the Political Union, who was additionally charged with making a 'seditious speech at Newtown' some weeks before! Powell and his co-defendants were represented in court by Hugh Williams and despite a spirited defence which made a mockery of the prosecution's case, which failed to prove that the defendants had planned the disorder, they were all found guilty.

What was the Newport Rising and how serious was it?

Chartism in Monmouthshire had its roots in a long tradition of dissent. Feeding on industrial and urban discontent, and hatred of the new poor laws, Chartism drew together elements of early trade unionism, Scotch Cattle Societies and radical nonconformity to form a movement with a new political focus. The leading Chartist in Newport was a local tradesman John Frost (d. 1877) who was elected a representative on the Chartist National Convention in October 1838. Frost was a prosperous and influential businessman who had been, successively, a councillor and mayor of, and magistrate and poor law guardian in, Newport. Unlike other Chartist leaders in Wales, Frost appeared to be a pillar of the establishment and a man in whom the authorities might have thought they could trust. However, Frost sympathised with the plight of the poor and dispossessed and he was an active campaigner against the workhouse system. He was a moderate who aligned himself with the 'Moral Force' movement, but, unfortunately for him, a majority of the 430 card-carrying Chartists in Newport were apparently won over to the 'Physical Force' camp by Henry Vincent who came to speak to them in April 1839: '... the working classes were the industrious classes, … the upper classes were the idle ones ... A rising of the people was a thing likely soon to happen ... death to the aristocracy! up with the people and the government they have established'. Inspired by this speech, which Vincent had delivered at meetings of local Chartist branches across south Wales with similar results, Newport's Chartists were ready for action. With Newport's Chartists at fever pitch all that was required was an excuse for them to rise which the arrest of Vincent by the town's magistrates in May provided.

Vincent's crime had been to defy a ban imposed by the town's magistrates on returning to Newport. They were so concerned by his earlier visit that they suspected trouble would flare up if he were to address local Chartists whose meetings had, in any case, also been banned. For good measure they also arrested three local Chartists who, together with Vincent, were found guilty of riot and affray and were sentenced to terms of imprisonment ranging from a year to six months. This miscarriage of justice enraged Newport's Chartists who determined to seek revenge on the authorities, particularly on the Mayor of Newport, Thomas Phillips, whom they regarded as their chief enemy. Local Chartists were angered by Phillips' support for the anti-Chartist organisation, the Association for the Protection of Life and Property, which suggested that they were no better than criminals.

I

II

III

IV

V

VI

VII

VIII

IX

X

85

I

II

III

IV

V

VI

VII

VIII

IX

X

It had been decided at a meeting of the Chartist National Convention in London to plan and execute a country-wide rising in which Newport was to play but one part. Unfortunately for the south Wales men, the national rising did not go ahead as planned but theirs did. Inflamed passions aroused by the treatment of Vincent and others made Frost's job of organising and controlling the Newport Chartists almost impossible. Added to that was the logistical problems in co-ordinating the action of other Chartist groups from as far afield as Blackwood (led by Frost), Blaina (led by Zephaniah Williams) and Pontypool (led by William Jones). What happened next is described in *The Monmouthshire Merlin* (9 November 1839):

> ... At about nine o'clock the cheering of many voices was heard in the distance, from the direction of Stow Hill, producing the utmost alarm, as evidenced by the countenance of those inhabitants who appeared at their windows. In a few minutes after, the front ranks of a numerous body of men, armed with guns, swords, pikes, bludgeons, and a variety of rude weapons,   5 made their appearance, and wheeled round the corner of the hotel, from Stow Hill, with more observance of regularity in movement than it is usual for rioters to display; – an observer, who saw the movement down Stow Hill, calculates that this body of Chartists must have amounted to five thousand men. When the head of the column arrived at the Westgate, the rear ranks   10 were at the house of Mr. Sallows, and they appeared to be almost twelve abreast. The leading ranks then formed in front of the house, and a large body made an attempt to enter the yard leading to the stables, but found the gate too strongly secured against them. They then wheeled to the portico of the inn, holding their guns and other weapons in a menacing manner ... The heat   15 of the conflict lasted about a quarter of an hour, when the defeated Chartists took to their heels in all directions – throwing away their arms, and abandoning their dead and dying ... Many who suffered in the fight, crawled away some with frightful wounds ... wildly crying for mercy ... others desperately maimed ... a few ... writhed in tortures, crying for water.

There also followed a report of the rising in *The Charter* (17 November 1839):

> At least eight thousand men, mostly miners employed in the neighbourhood (which is very densely populated) were engaged in the attack upon the town of Newport and ... many of them were unarmed. Their design seems to have been to wreak their vengeance upon the Newport magistrates, for the prosecution of Vincent and others, now lying in Monmouth goal, after   5 securing the town, to advance to Monmouth, and liberate these prisoners. The ultimate design of the leaders ... probably was to rear the standard of rebellion

throughout Wales, in hopes of being able to hold the royal forces at bay ...
According to the evidence now before the world, Mr. Frost, the late member

10 of the Convention, led the rioters, and he, with others, has been committed for
high treason. On entering Newport, the people marched straight to the
Westgate Hotel, where the magistrates, with about 40 soldiers were
assembled, being fully apprised of the intended outbreak. The Riot Act was
read, and the soldiers fired down, with ease and security, upon the people who

15 had first broken and fired into the windows ... About thirty of the people are
known to have been killed, and several to have been wounded.

Fig. 14
The Chartists' assault on the Westgate Hotel, Newport, 1839

The attack of the Chartists on the Westgate Hotel, Newport, Nov. 4th 1839

I

II

III

IV

V

VI

VII

VIII

IX

X

I

II

III

IV

V

VI

VII

VIII

IX

X

Frost, Williams and Jones, and around 60 other Chartists were tried and found guilty of insurrection, all but the first three being sentenced to terms of imprisonment or transportation. The three 'ringleaders' were sentenced to death though this was later commuted to transportation for life. Frost alone was to return to Newport from Australia (via the United States 1854-56) after being granted a pardon in 1854. On his return in 1856 Frost was given a hero's welcome but rather than involve himself in a decaying Chartist movement he left for Bristol where he lived the remaining 21 years of his life.

In the absence of a general rising across the country the Newport Rising was unlikely to succeed. Moreover, the fact that the authorities knew of the intended march on the town and were prepared with well armed to troops to confront the Chartists suggests that the organisation was riddled with informers. At the trial of Frost and his companions much of the evidence gathered by the Crown came from former Chartists who volunteered information in return for reward or immunity from prosecution. On the other hand, that the insurrection went ahead with the support of several thousand supporters suggests that the potential for an armed rising in Wales did exist. Certainly, the national government and local authorities were not only frightened by the events at Newport but were fearful of it happening elsewhere in Britain. Indeed, the failure of the Newport Rising did not herald the end of the movement. Resilient pockets remained in places like Merthyr, where two pro-Chartist periodicals were established – *Utgorn Cymru* and the *Merthyr Advocate*, Newport and the Monmouthshire coalfield. The desperate social and economic conditions and the anger over political disabilities out of which Chartism had sprung remained and although the movement continued to exist, it ceased to be prominent on a broad front becoming submerged into local politics. In Merthyr some former Chartists became founder members of the town's branch of the Independent Labour Party.

Advice and Activities

(i) General

Suggested Further Reading

A.H. Dodd, *The Industrial Revolution in North Wales* (Cardiff, 1951).

D. Egan, *People, Protest and Politics: Case Studies in Nineteenth-Century Wales* (Llandysul, 1987).

D. Egan, *Coal Society: The South Wales Mining Valleys, 1840-1980* (Llandysul, 1987).

A.H. John, *The Industrial Development of South Wales, 1850-1950* (Cardiff, 1950).

D.J.V. Jones, *Chartism and Chartists* (London, 1975).

D.J.V. Jones, *The Last Rising* (Oxford, 1985).

J. Lindsay, *A History of the North Wales Slate Industry* (Newton Abbot, 1974).

I. Wilks, *South Wales and the Last Rising* (London, 1984).

G.A. Williams, *The Merthyr Rising* (Cardiff, 1978).

Articles:

O.R. Ashton, 'Chartism in Mid-Wales', *Montgomeryshire Collections, vol. 62* (1971-2).

D. Egan, 'Wales at Work' in T. Herbert & G.E. Jones (eds.), *Wales 1880-1914* (Cardiff, 1988).

N. Evans, 'The Urbanization of Welsh Society' in T. Herbert & G.E. Jones (eds.), *People and Protest: Wales 1815-1880* (Cardiff, 1988).

A.V. John, 'The Chartist Endurance: Industrial South Wales, 1842-1868', *Morgannwg, vol. XV* (1971).

D.J.V. Jones, 'The Scotch Cattle and their Black Domain', *WHR,* vol. 5 (1971-2).

D.J.V. Jones, 'Chartism in Welsh Communities', *WHR*, vol. 6 (1972-3).

D.J.V Jones, 'Women and Chartism', *History,* vol. 68 (1983).

D.J.V. Jones, 'Scotch Cattle and Chartism' in T. Herbert & G.E. Jones (eds.), *People and Protest: Wales 1815-1880* (Cardiff, 1988).

M. Jones, 'Rural and Industrial Protest in North Wales' in T. Herbert & G.E. Jones (eds.), *People and Protest: Wales 1815-1880* (Cardiff, 1988).

G.A. Williams, 'The Emergence of a Working-Class Movement', in A.J. Roderick (ed.), *Wales through the Ages,* vol. 2 (Llandybie, 1960).

Research

1. Study working conditions in the coal, iron and slate industries and suggest how these might have contributed to protest movements in industrial Wales.
2. Look up the Factory Acts of 1833, 1844, 1847 and 1863. Determine how effective they were in improving working conditions.
3. Study the issue of child labour and the evidence collected by the Children's Employment Commission. What contribution did Lord (Ashley) Shaftesbury make to eradicating the 'evil' of child labour?

Issues for Debate

A good debate requires careful preparation and the most exciting debates are those which are played out in front of an audience and requiring a vote at its conclusion. Your task will be to present as persuasive an argument as is possible to sway the audience to vote for you. The key to success is a clear understanding of what the key words mean and how you intend to present your argument either fully written down in prose form to be read or, better still, in point form to act as prompts so that you talk to and make eye contact with your audience. Your argument needs to be woven around a series of points that can be supported by exemplar evidence. Remember, although you have to concentrate on your side of the argument, try to anticipate what arguments the opposition have come up with or how they might respond to your points if you are given a right of reply.

In some instances the debate could be played out in the form of a court case with your teacher acting as judge and your fellow students as jury (for the best results an impartial jury is recommended with little or no prior knowledge of the case to be tried). The cases for and against could be delivered in the form of a summing up after which the two opposing counsels could respond by interrogating each other. To involve those members of the class not acting as counsel or jury, the judge might invite each of them to ask a question of either the prosecution or defence. On completion the jury could then be invited to deliver its verdict i.e. finding for the most convincing case or argument.

Look at the following motions for debate.

1. Newport was a Riot and not an Insurrection?
State a case for and against this verdict.

Advice

The following advice should serve to help you prepare a case against the verdict. To help you begin, read the following extract of a report on the Newport Rising published in *The Times* (6 November 1839).

> We have called that by the name of a riot which should have been styled 'an insurrection', for a riot is, strictly speaking, some sudden outbreak of popular fury, arising from some excitement of the moment; while here there has been sufficient evidence to show that this was no momentary outbreak, but a long-planned insurrection, deeply organised, managed with a secrecy truly astonishing ...

The Times extract can serve as your introduction and focus for developing your supporting argument. Re-read the text and source descriptions of the Newport Rising on pages 84-87 and make sure you are clear in your own mind whether Newport was a riot or an insurrection. Support your decision with evidence taken from both text and sources in the chapter. Draw up a series of key points (no more than seven or eight) which will form the basis of your argument taking care to match the sources found to each of your points.

2. 'Riot or Revolution'. Which is the more accurate description of protest movements in nineteenth-century Wales?
State a case for and against this verdict.

Follow the same process for this second issue for debate. Here the issue is much wider than the first requiring you to research the background of the protest movements that affected Wales – Scotch Cattle, Chartism, the Merthyr Rising, Rebecca and The Tithe War [Read the relevant sections of Chapter 3 for the last two].

I

II

III

IV

V

VI

VII

VIII

IX

X

I

II

III

IV

V

VI

VII

VIII

IX

X

(ii) Examination Specific

Answering Essay Questions

Essays will be a central part of the way you study throughout your course and in the examinations you will use them to show your historical knowledge, skills and understanding. Before writing an essay it is essential to draw up a plan. The amount of detail in a plan will vary from student to student. For some it will only be a series of words or phrases which provide the key to each paragraph, while for others it will be a comprehensive set of notes indicating the direction and shape the essay is to take. Neither approach is wrong. It is up to you to find the most effective method for yourself. In essay planning, practice makes perfect!

Every essay should contain an introduction, a middle and a conclusion. The middle will be the argument – the main body of the essay – and will be by far the longest part of it.

- The introduction, particularly the first sentence, is often the hardest to compose. Remember that the introduction introduces the argument. It does far more than merely set the scene. It establishes the way the essay will develop. Think of the essay as a journey and the introduction as the time when you state which route you will be taking, and perhaps what might be seen on route. As you have now given your directions, you cannot change course midway.

The introduction is the first thing that the examiner will read and it is important to make a good impression at the beginning!

- A common problem facing students, particularly at the beginning of their course, is learning how to structure an essay. To begin with you must identify the key word[s] or phrase[s] in the essay, this will help focus your thoughts and should stop you straying from the point.

The following example is an essay involving the consideration of an historical interpretation.

'Poverty was the major problem of the age'.
[I.G. Jones, an historian specialising in the social history of Wales]

Q. How valid is this interpretation of the causes of popular protest in Wales during the period 1815-68?

Advice

The question demands that you deal directly with this challenging statement. You might agree or disagree with this historian's opinion but you have to be sure that there is sufficient evidence/material to argue for or against this interpretation.

You must always note any dates that might accompany an essay question for they set the parameters before and beyond which you should not stray. This essay therefore, requires sound knowledge of the more important popular protests of the period e.g. Scotch Cattle, Merthyr Rising, Rebecca Riots and Chartist protests. You must then evaluate the role of poverty in each e.g. the burden of the court of requests/debt, long pay system and low wages (Merthyr); general poverty, lack of secure employment and wage reductions amongst the industrial workers of the Gwent valleys (Scotch Cattle and Chartism); the toll-gates, greed of the toll-owners and the workhouse system (Rebecca).

Assembling this material should not be a problem but it will require sorting out into a structure in which repetition is kept to an absolute minimum. The best answers will employ an evaluative approach and present a coherent argument in which the issue of poverty is set against other contributing factors e.g. political motivation of Chartism and Merthyr Rising, the key roles of individuals such as John Frost (Chartism), Lewis Lewis (Merthyr) and 'Rebecca'; the influence of government tactics in escalating violence. Some thought must also be directed towards more general, but no less important, points such as evaluating the contribution of the radical tradition in Wales during the period.

I

II

III

IV

V

VI

VII

VIII

IX

X

I
II
III
IV
V
VI
VII
VIII
IX
X

The standard bearers washing their hands in calf's blood

Chapter III
Rural Change and Popular Protest, c. 1830-1895

1. Change

■ **Key Issue:**
Did Wales experience a Rural Revolution in the nineteenth century?

In spite of its rapid industrialisation during the nineteenth century Wales remained, at least until the last decade, a predominantly agricultural country. True the economic transformation of the nation was as remarkable as it was swift and though the rural/industrial balance altered drastically, historians need to guard against overstating the case for change. It is important to remember that the nature and pace of that change was not uniform and although there was massive growth in industry, it was the largest single economic factor in only a small proportion of the country, affecting an area of less than 30% of the entire land mass. Where Glamorgan and Monmouthshire witnessed an economic metamorphosis with its associated, and unprecedented, growth in population and urban development, the majority of the remaining counties of Wales did not. Although parts of Carmarthenshire, Pembrokeshire, Caernarfonshire, Flintshire and east Denbighshire experienced significant industrialisation, and in some areas measurable urbanisation, yet they managed to retain their rural character. Despite the growth of slate towns like Blaenau Ffestiniog, in which a third of the population of rural Merionethshire lived in 1881, coal and steel towns like Wrexham and tin-plate towns such as Llanelli, were nowhere near as large and populous as Merthyr Tydfil, Cardiff or Swansea.

Map 7

Relationship between Agriculture and Industry: The case of Wrexham.
Wrexham is the hub of a circle of villages, industrial to the west and
agricultural to the east, a combination not often seen

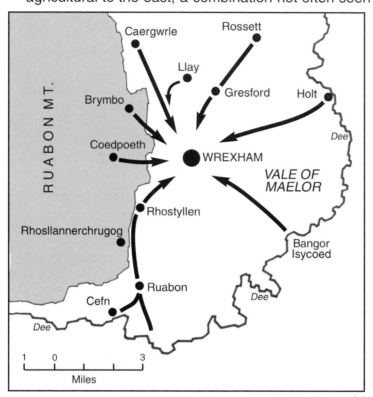

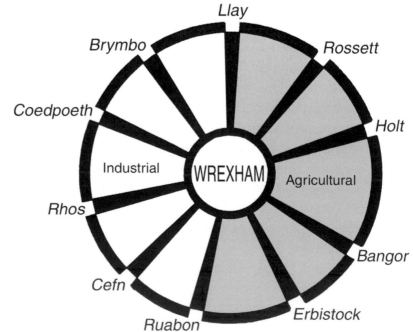

I
II
III
IV
V
VI
VII
VIII
IX
X

Yet if the territorial growth of industrial Wales has been over stated, certainly in the past, its impact on the demographic development of the nation has not. The population of Wales not only increased it moved, and *en masse*. Coupled with immigration and emigration, migration was a phenomenon of the nineteenth century which not only contributed to the industrialisation of the country but radically transformed the social and cultural nature of the nation also. Thousands moved from rural to industrial Wales and thousands more emigrated to England and beyond (USA) to be replaced by thousands of immigrants from England and Ireland. The result was two-fold: rural depopulation and urban/industrial ethnic mixing. In the countryside the power of the large landowning landlords was first challenged and then eclipsed by a rising, and largely urban, middle class of industry-rich, trade-rich and mercantile-rich men of political ambition. As power shifted away from the landowners and as agricultural prices fell the great estates were put under enormous pressure, they were becoming uneconomic and gradually they were broken up and sold. For the people who lived and worked in the countryside life did not change a great deal during the nineteenth century, they continued to suffer from periodic agricultural depressions, unemployment, low wages, poor housing and poverty. In political terms they were the forgotten people being the last group of workers to be given the vote in the Parliamentary Reform Act of 1884.

a) Rural Life and Economy

In descending order on the social scale were:

*   the great landowners who dominated the life and economy of the countryside and whose estates, until many were broken up in the early twentieth century, tended to be larger than 20,000 acres. Although there were relatively few of them they owned nearly 70% of the land.
*   the lesser landowners, squires and gentlemen, the majority of whom owned estates of between 1,000 and 3,000 acres. They had more in common with the great landowners than with those classes below them.
*   the freehold farmers who owned their land. The size of their farms tended to vary but the majority were relatively small averaging out at anything between 40 and 140 acres.
*   the tenant farmers who held their lands by leasehold tenure, the length and rent of which were determined by the terms of the contracts they signed with their landlords.

I

II

III

IV

V

VI

VII

VIII

IX

X

- the labourers who worked for the classes above them – the majority of rural folk who neither owned nor leased land.

What this meant in practice can be illustrated by taking Caernarfonshire in 1883 as an example.

According to the Census return of 1881, 99,000 people were engaged in agricultural work of whom 9,000 were women. Yet according to figures published in 1883 by John Bateman in his book *Great Landowners of Great Britain*, there were only 6,240 landowners in the county. Of these

- 14 were great landowners, four of whom held peerages, who between them owned 203, 331 acres of land;
- around 61 can be classed as squires and gentleman who owned 53,300 acres of land;
- roughly 1,503 were wealthier freehold farmers who owned 39,847 acres of land
- approximately 4,610 were poorer farmers, called cottagers, who between them owned a miserable 373 acres of land.

4,382 acres of land were owned by 52 different public bodies and institutions.

Because they owned no land tenant farmers and labourers were not included in Bateman's calculations but they probably made up the remaining 83,760 (excluding the women) engaged in agricultural work.

Table 4

Percentage of Working People Engaged in Agriculture, 1851-1911

	Males			Females		
	1851	1881	1911	1851	1881	1911
Wales	35.3	20.4	11.9	26.8	6.9	9.4
Anglesey	49.2	39.6	39.5	34.9	11.4	27.9
Brecon	40.8	35.7	23.9	26.2	5.4	12.9
Caernarvon	39.4	23.6	19.2	28.4	6.4	8.8
Cardigan	49.6	47.2	45.4	42.6	16.7	26.3
Carmarthen	46.2	29.5	21.3	38.0	12.7	21.3
Denbigh	44.9	26.7	21.6	27.8	6.3	10.9
Flint	24.6	15.4	17.7	21.6	5.3	8.7
Glamorgan	15.4	6.0	2.5	13.1	2.1	2.0
Merioneth	53.1	31.3	32.3	40.0	9.0	15.8
Monmouth	21.0	12.7	5.7	13.0	2.6	3.3
Montgomery	56.1	45.4	49.1	30.3	9.5	20.8
Pembroke	40.9	31.5	29.5	31.7	11.7	21.7
Radnor	63.7	56.9	52.6	39.4	5.0	13.5

Table 5

Graph showing the decline in the number of agricultural workers, 1841-1911

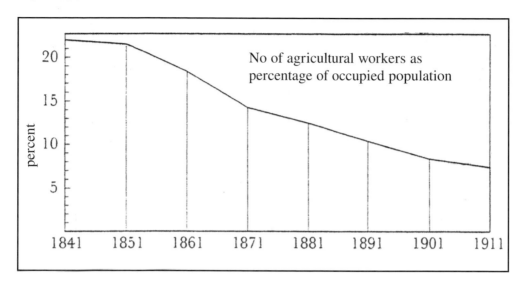

The landowning landlords enjoyed a life of wealth and privilege. Some were Englishmen who had little sympathy with their Welsh tenants and for whom their estates were nothing more than income-generating concerns. Welsh landowners too could be just as insensitive and both they and their English counterparts were often absentee landlords leaving the running of their estates to stewards or bailiffs. However, the gulf that existed between landlord and tenant was not entirely due to wealth and lifestyle, there was a cultural and religious difference also. The majority of landowners were monoglot-English speakers who did not and could not share in their tenants' attachment to their native culture. Many were Anglicans and their support for the established Church was at odds with their Nonconformist chapel-going tenantry. The antipathy (deep dislike) between them is captured in an article published in *Baner ac Amserau Cymru* (2 November 1887):

> It is almost as difficult to get hold of a white rook in Wales, or a white elephant in Bengal, as it is to find a kind landlord. A kind landlord! He is a lamb amongst wolves, a Liberal amongst Tories ... The common idea of a

landlord is a man who has the mouth of a hog, the teeth of a lion, the nails of
a bear, the hoofs of an ass, the sting of a serpent, and the greed of the grave.   5
The landowners of our country are, in general, cruel, unreasonable, unfeeling,
and unpitying men. It does not matter to them who gets drowned so long as
they are allowed in the lifeboat; it does not matter to them who suffer the
mortal pangs of poverty and hunger, if they have plenty of luxuries.

[Quoted in translation from an article by D. Oliver Edwards]

Life for both the freehold and tenant farmer was tough. It was their
misfortune that they were subject to the weather and to natural disasters.
For example, a series of poor harvests between 1837 and 1841 had badly
damaged the agricultural industry in Wales. Ruined crops were unsaleable,
the feedstuffs for livestock had to be bought in as did corn. To make matters
worse a fall in the price of cattle and sheep between 1839 and 1840, and
again between 1842 and 1844 hit farmers hard. Although the harvest of
1842-43 was good a corresponding depression in the iron and coal
industries added to farmers' woes when the demand for agricultural
produce fell. The problems resulting from bad harvests and depressed
prices were ably set out by William Day who wrote from Carmarthen in July
1843 to the Poor Law Commissioner in London George Cornewall Lewis,
'Barley, which last year fetched 6s/ (30p) [a] bushel, realises 3s/ 6d. (18p).
Other corn has fallen almost in the same proportion. Cheese from 4d. to 2d.
Butter likewise. A large farmer at Newscatle Emlyn, who has ordinarily
carried over 2 Cwt (101 kg) of butter per fortnight to Glamorganshire can
scarcely now sell this same quantity at the reduced price, once a month.
Horses are almost unsaleable'.

The fall in prices inevitably meant a fall in income and while this was hard
on the freehold farmers it was especially tough on the tenant farmers who
were still expected by their landlords to pay the same level of rent for their
lands and farms. One burden they did share was the tithe which was levied
or collected annually and amounted in most cases to a tenth of the farmer's
income. Before 1836 hard pressed farmers had had the choice of settling
their tithe payments in kind – in produce or stock – but this was stopped by
the Tithe Commutation Act which stated that henceforth only cash
payments would do. The tithe was intended to contribute to the upkeep of
the established State or Anglican Church but it was bitterly resented by a

people, the majority of whom, were not even members of that Church. They were Nonconformist chapel-goers, Baptists, Independents and Methodists, who began to powerfully challenge a centuries-old tradition which had no place in their lives. Refusal to pay resulted in seizure of goods, property, produce or stock to the value of the outstanding debt. In the worst cases, farmers might even suffer eviction from their farms. Their dissatisfaction over this, in their view, unnecessary and unjustified charge, was at the root of much trouble in rural Wales leading eventually to the outbreak of the so-called Tithe War in 1886. Another burden shared was the inflated toll charged by the Turnpike Trusts which again erupted into violence with the Rebecca Riots in 1839. In both instances, the protests and demonstrations were led by both freehold and tenant farmers but the bulk of the various protest movements were made up of their employees, the labourers.

The labourers were the poorest and least considered class in rural Wales. When times were tough farmers often resorted to the easiest way of reducing costs, by making their workers redundant. If the attacks on the toll-gates and tithes was a matter of principle for some farmers, it was an absolute necessity for the labourer. The farmer hoped to ease his financial burden by ridding himself of the payments but for the labourer the pressure of tithe and toll was a matter of survival. Sometimes they did not always see eye to eye as the following extract from *The Times*, dated 5 September 1843 and written at the height of the Rebecca Riots, makes clear:

> I hear that they [the labourers] are holding meetings every night on the hills in this county [Carms.] and Cardiganshire. They complain that the farmers pay them ill and treat them badly. They say to the farmers, 'We have heard your grievances and helped you to get them redressed; and now we will tell you ours'. I have heard of several meetings of this kind in which the labourers have pretty loudly grumbled at their treatment by the farmers, in being underpaid ... The farmers are beginning to express much alarm at these proceedings.

5

Written by Thomas Foster, a journalist working for *The Times* newspaper, he found it ironic that as the farmers had taken the law into their own hands and destroyed toll gates and opposed the authorities and the forces of law and order, the same should now happen to them by the disgruntled class

I

II

III

IV

V

VI

VII

VIII

IX

X

below them. What were the farmers to do? they could hardly turn for help to the authorities!

Foster had great sympathy for the poor labourer and he recalled in print what he saw on entering several farm labourers' cottages during his visit to Wales in 1843.

> [I] found them mud hovels, the floors of mud and full of holes, without chairs or tables, generally half filled with peat packed up in every corner. Beds there were none; nothing but loose straw and filthy rags upon them. Peat fires on the floors in a corner filling the cottages with smoke, and three or four children huddled around them. In the most miserable part of St. Giles, in no part of England, did I ever witness such abject poverty.
>
> They [the labourers] live entirely on potatoes and have seldom enough of them, having only one meal a day.

Perhaps there was a better life elsewhere.

Fig. 15
A labourer's Cottage in Nineteenth-century Cardiganshire

b) Migration

Why did people move?

People moved and rural depopulation occurred largely because of economic depression and declining employment opportunities in the countryside. As key economic activities steadily moved from the villages and the rural communities into the towns and the urban districts the people followed. Consequently, between 1840 and 1890 the number of agricultural workers in Wales fell from 73,300 to 44,900. In a report published by Seebhom Rowntree, *How the Labourer Lives* (1913), the reasons why people migrated and what happened to those left behind were clearly set out.

> The wages paid by farmers.... is in the vast majority of cases insufficient [not enough] to maintain a family.... in a state of ... physical [health]. The labourer's life is that of existing not living [being] starved mentally and emotionally. ...the sturdy sons of the village have fled, they have left behind the old-men, the lame, the mentally deficient, the vicious, the born-tired.

In 1913, government-commissioned Land Enquiry Committee published its report. Its findings made for grim reading.

> We can say that ... about one in every fifty of our male agricultural population found their prospects in the United Kingdom so poor that they decided to leave the country altogether. In some parts of the country we find villages from which the majority of the younger able-bodied men have emigrated and
> 5   it is generally the most capable and energetic who go.
> Side by side with emigration for the last thirty years and more, there has been a huge exodus of labourers into the large towns where wages are highest. The emigration and migration of the labourers have meant an increasing depopulation of the countryside. The rural exodus is not entirely due to low
> 10   wages. The fact that the colonial emigration agencies have advertised their own lands ... has ... been an important factor, and so, too, has the general dullness and monotony of life in many of our rural villages. We find that the two predominant causes are, first, the lack of outlook and prospects for the future. Secondly, the low wages and long hours, while the shortage of houses comes next in importance.

I
II
III
IV
V
VI
VII
VIII
IX
X

Where did the people move?

The majority of those who moved from the land remained within Wales. They moved mainly to those counties that had become heavily industrialised, to Glamorgan and Monmouthshire. Contained in a Report of the Commissioners into the State of Education in Wales, 1847, the following observation on the growing population of Merthyr Tydfil was made; 'The workmen who are perpetually immigrating, live together very much in clans, e.g., the Pembrokeshire men in one quarter, the Carmarthenshire men in another and so on ...'.

Table 6

Population of Wales and Per County, 1851-1911
(Calculated from Census Returns)

	1851	1861	1871	1881	1891	1901	1911
Wales	1,163.1	1,280.4	1,412.6	1,571.8	1,771.5	2,012.9	2,420.9
Anglesey	57.3	54.6	51.0	51.4	50.1	50.6	50.9
Brecon	61.5	61.6	59.9	57.7	57.0	54.2	59.3
Caernarvon	87.9	95.7	106.1	119.3	118.3	125.6	125.0
Cardigan	70.8	72.2	73.4	70.3	62.6	61.1	59.9
Carmarthen	110.6	111.8	115.7	124.9	130.6	135.3	160.4
Denbigh	92.6	100.8	105.1	111.7	117.9	131.6	144.8
Flint	68.2	69.7	76.3	80.6	77.3	81.5	92.7
Glamorgan	231.8	317.8	397.9	511.4	687.2	859.9	1,120.9
Merioneth	38.8	39.0	46.6	52.0	49.2	48.9	45.6
Monmouth	157.4	174.6	195.4	211.3	252.4	298.1	395.7
Montgomery	67.3	66.9	67.6	65.7	58.0	54.9	53.1
Pembroke	94.1	96.3	92.0	91.8	89.1	87.8	90.0
Radnor	24.7	25.4	25.4	23.5	21.8	23.3	23.6

I
II
III
IV
V
VI
VII
VIII
IX
X

Table 7

Net Gain or Loss per County by Migration, 1851-1911
(Calculated from Census Returns)

	1851		1861		1871		1881		1891		1901		1911	
	No. 000s	%	No. 000s	%	No. 000s	%	No. 000s	%	No. 000s	%	No. 000s	%	No. 000s	%
Wales	+9.1	+0.85	-19.8	-1.67	-49.5	-3.82	-52.1	-3.67	-17.8	-1.13	-9.4	-0.53	+98.5	+4.84
Anglesey	+1.2	+3.15	-5.0	-12.48	-5.0	-13.09	-2.4	-6.88	-3.2	-9.2	-1.5	-4.49	-1.9	-5.42
Brecon	-2.4	-4.27	-6.6	-11.18	-9.0	-15.27	-9.5	-16.64	-7.0	-12.85	-5.6	-10.32	-3.5	-6.53
Caernarvon	-2.5	-2.92	-4.5	-4.55	-2.6	-2.53	+1.2	+1.09	-8.5	-6.83	+2.8	+2.24	-4.9	-3.57
Cardigan	-9.4	-9.82	-9.3	-9.54	-10.2	-10.43	-11.3	-11.56	-15.7	-16.53	-7.3	-8.41	-3.7	-4.53
Carmarthen	-6.5	-7.23	-13.8	-14.60	-8.2	-8.52	-5.5	-5.38	-7.9	-7.07	-8.6	-7.30	+10.7	+8.63
Denbigh	+1.6	+1.69	+0.4	+0.38	-6.1	-6.16	-4.1	-3.91	-7.5	-6.60	-1.2	-1.07	-3.4	-2.65
Flint	-4.4	-10.79	-4.4	-10.67	-1.0	-2.45	-3.2	-7.36	-7.8	-17.04	-4.4	-10.26	+1.6	+2.60
Glamorgan	+41.9	+23.52	+44.2	+18.42	+19.0	+5.82	+30.3	+7.47	+77.5	+14.94	+41.0	+5.92	+92.1	+10.63
Merioneth	-4.2	-8.26	-2.8	-5.42	+1.7	+3.27	-1.5	-2.52	-10.7	-15.70	-5.2	-8.09	-8.4	-13.02
Monmouth	+9.6	+6.36	-6.1	-3.45	-7.2	-3.65	-21.7	-9.89	+3.7	+1.58	-5.1	-1.86	+34.4	+10.86
Montgomery	-7.6	-9.56	-7.3	-9.51	-6.6	-8.63	-11.1	-14.24	-15.8	-21.72	-8.7	-12.89	-6.6	-10.32
Pembroke	-4.7	-5.99	-5.7	-6.80	-13.8	-15.77	-9.4	-11.20	-11.6	-13.85	-7.2	-8.79	-5.5	-6.64
Radnor	-3.8	-11.81	-2.9	-9.19	-3.2	-15.07	-3.7	-18.78	-3.4	-18.48	+1.0	+6.06	-4.7	-23.16

Outside the country but within the British Isles, Welsh migrants settled in London and in the industrial regions of midland England. The USA however, proved the most alluring destination for Welshmen and women with ambitions to begin a new life. Historians have written a great deal about the huge social and cultural dislocation caused by migration but it was not all doom and gloom. According to Professor Brinley Thomas

> Instead of bemoaning the rural exodus, the Welsh patriot should sing the praises of industrial developments. In that tremendous half-century before the First World War, economic growth in Wales was so vigorous that the net loss of people by emigration was a mere 4 per cent... Few countries in Europe came anywhere near to that.

c) The Land Question

Although the economic grievances of Welsh-speaking, Nonconformist tenant farmers lay at the heart of the 'Land Question' it is almost impossible to separate this from the wider sense of political and religious exclusion. The Land Question encompassed grievances against grasping landlords, high rents, short leases, evictions, the Church and tithe and the lack of political representation. These were issues which had long troubled rural Wales but little had been done. This was to change after 1880 for four key reasons:

(i) the Liberal Party won, and continued to win, a huge majority of the Parliamentary seats in Wales. They were sympathetic to the problems facing rural Wales and as a party of government they had the power to change matters.

(ii) the Parliamentary Reform Act of 1884 gave tenant farmers and rural labourers the vote. They could now bring their influence to bear in politics.

(iii) the election in 1886 of Thomas Edward Ellis, as Liberal M.P. for Merioneth. The son of a Welsh-speaking, Nonconformist tenant farmer, his election, and of others like him, ensured a sympathetic voice in Parliament.

(iv) The foundation in 1886 of The Welsh Land League by Thomas Gee provided the leadership and support the farmers were looking for. As a newspaper proprietor and Nonconformist minister, Gee had the power to influence public opinion and he used this ruthlessly. Some in government blamed him for contributing to the tithe riots by encouraging the farmers to protest.

Ellis led the attack in Parliament on the largely Conservative-supporting landowners and he worked tirelessly to improve the lot of Welsh farmers. Twice, in 1887 and again in 1892, Ellis' attempt to introduce into the Commons a Welsh Land Bill designed to protect Welsh farmers from the worst excesses of landlordism – high rents, the tithe and evictions – both failed. Nevertheless, due, in part, to the pressure exerted by the large contingent of Welsh Liberal M.P.s, and also, in part, to the tithe riots, the government agreed to establish a body with the power to investigate the Land Question in Wales. Over two years (1893-95), the Royal Commission on Land in Wales gathered evidence from eleven hundred witnesses, visited selected areas and made recommendations in a published report (1896) running to over half a dozen volumes. Among those who gave evidence was Ellis himself.

> I am the son of a tenant farmer ... From boyhood I have had a strong and deepening conviction that the system under which land in Wales is cultivated requires drastic modification and reform. Here are some instances ...
> 1. Eviction for exercising independent judgement in politics ...
> 3. Dispossession of tenants owing to a whim of the landlord ...
> 4. Compulsory extortion of rent under the threat of eviction ...
> 5. The exaction of high, sometimes impossible, rents in times of severe economic depression ...
> 6. The uncertainty of obtaining compensation for improvement ...

Table 8

A Labourer's Budget in the Builth District, Mid-Wales.
(Royal Commission on Labour, *The Agricultural Labourer: Vol. II, Wales*, 1893)

Edward Jones, farm labourer, wife and five children, wages 16*s*; extra harvest and job work 2*s*, equal to 18*s*.

Rent	1*s* 3*d*
Flour, 28 lb	3*s* 0*d*
Tea, 1/2 lb	0*s* 11*d*
Sugur, 6 lb	1*s* 3*d*
Bacon and lard	2*s* 2*d*
Potatoes	0*s* 2*d*
Milk	0*s* 3*d*
Coal	0*s* 10*d*
Wool (gratis)	———
Butter	2*s* 2*d*
Salt, pepper etc.	0*s* 1*d*
Soap	0*s* 4*d*
Club money	0*s* 6*d*
Clothing	3*s* 9*d*
Butcher's meat	1*s* 0*d*
Total	17*s* 8*d*

I
II
III
IV
V
VI
VII
VIII
IX
X

The majority of the nine commissioners were sympathetic to the Welsh farmer and in their report they concluded '... that in Wales it is the tenant farming class that have hitherto borne the brunt of depression. In the majority of cases the tenant has during recent years, found it increasingly difficult to pay his rent ... Many tenant farmers have failed completely ... a very large number will shortly be face to face with the prospect of bankruptcy'. However, not everyone was sympathetic to the plight of the 'hard-pressed farmer' or even prepared to acknowledge that there was a 'Land Question'. In 1896 J.E. Vincent, a barrister employed by Lord Penrhyn to represent the interests of the landlords, published *The Land Question in North Wales* in which he stated

> ... the alleged Welsh Land Question is a plant of quite recent growth. Twenty years ago, nay, fifteen years ago, it was unheard of ... It may be asked how it came about that the appearance of a Land Question was brought about in a community having, on the whole, so happy a history ... The answer is to be found in the ... fact [that] the Welsh people, who are by nature as quiet and peaceloving a people as any in the world, were, during the decade [1880-90], in a state nearer to general lawlessness ... than during any other period of the century ... it is certain that until the anti-tithe agitation in Wales became acute, nothing whatsoever was heard about a Welsh Land Question ... Hence came it that Lord Penrhyn ... said, '... the agitation upon the Welsh Land Question was unreal in origin, and had not its source in any genuine sense of grievance on the part of the agricultural community.
>
> 5
>
> 10

Recommendations were made by the Land Commission, such as the setting up of a Welsh Land Court to deal fairly with disputes between tenant and landlord, but they were not acted upon because the commissioners who led the inquiry were split between the six Liberals and three Conservatives and they could not agree on the key changes that needed to be made. Two further attempts by the Liberals to introduce a Welsh Land Bill in 1897 and in 1898 failed. It took a World War (1914-18) and the setting up of a Welsh Church by the Disestablishment of the Church in Wales Act (1920) to finally put an end to the 'Land Question'.

2. Protest

■ Key Issue:

'Violence born of despair'. How accurate is this description of rural discontent and protest in nineteenth century Wales?

If Chartism was the protest movement of industrial Wales, Rebecca was its rural equivalent. Driven to distraction by the experience of poverty or the fear of it, paucity and pauperism, rural folk turned to the only means left to them to shake the ruling classes out of their seeming indifference to their plight – protest. Distress and discontent in equal measure had been an ever present problem for the authorities, the more so since the end of the war in 1815, but the particularly grim social and economic circumstances of the 'hungry 40s' had conspired to force otherwise law-biding and respectable men to do more than merely contemplate violent action. Landowning freeholders and land-renting leaseholders found themselves acting in concert with landless labourers, a class so near the bottom of the economic pyramid that a simple drought or wet summer could so easily tip them into the abyss of workhouse pauperism. Rebeccaism was, in large part, their answer to absentee landlords, insensitive toll-road owners and corrupt workhouse trustees.

One aspect of the Rebecca riots which is generally little known or not given due recognition was the anti-tithe grievance. The largely Nonconformist farmers of south-west Wales were as dissatisfied with paying the tithe (a tenth part of a landlord's or tenant's income paid to maintain the Anglican Church) as they were with paying the toll, but because the toll-gates were more visible and toll payments more pressing and their destruction more easily accomplished, the tithe issue was rarely at the forefront of either their demands or in the reporting of their activities.

However, unlike the toll issue which was largely resolved by Parliament in 1844, the tithe question continued to plague and anger hard pressed farmers, particularly those in north-east Wales, but it took another severe economic depression to sting them into action. The spark that lit the fire of the anti-tithe campaign was the foundation in 1886 of The Welsh Land League by Thomas Gee. The Welsh Land League was born of frustration

I
II
III
IV
V
VI
VII
VIII
IX
X

I

II

III

IV

V

VI

VII

VIII

IX

X

and though it made the tithe issue a central feature of its campaign this was just part of its aim to redress wider social, economic and political grievances. The so-called Tithe War erupted in north-east Wales in 1886 and it lasted until the issue was partly resolved by Parliamentary legislation in 1891.

a) Rebecca

(i) The Turnpike Trusts

Bereft of good roads and navigable rivers Wales was a country almost inaccessible to all but the hardy traveller and the entrepreneur with an eye for an opportunity. The Turnpike Trust was just such an opportunity both to improve and extend the dilapidated and chaotic road system and to make a handsome profit in the process. Whereas many of the early road entrepreneurs, some of whom were Merthyr ironmasters and Snowdonia slate magnates, were keen to promote their businesses and thus built reasonable roads, those who came later were more concerned with profit than improvement. This almost inevitably drew them into conflict with those for whom the roads were an essential means of conducting their business. The farmers of west Wales were among the first to express their displeasure at Trusts which were erecting toll-gates every few miles along a single highway, in the hope of raising revenue by exacting an ever increasing and bewildering range of tolls. It is probable that had the Trust roads been well-built and maintained they would not have attracted the protests they did, but in many cases they were quite simply appalling. 'Nothing but love of glory should tempt a man to pass along them' was the advice of one visitor who had the misfortune to travel by road between Carmarthen and Fishguard.

Besides the Trust roads, which even by the 1830s only accounted for no more than 30% of highways in Wales, there were also parish roads which, according to an Act of Parliament of 1555, were the responsibility of the respective parish communities. Forced labour, together with the added responsibility of meeting the cost of repair, were the order of the day for each parish which is why these roads were usually resented and generally neglected. By the beginning of the nineteenth century many of them had been reduced to dirt tracks, in fact many of them had never been more than that, and though they may have served the drovers well they were simply ill-equipped to cope with the transportation of industrial goods. Nor were they benefiting the farmers who used them, when possible, in preference to expensive Trust roads. Unlike the canal and railway, road building and repair went largely unregulated, being left to the private companies to do as they wished. In an effort to maximise profits and to prevent travellers by-passing Trust roads some companies adopted parish roads but in doing so they added side-bars and chains to raise revenue without necessarily improving them. Despite this, some of the Trusts were so badly run that they were actually losing money. It has been estimated that of the twenty-nine Trusts in south-west Wales in 1840, thirteen of them were either in debt or bankrupt.

It was not until long after the troubles and protests associated with Turnpike Trusts that the government eventually stepped in to co-ordinate a strategic programme of road building, repair and maintenance. But by this time the development of the railways had revolutionised the transportation system to such an extent that in Wales roads never really contributed to the industrialisation of the country as much as they could have done. Therefore, far from performing a service to the nation, by bringing distant parts of the country into closer contact with each other and assisting agriculture by supporting farmers in the transportation and trade of their livestock and produce, the chaotic road system was, if anything, an inhibiting factor.

(ii) The People Protest

Rebecca was a popular protest movement and a secret movement that sprang from a number of social, economic and religious causes. Its leaders organised attacks on toll-gates and workhouses and the properties of unpopular tithe owners. The movement originated and the first protests occurred in May 1839 on the Carmarthenshire-Pembrokeshire border. A group of some 400 men with blackened faces, dressed in women's clothes, armed with axes and sticks, and going under the name of 'Rebecca' and her 'daughters', gathered at Efailwen where they pulled down and destroyed the toll-gate. Attempts by the Whitland Turnpike Trust, which owned the gate and toll-house, to replace the toll-gate was met with similar destruction. When the Turnpike Trust decided to abandon the toll-gate at Efailwen the Rebeccaites also disappeared (but not before they had destroyed a further two toll-gates west of Carmarthen and possibly stormed the half-built

I

II

III

IV

V

VI

VII

VIII

IX

X

I

II

III

IV

V

VI

VII

VIII

IX

X

Narberth workhouse). Nothing more was heard of Rebecca until mid-November 1842 when newly-erected toll gates at Pwll-Trap and at the Mermaid Tavern, located on either side of the village of St. Clears, were stormed and destroyed.

By the beginning of January 1843 Rebecca Rioters had carried out no less than six separate attacks destroying toll-gates within a fifteen miles radius of St. Clears. By the beginning of February Rebecca had struck further west into Pembrokeshire and by April her daughters were operating across the Teifi in Cardiganshire.

Turnpiking provided a focus for discontent because it was visible and a tangible symbol of oppression. The toll-gates and the tolls charged by the various Turnpike Trusts were becoming a burden to hard pressed farmers many of whom were already suffering from severe economic pressures. The insensitivity of toll-road owners contributed to the growing discontent and one name in particular stands out, that of Thomas Bullin. With a successful career behind him in Trust management in England, Bullin struck out on his own and during the 1830s he bought up and leased a number of Welsh toll roads mainly through auction. His business methods were rigorous and efficient which, unsurprisingly, turned his farming 'customers' against him. Welsh farmers were particularly vulnerable to the exactions of tolls because they had no choice but to carry lime (to fertilize the soil) by cart to their farms and transport their produce to market. To make matters worse some farmers had to pass through the toll-gates of several Trust companies, each of whom demanded payments in full for the service. Had the roads been good quality and worth the expense of their upkeep then the farmers' anger might not have been as great as it was, unfortunately, some of the trusts were in financial difficulties and their solution to the crisis was either to erect more gates and/or increase tolls. As if to add insult to injury, some Trusts tried to force their 'customers' to repair certain roads by cynically using a law passed in the sixteenth century which required parishioners to maintain roads in their locality! However, as a government-led commission was later to discover, this was not the only cause of the riots.

Fig. 16
Illustrated London News: The Rebecca Rioters

THE WELSH RIOTERS.

Having swept all before them without so much as a rebuff by the authorities, who, in spite of deploying special constables to protect the toll-gates, seemed powerless to stop them, Rebecca and her daughters turned their attention to other perceived injustices such as tithes and the new poor law. Besides corrupt and insensitive workhouse trustees and employees, the farming communities of west Wales were particularly incensed by the so-called 'bastardy clause' of the Poor Law Amendment Act of 1834 which removed maintenance for unmarried mothers thus forcing them to starve or go into the workhouse. In February 1843 the master of the Narberth workhouse was sent three threatening letters warning him about the quality of the food given to the inmates. In June 1843 Rebecca sent threatening letters to both the Haverfordwest and Carmarthen workhouses and in one incident some 600 of Rebecca's daughters stormed the Narberth workhouse only to be thwarted in their attempt to burn down the building by

I
II
III
IV
V
VI
VII
VIII
IX
X

a detachment of troops of the Castlemartin Yeomanry. In Pembrokeshire Rebecca was particularly active adding high rents and enclosures to her list of grievances. In August 1843 a large crowd destroyed the pound of the manor of Slebech and released the animals which had been seized by Baron de Rutzen from one of his tenants for non-payment of rent.

Map 8

Rebeccaism: Attacks on Tollgates, 1839-44

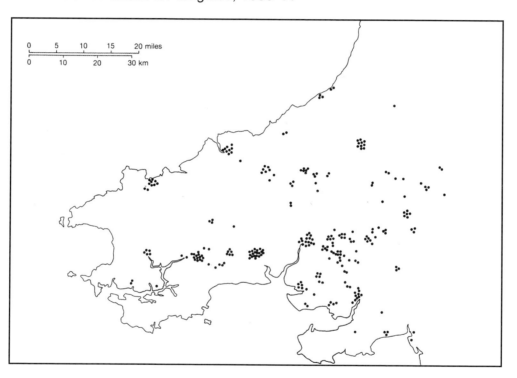

There were at least thirty-one other attacks in Montgomeryshire, Radnorshire and Breconshire.

Fig. 17
Landowners' appeal to the followers of Rebecca

On 19th June 1843, in their boldest move yet, Rebecca rioters marched in broad daylight through the streets of Carmarthen gathering about them the poor of the town. Led by Mike Bowen of Trelech and bearing placards with the word *Cyfiawnder* (Justice) on them, their aim was two-fold:

• to present the magistrates sitting in session in the guildhall with a list of their grievances
• to sack the town's workhouse.

The so-called 'Carmarthen Riot' was ended by the appearance of a troop of cavalry, the 4th Light Dragoons, who set about their task of breaking up the riot with their accustomed military efficiency. Yet, even in retreat, Rebecca was undaunted for on the very day they were rebuffed in Carmarthen a warning letter was issued to 'Ye Master of ye Union Workhouse Newcastle Emlyn' which stated that if he and 'the paupers that are under thy care' did 'not come out ... before next Wednesday' they would 'destroy it [the workhouse] wholly and woe be to thy body for we shall take care of thee that thou shalt not escape'.

I

II

III

IV

V

VI

VII

VIII

IX

X

The events at Carmarthen not only alarmed the already fearful authorities, it drew the attention of London-based national newspapers like *The Times* which dispatched one of its reporters to the area. The secrecy and the increasing level of destruction that accompanied the movement worried the government and, anxious to prevent the spread of 'Rebecca', it reacted in the only way it knew how, by brutal force.

Map 9

Distribution of Troops in south-west Wales, Oct. 1843-Feb. 1844

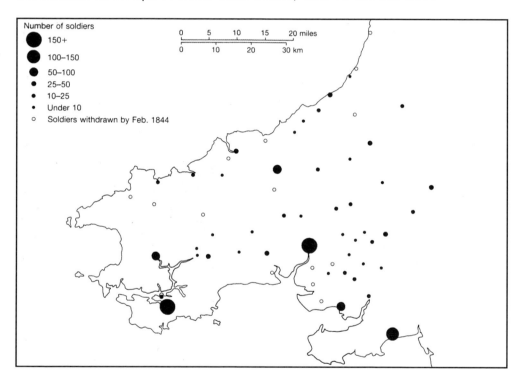

The plight of Welsh farmers was highlighted by Thomas Foster, correspondent for *The Times*, who came to south Wales to investigate the issue. Following exhaustive inquiries and having won the trust of the farmers, Foster sent a series of reports back to his newspaper on the unfolding events in west Wales. His reports are invaluable because they provide direct evidence of the views of Rebecca's supporters. This is an extract from an article published on 4 August 1843:

I II III IV V VI VII VIII IX X

5

10

15

The farmers loudly complain of the oppressive nature of the tolls, particularly on those roads originally parish roads, and which the trust adopted, placed turnpikes on them, and then called on the parishes to keep them in repair. They gave me an instance of a parish road between Llanelly and Pymbrae (Pembrey), a distance of five miles, on which a gate has been erected, and a sixpenny toll demanded for a horse and cart. A fortnight ago a bridge on this road was broken down by a flood. The trustees refused to do anything, and call on the parish to repair it. They say there is not a bye-lane of any sort by which a cart can get to the lime-kilns which has not a bar or a chain across it. They say if ever there is a lane by which one or two farmers can get to their farms without paying toll, an application is immediately made to the trustees to grant a bar on the lane, which is almost of course acceded to; that there is never a fair held in any of the villages or principal towns but that the toll contractor surrounds the town by every approachable access to it with a cordon of toll bars.

By the beginning of July Rebecca had widened her operations still further by crossing the county border into Glamorgan at Pontarddulais and Llangyfelach. However, here the movement met with its first serious reverse when an attack by over a hundred Rebeccaites on the toll-gate at Pontarddulais in September 1843 was thwarted by troops and police under the command of the Chief Constable of Glamorgan, Charles Napier. A number of prominent Rebeccaites were arrested, tried at Cardiff and sentenced to between seven and twenty years transportation. The reaction of both Rebecca and the authorities to the trial and harsh sentences was reported by Foster in *The Times* (20 September, 1843).

It was fondly hoped and indeed confidently predicted by both the magistrates and the police that it would put an end to Rebeccaism and that such would be the terror felt throughout the country that the Lady Rebecca would be so struck with the terror that the outrages would at once be put to an end. The effect has, however, been precisely the reverse. The Welsh are a peculiar people and they have become completely exasperated in consequence of their countrymen having been shot, as they say, by a villainous body of police.

Rebecca, however, continued. Sporadic rioting, some serious, was reported as late as the autumn of 1844 after which the movement gradually faded away.

I

II

III

IV

V

VI

VII

VIII

IX

X

I
II
III
IV
V
VI
VII
VIII
IX
X

(iii) The Nature of Rebecca

> And they blessed Rebekah, and said unto her, Thou art our sister, be thou the mother of thousands of millions, and let thy seed possess the gates of those which hate them.
>
> *[Book of Genesis, xxxiv, 60.]*

We shall never probably know the truth of why the movement came to acquire the name Rebecca. In the opinion of some historians the Bible may have provided the inspiration for naming the movement but it is as likely to have been as much accident as design since the trappings of disguise, secrecy, rhyming, threats, mock trial and the pantomiming that accompanied Rebecca sprang directly from the folk traditions of rural Wales. Stemming from earlier rural protests, the *ceffyl pren* was one such custom or tradition on which wooden cock-horse the effigies of the offenders against the community were mounted and paraded to the tune of some 'rough music'. Between the violence and destruction, the disturbances were also accompanied by much mirth-making, song-singing and ballad-writing. The riots spawned a number of ballads and balladeers such as Levi Gibbon and David Davies alias *Dai'r Cantwr*. Their ballads were intended to be more than mere entertainment for though they added to the sense of occasion they were a means of highlighting, mirroring or expressing the views of the community. Nor was this peculiar to south-west Wales. Other disturbances, riots and tumults throughout Wales had their ballads and balladeers. One might even argue that these working-class balladeers were the modern successors of the bards of old. Below is an extract (in translation) of a ballad by Levi Gibbon:

> Rebecca, like myself, was born in Wales
> In the parish of Mynachlog-Ddu - a bonny child.
> She grew up to be quite tall
> And she took complete possession of the gate at Efailwen.
> Constables and policemen came there
> To try and prevent Beca stealing the old gate
> And soldiers were in power for a month
> So that every gateman could keep his livelihood.

One of the most disturbing aspects of the Rebecca movement were the threats that it issued by letter to those it wished to intimidate. This had the desired effect serving to strike fear into recipients. In rural England also the 'Captain Swing' movement struck terror into the hearts of its victims by issuing threats like the one quoted. Compare it with the first 'Rebecca Letter' sent on 16 December 1842.

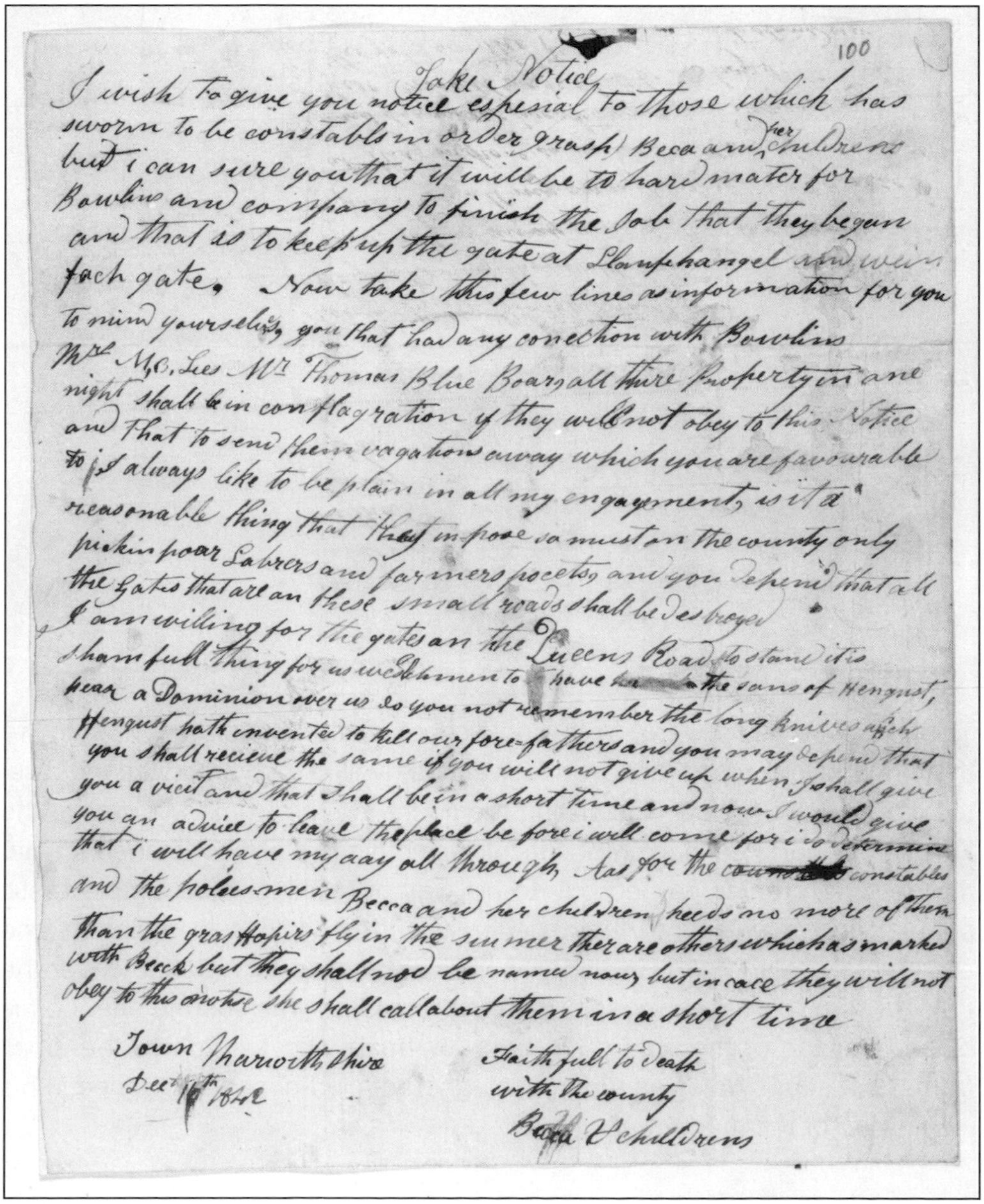

Fig. 18
The First 'Rebecca Letter'

I II III IV V VI VII VIII IX X

119

Fig. 19
The First 'Captain Swing Letter'

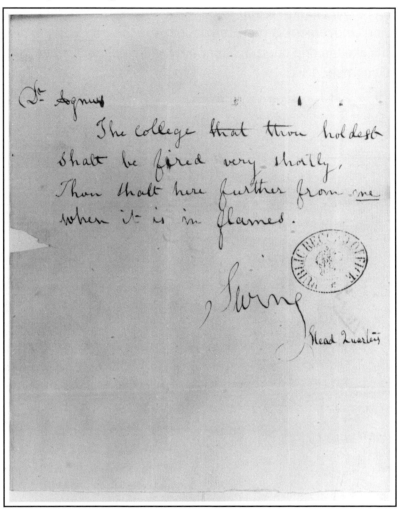

The Rebecca Riots were, in the opinion of David Jones, 'larger than we thought and less respectable, and for a time rivalled Irish affairs as the chief topic of debate in Westminster and the country'. The Prime Minister at the time, Sir Robert Peel had great difficulty in coming to terms with the fact that the riots were being carried out, to his way of thinking, by a simple rustic people who 'speaking of them generally, [are] novices in agitation and systematic outrage'. An English reporter dispatched to Wales to cover the riots for the Chartist newspaper the *Northern Star*, was soon to change his biased opinion of the rioters he met: 'Any man who sets down the small farmers of south Wales as a parcel of ignorant clod-hoppers for once in his life is wide of the mark'.

(iv) A contemporary view of the Causes and Consequences of Rebecca

Foster of *The Times* was of the opinion that the heavy-handed use of the police and army was merely serving to exacerbate (make worse) an already volatile (unstable) situation. He believed only a government-led commission could resolve the problem. This happened in October 1843 when a 'Royal Commission to Enquire into the Causes of Discontent in South Wales' was established. It spent five months gathering information and it reported its findings in March 1844. Below is an extract:

It is a matter of great satisfaction to state our belief that the disturbances of the country, though so widely extended, were not connected with political causes, and that nothing like a general spirit of disaffection, or organised hostility to the laws, pervaded the community. The excitement having been
5   first stimulated by a sense of local grievances, gradually spread to other districts in which similar complaints existed and the spirit, once roused, was perverted in some instances by evil disposed persons to aggressions of a more extensive and systematic kind.
It appeared generally, that the chief grounds of complaint were the
10   mismanagement of the funds applicable to turnpike roads, the frequency and the amount of the payments of tolls, and, in some cases, the vexatious conduct of toll collectors, and the illegal demands made by them: the increase in the amount payable for tithe under the Tithe Commutation Act ... the operation of the Poor Law Amendment Act, principally (though not exclusively) on
15   account of the high salaries of the officers, and the operation of the bastardy clauses: the administration of justice by the local magistrates and especially the amount of the fees paid to their clerks, and the progressive increase of the county rate ...
All persons acquainted with the condition of the country concurred in stating
20   that a succession of wet and unproductive harvests had very much reduced the capital of the farmers. They had been forced, during successive years, to buy the bread consumed in their families; and the money they obtained by the sale of stock, and the other produce of their farms, scarcely enabled them to make good various payments to which they were liable.
25   Concurrently with these difficulties, the price of sheep, cattle, and butter had fallen much below the average of preceding years, though, at the same time [as it is said] all rates, tithes and taxes had increased, the rent of land still remaining, generally, undiminished.
The Welsh farmers are, at all times, a frugal, cautious race, but by the
30   pressure of the circumstances we have described, they were rendered more than usually anxious to release themselves from even the smallest payments.

I
II
III
IV
V
VI
VII
VIII
IX
X

The publicity given the Rebecca Riots and the sympathetic report published by its own commissioners forced the government to act.

- In August 1844, barely five months after the publication of the Report, Parliament passed a Turnpike Act which established a Roads Board in each county to consolidate and manage the trust companies and appointed experienced surveyors to advise the boards. In addition, tolls were simplified and the toll on lime was halved.
- Indirectly, the riots contributed to other important legislation such as the passing, in 1845, of a General Inclosure Act which provided for the needs of smaller farmers should proposed agricultural changes affect them
- In 1847 a Poor Law Board was set up in order to make the working of the Poor Law more humane.

b) The Tithe Wars

In 1886 north-east Wales went to war, not in the conventional sense but in the time-honoured tradition of riot and violence. Not for the first time agrarian discontent provided the basis for trouble but one issue more than any other provided the spark – the tithe. In view of the depressed prices for agricultural produce, partly as a result of poor harvests and partly from increased competition from cheap imported foreign foods, farmers looked to ways of reducing their financial burden. Their focus fell upon the tithe rentcharge which had long been resented, but especially so in times of economic hardship and the more so in view of their Nonconformity. Encouraged by meetings organised by The Society for Religious Freedom, the tenant farmers of Denbighshire took to withholding the payment of tithe. This led to Court action in which the goods and stock of farmers unwilling or unable to pay the tithe in cash were seized or distrained and subsequently sold.

In his book *Memories*, published in 1889, Bishop (later Archbishop of Wales) A.G. Edwards of St. Asaph stated that 'The Welsh tithe war was motivated not by poverty but by politics'. In some respects he is correct since the tithe issue arose at the same time as the question of the disestablishment and disendowment of the Anglican Church in Wales was being actively pursued in Parliament by some Welsh Liberal politicians like Thomas Edward Ellis. Thomas Gee, the Nonconformist printer-publisher from Denbigh, and his Welsh Land League was also accused of encouraging the farmers to revolt by influencing public opinion against both Church and landowners. Unsurprisingly, the disturbances attracted widespread attention in the English press and provoked the interest of others anxious to understand the cause and nature of the so-called tithe war. A selection of extracts attempts to provide a contemporary view of events.

Examining the evidence: The Tithe Wars

Why were tithes opposed in Wales?

A

Farmers in Denbighshire are formulating their demands for the establishment of land courts in Wales ... Tithes, they say, are no longer tenths of the farm produce, but sixths, fifths and even fourths, and one speaker at a meeting held at Holywell yesterday went so far as to say that in one case a farmer had in three years paid tithes equal to one year's rent. In addition, the prices of stock and of wheat have fallen by one third, and so therefore they urge, rents must be reduced one third also.

[*Chester Chronicle*, 16 January 1886]

B

The agitation has arisen ... by the fact that it is an alien church, and includes but a small minority of the inhabitants. The payment of tithes to this Church is a badge of conquest which we are determined to shake off as soon as possible. The present state of agriculture is not the cause but the occasion of this

5   agitation...

... the Church Commissioners have insulted and angered my fellow countrymen to such an extent, by calling on the army and the police to protect them while collecting the tithe payments in full, that their behaviour ... will surely inspire the Welsh nation to ... hasten the disestablishment of the Church

10   whose leaders have shown no practical sympathy towards the farmers in their hardship.

[Evidence of Thomas Gee given before Commissioner John Bridge at the Committee of Enquiry into the Tithe Agitation in Wales (1887)]

I

II

III

IV

V

VI

VII

VIII

IX

X

C

Is it not unjust to compel Independents, Methodists, Baptists, Wesleyans, Unitarians etc. to contribute towards the support of the clergy of the Church of England ... Welsh tithes are taken out of the country to swell the revenues of English bishops, cathedrals and colleges ... The Bishop of Lincoln takes £400, ... the Bishop of Lichfield takes £766 ... and the Bishop of Gloucester £844. The deans and Chapters of Gloucester, Oxford, Winchester and Worcester the sum of ... £9,154.

[W. Thomas, *The Anti-Tithe Movement in Wales* (1891)]

D

In one sense, the anti-tithe movement was the Rebecca Riots over again, but this time in North Wales. During the distress of the forties, the south Wales farmers found it easier to relieve themselves of the payment of the turnpike tolls than of rates or rent; the unpopular gate-keeper was more easily combated than the rate-collector or landlord. In 1885-88, the north Wales   5
farmers regarded the tithe-owners in much the same way as the turnpike toll and the gate-keeper had been regarded by their south Wales bretheren a generation previously. ... payment of the tithe had been always, more or less, unpopular with the bulk of the people.

[D. Lleufer Thomas, *The Welsh land Commission: A Digest of its Report* (1896)]

How were tithes opposed in Wales?

E

A number of Cwm Eithin farmers resolved not to pay tithe at all unless a reduction was granted. The result was that on the eighteenth of May, 1887, the Ecclesiastical Commissioners decided to distrain on the goods of about eighty farmers who had refused to pay. The alarm was sounded, crowds gathered at the threatened farms and in many cases it was found impossible to   5
seize the goods.
In three farms, however, goods were distrained upon. This meant that a sale was to follow, and on June 1, 1887, there was a forced sale ... but not a penny was bid and the attitude of the crowd was threatening. ... In the circumstances the auctioneer and his companions were glad to get away with unbroken   10
bones. I have heard that they and their police protectors were escorted by some three hundred people along the road ... in the Corwen direction.
The 'invaders' were convinced that they were in serious peril and begged for their lives. They were told to kneel on the road and presented with the following declaration which they signed: 'We hereby promise not to come on   15
this business again in any part of England or Wales to sell for Tithes'. They were then made to take off their coats and to put them on wrong side out, to show their repentance.

[Hugh Evans recounting the history of his parish in his book *Cwm Eithin* (1931)]

F
Fig. 20
Daily Graphic: Tithe Disturbances in Denbighshire (29 August 1890)

I
II
III
IV
V
VI
VII
VIII
IX
X

G

On Thursday morning, a large force of police, numbering upwards of 100 men, drafted from Flintshire and Denbighshire forces, assembled [and] were joined by a full company of the 22nd Cheshire Regiment ...

The police drew their truncheons for a few moments and charged the mob right and left. About a dozen were carried out in an insensible condition. One man, Elias Hughes, a deacon in a chapel in the locality, who had been particularly active in the anti-tithe movement, was badly injured, his skull being cracked and his arm broken.

[Report on the riot at Mochdre in *The Flintshire Observer* (June 1887)]

H

As children we heard much talk of how the anti-tithe rebels marched from district to district, and from farm to farm when animals and property were sold to meet the demands ... Pretty effective ways were devised of obstructing the auctioneer and not everyone was a pacifist either, as the odd officer, escaping in haste, found to his cost.

[Rev. T.E. Davies, a Nonconformist minister, describing from memory the tithe war in Gwernogle, Cardiganshire.]

What was the solution?

I

In Denbighshire there is an almost universal consensus of opinion among law-biding persons to the effect that peace cannot be restored by anything short of either disestablishment or a measure casting the tithes, in the first instance, upon the shoulders of the landowners.

[J.E. Vincent, *Letter from Wales* (1889)]

How was the tithe issue resolved?

In 1891 Parliament passed The Tithe Rent Charge Act which stated that in future the tithe must be paid to the Church by the landlords rather than by the tenant farmers. Although unscrupulous landlords raised their tenants' rents to cover the cost of the tithe, the disturbances died down because an important principle had been won. The Disestablishment of the Church in Wales in 1920 went a long way to resolving the issue permanently, though this was not finally done until the abolition of the tithe in 1936.

I
II
III
IV
V
VI
VII
VIII
IX
X

Advice and Activities

(i) General

Suggested Further Reading

D. Egan, *People, Protest and Politics: Case Studies in Nineteenth-Century Wales* (Llandysul, 1987).

D.W. Howell, *Land and People in Nineteenth-Century Wales* (London, 1978).

J.G. Jenkins, *Life and Tradition in Rural Wales* (London, 1976).

D.J.V. Jones, *Before Rebecca: Popular Protests in Wales, 1793-1835* (London, 1973).

D.J.V. Jones, *Rebecca's Children: A Study of Rural Society, Crime and Protest* (Oxford, 1989).

D. Williams, *The Rebecca Riots: A Study in Agrarian Discontent* (2nd. ed., Cardiff, 1986).

Articles:

A. Conway, 'Welsh Emigration in the Nineteenth Century', in A.J. Roderick (ed.), *Wales through the Ages*, vol. 2 (Llandybie, 1960).

D.W. Howell, 'The Agricultural Labourer in Nineteenth-century Wales', *WHR*, vol. 6 (1972-3).

D.W. Howell, 'The Impact of Railways on Agricultural Developments in Nineteenth-century Wales', *WHR*, vol. 7 (1974-5).

D.W. Howell, 'The Rebecca Riots' in T. Herbert & G.E. Jones (eds.), *People and Protest: Wales 1815-1880* (Cardiff, 1988).

I.G. Jones, 'People and Protest: Wales 1815-1880' in T. Herbert & G.E. Jones (eds.), *People and Protest: Wales 1815-1880* (Cardiff, 1988).

D. Williams, 'Rural Wales in the Nineteenth Century', in A.J. Roderick (ed.), *Wales through the Ages*, vol. 2 (Llandybie, 1960).

J. Williams, 'The Move from the Land' in T. Herbert & G.E. Jones (eds.), *Wales 1880-1914* (Cardiff, 1988).

I
II
III
IV
V
VI
VII
VIII
IX
X

Research

1. Look up the causes, course and consequences of the 'Captain Swing' movement in England (culminating in the 'Swing Riots') and compare it with the Rebecca movement in Wales. Note the similarities and differences between them.
2. Look up the following key figures involved in the tithe dispute i) Thomas Gee ii) J.E. Vincent. Write a short biographical sketch on each taking care to emphasise their attitude and contribution to the tithe dispute.

Issues for Debate or Discussion

1. The title 'Tithe Wars' dignifies what would otherwise have been regarded as nothing more than a squalid squabble over tax collection by the Church. Debate the merits of this provocative statement.
2. 'Chartism was a truly political movement, inspired by a theory; Chartism was a plan; Beca was a commotion'. Debate the validity of this statement by the historian R.T. Jenkins.

(ii) Examination Specific

Answering Source/Document Questions

Working with contemporary sources of evidence has become an integral part of study at GCSE and AS/A level. At AS/A level you will be required to answer questions on single-sources (usually between 20 and 35 lines in length) and multi-sources (normally five or six in number ranging from 3 to 6 lines in length). To be successful you need to acquire the necessary skills. Take these steps:

(i) understand the content of the source[s]

(ii) analyse (examine in detail) the information by breaking it down into component parts depending on the questions asked (how, why, what, which, when).

(iii) compare and contrast (similarities and differences) sources

(iv) interpret (explain the meaning) their content by inference and deduction

(v) evaluate by assessing their usefulness and reliability.

The following basic hints should enable you to deal effectively with source-based questions.

(i) Read the source[s] carefully. You will find that the single-source extracts are longer than those you have been used to at GCSE, so it will be good practice to get into the habit of reading them two or three times before answering the questions.

(ii) Note the language and tone of a source as you read it. The primary sources you will encounter may not be easy to understand. The language and written style can often prove very difficult. This is not to say that secondary sources are significantly easier but they are usually more accessible. When working with sources at home or in class, use of a dictionary/glossary is essential. With practice you will soon became familiar with the sources and the language for your period of study.

(iii) Note the attribution (the identity of the writer) and date of each source you read. Knowing who wrote it and when is crucial to answering questions on usefulness and reliability. In time you will became familiar with the source-writers for your period of study.

(iv) Ask yourself why the source was written and for whom. Was it written for a particular purpose? Determining this will help you decide if it is likely to be biased or not which may affect its reliability.

(v) Analyse the source[s] and decide whether the content is factual or opinion? It is likely that in most cases sources will contain elements of both. Guard against being too pessimistic. Just because a source is written by an eye-witness who expresses his opinion does not mean the source is biased and therefore of no value to the historian. Opinion can be just as useful as fact and vice-versa.

Look at the following example:

Q.1. Read the source on page 121 and answer the following questions on the Rebecca Riots.

a) Explain briefly the meaning of the phrase 'the vexatious conduct of toll collectors'? (L.11-12) (4 marks)

b) What information may be inferred from the source about the injustices suffered by those who took part in the riots? (8 marks).

c) How useful is the source to an understanding of the nature of the protest inspired by the Rebecca movement? (20 marks).

I

II

IV

V

X

Advice

a) Refers to the greedy and high-handed way toll keepers were collecting their tolls from those who could least afford to pay.

b) The causes of the riots were put down to the mismanagement of the turnpike trusts e.g.

- money raised not being spent on road improvement;
- the frequency with which tolls were increased and collected;
- the unsympathetic attitude of toll collectors together with some instances of illegal conduct on their part;
- the increase in and collection of tithes;
- the poor laws and the workhouse system;
- corruption of local magistrates.

c) The source gives a good insight into the actions of Rebecca rioters and the impact they had on the area. It provides a detailed account of the grievances of local farmers which contributed to causing the riots. The source is also sensitive to other problems like the weather and other natural phenomenon putting added pressure on the farmers, all of which was made worse by the worsening economic situation. The source is a serious response to the riots, the causes of which the authors have been detailed to investigate. However, the source is limited in the way that it dismisses too easily other potentially contributing factors like political causes. Nor does the source say anything about the heavy-handed reaction of the authorities to the riots. The source also fails to present the wider picture preferring instead to highlight what it terms are the 'local grievances' of the rioters. There is no hint of such unrest elsewhere in Wales or any links between Rebecca and Chartism. To judge from the source alone one may be tempted to think that this was an isolated event peculiar to south-west Wales only.

Answering Synoptic Essay Questions

Synoptic essay questions may sound daunting and different from the traditional open-ended essay questions but they are not. Synoptic assessment requires students to evaluate and analyse change over time so you will be expected to draw together, where appropriate, the political, social, economic, religious and cultural aspects of the topic of study. In the case of a Period Study, such as England and Wales 1815-1914, you will be expected to demonstrate a synoptic approach to the question by evaluating and analysing a topic over a century. In the case of an In-Depth Study, such as Reform and Protest in Wales c.1830-48, the question will be presented as an historical interpretation which you will be required to assess and evaluate by means of an open-ended essay whilst demonstrating a synoptic approach but over a shorter period of time.

As you will see from the examples set out below, the advice you were given on answering open-ended essay questions at the end of the last chapter is sound.

Look at the following example:

'Protest movements were primarily the result of economic and social hardship rather than the results of any deep seated popular demand for political power'. [D. Neils, an historian writing in a general survey of the period, *Nineteenth-Century England* (1992)]

Q. Discuss this interpretation of the nature of popular protest movements in Wales and England during the period 1830 and 1848.

Advice

The key words in the question are interpretation (opinion) and nature (what was it). You could begin by either agreeing or disagreeing with the writer's opinion and then shaping your argument on that basis. On the other hand, it is wiser perhaps to approach such questions in a 'to what extent' way so that you write an essay which will present both sides of an argument, i.e. protest movements may have been the result of economic and social hardship but you cannot dismiss entirely the possibility that there was a demand for political power. You will need to draw on your knowledge of the protest movements you have studied and think critically about their causes, as well as their consequences, and the reactions of contemporaries both in and outside of authority.

You should also engage in a discussion of the attribution by noting the status of the writer and the date the statement was made. As an academic historian he should be in a position to come to a sound judgement based on extensive research. Depending on the date, it might be argued that historical interpretations can change over time.

I
II
III
IV
V
VI
VII
VIII
IX
X

I

II

III

IV

V

VI

VII

VIII

IX

X

Chapter IV
Social Reform and Social Issues

It would be difficult, if not impossible, to exaggerate the scale of social change in nineteenth-century Wales. The pace of that change in the period from 1815 to 1914 was so rapid and so complete that it quite literally witnessed the transformation of Welsh society. Nor was this 'transformation' merely a 'Welsh' phenomenon, Britain, Europe and the wider world too changed as did Wales' place within it. As one might imagine, the subject has the potential to be vast, almost limitless, therefore it behoves (is the duty of) an author or historian to set limits in order to make his study accessible and meaningful to the reader. The aim of this chapter is not to cover all aspects of the subject but to introduce students to some of the main themes of nineteenth and early twentieth century social history that have been outlined recently in books and articles. This chapter has sought to chart the social 'transformation' of Wales by examining five themes which may be regarded as representing the core of what a social historian may use to measure change in a civilised society – by means of its health, education and religion and by its treatment of its poor and criminally delinquent.

1. Health

■ **Key Issue:**
How effectively were the problems of public health and sanitation in Wales dealt with in the nineteenth century?

a) Contemporary Attitudes

Had Victorian Welshmen the means, and the will, to inquire of their compatriots what they considered to be the most pressing social issues of

I
II
III
IV
V
VI
VII
VIII
IX
X

133

their day, it is likely that for the majority, public health would not have figured on their list of priorities.

Had they been disposed to think on the matter, and only the middle and upper classes had the luxury of time to do so, then doubtless crime and the fear of crime, poverty, unemployment and the means to feed, clothe and house their loved ones would have been at the forefront of their minds. This is not to suggest that health was not an issue of vital importance to the population at large, of course it was, but it was very much more of a personal than a public concern, the latter being too abstract a concept for those lacking the educated intellect to make sense of it. Life for the working and poorer classes was hard and in the daily toil and travail of grinding out an often miserable existence, they tended, with the active encouragement of the Church, to accept their lot (of course, when the poor could no longer 'accept their lot' the result was Rebecca and Chartism).

The misery of ill-health, the anguish of pain and the curse of early death were regarded as some of the more fateful hazards of living about which they could do little or nothing. They had neither the time, the education nor the means to apply pressure, political or otherwise, on those with the power to effect changes in matters of public health. Indeed, what demands could the working class make when those on whom they were made, the middle class, were themselves often unsure of how best to proceed. Even the best scientific minds of the day could not, as yet, explicitly show how filth caused sickness or explain the link between poverty and ill-health. That they, and the social reformers who supported them, were certain that such links existed were regarded as insufficient grounds for government legislation or intervention. Public health projects, where they existed, continued to be organised and funded at local level, often at the instigation of enlightened entrepreneurs or social reformers. Therefore, only gradually did universal ignorance in matters of public health give way to a growing awareness of the importance of better housing and good sanitation.

b) Problems in Public Health: Cause and Consequence

It is possible to argue that there had always been a public health problem. The plagues, sicknesses and other disease-epidemics of previous centuries had long taken their toll on a people inured to suffering. Nevertheless, the reason why public health came to constitute, as one historian put it, 'a gigantic problem in Victorian Wales', was mainly on account of the higher mortality rate caused by the increasing frequency of epidemic outbreaks. True, the population was many times greater than had been the case in earlier plague-ridden centuries but the percentage number of estimated deaths per thousand had hardly declined in line with this population growth. People continued to live in appallingly unhealthy conditions but the problem was exacerbated by the rapid urbanisation of Wales which was itself a consequence of the equally rapid industrialisation of Britain. This shift of the population away from a rural to an urban-industrialised environment is regarded by historians as fundamental to understanding the changing patterns of health in Victorian Wales. The growth of towns during the second half of the eighteenth and first half of the nineteenth centuries occurred too quickly, was haphazard and took place without any form of building regulation. As a result, by the middle of the nineteenth century, the authorities were faced with dangerously insanitary conditions caused by poor housing, overcrowding, impure water supplies and the almost total lack of means for the disposal of sewage and household refuse.

Such appalling conditions no doubt still prevailed in the countryside but here they might be better tolerated in sparsely populated villages where the volume of human refuse was inconsequential in comparison to largely overpopulated towns like Merthyr Tydfil. By the same token, when fatal epidemics occurred the rural death rate paled in comparison with urban mortality rates the horror of which, by the sheer number of corpses involved, was compounded by the visual impact of so many burials. In October 1854 the vicar of Dowlais, the Revd. E. Jenkins, wrote 'I preached three times on Sunday and three times yesterday – and had not much sleep for two nights. There were 18 funerals yesterday. Eleven at the same time in the churchyard at the Pant. There are several later today'. This may account for the fact that contemporaries considered life in the country as being considerably healthier than in towns when in truth the benefits were, in most cases, little better than marginal. Certainly, when the writer and traveller George Borrow visited Wales in 1854 he lamented leaving the delightfully scenic little villages of mid-Wales populated, as he saw it, by robust and healthy looking rustics, for the grim reality of the industrial towns of the south filled to the brim with 'rough savage-looking men'. He was appalled by the sight that greeted him on reaching Neath which account he published in his book *Wild Wales* (1862).

I

II

III

IV

V

VI

VII

VIII

IX

X

I

II

III

IV

V

VI

VII

VIII

IX

X

... an extraordinary scene presented itself to my eyes. Somewhat to the south rose immense stacks of chimneys surrounded by grimy diabolically- looking buildings, in the neighbourhood of which were huge heaps of cinders and black rubbish. From the chimneys, notwithstanding it was Sunday, smoke was proceeding in volumes, choking the atmosphere all around. From this 5 pandemonium, at the distance of about a quarter of a mile to the south-west, upon a green meadow, stood, looking darkly grey, a ruin of vast size [Neath Abbey] with window holes, towers, spires, and arches. Between it and the accursed pandemonium, lay a horrid filthy place, part of which was swamp and part pool: the pool black as soot, and the swamp a disgusting leaden 10 colour. Across this place of filth stretched a tramway leading seemingly from the abominable mansions to the ruin. So strange a scene I had never beheld in nature. Had it been on canvas, with the addition of a number of diabolical figures ... it might have stood for Sabbath in Hell devils proceeding to afternoon worship, and would have formed a picture worthy of the powerful 15 but insane painter Jerome Bos.

As horrible as he found Neath, Borrow had yet to reach Merthyr Tydfil! Clearly, such horrific industrial scenes were regarded by the country-bred Norfolk gentleman as unnatural and his sympathy for the people who lived and worked in places like Neath, Swansea and especially Merthyr Tydfil is, elsewhere, made plainly evident. He was repelled by his experience of Merthyr Tydfil: 'I went through a filthy slough, over a bridge, and up a street, from which dirty lanes branched off on either side, passed throngs of savage-looking people talking clamourously, shrank from addressing any of them'. He found the 'houses in general low and mean, and built of rough grey stone' and though the town 'can show several remarkable edifices' they were, in his view, 'of a gloomy, horrid satanic character'! Nor, it seems, could Merthyr easily escape its past for though the town had undergone much improvement in the twenty-five years since Borrow's visit, *Black's Picturesque Guide to Wales* was still able to report in 1881 that 'The populous town which, with astonishing rapidity, has sprung into existence was, until lately a shapeless, unsightly cluster of wretched dingy dwellings'.

Borrow was no scientist nor was he, consciously at least, a social reformer but even his untrained eye, and untrammelled opinions, were witness to the effects of pollution. Leaving Caerffili for Newport he states that, 'The scenery, [somewhere near Bedwas] soon became very beautiful – its beauty, however, was to a certain extent marred by a horrid black object, a huge coal work, the chimneys of which were belching forth smoke of the densest description'. As if the resultant air pollution was not bad enough, Borrow was equally saddened and shocked by the state of the river Rhymney which 'was filthy and turgid owing ... to its having received the foul drainings of the neighbouring coal works'. Nor was industrial waste the only pollutant, a report compiled in 1845 on Merthyr Tydfil [*Second Report of Commissioners of Inquiry into the State of Large Towns and Populous Districts*] listed the human waste that could be found in the nearby river Taf rendering it unfit for use by the town's population either for bathing, washing let alone drinking. The report concluded that Merthyr 'containing at present above 37,000 inhabitants' was a town 'without any public care for the supply of water, drainage or cleansing' and that the people were exposed to disease 'from the filth so abundant in it'. Bangor and Cardiff too had their public health problems. Surveys conducted on behalf of the General Board of Health in 1849 and 1850 respectively concluded that Bangor

> consist of both streets and houses being in a filthy and unhealthy state, the yards being small and having privies in them, from which a disagreeable and unhealthy smell is emitted, and from which contagious diseases have frequently arisen. To several of the houses, especially in Glan-yr-Afon, no privies are attached. The streets generally are rendered disagreeable from their want of being properly cleansed in the winter, and watered in summer.
> [Report to the General Board of Health on ... the Borough of Bangor by G.T. Clark, London, 1849]

Cardiff fared little better where, according to the survey,

> the consequences [of unregulated and poorly constructed building] is what could only be looked for under such circumstances, floods, swamps, filth, miasma, ague and other disorders, in fearful abundance ... The present drains throughout the town would be almost entirely useless in any future system of refuse-drainage. ...Nothing can be worse than the house accommodation provided for the labouring classes and the poor in this town; and the overcrowding is fearful, beyond anything of the kind I have ever known of.
> [Report to the General Board of Health on ... the Town of Cardiff by T.W. Rammell, London, 1850]

The almost total absence of proper sanitation was compounded by the equally dire consequence of ignorance. People, generally, were unaware of the health hazards and they continued to behave in a manner calculated to

I

II

III

IV

V

VI

VII

VIII

IX

X

I
II
III
IV
V
VI
VII
VIII
IX
X

perpetuate their misery. Despite the construction of a new reservoir at Portfield to serve the inhabitants of Haverfordwest, within a decade the *Pembrokeshire Herald* reported that it had become polluted by 'newts, leeches, decaying animals and vegetable matter'. In spite of entreaties to the contrary, it was calculated that the population of the Rhondda Valley was continuing to pollute the soil with upwards of 3,000 tons of excrement annually. In mitigation one is bound to say that though some might complain of the more obvious signs of urban decay, those that more readily offended the senses such as the smells and sights of filth, the local authorities were often reluctant to act. This was motivated in part by obscurantist views that disease was due to 'atmospheric forces' or 'divine providence' but the root cause of their apparent inertia can be found in the generally-held principles of *laissez-faire* the basis of which revolved around a policy of non-interference in economic and social matters. In this respect, local authorities took their lead from national governments which fully endorsed the doctrine of economic and social individualism. Of course, cynics might cite cost as the true basis of *laissez-faire* in matters social, since action in response to public health issues almost inevitably required capital outlay for improvements. Landlords, employers and rate-payers (mainly the well-to-do who also formed the core of most local authorities) were united as one in their reluctance to defray the cost of such improvements. Unless compelled to do so, and a like-minded central government was hardly likely to force them, many local authorities were content to leave matters lie in the hope that the problems would right themselves which, at the necessary expense of the poor and vulnerable, it inevitably did. Epidemics came and went, crises passed and life returned to its usual pattern until the next time.

The consequence was, of course, an ever widening and more frequent cycle of death and disease about which local and national authorities were increasingly becoming concerned. Concern turned to alarm when, in 1831-2, the country was swept by a cholera epidemic the arrival of which had been rumoured for weeks before it struck. Sweeping across Europe the Asiatic cholera cut a swathe of death through rural and urban communities but it was among the latter, in the populous environs of industrial towns, that it caused greatest carnage. Its first reported strike in Wales occurred in May 1832 (some seven months after its first reported strike of a British town, Sunderland in October 1831), when cases were recorded in Flint. By the time the epidemic had run its course, some six months later, it had covered the whole of the Principality causing the deaths of some 455 people. The worst hit towns in Wales included Swansea with 152 deaths and Merthyr Tydfil where 600 people were reportedly infected of whom 160 died. In north Wales, Denbigh was hardest hit suffering 47 deaths and in all some 95 people across the region succumbed to the disease. The irony is that the cholera epidemic, given its 'fearfully sudden destruction' as one contemporary headline put it, killed less people than either typhus or dysentery which were, along with other zymotic diseases (caused and spread by germs) endemic killers. Cholera Morbus, to give it its scientific label, had succeeded where the other equally fatal epidemics had failed, it roused public opinion which in turn put pressure on central government to act. This was due partly to the powers of newsgathering and its dissemination through the newspapers, partly by word of mouth and to the heightened state of anxiety in anticipation of the disease, which had been tracked across Europe, reaching British shores. The government's response was, if anything, half-hearted and though some public health measures were enacted, such as the Water Act intended to improve the supply of fresh water and the compulsory creation of 800 local boards of health in England and Wales, they were but temporary, being allowed to lapse once the danger had passed.

Inevitably cholera morbus returned and when it struck in 1848-9 it was more deadly than before. Reaching Edinburgh in October 1848 it soon spread to Wales striking first in Cardiff in May 1849 where 396 victims perished. In the first six months of the epidemic sweeping England and Wales it claimed over 53,000 lives, by its end nearly 130,000 had fallen victim to the scourge. Merthyr Tydfil suffered worst in Wales with a reported death toll of 1,682. In the following extract from her daily Journal, dated 31 July 1849, Lady Charlotte Guest, the enlightened wife of a wealthy local ironmaster, recounts the scene in her beloved Merthyr.

> I am sorry to say that the accounts of the cholera at Dowlais are fearfully bad. They are beyond anything I could have imagined, sometimes upwards of twenty people dying in one day, and eight men consistently employed in making coffins. Poor Miss Diddams, one of our Infant School Mistresses is dead. One of the medical assistants sent down from London is dying and the whole place in a most lamentable state. I am greatly grieved at the conditions of my poor home.
>
> [Earl of Bessborough (ed.), *Lady Charlotte Guest: Extracts from her Journal, 1833-52* (1950)]

I
II
III
IV
V
VI
VII
VIII
IX
X

There were further cholera outbreaks in 1854, the year of Borrow's four-month visit to the Principality though he does not mention the disease, and again in 1865-6. The following table gives some indication of the mortality rates suffered by some towns and districts in Wales.

Table 9

Cholera Deaths in Welsh towns and districts, 1832-66.
[Figures quoted in Creighton's *History of Epidemics in Britain and the Registrar-General's Office*]

Towns	1832	1849	1854	1866
Caernarfon	30	16	N/A	75
Cardiff	N/A	396	225	76
Merthyr Tydfil	160	1,682	455	229
Newtown	17	N/A	19	N/A
Swansea	152	262	N/A	521

As horrific as were the number of deaths recorded they take no account of the many more who contracted the disease, suffered its ill-effects but lived. For example, in Ystalyfera in 1866 the local physician attended nearly a thousand cases of which 95 proved fatal.

Fig. 21
(i) 'A Court for King Cholera', *Punch* cartoon (1864) and (ii) a ballad entitled
Ymweliad Y Cholera (c.1865)

A COURT FOR KING CHOLERA.

YMWELIAD y bvd ynyd riadr

CHOLERA;

YNGHYD A

Galwad ar bawb i ymofyn am
gymod â Duw cyn eu symud
i'r byd tragwyddol.

GYMRY anwyl, dwys ystyriwn
Yn ein beddau'n fuan byddwn,
Cawn rybyddion bob diwrnod
I ymbar'toi a bod yn barod.

Mae pechodau'r wlad yn gwaeddi
Am i farnau Duw ddod arni,
A phob un galedo'i galon
Deimla'r farn mewn modd echryslon.

Plaau'r Aifft roed i rybyddio,
Er darostwng calon Pharo,
Ond trwy bara i ymgyndynu,
Y môr coch a wnaeth ei foddi.

Cora, Dathan, ac Abiram
Lyncwyd am eu buchedd wyrgam,
Ond er gweled Duw'n ymddigio
Dyn ni fynai blgyu iddo

The Visitation of the Cholera;
and a call for all to seek to be reconciled with
God before they are taken to everlasting life.

Dear Welshmen, let us seriously reflect
Soon we will be in our graves,
We are warned each day
To prepare ourselves and be ready.

The sins of the country shout
(inviting) God's retribution
And each one who hardens his heart
will feel the judgement in a terrible way.

The plagues of Egypt were sent to warn,
And bring humility to Pharaoh's heart,
But because he was still reluctant
The red sea drowned him.

Korah, Dathan and Abiram
Were swallowed because of their crooked ways,
But although God could be seen to be vexed
Man was not willing to submit to Him.

Cholera was a particularly frightening disease, made more so by the often hysterical reaction to it, but it was only one of a number of endemic killers – typhus, typhoid, dysentery and tuberculosis – which preyed on the population at large. According to one medical historian typhus was

> The most persistent and devitalising fever of the first half of the nineteenth century. Greatly encouraged by hunger, dirt, and overcrowding, it is carried in the faeces of lice which dry to a light dust thus enabling a person to become infected by breathing in the dust, or by a scratch on the hand.
>
> [Quoted in K. Strange, *Merthyr Tydfil in the 1840's*]

I

II

III

IV

V

VI

VII

VIII

IX

X

It has been estimated that in Merthyr during the 1840s typhus caused the deaths of 1 in 9 of the town's population but tuberculosis proved infinitely more deadly accounting for 1 in 5 during the 1850s. Although no single factor may be said to cause the disease, poverty, and its associated evils of overcrowding and under-nourishment, was at the root of the problem. According to one eye-witness, a provincial physician named Richard Howard,

> Although death directly produced by hunger is rare, there can be no doubt that a very large proportion of the mortality amongst the labouring classes is attributable to deficiency of food as a main cause, aided by too long continued toil and exertion without adequate repose, insufficient clothing, exposure to cold and other privations to which the poor are subjected.
>
> [Quoted in K. Strange, *Merthyr Tydfil in the 1840's*]

Howard's conclusions were supported by no less a physician than Dr. Edward Smith, assistant to Dr. Simon the government's chief Medical Officer, a post established in 1859. Visiting north Wales in 1863, which included the towns of Conwy, Denbigh, Dolgellau and Machynlleth, Smith concluded that the diet of the labouring classes was 'inferior in almost every respect and in no way sustainable of good health'. They ate few vegetables, some cheese, little butter and meat rarely; bread, milk and oatmeal seemingly forming the bulk of their dietary consumption.

Poverty, poor diet and disease contributed much to the appallingly high infant mortality rate which, as one might expect, was greater in urban than rural districts. Nevertheless, some rural districts suffered more than others it seems and if the diary of Thomas Jenkins (d. 1871) is anything to go by then Llandeilo and its environs was particularly hard hit. An undertaker by trade, though a man of many parts it seems, with engineering and bridge-building at the centre of his interests, Jenkins is uniquely placed to report on the infant mortality rates in his locality. His diary, kept religiously from 1826 until a year before his death, is an useful tool for historians for he invariably gives the ages of those whom he buries, infants and adults, the times of the year in which they died and speculates on the cause of death if an official report from the local medical practicioners was not forthcoming. As a counter-balance to the overwhelming data and statistical evidence regarding the cholera outbreaks, not once does Jenkins mention the disease and nor it seems was the town greatly affected by any of the epidemics. Besides smallpox, 'dropsy' and ill-defined 'fevers', outbreaks of scarlet fever seems to have been the greatest burden suffered by the folk of Llandeilo. Between August 1844 and February 1845 no less than five children, aged from 3 to 9 years, died of scarlet fever one of whom was the diarist's own son, his daughter having recovered. The boy's treatment was in the care of local physician Dr. Prothero 'who ordered his head to be shaved and bathed with cold salt water and leeches applied to his temples'. Needless to say within nine days of contracting the illness the patient died. Primitive medicine dispensed by well-meaning but ill-equipped physicians often proved as much a hindrance to recovery as the effects of the illness itself. It is sad to reflect on the fact that of the four children known to have been born to Dr. Prothero, in whose care the health of a fair proportion of the townsfolk rested, not one survived beyond the age of 11 years.

Table 10

Major Epidemic Diseases of the Victorian Era

Cholera	a severe intestinal infection causing violent vomiting and diarrhoea.
Diptheria	a throat infection causing a mucus-like membrane to block the victim's air passages.
Measles	an acute infectious viral disease marked by red spots on the skin.
Pneumonia	bacterial infection causing inflammation of the lungs.
Scarlet Fever	a throat infection accompanied by a red blotch-like skin rash.
Small Pox	the most contagious of all diseases, marked by fever and pustules leading to disfiguring scars.
Tuberculosis	a wasting disease particularly affecting the lungs.
Typhoid	a severe stomach infection transmitted by polluted water.
Typhus	similar to typhoid but transmitted by lice.
Whooping Cough	an infection of the throat and lungs, particularly affecting children.

I
II
III
IV
V
VI
VII
VIII
IX
X

c) Remedy through Reform

If, as is widely believed, the cholera outbreak of 1831-2 was largely responsible for stimulating interest in social and sanitary conditions in the 1830s, it took central government another decade to act decisively in the cause of public health. It has been suggested that the reasons for this retarded response to the public health problem were four-fold: technical, financial, ideological and political. A shortage of skilled engineers, disagreement between technical 'experts' and the sheer scale of the task involved in supplying piped water to large towns and cities simply added to the often monstrous cost of providing sanitary services. Ideologically and politically those in authority were gripped by the principles of non-intervention so that taxing the few for the benefit of the many was, for many, simply too radical and unorthodox.

The catalyst for change, besides the cholera epidemics, was the work of social reformers like Edwin Chadwick (d. 1890), who devoted himself to the cause of the poor, and the formation of like-minded propagandist organisations such as the statistical societies, the first of which was established in Manchester in 1833 with the object of discussing 'subjects of political and social economy and for the purpose of statistical inquiries'. Characteristic of the enquiring and reforming climate of the 1830s soon other large towns and cities across England and Wales formed their own statistical societies. Their purpose was not only to investigate the conditions of life in urban districts but also to disseminate their findings to a wider audience which included central government reforms.

Their work, and pressure, bore fruit in 1837 when the government passed the Registration Act which led to the foundation of the Registrar-General's Office. Charged, primarily, with collecting accurate statistics on the death-rate social reformers and government ministers alike were, for the first time, given the opportunity to measure and analyse statistical data which might form the basis of future campaigns or policies. By 1840 the government was able to publish the first reliable index measuring the death rate in each of the 48 registration districts into which Wales had been divided as a result of the 1837 Act.

The indices drawn up for the period 1840-60 indicated that the average death-rate for Wales was 22 per 1,000 and for England 23 per 1,000.

Naturally, the mortality rates varied, quite considerably in some cases, from district to district and in 1850 it was calculated that 8 of the 48 registration districts had death rates above the national average, they included Pontypool (23 per 1,000), Newport (24 per 1,000), Cardiff (30 per 1,000) and, top of the league, Merthyr Tydfil (34 per 1,000).

Infant mortality rates were also published and in the period 1837-50 the ratio of deaths to 1,000 live births for England and Wales was 150. This ratio rose to 156 in the following decade and did not show signs of falling until after 1880. Although the surge of interest in such social investigations slackened off somewhat after 1860 they did not cease entirely as is made plain with the foundation of the National Association for the Promotion of Social Science which divided its interests into education, public health and 'social economy' and which met regularly until 1886.

Edwin Chadwick was one, if not the, leading reformer of his day, and, by virtue of his office, he was appointed secretary of the Poor Law Commission in 1834, and because of his connections in Parliament, he was uniquely placed to report on the health problems associated with poverty. His task was, in part, to change attitudes and to confront the authorities with irrefutable evidence of the debilitating effects of ill-health. This is what he did in 1842. *His Report ... on an Inquiry into the Sanitary Condition of the Labouring Population of Great Britain*, is justly hailed as a landmark in the growth of national social consciousness:

- It contributed to the formation in 1844 of the Health of Towns Associations, voluntary bodies which sprung up in various urban centres across England and Wales.
- It acted as a spur to the appointment of a Royal Commission to inquire into 'the State of Large Towns and Populous Districts' which reported its findings in 1844-5.

Making powerful use of statistical data collected by the Registrar-General's Office and provided by local statistical societies, Chadwick was able to prove, nearly eight years before a scientific link was established by London doctor John Snow in 1849, that the 'disadvantaged masses' huddled together 'ghetto-like', in the most insanitary parts of towns and cities, suffered most from epidemic diseases. Faced with this evidence, and the renewed cholera outbreak in 1848, the government had no choice but to legislate in line with Chadwick's demands that local authorities be 'forcefully

I

II

III

IV

V

VI

VII

VIII

IX

X

encouraged' to provide safe water supplies, proper sewage disposal, clean streets and 'the removal of nuisances and the like'.

The Public Health Act of 1848, viewed by some historians as 'the starting point of a revolution in sanitary matters', was far from the comprehensive legislation envisaged by Chadwick. According to the terms of the Act local authorities would be encouraged or advised rather than compelled to comply with government directives on matters of public health. Of greater concern, was the fact that local authorities were only obliged to set up boards of health if 10% of the ratepayers petitioned for one or if the death rate exceeded the national average. Before local boards of health could be established reports on the sanitary conditions of the districts concerned had to be prepared by properly qualified officers. The time taken and the expense incurred in preparing these reports, acted sometimes as a disincentive for local authorities to participate in the scheme. Such was the case in the cathedral city of St. David's when, incredibly, the council treated as a 'joke' a request by the inhabitants for a public water supply, and this as late as January 1910!

Despite its shortcomings, the 1848 Act set the basis for future improvements and over the next thirty years no less than three Public Health Acts were passed by Parliament, in 1859, 1872 and 1875. As a direct consequence of these acts:

- 1859 saw the creation of a Medical Committee to which was attached the first permanent Medical Officer charged with the task of advising the government in matters of health.
- In 1872 urban and rural Sanitary Districts were established across the country which made more effective the provision of state health care and the gathering of statistics.
- The 1875 Act passed by the Disraeli government made compulsory the registration of all Regional and Local Medical Officers and, moreover, it ensured that they were properly qualified medical personnel.
- By 1888 not only had a Society of Medical Officers been established but they were publishing annually a Journal, *Public Health*, which enabled health districts to be compared and information shared. As the following table reveals there was other equally significant legislation passed during the latter half of the century which widened the issue of public health.

Table 11

Principal Acts of Parliament Concerning Public Health

1832	The Water Act
1837	Registration Act
1847	The Town Improvement Clauses Act
1848, 1859, 1872, 1875	Public Health Acts
1848, 1854	Nuisances Removal and Diseases Prevention Acts
1851	Workmen's Cottages Act
1866	Sanitary Act
1868, 1875	Artisans' Dwellings Act

Swansea was among the few urban authorities in Wales to take full advantage of the Artisans' Dwellings Act to rid itself of slum housing by compulsory purchase which enabled Gamwell's *Guide to Swansea* (1880) to sell the town as a resort for visitors: 'Until some months ago, the whole of the neighbourhood between middle High Street and the Hill was covered with small, unsightly, unhealthy houses ... All these wretched habitations have now been swept away ... Other unhealthy areas have been cleared at Greenhill, Frog Street and Cross Street'.

Disappointed by the feeble terms of the 1848 Act, Chadwick continued to press for more radical action and in doing so he made powerful enemies not least among his colleagues on the newly-established General Board of Health (1848), of which he was a commissioner, who resented his often tactless and obtrusive manner. Partly in consequence of this the Board was wound up in 1854. Chadwick had made enemies elsewhere particularly among the class of industrialists, businessmen and other substantial employers who regarded him and his aims, let alone the expense to which they might be put, with grave suspicion. Their concern was, in many respects, justified for as Chadwick himself admitted public health schemes did not come cheap.

It has been calculated that between 1848 and 1875 something approaching £1.2 million was spent by local authorities, often in partnership with private enterprise, on sewerage, drainage and piped water supplies. In local terms,

I

II

III

IV

V

VI

VII

VIII

IX

X

public health expenditure varied from town to town and much depended on their size and the seriousness of the conditions therein.

- **Bangor** ratepayers were required to foot a bill of nearly £8,000 for essential work
- **Cardiff**'s townsfolk had to find close on £100,000.
- In light of the damning reports on **Swansea**'s public health problems – by Sir Henry De La Beche in 1845 and G.T. Clark in 1849 – over £200,000 was spent over the next twenty years.
- Although equally damned by report – T.W. Rammell in 1850 – and twice the size of Swansea – according to census a population of 46,378 in 1851 as opposed to 21,533 – a little less than £175,000 was spent in the same period putting right **Merthyr**'s public health problems. According to Neil Evans Merthyr's problems stemmed from the fact that 'lacking in government and in middle-class aggression, the power and parsimony of the great ironworking concerns prevented any real progress' (N. Evans, 'The Urbanization of Welsh Society' in *People and Protest: Wales 1815-1880*, 1988).

By the end of the nineteenth century the nation's health had been significantly improved yet there remained a great deal to do and the issue was certainly not resolved to the satisfaction of Chadwick's successors in the field of social reform. True, Swansea's chief medical officer was able to report that whereas the death-rate in 1848 had stood at 23.5 per 1,000 by 1899 it had improved to 18.3 per 1,000. On the other hand, some basic lessons had yet to be learnt and as late as 1893 Rhondda's chief medical officer reported on the pollution found in the river which 'contains a large proportion of human excrement, offal and entrails from the slaughterhouse, the rotten carcasses of animals, cats and dogs and street refuse'. Nor was the populous and industrialised Rhondda valley alone in this respect, as the report of the chief medical officer for Haverfordwest, published in October 1910, makes clear. He complained bitterly of the casual non-observance of simple rules of hygiene by the inhabitants, and this from a man who was by profession a veterinary surgeon! This strikes at the heart of the issue for, in spite of half-a-century of parliamentary legislation devoted to improving the health of the nation, its success rested on the co-operation of the public in whose continued ignorance, rather than in government neglect, lay the final stumbling block to progress.

2. Poverty

■ Key Issue:
How much of a problem was poverty in nineteenth-century Wales and how was it dealt with?

a) Attitudes to the poor and the treatment of poverty

> Poverty, something experienced only by the lower classes, but defined in legislation by the ruling classes, was the major problem of the age.

Professor Ieuan Gwynedd Jones' definition of poverty is deliciously ironic and is a truism that may be applied to any age or period in history. It was undoubtedly a major problem in nineteenth-century Wales but no more or less so than in previous centuries. The average twelve year old school child can, if pressed, recount chapter and verse on the problems of the poor in Tudor times and on the measures taken by Elizabethan government to solve them. In Elizabethan society poverty was regarded almost as a disease, and a self-inflicted one at that, the sufferers of which needed sharp corrective treatment. The poverty-stricken masses were divided into two classes of able-bodied – physically well and active but unemployed – and impotent poor – the old, the sick, the handicapped and the young – the latter gaining a mean measure of compassion in a society not noted for its humanitarianism. Whipping, branding and virtual incarceration in a house of correction or workhouse was usually the lot of the able-bodied poor whilst their impotent brethren might look forward to some support from private charities. Self-help was promoted as a cheap and effective way of dealing with small numbers of poor, licences were issued giving the fortunate few the legal right to beg for a living. Unfortunately, Elizabethan measures to 'cure' poverty were too few, too poorly funded and too small-scale to deal with a rapidly expanding and increasingly volatile problem. Vagrancy, riot, crime and general unrest forced an increasingly perturbed government to act and it did so by legislating a series of poor laws culminating in the Poor Law Act of 1601. This Act required each parish to take responsibility for its own poor and its administration was entrusted to the parish priest and Justices of the Peace. In an effort to tackle vagrancy the Act of Settlement of 1662 was passed which stated that, henceforth, the 'wandering' poor

I
II
III
IV
V
VI
VII
VIII
IX
X

I

II

III

IV

V

VI

VII

VIII

IX

X

would be required to return to and be supported by the rate-paying parishoners of the parishes in which they were born.

The Poor Rate was levied by few parishes in Wales the majority of which had, by tradition, long shouldered the burden of poor relief. Welsh communities coped because the numbers of poor per parish remained relatively low which meant they were not an obvious burden on the often public spirited parishoners who supported them largely by means of the church collection on Sundays or through bequests by local gentry. However, rapid industrialisation, urbanisation, demographic and economic changes contributed to massive social dislocation which inevitably impacted on the poor, not least in swelling their number, with the result that between 1760 and 1820 the poor rate for England and Wales increased by over 400%.

In becoming a greater financial burden the poor were propelled to the forefront of parishoners minds which tended to diminish their sympathy and increase their parsimony. A culture of shame evolved where those seeking poor relief were reminded of their destitution and thereby deliberately disgraced by being 'on the parish'. In Cowbridge in 1770, for example, the poor were required to wear badges indicating that they were paupers. The poet, writer and Independent minister Robert Thomas, better known by his bardic name Ap Vychan, recounted with anger the day, in 1817, his aged, bedridden and fever-sick father, himself no mean poet and man of letters, was deprived, by the overseer of Llanuwchllyn, of his one luxury, his mattress. A harshly enforced means test ensured that those seeking poor relief were denied help if, as was decided in Dolgellau in 1822, there was 'a clock or any useless furniture in the house'.

It is perhaps an indictment on a society that calls itself civilised that Victorian social reformers were faced with largely the same problems that confronted their Elizabethan predecessors more than 300 years before. Equally indictable is the fact that attitudes had changed little during that period, the poor were still viewed with suspicion by those charged, by their relative wealth, to relieve them of their poverty. If reluctance and resentment tended to characterise the attitudes of the average rate-payer, upon whom fell the burden of funding initiatives for poor relief, the state and its judicial system had even less charity to spare.

There was a generally-held belief that poverty was a sign of bad character for which the poor ought to be punished, and punished they were, being subjected to a penal system which seemed to revel in its cruelty, which was apparently devoid of humanity but which, ultimately, had no answer to the problem it sought to eradicate. By 1822 more than 150 crimes listed in the statute book were punishable by death. Some of the more absurd included impersonating a Chelsea Pensioner, defacing Westminster Bridge, theft of a sheep, stealing articles worth more than 5 shillings (25p), even stealing a silk handkerchief might result in hanging! That crime went hand-in-hand with poverty was an acknowledged if not an established fact and in spite of the repressive measures taken to tackle the one – crime – they were almost bound to fail if the symptoms of the other – poverty – were not addressed also. For example, it has been convincingly shown that it was mainly the dire poverty suffered by the farmers and labourers in south-west Wales in the 1830s and 1840s that led to the Rebecca Riots. Consequently, fear of social unrest and possible revolution convinced the government that the Old Poor Law (1601), which had remained largely intact and only ever intended for times of crisis, required urgent amendment.

b) Penury and Policy: The Poor Law Amendment Act,1834

The first steps to amending the Old Poor Law were taken in 1832 when a Commission of Inquiry was set up to examine critically the system of poor relief as operated throughout the country. The commissioners found wide variations in the structure and administration of the Poor Laws ranging from the system first ventured in 1795 by the magistrates of the parish of Speenhamland in Berkshire, which involved payment of poor relief in cash to supplement inadequate wages, to that used in the parish of Southwell in Nottinghamshire in the 1820s by which relief was given only to those poor who agreed to accept the strict regime of the workhouse. In 1834 the Poor Law Commission published its report in which it recommended, among other things, adopting the Southwell system of poor relief. The following extracts taken from the *Report of the Royal Commission on the Poor Laws* (1834) give some hint as to the attitudes adopted by the commissioners.

> We recommend ... the appointment of a Central Board to control the administration of the Poor Laws ... that ... Commissioners be empowered ... to frame and enforce regulations for the government of workhouses ... and that

I

II

III

IV

V

VI

VII

VIII

IX

X

I

II

III

IV

V

VI

VII

VIII

IX

X

such regulations shall, as far as may be practicable, be uniform throughout the country ...

The first and most essential of all conditions ... is that his (the able-bodied pauper) situation on the whole shall not be made really or apparently as eligible as the situation of the independent labourer of the lowest class ... All relief whatever to able-bodied persons or to their families, other than in well-regulated workhouses ... shall be declared unlawful, and shall cease.

The government responded by passing the Poor Law Amendment Act the main terms of which stated that
1. no able-bodied poor were to be given outdoor relief
2. workhouses were to be constructed in each parish
3. parishes could, if desired and to defray cost, band together to form unions – 48 were set up in Wales
4. the rate-payers of each parish or union had to elect a Board of Guardians to administer the provisions of the Poor Law
5. the Guardians were required to oversee the workhouse and to collect the poor rate
6. a Poor Law Commission of three men be established to regulate and supervise the working of the Act.

Map 10

Poor Law Unions and Workhouses, c. 1871

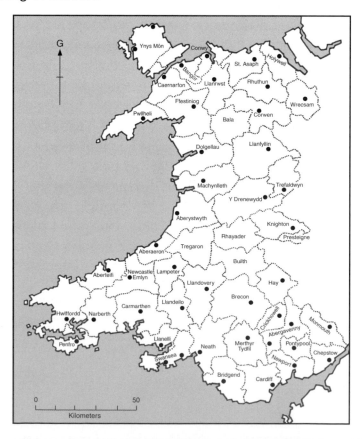

Fig. 22
Desperation and Despondency: a street scene in an urban slum (1870)

The architect of the Act was Edwin Chadwick and in recognition of his work for the Commission of Inquiry 1832-34 he was appointed secretary to the Poor Law Commission, a post he held until 1846. During his tenure Chadwick endured savage criticism for what was perceived to be his over-confident faith in the Act and his stubborn refusal to amend it even in the

I
II
III
IV
V
VI
VII
VIII
IX
X

face of evidence showing its flaws. The most serious flaw in the Act revolved around the principle of reducing costs which, statistically at least, it achieved with spending on the poor down from £7 million in 1831 to less than £5 million in 1851. In local terms, spending on the poor varied considerably, for example

- the Swansea Union, consisting of 27 parishes and a population of around 31,000, expended £6,859 between 1834-36 (its nearest neighbour)
- the Neath Union consisting of 29 parishes and a population of approximately 23,500 spent £7,510.

However, the cost in human terms was incalculable for in the drive to reduce spending some Boards of Guardians sacrificed the health and welfare of the workhouse poor by denying them a staple diet. The worst case occurred in Andover in 1845 where it was discovered that the inmates of the parish workhouse were so hungry that they fought each other to eat the rotting marrow of the bones they were employed to crush. The so-called Andover Scandal caused such an outcry that an embarrassed government tried to deflect criticism by shifting the blame on to the Poor Law Commissioners and then replacing them and their Commission by establishing a Poor Law Board in 1847. Nothing daunted Chadwick resigned his secretaryship of the now-defunct Poor Law Commission in 1846 and turned his attention to sanitary reform becoming an influential member of the newly-established General Board of Health in 1848 – until that too was wound up in 1854!

The Poor Law Amendment Act of 1834 may have signalled a change in policy but it did not herald a change in attitude, if anything attitudes towards the poor hardened. The Act required that conditions in the workhouses be made as 'less desirable' as possible so as to deter the 'indigent' poor. Consequently, a strict daily regime was introduced, families were split up and severe spending limits imposed, indeed, no fit or 'able-bodied' person was to receive money or other kinds of help from the Poor Law authorities except in a workhouse. The New Poor Law (1834) may be seen as a final solution to the problem of pauperism, which, it hoped, would not only reduce the cost of provision of relief, but would also improve the moral character of the poor and labouring classes.

In common with other prominent social reformers of his day, Chadwick was convinced that outdoor relief undermined the labourer's will to fend for himself and so he intended that help should only be given inside a workhouse 'in conditions that were below the lowest standard of living outside the workhouse'. He held the firm opinion that the so-called 'workhouse test', would deter all but the destitute and 'deserving poor' from applying to 'go on the parish' and that it would restore the principle of work by requiring paupers to perform a service in return for relief.

Even those of a more charitable disposition found they held much in common with Chadwick's views. In 1869 the newly-established Charity Organisation Society, founded with the express purpose of co-ordinating the various efforts of the poor relief organisations, made a clear distinction between the 'deserving' and 'undeserving' poor. In its annual report for 1876, the Charity, set up by a group of wealthy philanthropists who believed the poor could best be helped by giving them the means to help themselves, reminded its subscribers of its purpose:

The poor should meet the ordinary problems of life, relying not on charity but on their own thrift and self-help. The worker knows that:
1. temporary sickness will sometimes visit his household
2. times of slackness of work will occasionally come
3. if he has a large family his resources will be taxed to the utmost
4. old age will make him incapable of work.
All these are the ordinary problems of life. If the worker thinks they
will be met by State aid he will make no effort to meet them himself.

Almost inevitably, such views and the Poor Law that inspired them, attracted as much criticism as support, even praise in some quarters, as may be gauged by the reports and editorials in local newspapers. *The Cambrian*, published in Swansea, offered its support for the Poor Law while *The Carmarthen Journal* and, in north Wales, *The Chronicle*, attacked it as a gross violation of peoples' rights. The most vitriolic attack on the Poor Law came in the English newspaper *The Northern Star* (7 June 1845) which stated that

> ... the denial of all relief, except on terms that would deter everyone but the soul-destroyed starving slave ... the institution of the workhouse test ... classification ... separation ... 'scientific' dietaries ... all this was well-calculated to make the labourer offer his services for almost any amount of wage, sooner than subject himself to the cruelties which awaited him...

I

II

III

IV

V

VI

VII

VIII

IX

X

155

Fig. 23
Contemporary cartoon illustrating the Poor Laws (1836)

Fig. 24
'Just-Starve-Us Workhouse' by George Cruikshank (c. 1837)

Despite the criticism the government remained firm and committed to the Act. In the same year it received over 250 petitions signed by more than 225,000 people calling for the repeal of the Act, the government responded by publishing the Report of the Select Committee of the House of Commons on the Poor Laws (1838) which stated that 'the committee are convinced that the utmost benefit has resulted from the general adoption of this system of relief, and they strongly recommend that it should in future be adhered to, subject to occasional departures ... under the pressure of special circumstances ...'.

In the face of government intransigence those opposed to the Poor Law turned either to peaceful protest or to violence and, unsurprisingly, the workhouses, nicknamed *Bastilles*, became obvious targets for destruction. In January 1839 a baying mob, whose motives, it has to be said, were mixed and not entirely focused on the plight of the poor, attempted to burn down the newly-built workhouse at Narberth. Although the workhouse was repaired there was to be no change in the attitude of those charged with its 'efficient' administration. In 1900 the Narberth guardians took the decision to reduce spending on paupers, a policy which was still in evidence as late as 1924 when, according to a disapproving *Pembrokeshire Herald*, they turned down a suggestion for installing electric light in the workhouse being, in their view, 'the wrong time to go in for luxuries'! Nor were the Narberth guardians alone in stigmatising the poor, in an effort to discourage persons from seeking relief, in May 1872 the Pembroke guardians published a list of paupers in the local, and very pliant, press (none other than the *Pembrokeshire Herald* in its pre-social conscience guise!).

Aside from violence there was much peaceful protest against the Poor Law and in this the local gentry, particularly in rural Wales, were to the fore. Many of those elected to serve on the Boards of Guardians were drawn from the landowning classes, families who had a long tradition of dispensing charity to the poor, and they resented the intrusion of central government and the centralisation of poor relief under the Poor Law Commission. In Cardiganshire, for example, the local Boards of Guardians resisted efforts to reduce or cease altogether outdoor relief and in some instances, at Lampeter and Tregaron, they had yet to build a workhouse. The Poor Law Commission and, from 1847-1871, the Poor Law Board (from 1871 the Local Government Board), lacked the necessary powers to compel parish unions to carry out its wishes and in Wales it was more often ignored than complied with. This is not to suggest that all parish unions, their administrators and their workhouses were inefficient, deficient or inhuman, many were praised when inspected by commissioners appointed by the government to survey the workings of the Act in 1844. The Commission of Inquiry for Wales found many instances of good practice such as the provision of chaplains for religious services, gardens for inmates to grow their own food, doctors and nurses for improved medical care and teachers for instructing the children of the poor. Aberystwyth and Cardigan were singled out for especial praise particularly in their provision of a good healthy diet for inmates. If the reports in the *Llanelly and County Guardian* are typical then the inmates of the town's workhouse could count themselves among the most fortunate paupers in Wales, enjoying as they did the rich and charitable bounty of the local landowning gentry, the Nevills and Stepneys.

> Easter Treats [1864] - On Good Friday last, Mrs. Nevill kindly gave the inmates of the Llanelly Union Workhouse a festivity of good tea and hot cross buns. On Monday last, Col. Cowell Stepney sumptuously feasted them with roast beef, plum pudding, and *cwrw da*, together with a supply of tobacco for the old men, and oranges for the children. ... ample justice was done by the inmates to the good things provided for them.

> New year's day at the Workhouse [1869] – It is a fact, and a tragic one, that 80 per cent if not more of the female paupers of our country are what they call living to drink. Life in the workhouse, of course, is full of sameness and very uneventful, except for those very few occasions when some kind-hearted gentlemen ... conspire to rid the Workhouse of its glooms and the hearts of the inmates of their sorrows. One of these occasions was New Year's Day.

The brutal, and boring, reality of life in the majority of workhouses, only hinted at here, was quite different as is made clear in a report compiled by a Royal Commission on workhouses in 1909:

> We have found respectable old women annoyed by the presence of noisy and dirty imbeciles. We have ourselves seen... pregnant women, who have come in to be confined, compelled to work side by side with women so physically deformed as to be positively repulsive... We have more than once seen young children in bed with minor ailments next to women of bad character under treatment for contagious disease, whilst other women in the same ward, were in advanced stages of cancer and senile decay.

This highly critical report recommended urgent and far reaching reforms or, failing that, the abolition of workhouses. In the event, abolition took another twenty years.

c) Booth and Rowntree

By the late nineteenth century the issue of urban poverty was attracting a great deal of critical comment. One of the pioneers of social reform was a wealthy and successful Liverpool shipping merchant Charles Booth (d. 1916) who spent over fifteen years gathering information on the lives of working people in London. His intention had been to disprove the image of grinding poverty that some social reform movements, most notably the Social Democratic Federation established in 1881, said existed in Britain's towns and cities. Faced with the horrible reality of what he found, Booth had to admit his error and between 1891 and 1903 he published the results of his work in 17 volumes entitled *The Life and Labour of the People of London*. Booth calculated that:

- 30.7% of the population were living in poverty
- only 0.9% were responsible for their poverty-stricken existence. He believed that £1.05 per week was just sufficient for a 'moderate family' to survive and that the state should help more directly the 'honest poor'.

Seebohm Rowntree (d. 1954), a wealthy chocolate manufacturer from the north, carried out a similar survey based on a house to house study in his home city of York. His research published in 1901 under the heading *Poverty: A Study of Town Life* indicated clearly the cyclical nature of poverty – its incidence varying with the trade cycle of prosperity and slump and the cycle within the wage-earning household. According to Rowntree's calculations there were two kinds of poverty; primary and secondary:

- Those suffering primary poverty were mainly without work and consequently without the means to fund the four basic requirements – food, fuel, shelter and clothing.
- Secondary poverty affected mainly those in low paid or casual employment who earned just enough to pay for the basic necessities but not for items like medicine. He concluded that 9.9% of York's population were living in primary and 17.9% in secondary poverty.

I
II
III
IV
V
VI
VII
VIII
IX
X

Booth and Rowntree did more than most to contribute to a change in attitude to the relief of the poor. According to an editorial in the *Observer* newspaper, dated 20 December 1891, 'Mr. Charles Booth's paper on State pensions for the aged poor ... proves that the pauperism which is most probably not, as we have all been taught, due to drunkenness, vice and laziness but to ... sickness and old age. These, according to Mr. Booth's unimpeachable figures, are the chief cause of poverty'.

d) The Liberal Government Welfare Reforms, 1906-1914

The Liberal leader Campbell-Bannerman was shocked by the reports and he used Rowntree's figures for York to estimate that nearly 33% of the British nation were living below the poverty line or as he put it 'on the verge of hunger'. Determined it seems to right the wrongs of the past, the Liberals set themselves the task of social welfare reform.

The Liberal's massive election victory in 1906 gave them a mandate to carry through radical reforms at the root of which was the idea that state benefits should be paid in addition to, but separately from, the Poor Law. The core of the Liberal's reform programme revolved around three pieces of legislation:

1) the Workmen's Compensation Act (1906) – employers to compensate workers injured or diseased as a result of their work
2) the Old Age Pensions Act (1908) – a means tested pension for people aged over 70
3) the National Insurance Act (1911) – part 1 set up a National Health Insurance scheme for workers unable to work due to illness while part 2 established the principle of dole for the unemployed workers, though initially its provisions were limited to those employed in the construction industry.

Although the measures offered minimal help to those in need they did more to alleviate poverty than any government-backed legislation during the whole course of the nineteenth century. They were important first steps towards a welfare state, and though never intended as such by the Liberal government, who saw them as an end in themselves, they amounted to a considerable erosion of the principles of *laissez-faire* especially as embodied in the 1834 Poor Law.

Fig. 25
'The New Year's Gift', *Punch* welcomes the Old Age Pension (1909)

THE NEW YEAR'S GIFT.

I
II
III
IV
V
VI
VII
VIII
IX
X

Apart from the introduction of Old Age Pensions, perhaps the most significant element in the Liberals' approach to the whole issue of welfare reform was the so-called 'People's Budget' of 1909. In order to raise revenue to pay for the government's welfare reforms, particularly the costs associated with Old Age Pensions, the Chancellor of the Exchequer, David Lloyd George, planned to increase taxation on the propertied classes, e.g.

- income tax to be raised to 5p (2p) in the pound on annual incomes up to £3,000
- a new higher tax of 1s. 3p (8p) in the pound on incomes over £3,000
- death duties on estates worth over £5,000
- a tax of 20 per cent on the unearned increase in property values when land was sold or exchanged.

In this way the Liberals hoped to raise over £16 million a large part of which would be spent on their social and economic reforms. The Conservatives in the Commons and the aristocratic-wealthy Conservative supporters in the Lords, together with the property-rich classes outside Parliament, opposed the Liberal budget of 1909 but failed to stop it. Lloyd George defended his budget in a speech given in the House of Commons:

> This is a War Budget. It is for raising money to wage implacable warfare against poverty and squalidness. I cannot help hoping and believing that before this generation has passed away we shall have advanced a great step towards that good time when poverty and wretchedness and human degradation which always follow in its camp will be as remote to the people of this country as the wolves which once infested the forests.

For more than a century before 1906 Britain had topped the world's league of wealthiest nations, her industrial and commercial strength had dominated the world's markets for much of the nineteenth century. British political, military and naval power had triumphed and secured for the country a large overseas Empire rich in resources. Confident, wealthy and secure, Britain seemed capable of overcoming the most difficult of problems. Yet for all her success abroad she failed to conquer the problems of poverty and social deprivation at home. Edwardians were faced with solving a social problem that Victorians had failed to resolve, the Liberal's social welfare measures did much to move the philosophy of the country away from self-help to state help which, in time, impacted upon the causes rather than the symptoms of poverty.

Table 12

Principal Social and Economic Reforms

1906	**Workmen's Compensation Act** employers to compensate workers injured or diseased as a result of their work.
1906	**Trades Dispute Act** protected union funds from claims for damages arising from strikes.
1907	**Measure for Prison Reform** ended imprisonment for debt and introduced probation service.
1908	**Old Age Pensions Act** a means tested pension for people aged over 70.
1909	**Trade Boards Act** laid down minimum wages in so-called 'sweated' industries (e.g. clothing trade).
1909	**Measure for Labour Exchanges** helped unemployed to find work.
1909	**Development Commission** to organise the better funding of state welfare.
1911	**Shops Act** established legal right of shop workers to a weekly half-day holiday.
1911	**National Insurance Act** provided financial assistance for men unable to work due to illness and established the right to dole for the unemployed.
1913	**Trade Union Act** legalised union funds being used for political uses.

I

II

III

IV

V

VI

VII

VIII

IX

X

3. Crime

■ Key Issue:
How serious a problem was crime and how effectively did government deal with it?

a) Definition

According to *The Oxford English Dictionary* crime is defined variously as

> **1 a** an offence punishable by law
>   **b** illegal acts as a whole (resorted to crime)
> **2**   an evil act (a crime against humanity)
> **3**   a shameful act

These definitions appear so straightforward as to warrant little attention beyond their comprehension but this would be to ignore the fact that what constitutes a 'crime' in one period may not necessarily do so in another. Indeed, in any period a bewildering variety of forms of behaviour have been criminalized – the prosecution of Roman Catholic recusants in the Elizabethan period – or categorised as deviant – convictions for witchcraft were still possible as late as the 1730s. For example, while we might regard strikes and peaceful protest as a legitimate means of drawing attention to widely-held grievances, the early Victorians would almost certainly have not. To them, workers' strikes and popular protest, peaceful or otherwise, were regarded essentially 'evil' acts calculated to end in a 'revolutionary' frenzy of death and destruction. Consequently, the authorities reacted, more often perhaps over-reacted, with such ferocity and repressive zeal, turning a deaf ear to petitions and the like, that strikers and protesters themselves resorted to violence.

The strike in 1816 by miners in Tredegar was initially peaceful but as their numbers swelled beyond what the local authorities considered acceptable – the Riot Act of 1715 regarded 12 or more persons 'tumultuously assembled' as unacceptable! – panic-stricken, they called in the army (which consequently exacerbated) the situation. Within days what had originally been a protest over wage-cuts had turned into a rioting-mob of around 8,000 confronted by 120 well-armed soldiers of the 55th Regiment and Swansea Cavalry. The inevitability of violence, intimidation and property destruction attached to mass movements like workers' strikes and protests merely served to confirm the deep-seated prejudice of those in authority that crime, committed in the main by individuals in what might be termed minor social-domestic circumstances, was an endemic feature of life for the lower classes and, like cancer, needed to be cut out of society and destroyed. Little effort was made to understand the causes of crime much less sympathy for the convicted even if, for example, hunger were proved to be the chief motivation for theft or wage-cuts and unemployment for protest. As a result of this growing preoccupation with crime it soon came to be regarded as a serious social problem.

If the substance and nature of nineteenth-century crime cannot easily be defined, its punishment, which varied in its intensity and severity, may also defy simple explanation. Indeed, the Victorians and their predecessors seem to have had difficulty in deciding what constituted 'serious' crime, meriting the severest punishment, let alone what might be considered, today at least, minor crimes requiring no more than a fine or caution. Influenced still by the so-called 'Bloody Code' of the eighteenth century, the early nineteenth-century judicial system was designed deliberately to be harsh, repressive and public in order to deter crime and criminals. Consequently, by the early 1820s in excess of a hundred and fifty crimes were punishable by hanging, ranging from pick-pocketing, demanding money with menaces to cutting down trees in an orchard and various forms of vandalism and begging. When lawyer and M.P. Samuel Romilly attempted to introduce a Bill into Parliament in 1810 which would have abolished the law making the theft of five shillings from a shop a capital crime, it was thrown out by the House of Lords!

Fear lay at the root of this vindictive judicial system, fear of revolution in part among the ruling élite, but also a general fear of crime against persons and property for which death, transportation or incarceration with hard labour seem to have been the preferred methods of punishment. The fact that crime levels rose alarmingly during the early nineteenth century, mainly as a result of the mass demobilisation of men from the armed forces after 1815, did little to calm the fears of the propertied classes who came to believe in the existence of a 'criminal class'. 'There is a distinct body of thieves' suggested one contributor to *Fraser's Magazine* in 1823, 'That may be known almost by their very gait in the streets'. Prejudiced by such preconceived notions on the nature of contemporary criminality, the wealthy,

I

II

III

IV

V

VI

VII

VIII

IX

X

165

I

II

III

IV

V

VI

VII

VIII

IX

X

ruling and propertied classes were either disinterested or actively hostile to those advocating reform of the judicial system. Consequently, reformers like Sir Samuel Romilly (d. 1818), Sir James Mackintosh (d. 1832) and Sir Robert Peel (d. 1850) were faced by determined opponents who disagreed with their demands for a liberalisation of the criminal justice system.

b) Causes and Nature of Crime

> If the poor cannot procure employment, and are not supported, they must commit crimes or starve.

So stated Robert Owen (1816) who was of the firm opinion that poverty was a primary cause of crime. However, the government disputed this, publicly at least, and in a report compiled by a Royal Commission on Crime in 1839 it was suggested that among its root causes were drink, profit, 'a natural propensity by the indigent to mischief' and the 'attractions' of a criminal life. Privately, there were many in the government who acknowledged that some link existed between poverty and criminal behaviour though they seemed at a loss on how best to tackle the problem. The Poor Law Amendment Act (1834) was as far as they were prepared to go, thinking its provisions would have sufficient impact on crime levels as to obviate the need for further legislation. Even Sir Robert Peel, among the first to tackle the injustices of the Penal Code during his period as Home Secretary (1822-27), did not fully understand the nature of crime. Nevertheless, his reforms were a step in the right direction, he abolished the death penalty for over a hundred offences, enabled judges to give less than the death sentence for non-killing crimes, simplified the recruitment of juries and established the Metropolitan Police Force, but his work tended to deal with the symptoms rather than the causes of crime.

To judge from contemporary reports and judicial records (see Table 13), the most commonly committed crimes were, in order of seriousness, drunkeness, assault, stealing, vagrancy, malicious damage to property, and, in the industrial towns but especially Merthyr, prostitution. The list indicates a strong correlation between crime and the lower classes and so it has been proved in a number of local research studies. In her research of crime and protest in Pembrokeshire (1815-1974) Audrey Philpin states 'One of the most remarkable aspects of nineteenth-century crime in Pembrokeshire is the almost total absence of evidence of law-breaking amongst the middle and upper classes. In over two hundred cases of men appearing at Quarter Sessions between 1820 and 1837, only six could even remotely be judged to be men of means. Of these, five were described as "farmer" and one as "schoolmaster"'. The same was true with regards to middle and upper class females. 'Of over 3,000 cases studies between 1820-1900, there were sixty categories of work specified; almost all were for menial occupations such as mantua-making, domestic service, labouring, colliery work, shepherding, basket-making, quilting, brewing and the like.' Crime records have as much to teach the occupational structure of Victorian society as about Victorian morality.

Table 13

Calendar of Prisoners at Swansea Prison, 1851

1	William Jones	42	Stealing bacon	Two years to hard labour
2	Richard Hillier	21	Sheep-stealing	Eighteen calendar months
3	William Thomas	44	} Same	Eighteen calendar months
4	William Meyrick	34		
5	Anne Owens	29	Concealment of birth	One year to hard labour
6	Hugh Lewis	23	Horse-stealing	Two years each to hard lab
7	Bennett Williams	22		
8	John Williams	27	{ Stealing from the }	{ Six calendar months each
9	John Thomas	25	person	first three days of each n
10	James Taylor	27		days of sentence solitary
11	David Roach	30	Malicious assault	Eighteen calendar months'
12	Henry Jones	22	{ Stealing from the } person	{ Six calendar months to h two days of each month of sentence, solitary
13	Maria Grubb	23	Stealing cotton print	Same
14	Mary Davies	62	Misdemeanour	Six months to hard labour
15	Morgan Bowen	24	Horse-stealing	Two years' hard labour
16	Thomas Jones	24	Housebreaking	{ One year to hard labour, alternate week in solitu
17	Phillip Neagle	17	Stealing clothes	{ Six calendar months' ha three days of each mon
18	Samuel Lloyd	25	{ Obtaining money by } false pretences	{ Four calendar months' days of each week, and sentence solitary
19	Owen Morgan	55	Sheep-stealing	Two years to hard labour
20	Ruth Rees	19	Receiving stolen money	{ Four calendar months to days of each alternate v
21	William Edmunds	22	Bastardy	{ Three calendar months' pay £4 19s.
22	John Christy	23	Uttering base coin	{ Three calendar months' days of each alternate
23	David Thomas	50	Stealing fire bricks	Two calendar months to ha
24	Charles Dowdell	22	,, a coat, &c.	Same
25	William Langdon	33	,, beef	Same

I

II

III

IV

V

VI

VII

VIII

IX

X

There were few cases of murder or manslaughter and nor did the Welsh erupt in revolution, which fear preoccupied central government for much of the second quarter of the century. Since protest was equated with crime, successive Home Secretaries, Lords Melbourne (1830-34) and Russell (1835-39), were out of sympathy with what they regarded as the wild and insurrectional Welsh, pointing to the Scotch Cattle (c. 1820s-30s), Merthyr Rising (1831), Newport Rising (1839) and Rebecca Riots (1838-44) as evidence of their uncivilised nature and natural tendency to criminal behaviour. Such prejudiced assumptions were given concrete form in the pages of the infamous Blue Books of 1847 which may have been intended primarily to survey the state of education in Wales but, by exceeding its brief, presumed to pass judgement on the state of Welsh society. This unflattering view of the Welsh caused outrage and encouraged some to respond with facts and figures purporting to show that Wales was in fact a law-abiding country. According to one historian, T.I. Ellis, Henry Richard (d. 1888), one time minister of religion and subsequently Liberal M.P. for Merthyr, 'sought to interpret Wales to the English; he wrote to the English press to explain the Rebecca Riots, and in 1866 published a series of letters upon the social and political condition of Wales'.

> For the last hundred or hundred and fifty years, there is probably no part of the United Kingdom that has given the authorities so little trouble or anxiety. Anything like sedition, tumult, or riot is very rare in the Principality ... the normal condition of the Principality is one of profound calm, rarely ruffled even by a breath of popular discontent. There is no part of the country probably where the hand of authority is so little seen and so little needed.
> [Henry Richard, *Letters on the Social and Political Condition of the Principality of Wales* (1st, ed., 1866)].

Even at the height of the Rebecca Riots, the Welsh were, in the opinion of Walter Griffith (d. 1846) of Tal-y-sarn in Caernarfonshire and much travelled lecturer for the Anti-Corn-Law League, 'difficult to agitate'. Nevertheless, it required more than mere sentiment and uncorroborated comment to convince the English establishment and press that their Welsh neighbours were no whit less law-abiding than they claimed their people to be. This came in the form of statistical evidence gathered together by Henry Bruce, Lord Aberdare, and Home Secretary (1869-73) in Gladstone's Liberal government which claimed to show that the Welsh were indeed less criminally inclined than any other part of the United Kingdom. Today, historians are disinclined to accept at face value Aberdare's figures suggesting that when modern methods of calculation are taken into account Welsh crime figures, in percentage terms, were not much less than, and after 1881 were in fact on a par with, those for England.

One of the most striking aspects of crime in Wales and England during the nineteenth century was the rise in the incidence of juvenile crime. Orphaned and abandoned children had little choice but to fend for themselves and they did so, as was graphically described in Charles Dickens' novel *Oliver Twist* (1837), by turning to stealing. Novelist, essayist and social critic, Dickens had worked as a journalist in the law courts and his utter revulsion of what he witnessed inspired him to write novels in which he actively campaigned for reform of the 1834 Poor Law, the prison system and the law. His concern at the number of juvenile delinquents was shared by others most notably Dr. Barnardo who in 1867 founded the East End Juvenile Mission for the care of sick and destitute children. In 1876 he calculated that there were some 30,000 children sleeping rough in London alone. The industrial towns of Wales too had their juvenile delinquents who contributed to upping the crime statistics. The report carried in *The Cambrian* newspaper (1852) is typical of the problems encountered by the authorities in Swansea:

> Daniel Leary, an Irish boy who is a confirmed beggar was charged with begging in Singleton Street on Monday evening ... it appeared he was not only annoying persons as they passed by begging, but was drunk – Mr. Superintendant Tate said that the boy was a notorious beggar – that he had been several times cautioned by the Mayor, but to no purpose – Mr. Dillwyn after giving him a severe reprimand sent him to the House of Correction for three days – a sentence which made the boy cry considerable.

Even in rural Pembrokeshire children figured prominently in the gaol records of the town of Haverfordwest. Between 1820 and 1863 around 208 children, the majority with their mothers, were admitted to the town's jail. Indeed, they seem at times to have been unwitting accomplices to crime as is shown in the case, in 1832, of ten-year-old William Michael Burns who was with his mother Mary when she broke into a house in Robeston Wathen to steal 'foodstuffs and goods'. Both were convicted and condemned to

I
II
III
IV
V
VI
VII
VIII
IX
X

death, their sentences being commuted later to a year's imprisonment for '12 calendar months to hard labour'. After serving six months the youth was removed to the town's workhouse.

Table 14

Indictable crime in Cardiganshire, Carmarthenshire and Pembrokeshire, 1805-50

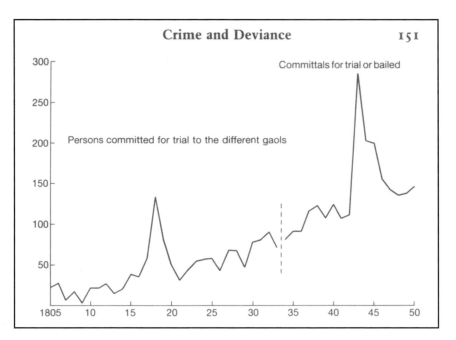

c) Forces of Law and Order

In 1815 the forces of law and order were nowhere near as organised as they are today. There was no police force in the modern sense and, with the possible exception of Fielding's mid-eighteenth-century 'Bow Street Runners', no method of criminal detection. 'Thief-taking' was a local business, which was organised on a county basis with a high constable assisted by unpaid parish or petty constables appointed by the justices of the peace. Every citizen of 'good character' was liable to serve as a constable but the system tended to recruit older less fit men unencumbered by their daily employment. Despite the weaknesses of the system it tended to work well in less populous rural districts once the regular haunts of criminals were known. However, with the rapid industrialisation and urbanisation of Wales the system soon reached breaking point. The old system of borough 'watchmen' simply could not cope with the huge increase in town populations. When large scale demonstrations and riots occurred the authorities resorted, as they had done in the past, to calling in the army. Yet, the increasing frequency with which troops were deployed in Wales between 1815 and 1850, concerned the authorities who sought an alternative method of 'policing'.

Unfortunately, proposals for introducing a more organised method of policing often foundered on the rocks of public opinion which was suspicious and hostile to the idea. Even Parliament, sensitive to the opinion of its electorate, composed almost entirely of well-to-do men from the middle and upper class, was initially reluctant to establish a police force. In 1818 a Parliamentary committee on policing reported that 'the police of a free country was to be found in rational and humane laws, in an effective and enlightened magistracy ... above all in the moral habits and opinions of the people'.

With the rapid increase in the incidence of crime the government was eventually moved to act and in 1829 Sir Robert Peel established the first 'modern' police force in the country (though he had previously set up the Irish Constabulary in 1822). Although only intended for London, the Metropolitan Police Force had set a precedent that could, and would, be followed elsewhere in the country. Its influence in Wales was, at first, subtle and peripheral. For example, in 1831 three officers of the Metropolitan Police were sent to Denbighshire to investigate attacks on local coal owners. In the same year six officers were sent to Carmarthen to deal with riots connected with the general election. Their efficiency and attention to duty so impressed the town's authorities that they invited one of the six, John Lazenby, to remain and help set up their own police force. His task was a massive one and, in the face of determined opposition, it took fully five years to properly establish a borough police force. A flavour of local opinion is captured in the following letter which appeared in the *Carmarthen Journal* in September 1836.

> The Police force is now composed of persons who, to say the least, do but give authority to the old adage, 'set a thief to catch a thief', riotous and disorderly conduct among them is of so frequent occurrence as to call forth even the indignation of the magistrates themselves. This is in character. What more could be expected from men who have been dreaded by every peaceful inhabitant of the town.
>
> 'A Respectable Inhabitant'

I

II

III

IV

V

VI

VII

VIII

IX

X

I

II

III

IV

V

VI

VII

VIII

IX

X

Under the terms of the Municipal Corporations Act of 1835, every town in England and Wales was required to appoint watch committees which in turn were to to be responsible for setting up local police forces following strictly Peel's Metropolitan model. Many towns in Wales, and at least four counties between 1839 and 1845 – Carmarthen, Denbigh, Montgomery and Glamorgan (Map 11) – did so but even those slow to react to the directive, usually on account of the cost to rate-payers (see fig. 00), were required to do so by the County and Borough Police Act of 1856. Historians suggest that the more peaceful and settled conditions of the second half of the nineteenth century was due, in part, to the establishment of the county police forces. Certainly there were fewer incidents of riot and mass protest demonstrations and yet, paradoxically, crime statistics show an increase which might suggest a more, rather than a less, lawless society. However, the increase is probably to be explained by the fact that the police forces became more professional and successful in the detection, especially with the founding of the Criminal Investigation Department in 1878, and prosecution of crime. By the last quarter of the century the police, largely by virtue of their careful cultivation of their image as a 'consensual' body, had succeeded in overcoming the suspicions of the middle class and were soon accepted by the majority of the working classes.

Map 11

County Police Forces by 1856

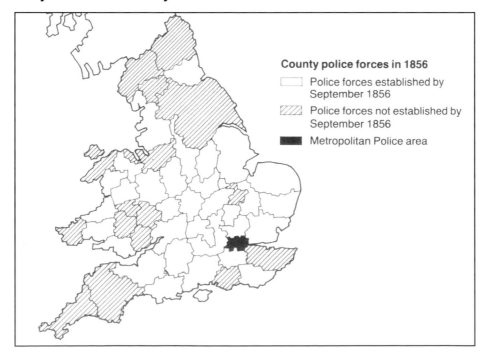

Fig. 26
No Police Poster (Aberystwyth)

NO POLICE!!

WELL DONE ABERYSTWYTH BOYS!

Your Month's Trial is past; and right nobly have you acquitted yourselves! Your behaviour has been admirable; your conduct deserves the utmost praise. The quiet, peaceable, and orderly state of the Town, is the greatest credit to you. It has been emphatically the MOST peaceable and happy Month enjoyed by the Town of Aberystwyth for Years! Even the Trees on the North Parade, so lately the objects of silly revenge, have not been touched. This is as it ought to be. Whoever destroys or injures them, is an Enemy to the Town, and an Abettor of the detested Police System! The fact of a Row of beautiful Trees growing there, cannot injure or annoy one single individual; nor could their removal benefit any one. There let them remain. Does not your voice already echo, Yes, there they shall remain!

Your conduct hitherto is a guarantee for the future; for to no one single act of disorder can even the finger of envy point! This has raised your character immeasurably; and proved, beyond the possibility of contradiction, that the Inhabitants of Aberystwyth do not require the surveillance of a couple of Bludgeon-men to keep them from becoming Pickpockets and Thieves. The question at the beginning of the Month was,

Police or No Police?

That problem has been solved; the question is answered. The Watch Committee appealed to the Town. The Inhabitants have responded---they have supplied the answer; and that answer is,

NO POLICE!!

The state of the Town for the last Month has proved to the satisfaction of the most timid and incredulous, that they were not required. As far as Aberystwyth is concerned, the Cutlasses and Truncheons of hired Spies may henceforth be consigned to oblivion in the Commissioners' Yard, along with rusty old Iron, rotten Timber, and broken Pipes, as perfectly useless Lumber, and Relics of bygone days.

PERSEVERE IN YOUR PRAISEWORTHY CONDUCT!

THE £200 WILL BE SAVED, And the Victory won!

April 6th, 1850.

E. WILLIAMS & SON, PRINTERS, ABERYSTWYTH.

I II III **IV** V VI VII VIII IX X

d) Punishment of Crime

> Without law and courts to enforce it, each one of us would be free to push
> and bully our fellow citizens and, which may be thought more important, our
> fellow citizens would be free to push and bully us. The justification for law,
> the courts, and law is that they protect us from unfair and oppressive actions
> by others. But if we are to have this protection, we must ourselves accept that
> the law applies to us too, and limits our freedom.
>
> [Extract of a speech by Sir John Donaldson, President of the Industrial
> Relations Court, 1972]

Few of us would disagree with this but what if the law is itself abused and manipulated by the authorities so that it became the bully? In the eighteenth and first part of the nineteenth century the law was legislated and enforced by men who had little sympathy for or understanding of those upon whom it was pronounced. It was seen and used as a means to protect property and quell unrest, its penalties were deliberately savage in order to deter criminal acts. The law was little interested in the causes of crime merely in its punishment. Poverty, starvation and destitution were often regarded as the fault of the sufferers and they were rarely accepted as mitigation for crimes committed. The death penalty remained the single most important punishment available to the authorities and it was dispensed for a wide variety of crimes from the ridiculously petty to the seriously malicious. However, by the late 1820s it was clear to all but the most obstinate that its use was having little effect on the incidence of crime and in truth, in many areas of the country magistrates and juries had long avoided passing sentences of death for what they were coming to regard as 'petty' offences. The reform of the criminal code was first seriously undertaken during Lord Liverpool's ministry under the firm direction of his Home Secretary Sir Robert Peel. Besides removing the death penalty for a large proportion of crimes, prisons and transportation were increasingly seen and used as alternative methods of punishing offenders who might otherwise have been hanged under the old 'Bloody Code'.

In 1823 James Mill, father of the famous utilitarian and liberal philosopher John Stuart Mill, submitted an article on prisons for inclusion in the *Encyclopaedia Britannica* which suggested that the purpose of imprisonment should be 'reform by industry'. It was a bold suggestion which looked towards rehabilitation rather than simply punishment. Hitherto prisons had been little more than unsanitary death traps ridden by disease. It was less a place of punishment as a place of confinement for short periods usually before trial or sentence. However, its use and the numbers incarcerated increased significantly during the latter half of the eighteenth and early part of the nineteenth century which inevitably led to problems, the most pressing being the lack of funding, badly maintained buildings and a dearth of properly trained staff. In Carmarthen and Haverfordwest, for example, the remains of their respective medieval castles were converted for use as prisons. The living conditions within them were scandalously unclean and unhealthy and no wonder when the majority of those committed to prison were themselves 'dirty' and suffering from ill-health. According to the Surgeon's Record Book, 1820-35, for Haverfordwest castle prison many of those convicted of vagrancy, who made up more than half of the prisoners incarcerated at any one time, suffered from malnutrition, fleas, lice, venereal disease and the 'itch', probably scabies. In line with Mill's suggestion the government encouraged local prisons to find useful employment for their inmates and by 1826 Haverfordwest was among the first Gaols in Wales to install a treadmill.

Between 1821 and 1858 the register of prisoners for Haverfordwest Gaol records some 8,182 convicts, committed to its care of which 1,663 were females, making up 20.3% of the prison population. The ages of those serving sentences ranged from 12 to 73 and their crimes varied from prostitution, theft, bastardy and the desertion of children. Two examples must suffice to illustrate the types of females who might expect to be housed in the prison:

• The first concerns Charlotte Havard, 'a well known recidivist' according to Audrey Philpin 'who appeared regularly before early nineteenth-century Pembrokeshire courts'. On entering Haverfordwest prison in January 1829 her list of crimes were noted down in the Gaol Register, she being described as 'a rogue and a vagabond, conducting herself in a riotous manner in the streets, being a prostitute, and biting the thumb of Rebecca Evans in a fight'. It is difficult to know whether she was convicted for idleness, disorderly conduct, for vagrancy, prostitution, breach of the peace or common assault?

• The most tragic case listed in the prison register, but by no means uncommon, was that of 12 year-old Mary Anne Reynish. On 26 May

I

II

III

IV

V

VI

VII

VIII

IX

X

I

II

III

IV

V

VI

VII

VIII

IX

X

1826 she was given 'one months imprisonment to hard labour, for Leaving her Service'. Those placed in domestic service by parish guardians had no choice but to work as directed, to leave without permission was tantamount to committing a criminal act. She served her time and was released on 28 June but less than three weeks later she was again apprehended for 'leaving her Service' for which she received 'three months imprisonment for hard labour' which, in Haverfordwest, meant the treadwheel. Three days into her sentence she was punished by the prison governor Thomas Jones with solitary confinement on account of the fact that '... while at work on the wheel [she] made a noise by calling out to her fellow prisoners, for which offence I confined her to a dark cell for 4 hours'.

Such inhumane treatment of prisoners, confirmed by the passing of the Prisons Act 1865 – 'hard labour, hard fare and a hard board' – continued until the passing of the Prisons Act of 1877 which 'nationalised' and regulated all prisons across the country. The worst run or uneconomical prisons were closed down, 53 in all, of which seven were in Welsh counties, namely, Anglesey, Brecon (reopened in 1881), Cardiganshire, Flintshire, Merionethshire, Montgomeryshire and Radnorshire.

Fig. 27
Cardiganshire Constabulary Record Book (1904)

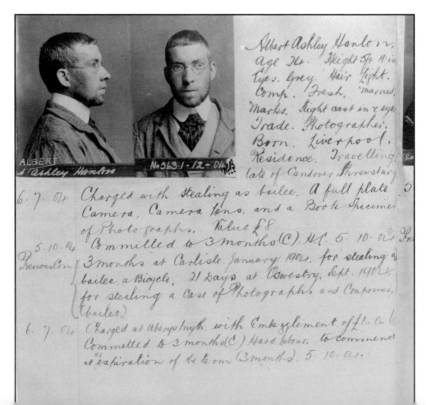

The Transportation Act of 1779 systemised a form of punishment which dated back to 1650. Its purpose, to remove the criminal from society for at least seven years (but usually for life) and to be used as a means of cheap slave-labour in the colonies, was taken up by nineteenth century reformers as a more humane and alternative method of punishment. In 1808 Sir Samuel Romilly introduced a Bill into Parliament which would abolish hanging in favour of transportation for pickpockets, it was accepted. Between 1788 and 1868 (when it ended) nearly 160,000 convicts were transported to Australia of which some 26,000 were women. During the same period close on 300 women and 800 men were transported from Wales. The conditions aboard ship were such as to result in the deaths of upwards of 20% of those transported before they even reached the penal colony of Australia. Once there, conditions were no less harsh and severe, though after sentence had been served they were given the opportunity to begin a new life 12,000 miles from home. Unsurprisingly perhaps, very few of those transported ever came home to Wales.

The humanization of the criminal code gradually led to more appropriate sentencing for offenders and a reform of the penal system which resulted in better treatment of prisoners. In 1902 the treadmill was abolished and in 1917 the flogging of prisoners for misdemeanours ceased. In 1907 probation was introduced for young offenders as an alternative to imprisonment. The end result was that by 1910 the proportion of serious offenders, mainly involving crimes against property rather than persons, sent to prison in England and Wales had almost halved. It has been calculated that by the beginning of the First World War a third of the prison population was composed of drunks with another quarter made up of beggars.

I

II

III

IV

V

VI

VII

VIII

IX

X

Advice and Activities

(i) General

Suggested Further Reading

R. Davies, *Secret Sins: Sex, Violence and Society in Carmarthenshire 1870-1920* (Cardiff, 1996).

D.J.V. Jones, *Crime, Protest, Community and Police in Nineteenth-Century Wales* (London, 1981).

D.J.V. Jones, *Rebecca's Children: A Study of Rural Society, Crime and Protest* (Oxford, 1989).

I.G. Jones, *Explorations and Explanations: Essays in the Social History of Victorian Wales* (Llandysul, 1981).

I.G. Jones, *Health, Wealth and Politics in Victorian Wales* (Llandysul, 1987).

I.G. Jones, *Mid-Victorian Wales* (Cardiff, 1992).

W.R. Lambert, *Drink and Sobriety in Victorian Wales, c.1820-c.1895* (Cardiff, 1983).

Articles:

G.P. Jones, 'Cholera in Wales', *NLWJ*, vol. X (1957-8).

Issues for Debate/Discussion

1. State a case **for** and **against** the Poor Law Amendment Act of 1834.
2. 'The scale of social change in nineteenth-century Wales has been grossly exaggerated'. Discuss.
3. Discuss the validity of Professor Ieuan Gwynedd Jones' definition of poverty on page 147.

I
II
III
IV
V
VI
VII
VIII
IX
X

(ii) Examination Specific

Answering Structured Questions

Q.

a) Explain briefly the system used for the relief of paupers in Wales and England before 1834 (24 marks).

b) To what extent did the Poor Law Amendment Act, 1834, alter radically the treatment of the poor in Wales and England? (36 marks).

Advice

In order to answer these questions successfully you need first to seek out and identify the key words. They are a) 'system' and 'relief', and b) 'alter radically' and 'treatment'. Once you have done this you should consider the following advice for each of the questions.

a) The examiner is seeking to test your historical knowledge and understanding, therefore you should begin by clearly establishing the fact that the administration of poor relief was parish-based and varied as widely as facilities. In some parishes the administration was in the hands of elected members, while in others an overseer was paid. Mention should be made of the Speenhamland System, the use of workhouses and outdoor relief. Some parishes paid dole without any expectation of return while others put paupers to work on roadbuilding or quarrying.

b) Here your ability to evaluate and analyse is being tested, therefore it is important to remember that marks will be awarded both for the factual content of your answer and for the analytical skills you display. Your answer should explain, evaluate and analyse the main changes to the treatment of the poor brought about by the Poor Law Amendment Act. Your answer should consist of the following elements:

- the development of the workhouse test for indoor relief;
- the establishment of a Central Board led by three commissioners;
- the grouping of parishes into unions;
- that each union controlled relief in its area and had to establish a workhouse;
- a Board of Guardians was to be elected by ratepayers of the union;
- conditions inside workhouses were austere and degrading and designed to discourage poor seeking aid.

In order to gain between 6-9 marks your answer must clearly demonstrate an understanding of these factors and not merely a narrative response focusing on details of the treatment of the poor.

Answering Essay Questions

Q. Assess the progress which had been made by 1850 to meet the growing demand for improvements in public health.

Advice

If you ignore the key words you are likely to write a narrative/descriptive essay on public health in general in which you might well impress with your knowledge but fail to address the issues raised by the question. Your essay has to be carefully structured to ensure that you plan your answer around the key words. In this way you will ensure that your essay has

  (i) identified the individuals and/or groups responsible for 'the growing demand'
 (ii) indicated the nature of the improvements demanded in public health by these individuals and/or groups
(iii) assessed the scale of the progress made – did the improvements meet the demands etc.

You should also set a limit to the essay so that you feel in control and don't lapse into filling up the paper with irrelevant detail or 'waffle'.

Remember to support your statements/points by providing examples.

Now for the conclusion. Like the introduction this is a vital part of the essay because you are leaving the examiner with the final impression of what you have written. Some of the best conclusions are short. Your aim should be to summarise clearly your main argument and to show how and why it agrees or differs from the essay title.

Chapter V
Education and Religion

1. Education

■ Key Issue:
What was the nature of education in Wales and how did it change?

a) Schools, Schooling and Scholars before 1847

It was not until the 1830s that the state began to take a serious interest in education. Prior to this, education, for the non-privileged, was voluntary in nature and philanthropic in provision, relying on charity, goodwill and not a little inventiveness. The charity and goodwill were largely provided by religious groups, the Established Church and the Nonconformists. Each had their own schools and academies, and each sponsored, supported or supplemented other educational ventures. Schooling was provided by the talent and genius of individuals who pioneered new educational initiatives. Gruffydd Jones (d. 1761) was one such pioneer, an Anglican clergyman from Llanddowror who set up a system of education across Wales that was cheap but effective. His Circulating Schools visited just about every parish in the country over a 45-year period.

- The teachers were committed, industrious, mobile and flexible being prepared to use whatever building or room came to hand.
- They taught, largely through the medium of Welsh, the basics of reading (mostly devotional in form and content), writing and simple arithmetic.

Jones' schools had set a very important precedent which might be followed in the future, but more importantly, they had demonstrated that there was an enthusiasm, even a demand, for education in Wales.

There had long existed fee-paying grammar schools in the Principality, many dating back to the Elizabethan period, but they, and their rigid, classically-based syllabi, were for the wealthy and socially well-connected élite. Those with academic talent but little else had to rely on the influence

I
II
III
IV
V
VI
VII
VIII
IX
X

I

II

III

IV

V

VI

VII

VIII

IX

X

and pecuniary support of patrons if they wished to enter these havens of learning. Few managed to realise their scholastic ambitions in these 'secondary' schools settling instead for instruction in the 'elementary' sector. Indeed, elementary education was equated with mass education or, to put it another way, it was thought suitable for the education of the masses – learning by rote and subject to mechanical obedience added up to fine factory fodder. Industrialists viewed as suspicious proposals to educate the masses, believing an educated workforce was more likely to stir up trouble – they might form trade unions and challenge the power of the employer! On the other hand, they could see the value of a basic 'workers' education so long as it was cheap. Hence the introduction of the monitorial system which involved using the older children to teach the younger ones. As Andrew Bell, the pioneer of the movement, stated 'Give me twenty-four pupils today, and I will give you twenty-four teachers tomorrow'. The system is estimated to have cost a mere 7 shillings a year to educate a child. Consequently, works schools were established in Wales such as

- at Blaenavon in 1816 which catered for the children, many of whom worked in the industry, of the ironworkers.
- Soon schools were founded by employers in the copper, tin-plate, coal and slate industries and by 1870 an impressive 134 works schools had been established.
- In north Wales the slate quarrying schools were provided by quarry owners for their largely Nonconformist employees who paid a small fee towards their upkeep. Arguably the largest employer of slate-quarrying labour, Lord Penrhyn, paid for and maintained free of charge schools for the boys and girls of his employees. The quality of education available in these schools varied enormously, one only has to read Daniel Owen's (d. 1895) semi-autobiographical novel *Hunangofiant Rhys Lewis*, to appreciate the horrors of early nineteenth-century schooling in north Wales when in the incapable hands of the likes of the infamous *Robyn y Sowldiwr*.
- By 1875 134 work's schools had been established across Wales.

Among the more enlightened industrialists was Robert Owen (d. 1858) of Newtown who founded nursery and elementary schools for the children of his workers in his Lanarkshire mills. Indeed, he advocated the setting up of a national, state-run system of education but his ideas were met with cynicism and criticism. To the rich, the privileged and the self-made men who inhabited Parliament, this smacked of state control, and they were committed to the principles of *laissez-faire*. Unfortunately for Owen his ideas were simply too 'radical' and his publication *A New View of Society* (1817) was too soon after the French Revolution and Napoleonic Wars. Taking his inspiration from the cry of the French revolutionaries that education should be 'universal, compulsory, gratuitious, and secular', he was accused of being a menace to society.

Nevertheless, there were many in Parliament who shared in the spirit of Owen's vision, like Lord Brougham who advocated working-class or 'popular' education which would embrace adults as well as children. In 1816 he moved for, and was granted, the power to conduct an inquiry into 'the education of the lower orders'. In his *Reports of Committee on the Education of the Lower Classes* 1818, he put forward proposals for funding (state grants irrespective of denomination), management (to be run by Anglican clergymen), teaching (non-denominational); he was attacked by both Anglicans and Nonconformists and so nothing came of his intended education (Parish Schools) bill of 1820. His attempt to reach a consensus between Anglican and Nonconformists on education failed and in the bitter aftermath of his report Brougham's request for a royal commission to investigate the work and funding of educational charities was turned down. Nothing daunted Brougham continued to work for the cause of universal education and he was instrumental in founding the Society for the Diffusion of Useful Knowledge (1825) and the University of London (1828).

Meanwhile, in Wales Gruffydd Jones' legacy of educational endeavour had been taken up by two societies:

  i) The National Society for Promoting the Education of the Poor in the Principles of the Established Church (1811), founded by the Anglican Church.

In view of the peoples' Nonconformist loyalties, the Church's National Schools faced a tough time and their aim to establish a school in every parish often foundered on the rocks of sectarian rivalry. Nevertheless, they persisted and with the overwhelming backing of the Established Church they succeeded in founding 33 National Schools across Wales by 1817.

  ii) The British and Foreign School Society (1814), founded by the Quakers

These British Schools were less successful and by 1819 only 15 had been established, all but two of which were to be found in the south.

According to historian Gareth Jones, 'The schools shared the universal problems of elementary education – grossly inadequate funding, untrained and amateurish teachers and a clientele who were not at all convinced of the necessity for the little amount of schooling which they were being offered'. The 'clientele' were subjected to rote learning of the three Rs and, in the National Schools, instructed in the principles of the Anglican Church. Therefore, rudimentary and basic best sums up the educational experience of the majority of pupils, which might explain why so many failed to attend regularly. The most vital and energetic part of their learning could usually be associated with religious teaching but the religious content in their elementary education was frequently a bone of contention because it was viewed as vaguely propagandist by Nonconformists. In contrast, the British Schools had early taken the decision to ensure that their religious teaching would be non-denominational.

Until 1833 it was the equation between the funding and the founding of schools that proved the most intractable problem in the Welsh education movement. The National Schools had always had the edge in funding over the British Schools because they were sometimes generously provided for by wealthy landowners or industrialists who were nearly always members of the Established Church. Sunday collections, charity donations and other money-raising schemes underpinned the continued existence of the few schools that had been established in Wales. By 1833, 146 schools had either been founded by or affiliated to the National Schools Society catering for over 13,000 pupils.

After 1833 the funding crisis diminished steadily when state-aid became more readily available. Beginning with a first-ever grant of £20,000 to be divided equally between the schools of the National and British Societies, the government was increasingly, if sometimes, reluctantly drawn ever deeper into educational issues. Its plan was simple, to aid local projects such as school building with a grant which was to be matched from funds raised locally. Unfortunately, the majority of Welsh parishes were too poor and could not compete with this 'match-funding'. Consequently, it has been estimated that in the period 1833-36 no more than £4,000 of £60,000 made available by the government found its way into the Principality. For example, Carmarthen's National School was given a grant of £80, Llanbedr (Caernarfonshire) received £47, while Llanllwchhaearn (Cardiganshire) and Llansantffraid (Denbighshire) received £40 and £30 respectively.

Table 15

Funding Levels of Schools in Wales per County, 1833-35
(Annual report of the National Society, 1836)

County	Schools	Attendance	Treasury Grant, 1833-5 (£)	National Society Grant, 1833-5 (£)
Anglesey	32	2,547	156	269
Brecon	13	1,837	153	249
Cardigan	16	953	93	382
Carmarthen	41	2,421	533	614
Caernarvon	45	2,738	88	627
Denbigh	32	2,984	566	942
Flint	43	4,704	524	1,195
Glamorgan	39	2,365	166	759
Merioneth	15	996	91	87
Monmouth	35	1,994	523	885
Montgomery	20	1,228	63	885
Pembroke	16	985	553	332
Radnor	7	307	50	70
TOTALS	354	26,059	£3,559	£7,296

Dissatisfied with the slow progress and often dubious quality of schools and teaching in Wales some took matters into their own hands calling on their fellow Cambrians to act in the cause of education. In 1843, the renowned educationalist, and one-time clerk in the Poor Law Commission, from Llangeinwen on Anglesey, Hugh Owen (d. 1881) published his now-famous *Llythyr i'r Cymry* or 'Letter to the Welsh People' in which he criticised the inadequate provision of day-schools and good-quality school-masters in Wales. Serving as their agent for Wales, he campaigned vigorously on behalf of the British Schools Society and he met with much success in north Wales where the number of schools established reached 31 by 1846. In the same year Owen became honorary secretary of the Cambrian Educational Society which purposed the advancement of education across Wales, including the training of teachers. Nor was Owen alone for in London also

I

II

III

IV

V

VI

VII

VIII

IX

X

the government was waking up to the enormity of the task that confronted them.

In 1839 Dr. Kay (later Sir James Kay-Suttleworth) was appointed secretary to the Committee of the Privy Council (a body set up to supervise the spending of the annual grant to education) and his aim, as he told the Home Secretary, Lord Russell, was to ensure 'the claims of the civil power to control the education of the country'. During the next ten years he helped establish a system of school inspectors, grant-aid for day schools currently funded by voluntary contributions and non-denominational religious instruction and better training for teachers. As a result, Parliament raised its annual education grant from £20,000 to £30,000 in 1839, then to £100,000 in the early 1840s and finally to nearly £550,000 by the later 1850s. Not without good reason is Kay-Suttleworth regarded as the 'founder of the English education system' since his work helped establish a national system of elementary schools in England.

b) Report [of the Blue Books] into the State of Education in Wales, 1847

Education before the Blue Books and education after them – this is how historians generally approach the study of education in nineteenth century Wales. That they do this is largely on account of the power, persuasion and controversy associated with the government's Commission of Inquiry into the State of Education in Wales that inspired the so-called Blue Books (This refers to the fact that the Commission's findings, published in three volumes, were bound in Blue). Of course, this suggests that they had a massive impact on education in Wales, that, as a result of their publication, Welsh education was radically transformed. Certainly, there were changes, there were even far-reaching reforms and by the end of the century the education system in Wales was significantly different to what it had been at the beginning, but how far this can be claimed to be directly the result of the recommendations contained in the Blue Books remains a matter for debate.

In the furore that followed their publication, critics and supporters alike tended to lose sight of what should have been the central issue, namely, education. Instead, they concentrated their energies on debating or arguing, defending or attacking, minimising or exaggerating the social, political, cultural, religious and linguistic issues covered in the report. Education was hardly ignored but it had been firmly pushed aside, and became simply one of a number of issues requiring attention as a result of the findings contained within the Blue Books.

The Report of the Commissioners of Inquiry into the State of Education in Wales was intended to be, and was largely completed as, an investigation into the provision (or lack of it) of educational facilities in the Principality, to judge the quality of that provision and to make recommendations for its improvement. In order to assist the research and data collection process Wales was divided up between the commissioners each of whom had the help of assistants, ten in all – Carmarthenshire, Glamorgan and Pembrokeshire was assigned to Ralph Robert Wheeler Lingen, Brecknockshire, Cardiganshire, Radnorshire and Monmouthshire to Jelinger Cookson Symons while the counties of north Wales – Merioneth, Caernarfon, Denbigh, Flint, Montgomery and Anglesey – were assigned to Henry Vaughan Johnson. That they may have exceeded their brief, no doubt with the best of intentions, to comment on other related social issues, which the commissioners would have defended as just and relevant, has attracted more attention and criticism than its pronouncements on education. Its findings generated debate, causing some even to hate the commissioners involved – Lingen, Johnson and Symons – and was taken up as a cause by Welsh political and religious groups who saw within its pages an attack on the Welsh way of life. Unfortunately, all this bitterness tended to muddy the educational waters in which domain the report makes some sober judgements, making for uncomfortable reading at times, but only rarely can we impugn the accuracy or integrity, if not the authority, of its findings. What the compilers lacked in sensitivity they largely made up for in objectivity which makes for an important document within which the data compiled is meat for the historian's table.

Did the commissioners exceed their brief as has sometimes been alleged?

The answer is probably not. They were instructed to conduct their inquiry with reference to the social condition of the areas which they investigated – 'In reporting on the number and description of schools in any district, you will not fail to keep in mind the amount, character, and condition of the population'. This they did. In fact, the commissioners took their roles very seriously for as Symons commented 'I conceive my province to be less that

I

II

III

IV

V

VI

VII

VIII

IX

X

187

of an inspector of schools than an inquirer into education. I have deemed the mental condition of the children the primary object of my attention'. Lingen, probably the least sympathetic of the three, believed it was his mission to dig a little deeper. For example, he reported on Landshipping Day School (Pembrokeshire): 'On 8th January I visited the above school. It was held in a small and wretched room ... and was kept by a person who had formerly been a shop-keeper, but had failed in business and therefore taken to school-keeping ... The master was an old man and apparently very ignorant'. Nor was the situation any better in the north where, according to Johnson, 'The teachers in North Wales are in fact drawn from the lowest class in society which contains individuals competent to read, write and cipher' [ie. do simple arithmetic]. In the south-east too Symons found fault with the teachers, 'If the competency of the Welsh schoolmaster is to be measured by the standard of the popular estimation of his duties, perhaps almost as many exceed as fall short of it'. This was typical of what the commissioners found across Wales, badly maintained or inappropriate school rooms, poor quality teachers and teaching and an inadequate syllabus. The poverty and general social deprivation of the children, their parents and the communities at large were factors the commissioners could hardly ignore. In speaking of Tregaron, Symons spares neither its people nor his readers the horror he witnessed there: 'I think the extreme filthiness of the habits of the poor, though observable everywhere, are as striking in this place, if not more so, inasmuch as in a town it might be expected that a little more of the outward observances of cleanliness and decency would be met with'.

Of course, it was not all doom and gloom, many schools, teachers and pupils were justly praised. They paid particular tribute to the work of the Sunday Schools, Lingen stating that, 'These schools have been almost the sole, they are still the main and most congenial, centres of education'. Johnson too was impressed, 'However, imperfect the results, it is impossible not to admire the vast number of schools which they [Dissenters] have established, the frequency of the attendance, the number, energy and devotion of the teachers, the regularity and decorum of the proceedings, and the permanent and striking effect which they have produced upon society'. They were guarded in their assessment of the educational merits of these schools since they found that many pupils were taught to repeat by rote verses from the Bible. That said, Johnson was sure that matters might

I
II
III
IV
V
VI
VII
VIII
IX
X

have been much worse if there had been no Sunday Schools; 'As the influence of the Welsh Sunday-Schools decreases the moral degredation of the inhabitants is more apparent. This is observable on approaching the English border'. Yet, for all their praise, the underlying bias, other historians prefer the more emotive word prejudice, of the commissioners was always with England and things English. Consequently, Wales and the Welsh tended to suffer in comparison and an example may be instanced by Lingen's comments on the system of education he found in south-west Wales;

> I have no hesitation in saying that a child might pass through the generality of these schools without learning either the limits, capabilities, general history, or language of the empire of which he is born a citizen, and this is the kind of knowledge which I consider to be the province of Geography, English History, English Grammar and English Etymology in elementary schools.

This is not to suggest that schools, teachers and syllabi were better in comparable districts in England, they were not. In Manchester for instance, a government report commented on the general ignorance found when questioning pupils on subjects taught on the curriculum, which was put down to poor quality teaching and the often indifferent attitude of parents and pupils to learning.

What is perhaps surprising is the number of schools found to be operating in Wales, for besides the day schools founded by the National and British Societies there were many small, privately run institutions. In Pembrokeshire, for example, Lingen reported on some 211 'institutions of learning' while in Glamorgan he found 373 schools operating, of which well over 100 were deemed to be unfit or unsuitable. The same was true in north Wales where a sympathetic Johnson wondered why pupils bothered to attend such awful schools especially in some villages where the parents were so poor they had 'no clothes in which to send their children to the school if they desired to do so'. In his view,

> It appears that considering the extremely small value of the instruction given compared with the expense, and considering the materials for instruction and the qualifications of the teachers, the scholars cannot reasonably be expected to be more numerous, more regular in their attendance, or to expend more time in an employment so unprofitable.

I
II
III
IV
V
VI
VII
VIII
IX
X

In Symons' view the Welsh attended school because they were eager to learn since 'they desire it to the full extent of their power to appreciate it'. Indeed, in his view 'They learn what they are even badly taught with surprising facility' and, given the right instruction, he believed they were capable of high achievement. He found the children of Monmouthshire to be particularly able in arithmetic stating – 'I have witnessed more proficiency after a small amount of instruction than I ever witnessed in any schools either in England or on the continent'. His praise for the Welsh sometimes overflowed but he was clearly impressed by what he witnessed – 'I can speak in very strong terms of the natural ability and capacity for instruction of the Welsh people. Though they are ignorant, no people more richly deserve to be educated'.

c) Education, Educators and the Educated after 1847

The second half of the nineteenth century may fittingly be described as the 'Age of Educational Reform' or, perhaps more appropriately, the 'Era of the Education Acts'. The period witnessed concerted government action which, in conjunction with the works of voluntary and religious groups, changed the educational landscape forever. The acts, codes and new initiatives tend always to be called after the names of the statesmen and politicians who introduced them, e.g. Robert Lowe's Revised Code (1862), Forster Act (1870).

Table 16

Principal Education Acts and Measures

1833	First annual government grant for education	£20,000 voted by Parliament to support and develop educational initiatives in Britain
1839	Cabinet Committee formed	to monitor spending on education
1858	Newcastle Commission	reports on inadequate provision
1862	Robert Lowe's Revised Code	recommended 'payment by results
1870	Forster Education Act	existing voluntary schools to be supported - schools' boards to be elected by local ratepayers to administer new schools and provide non-denominational education school boards given power to make attendance compulsory
1876	Sandon Education Act	penalised parents who kept their children from school
1880	Mundella Education Act	compulsory schooling for children under the age of 13
1889	Welsh Intermediate Education Act	created new system of schools to bridge the gap between elementary and higher education
1891	Government Grant	established free elementary education
1902	Balfour Education Act	school boards replaced by 144 Local Education Authorities run by the county and Borough Councils
1907	Welsh Department in the Board of Education founded.	
1918	Fisher Education Act	school leaving age raised from 12 to 14

I

II

III

IV

V

VI

VII

VIII

IX

X

I
II
III
IV
V
VI
VII
VIII
IX
X

The period of reform and reorganisation began inauspiciously enough when **Lowe's Revised Code** was adopted in **1862**. Its primary aim was to control government spending on education, which was beginning to worry ministers.

By the early 1860s Wales had upwards of 300 British Schools and over a 1,000 National Schools each of which now competed for a slice of the funding cake. The system was divisive and hated by schoolmasters and pupils alike but future funding depended on good results and favourable reports so schools had little choice but to fall in line. After one such inspection in 1868 the British School in Pembroke Dock had a tenth of its income deducted because it was reported that 'the elementary subjects are imperfectly taught. The writing is particularly defective'. The Welsh language was perhaps the most obvious casualty of this system since the inspection revolved around the pupils' facility in reading, reciting and writing in English.

W.E. Forster's Education Act quickly followed. It attempted, in part, to undo the damage caused by Lowe's Code but the funding issue remained to plague future government initiatives in education. The Act continued to make government grants available to pre-existing British and National schools in Wales and where there were gaps locally-elected School Boards would be set up with the power to raise money on the rates. In this way the government hoped to provide a nationwide network of efficiently-run and regularly inspected elementary schools for all children up to the age of thirteen. These were never intended as 'primary' schools in the sense that we understand them simply because 'intermediate' or 'secondary' education was thought still to be the preserve of middle and upper class children.

To cater for the needs of secondary or grammar school pupils in Wales the government passed the Endowed Schools Act in 1869 which provided funding and support. Although intended to calm the tension between Anglicans and Nonconformists by making religious instruction non-compulsory in Board Schools or, if it was taught, non-denominational, Forster's Act failed. *The Pembrokeshire Herald* expressed its opposition to the Act on this issue:

we have carefully perused the Act ... it is, in our opinion, a bad Act ... it has this one dark blot upon it – that it casts a slight upon the Christian religion, and is in plain and direct contradiction to the principles inculcated by the inspired word of God ... it affords a kind of legal recognition of every form of unbelief, and even of Atheism'.

Fig. 28
Punch pokes fun at Forster's Act (1870)

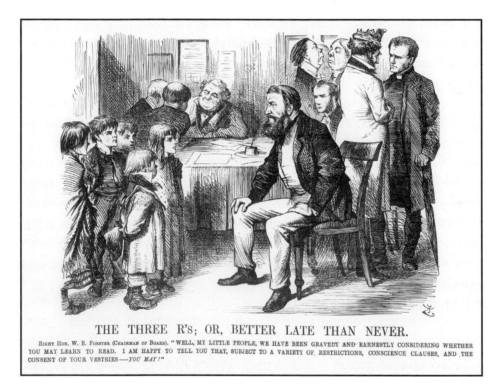

THE THREE R's; OR, BETTER LATE THAN NEVER.

Right Hon. W. E. Forster (Chairman of Board). "WELL, MY LITTLE PEOPLE, WE HAVE BEEN GRAVELY AND EARNESTLY CONSIDERING WHETHER YOU MAY LEARN TO READ. I AM HAPPY TO TELL YOU THAT, SUBJECT TO A VARIETY OF RESTRICTIONS, CONSCIENCE CLAUSES, AND THE CONSENT OF YOUR VESTRIES—*YOU MAY!*"

Unlike British Schools, Anglican National and Roman-Catholic Schools opted to retain their independence and so remain outside the provisions of the Act and by refusing to be incorporated into the School Board system which effectively denied them access to funds raised on the rates. They thought this to be unfair since they could not compete with wealthier School Boards. However, Nonconformists in those areas deemed well-provided for in terms of school places were denied the power to elect a School Board which meant that its children continued to attend National Schools where they were, in the words of historian John Davies, 'drilled in the catechism of the Church of England – a splendid way in which to rear a rebel, as Lloyd George's career bears witness'.

I

II

III

IV

V

VI

VII

VIII

IX

X

In **1876** and **1880 Lord Sandon's Act** and **A.J. Mundella's Education Act** imposed universal compulsory schooling for all children under 10 stating that it was the duty of all parents to ensure that their children received regular instruction in reading, writing and arithmetic. As the provision of elementary education widened its influence deepened which led to demands for something more than 'basic' or 'elementary' education. In 1881 H.A. Bruce, Lord Aberdare, was put in charge of a commission to investigate intermediate and higher education in Wales.

As a result of the commission's work, though it took fully eight years to implement, in **1889** the **Welsh Technical and Intermediate Education Act** was passed – 'one of the most influential pieces of legislation in the history of Wales' is the opinion of one historian – which effectively introduced a secondary system of education in Wales. Where existing grammar schools wished to be incorporated into the system they were absorbed to become county schools but elsewhere schools had to be purpose-built, the first being in Caernarfon in 1894. Despite modest government funding it fell to local education committees to provide additional money, usually by voluntary subscription. However, entreaties for cash donations from the locally rich and powerful sometimes met with an ignorance that defied belief. When one leading landowner in Pembrokeshire was asked to contribute to building a new school in 1891 he refused on the grounds that 'In my humble opinion there is too much education at the present day for the good of the county'.

The Aberdare commission also recommended state-aid to help establish two universities in Wales – one in north Wales (Bangor being the preferred site) and the other in south Wales (Cardiff eventually being chosen). This was tacit recognition of the fact that higher education in Wales had been sorely neglected by the government, having been left entirely to the voluntary sector. That Wales had come to have institutions of higher education was due, in large part, to the ceaseless efforts of a committed group of enlightened philanthropists, prominent among them was Hugh Owen who helped found the Principality's first university at Aberystwyth in 1872. Owen's pioneering work in education cannot be exaggerated, he was among the first to recognise the fact that if the number of elementary schools envisaged ever got established there would need to be a corresponding expansion in the numbers of teachers.

Teacher training became a focus for action and first in the fray was the Anglican Church which founded colleges in Carmarthen in 1848 and in Caernarfon in 1849. The Nonconformists followed suit and in 1856 Bangor Normal College was established admitting students for the first time in 1858. Between 1858 and 1862 a further three colleges were set up by the congregationalists in Carmarthen, Brecon and Bala.

In **1902 Balfour's Education Act** tried to improve the administration of education in the provinces by abolishing the School Boards (there were 320 in Wales by 1900) and replacing them with a more efficient system of Local Education Committees which were to be run by the newly-created county councils (set up in 1888). However, Nonconformists were angered by the fact that it made ratepayers money available to the hitherto voluntary-aided Catholic and Anglican schools. This led to the so-called 'Welsh Revolt' against the Balfour Act organised by Welsh Liberal M.P.s led by Lloyd George. As part of this 'revolt' a number of Liberal-controlled county councils refused to enforce the provisions of the act. The government hit back by passing the **1904 Education (Local Authority Default) Act** which became known as the **'Coercion of Wales Act'**. Threats and counter-threats were made on both sides and serious confrontation was only averted when the Conservatives fell from power.

Within a year of winning the 1906 election the Liberals had passed a new measure which tried to open up fee-paying grammar schools to all children no matter what their social background or financial situation. All grammar schools which received public money from the rates had to provide free places for up to a quarter of its pupils. Elementary school children had to compete for these free places by passing an entrance exam, the scholarship. Children aged between 10 and 12 were eligible. After 1944 this was known as the eleven-plus. With these reforms the Liberals hoped to provide all children with a ladder of opportunity, an aim re-inforced by **Fisher's Education Act (1918)** which made schooling compulsory for all children up to the age of 14.

I

II

III

IV

V

VI

VII

VIII

IX

X

Fig. 29
'A peep into the Future': Cartoon in the *Western Mail* (1904)

Fig. 30
Demonstration against the Liberal Education Bill (1906)
The *South Wales Daily News* supported the Education Bill. However, the Church opposed it because teachers would no longer have been compelled to teach religious instruction

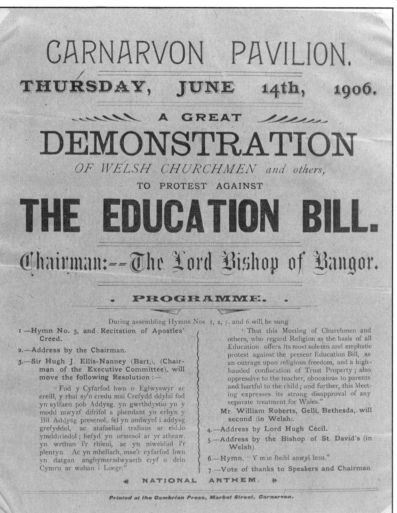

In **1907 The Welsh Department of the Board of Education** was set up. *The South Wales Daily News* welcomed the new department stating that it had established Welsh Home Rule in education. A distinguished Welsh scholar Owen M. Edwards was appointed the first Chief Inspector of Schools in Wales. It was hoped that this new department run by Welshmen would be more sympathetic to the teaching of Welsh subjects which had been largely ignored. Subjects such as Welsh history, literature and the Welsh language had been neglected in favour of English history, literature and language. In some schools even the speaking of Welsh was positively discouraged either by coercion or humiliation, for example in the school at Llanuwchllyn the future Chief Inspector of Schools in Wales was himself subjected to the hated 'Welsh Not' which involved having a wooden sign hung around his neck. Although the Welsh Not has entered the folklore and become part of the fiction of Welsh history there is no doubt that it existed, if not as widely used as was once thought, and that it came to symbolise the denigration of things Welsh. As this extract from a publicity pamphlet issued on St. David's Day in 1915 by the Welsh Department of the Board of Education makes clear, those who hoped for a more active policy on the teaching of 'Welsh' subjects in schools were to be to be disappointed:

Question: 'How can Welsh children uphold the Welsh Language?'.
Answer: 'By speaking, by reading and by writing it whenever they can – at home or abroad, at work or at play. A good knowledge of Welsh is a thing to be proud of, and all Welsh children should praise their mother tongue accordingly'.

Fig. 31
Pupils pose for the camera. Acrefair Board School, Denbighshire (1905)

I

II

III

IV

V

VI

VII

VIII

IX

X

I

II

III

IV

V

VI

VII

VIII

IX

X

The spread of literacy, in Welsh as well as in English, led to a demand for reading material beyond that normally provided by denominationally-run schools. Bibles, scriptures and other devotional literature were set aside in favour of newspapers, magazines and books, all of which enjoyed a boom in sales.

- Newspapers became especially popular because they were cheap, informative and entertaining. In 1910 there were 28 national daily and 9 evening newspapers the most popular being the *Daily Mail*, founded in 1896 and the *Daily Mirror* in 1904. *The Mail's* motto was 'explain, simplify and clarify'.

- A little more expensive but no less popular were the weekly magazines like *Punch*, the *Illustrated London News* and *Lloyd's Weekly News*.

- Wales too had its newspapers the most popular in Welsh being the weekly *Baner ac Amserau Cymru* and *Y Genedl Gymreig* for which a young Lloyd-George contributed many articles.

- The only truly Welsh national newspapers were the *South Wales Daily News* a pro-Liberal publication and its arch rival the Tory *Western Mail*.

- There was also a group of local newspapers like the *Cambrian Daily Leader*, the *Rhondda Leader* and the *Merthyr Times* of south Wales and the *Herald Cymraeg* and the *Caernarvon and Denbigh Herald* in the north.

Newspapers provided a better educated working class with the means to question the world around them and the opportunity to widen their horizons.

2. Religion

■ **Key Issue:**
'A deeply religious but divided nation'. How accurate is this description
of Wales and the Welsh?

a) The Religious Census of 1851

From these facts there are some inferences that are obvious and irresistible.
They prove – First, that the Church of England is not the Church of Wales.
Secondly, that but for the exertions of the Nonconformists, Wales would have
been at this time, as regards its spiritual interests in a most pitiable plight.
[The Welsh] amid poverty, isolation, and discouragement, have provided
themselves with more ample means of religious worship and instruction than
can be found, perhaps, among any people under the face of heaven.

> [Henry Richard, *Letters on the Social and Political Condition of the
> Principality of Wales* (1866)].

Henry Richard's confidence in portraying the Welsh as a deeply religious
nation, certainly more religious than the English!, the vast majority of whom
owed little loyalty to the Established or Anglican Church was as a result of
the findings published in the Religious Census of 1851. The *Census of
Religious Worship of 1851* was a truly remarkable exercise and was the
first of its kind to be undertaken. Although historians now argue over its
usefulness and sometimes dispute the reliability of its statistics (it was as
controversial then as now) it contains such a wealth of detail that it cannot
be ignored. At the very least it serves as a convenient starting point for
historians wishing to survey and study the form, nature and 'popularity' of
religion in Wales.

Given its shortcomings – it was a voluntary exercise, dependent on the
goodwill and integrity of the persons taking it, it provided a 'snap-shot' only
of religious attendance on the last Sunday in March and not every place of
worship in Wales was listed – the Religious Census proves beyond the
shadow of a doubt that Richard was correct in stating that 'the Church of
England is not the Church of Wales'. For every Anglican in Wales there
were roughly three who attended the various Nonconformist

I

II

III

IV

V

VI

VII

VIII

IX

X

denominational chapels, mainly, though not exclusively, Baptists, Independents and Methodists.

Wales had a long, and strong, tradition of dissent in matters of religious doctrine and worship dating back to at least the latter half of the seventeenth century. Although originally an imported creed from across the border the dissenters quickly established themselves in Wales, in part, because their moralistic and serious approach to religion appealed to the Welsh but also on account of the evangelic vitality of their worship. During the eighteenth century the older dissenting sects, the Baptists and Independents, and, what may be termed, the newer dissenters, the Methodists, found many converts among Welsh-speaking communities because they purposely associated and consciously identified themselves with things Welsh. Native culture, language and sense of 'patriotism' were taken on board and never ignored but shaped and fashioned to meet the needs of Nonconformist congregations. By comparison the Church of England, richly endowed, privileged and supremely (over?)-confident, had seemingly lost touch with the ordinary people. True, the Established Church could still count on the external support of the majority of the upper classes in Wales but, bar a few of the more active and deeply religious Anglicans, the Church had long ceased to meet the religious needs of the *gwerin*.

The extent to which Nonconformity had apparently seized the hearts and minds of the Welsh, or at least gave that impression, is illustrated by the unself-conscious way in which Henry Richard, and others, tended to equate the Welsh public with the Nonconformists. In 1831, twenty-years before the publication of the Religious Census, Arthur James Johnes (d. 1871) of Garthmyl in Montgomeryshire, later a county court judge, won a prize offered by the London-based Cymmrodorion Society for an essay on the causes of dissent in Wales. The fact that in the following year an expanded edition of the essay entitled *The Causes which in Wales have produced Dissent from the Established Church* was published, testifies to the strength of interest in Welsh religious affairs.

Again, in the Blue Books controversy of 1847 it was the Nonconformists who came out most strongly in defence of the people, probably because they stood accused alongside the three quarters of the population they represented. This suggests that by the nineteenth century it was not so much a question of, were the Welsh Nonconformist? but why were they? The Religious Census of 1851 merely served to confirm, more emphatically than expected perhaps, that the Welsh were predominantly Nonconformist in religion. It was never intended to find the causes or the reasons why this was or should be so but this did not deter the Nonconformists from using its statistical detail to support conclusions of their own. Some of the most popular reasons put forward for the success and strength of Nonconformity were

• the popularity of the Sunday School,
• the impact of preaching in Welsh
• their ability to set up a chapel almost anywhere.

Moreover, they used the Census data to attack the Established Church and to support their argument that it had lost the moral right to speak on behalf of the people of Wales.

Unsurprisingly, the Anglicans refuted the findings of the Census, concentrating on its weaknesses and deficiencies, to explain what, in their view, was a fundamentally flawed survey, the value of which was greatly diminished as a result. Nevertheless, the Church was well aware that it had serious problems, many of which long pre-dated the nineteenth century. Neglect, abuse, absenteeism, not a little corruption, class distinction and bias and the predominant use of English as the medium of instruction all combined at various times to denigrate the Church in the eyes of the faithful. Needless to say there were exceptions, great Anglicans who did much good, but in general the quality of religious worship was simply not there.

By the first half of the nineteenth century, the Church had failed to keep up with the pace of change. As the new industrial towns grew up its parochial system proved too inflexible and inadequate to take advantage of the growth in the number of potential worshippers. Too few churches were being built because they were geared up to serving a predominantly rural population. To create new parishes required an act of Parliament which would take time and require much debate.

According to the Census the Church had 1,180 places of worship as opposed to the Nonconformists' 2,769. Unencumbered by such restrictive things as parish boundaries and central control the essentially decentralised Nonconformists could erect a chapel wherever the demand was greatest. The building itself did not matter, initially it might be a barn, a

I
II
III
IV
V
VI
VII
VIII
IX
X

I

II

III

IV

V

VI

VII

VIII

IX

X

cottage, a farmhouse even an inn! This flexibility, the evangelical nature of their faith, the touring preachers, meant that they were able to take religion to the people rather than the people coming to them.

Were the Welsh, as Henry Richard claimed elsewhere in his publication, more religious than the English? According to the 1851 Census the answer was yes. This conclusion is drawn from arguably the most reliable data supplied by the Census, the so-called 'sittings' which refers to the number of people each denomination could accommodate within its respective churches or chapels. Thus, it was calculated that in England only around 51.4% of the population could be seated in places of worship compared to 75% in Wales. Of course, this national average hides the fact that some counties in Wales could accommodate more worshippers than others. For example, largely-rural Denbighshire could accommodate 94% of its population while, at the other end of the scale, industrialised Glamorgan could find room for 63.3% of its people within its places of worship.

Naturally, the raw data from the Census can tell next to nothing of the depth of religious fervour or feeling of those attending church or chapel on the day in question (30th March 1851), or whether they were regular or occasional attenders.

What perhaps should have been of greater concern to both Anglican and Nonconformist was the relatively significant number of people who were unaffiliated to any religious denomination and who attended no place of worship. This was particularly marked in the newly-industrialised and urbanised south-east where large numbers of immigrant families had settled, often swamping indigenous populations and cutting across older established denominational lines. However, such was the sectarian bickering between Church and Chapel, even between Nonconformist sects themselves, that this sometimes escaped their notice or did not receive the attention it deserved. On the other hand, it was not as yet an obvious or widespread problem but the potential remained for growth in terms either of religious apathy or atheism. In the interim, while *The Cardiff and Merthyr Guardian* could report with horror (25th May 1850) on 'the drinking, the debauchery, the spending there was' in Aberdare, a government report compiled in Merthyr (1842) by a clerk of the Plymouth Ironworks could say with unaffected enthusiasm that 'the majority of our population is decidedly religious'.

Table 17

Number of Sittings Provided by Welsh Denominations, 1851
(Census of Religious Worship 1851. Report and tables, 1853)

County	Church of England	Independents	Baptists	Wesleyan Methodists	Calvinistic Methodists	Total
Monmouthshire Popn: 177,130	39,215 % 22.1	14,135 % 8.0	28,377 %16.0	16,606 % 9.4	7,179 %4.1	116,266 % 65.6
Glamorgan Popn: 240,095	39,324 % 16.4	38,378 % 16.0	30,475 % 12.7	11,902 % 4.9	27,921 % 11.6	152,088 % 63.3
Carmarthenshire Popn: 94,672	22,321 % 23.6	20,088 % 21.2	9.785 % 10.3	3,757 % 4.0	14, 399 %15.2	70,976 % 75.0
Pembrokeshire Popn: 84,472	25,367 % 30.0	14,323 % 16.9	13,125 % 15.5	6,909 % 8.2	5,701 % 6.7	67,004 % 79.3
Cardiganshire Popn: 97,614	21,569 % 22.1	15,267 % 15.6	11,291 % 11.5	3,666 % 3.7	22,053 % 22.6	82,335 % 84.3
Brecknockshire Popn: 59,178	17,842 % 30.1	9.892 % 16.7	8,739 % 14.8	3,840 % 6.6	6,733 % 11.4	48,746 % 82.4
Radnorshire Popn: 31,425	13,204 % 42.0	2,102 % 6.7	3,165 % 10.1	1,731 % 5.5	1,385 % 4.4	22,802 % 72.6
Montgomeryshire Popn: 77,142	22,362 % 29.0	9,910 % 12.8	4,167 % 5.4	10,481 % 13.6	12,796 % 16.6	62,886 % 81.5
Flintshire Popn: 41,047	10,660 % 26.0	4,933 % 12.0	1,402 % 3.4	6,749 % 16.4	6,542 % 15.9	32,177 % 78.4
Denbighshire Popn: 96,915	36,535 % 31.5	10,507 % 10.8	7,235 % 7.5	11,872 % 12.2	25,921 % 26.7	91,177 % 94.0
Meirionethshire Popn: 51,307	8,895 % 17.3	7,212 % 14.0	1,934 % 3.8	3,299 % 6.4	13,550 % 26.4	35,161 % 68.3
Caernarfonshire Popn: 94,674	24,096 % 25.4	12,892 % 13.6	4,786 % 5.0	9,207 % 9.7	38,284 % 40.4	85,199 % 90.0
Anglesey Popn: 43,243	8,654 % 20.0	4,606 % 10.6	2,718 % 6.3	2,506 % 5.8	12,912 % 29.8	31,725 % 73.4

b) Aspects of Popular Belief: Revivals and Revivalism

I have been here eleven years [1848-59]. Almost all the miners used to be drunkards and Sabbath-breakers. They would come to their work on Monday with bruised faces and black eyes. The change is beyond anything I ever knew. I saw great revivals in Cornwall but none to compare with the present awakening in these parts. There is scarcely a house without its family altar.

[J.J. Morgan, *The '59 Revival in Wales* (1906)]

I
II
III
IV
V
VI
VII
VIII
IX
X

To judge from the comments of contemporaries the power and influence of a truly religious revival was simply breathtaking. It was an awe-inspiring experience, divinely inspired, miraculous even, which could, and frequently did, change lives. In the short term, revivalism was an almost irresistible force which tended to sweep all before it, but in the long term its effects, and the religious devotion it engendered, might wane with the passage of time. They might be local affairs, such as at Beddgelert in 1817-19 or more widespread and influential like the Great Revival of 1904-5. Of course, religious revivals were nothing new, they had a history which stretched back to the medieval period and beyond but it was the mass appeal and longevity of the 'modern', post-eighteenth century, revivals which set them apart.

The Great Revival of the second half of the eighteenth century which witnessed the foundation of Methodism in England (Wesleyan Methodism,1784) and Wales (Calvinistic and Wesleyan Methodism, 1811) had a profound effect on the people which left a lasting impression on both converted and critic. Edward Williams or Iolo Morganwg (d. 1826), literary forger and founder of the modern *eisteddfod*, was far from impressed by the change wrought by conversion to Methodism. In a letter to a friend (1799) he observed that 'North Wales is now as Methodistical as South Wales, and South Wales as Hell'. Love them or loath them, revivalists and revivalism were very much a feature of life in nineteenth-century Wales, so much so that foreigners too could not help but take note of their existence and influence. One such was Ralph Lingen, one of the authors of the infamous Blue Books, who stated that the Welsh were often subjected to, what he called, 'the strange and abnormal features of a Revival'! That said, they were well-meaning devotional events which were nearly always a force for good.

There were six major revivals, i.e. affecting more than one county or region of Wales, during the nineteenth and early part of the twentieth century – 1828-9, 1831-2, 1837-42, 1849, 1859 and 1904-5 – each of which was inspired by particular themes or problems in society such as temperance, health or poverty. The *gwerin* wanted to be comforted, they begged for answers, they wished for guidance but, above all, they hoped for security in this life and salvation in the next.
- The **1828**-9 revival which began in Caeo in the heart of rural Carmarthenshire was inspired by rural poverty but as it spread to the industrial towns and districts of Neath and Swansea it took its inspiration

from industrial poverty, the unemployed, the depressed and the discontented. In any other circumstance such conditions might have erupted into violence, strikes, even revolution, but due to the essentially conservative nature of dissent and the calming influence, at least in matters outside religion, of the revivalist preachers, the religious revivals acted as pressure valves, as a force for social control in some areas.

- The so-called 'cholera revivals' of **1831-2** and **1849** were largely, though not exclusively, a result of the deadly Asiatic epidemics. As the disease spread and the death-toll rose, so fear gripped the nation, churches and chapels quickly filled and those in search of salvation were converted.

- Temperance was the key to the revival of **1837** and because this was a more tangible issue which the church could do something about, unlike cholera!, its intensity outlasted initial conversion. Beginning in Bala, the movement spread quickly through the rural hinterland of north and south Wales but slowed up considerably when it reached the industrial districts of the south and north east. Here hard drinking and hard living were synonymous with workers employed in heavy industries and mining, and despite the best efforts of temperance societies they never managed to eradicate drinking though they did help control it. For example, in 1881 the government was persuaded to pass the Welsh Sunday Closing Act for which there was solid support in the north and much support even in the industrialised valleys of the south. An opinion poll held in Mountain Ash claimed that over 90% of those questioned favoured the closure of public houses on Sundays.

Arguably the two greatest, if not necessarily the most influential, revivals took place in **1859** and **1904-5** and both were inspired less by secular matters as by true religious devotion.

- Beginning in rural north Cardiganshire, the revival of **1859** was unashamedly theological in form, content and intent, almost harking back to a perceived 'simpler', less complicated religion of the pre-industrial era.

- On the other hand, the so-called 'Evan Roberts' revival of **1904-5** was born in the industrialised south at Loughor having been influenced by a smaller-scale revival in southern Cardiganshire. Here was a vital, youthful even strident movement which was characterised by a public showing of spiritual conversion followed by regular prayer meetings and

I

II

III

IV

V

VI

VII

VIII

IX

X

Bible classes. Roberts, an ex-collier, was a charismatic speaker who was particularly successful in recruiting large numbers of women to the movement. Part of the reason for the phenomenal spread and success of the revival was due to extensive newspaper coverage. In November 1904 the editor of the Nonconformist periodical *Y Goleuad* wrote 'Blessed be the *Western Mail*'. Its short-term effects were quite startling – 80-90,000 additional converts attending places of worship, the last large-scale building or renovation programme of chapels, a marked decline in theatre and eisteddfod-going and even the closure of some rugby clubs such as at Ammanford and Creunant – but after 1906 it merely fizzelled out.

Thus, religion acted as a focal point of social conscience where people could express their concerns, worries and fears. It might also act as a catalyst for change with religious leaders bringing pressure to bear on local and national authorities to act in the interests of the people. As we have witnessed in an earlier chapter, there was a close relationship between religion and radicalism, where the politics of dissent was making its mark in Parliament. In the cultural, educational and recreational fields too religion played, probably, a more crucial part. As historian John Davies has said,

> ... it is difficult to realise how central religion was to vast numbers of the Welsh people at the beginning of the [20th] century. At that time, the extent of the activities of the Welsh places of worship was amazing. They were served by 4,000 ministers and priests; they could draw upon the assistance of 25,000 deacons ...; 11,000 sermons were preached in them every Sunday; their Sunday Schools were attended by almost half the population; at least two million meetings were held annually in their vestries and halls; their members bought countless commentaries, hymn books and religious periodicals'.

c) The 1904-5 Revival

The religious revival of 1904-05 which gripped parts of Wales was the last of the great revivals. It was, in many ways, different from revivals which preceded it, and indeed, contained several features unique to it. For example, in the opinion of Tim Williams, one of the key features that made it different was how it '... was dominated by working-class youth, and by women, and this in a Society which offered women almost no paid employment prospects, so that chapel-going was virtually the only possible and indeed permissible activity outside the family domain'.

This revival, as David Jenkins has pointed out, caused an association to be made between those who had been awakened, '... ministers and laymen, men and women, young and old, regardless of their moral standing and regardless of denominational boundaries, *vis-a-vis* those who had not been awakened. People became prominent not because they were the official or elected leaders, but because they had been aroused'.

Below are a selection of sources which offer a varied contemporary view of the main features of the revival and its chief architect.

Fig. 32
Evan Roberts and fellow Revivalists from Loughor

Examining the evidence

A

> There were remarkable scenes of religious ecstasy. Strong men wept and groaned; women cried and sobbed ... spontaneously bursting into prayer and sacred song. Others rocked themselves in paroxysms of fervent emotion. It would puzzle the keenest critic to say precisely what it is that gives the young revivalists such power to stir the souls of his hearers.
>
> [*Cambrian Daily Leader*, 18 November 1904]

I
II
III
IV
V
VI
VII
VIII
IX
X

B

Whereas it is the work of the Revival to blast the stones in the quarry, it is the task of the settled ministry to dress them. In 1859 there was a similar explosion, between 60,000 and 100,000 converts having been made, rough stones most of them. It has taken forty years of labour on the part of the ministers to dress them and fit them in the spiritual temple ...

[Rev. Dr. C. Jones, reported in the *Western Mail*, 22 December 1904]

C

Someone in the body of the chapel started a hymn ... Evan Roberts awoke as if from a trance and said, 'Stop! Stop! ... There is an obstacle here which must first be removed'. It transpired that the obstacle was disobedience of those who were church members. He asked them all to pray ... This had gone on for some time when Mr. Roberts said the difficulty had passed off, and   5 that they might now sing. Throughout the chapel people might be seen speaking to their neighbours and ... hymns were sung with great emotion.

[D. Awstin, *The Religious Revival in Wales* (1905)]

D

He rose and held up a Bible, asking, 'What is this?' Many answered 'A Bible', another said 'The Word of God', 'Yes', he said, 'but there is one present tonight who denies it' ... Evan Roberts called on the doubter to rise and immediately confess ... as it was not possible for the worship to proceed while he was there. 'If he does not confess I shall probably have his name,   5 and once God gives me his name I shall announce it. He is a young man of twenty five.' And then. 'I have been given his name it is ...'. There was a loud wailing and tumult in the chapel ...

[Eyewitness account of a revival meeting recorded in a National Library of Wales Mss. (1905)]

E

Fig. 33
Revival Service in a Coal Mine (c.1904) as depicted by J.M. Staniforth

F

Fig. 34

Western Mail: Evan Roberts' Revival Meetings

MR. EVAN ROBERTS' MEETINGS.

REVIVAL.

WONDERFUL RESULTS OF THE MOVEMENT.

CONVERSIONS NUMBER OVER SEVENTY THOUSAND.

Place	No.
Aberaman	238
Aberavon	325
Aberbeeg	155
Abercrave	57
Abercwmboy	140
Abercynon	630
Aberdare	715
Abergwynfi and Blaengwynfi	420
Aberkenfig	256
Abernant	97
Abersychan, Pontnewynydd, Talywain, Garndiffaith, and Varteg	453
Abertillery, Sixbells, and Cwmtillery	2,342
Abertridwr	98
Aberystwyth and district	220
Barry	424
Bargoed	162
Beaufort	100
Bedlinog	182
Bedwas	38
Blackwood	340
Blaenavon	810
Blaencwmin (Pem.)	6
Blaengarw	545
Blaenpennal	15
Blaina	878
Bontnewydd (near Amph)	15
Bridgend	270
Briton Ferry	406
Bryncethin	86
Brynmawr	274
Brynmenin	22
Builth Wells	103
Burry Port	264
Bwlchyllan	30
Caerphilly	685
Capcoch	45
Cardiff	1,068
Cardigan and district	55
Carmarthen	300
Cefncribbwr	75
Cilfrew and Coytant.	101
Cilfynydd	721
Clydach (Brecon)	56
Clydach-on-Tawe	270
Clydach Vale	689
Coedpoeth	70
Coity	23
Cowbridge	26
Coychurch, Treos, and Llangan	70
Crickhowell	91
Crosshands and Tumble	276
Croeskeys	506
Crumlin	18
Cwmaman	565
Cwmamman (Carm.).	471
Cwmbach	374
Cwmbran	172
Cwmdare	91
Cwmgwrach	141
Cwmllynfell	120
Cwmpark and ...dif	135
Cymmer	79
Dowlais and Penydarren	1,365
Drefach and Velindre	89
Ebbw Vale	1,500
Ferndale and Blaenllechau	700
Ferryside	17
Fforestfach & Cockett	296
Fishguard	120
Fleur-de-Lis, Pengam, and Gilfach	214
Freystrop	35
Froncysyllte (N. W.)	60
Gadlys	147
Gelligaer	17
Gilfachgoch	451
Gilwern and district	60
Glyncorrwg	135
Glyn-Neath	450
Goodwick	20
Gorseinon	304
Gowerton and Waunarlwydd	341
Gwaen-cae-Gurwen	20
Irsfal	262
Haverfordwest	90
Heolycyw	22
Hirwain and district	327
Hopkinstown	84
Kenfig Hill	408
Kidwelly	191
Lampeter and district	110
Landore	748
Laugharne & Plasket	80
Llanbradach	194
Llanddewi-Brefi	40
Llandilo (Pem.)	12
Llandovery	87
Llandrindod Wells and Howey Village	10
Llandysul and district	114
Llanelly, Loughor, and Felinfoel	1,317
Llanelly Hill (Brecon)	90
Llangattock	53
Llangeitho	45
Llangennech	66
Llangollen (N. W.)	84
Llangyfelach	24
Llanharan	245
Llanhilleth	162
Llanidloes	27
Llannon	17
Llansamlet	274
Llantwit Major	138
Llwydcoed	87
Llwynhendy	109
Llwynpiod	25
Llwynypia	112
Machen	209
Maesteg	2,115
Maenclochog	60
Maesycwmmer	186
Maindee (Newport).	6
Mardy	680
Merthyr	760
Merthyr Vale	874
Middle Hill (Haverfordwest)	38
Milford Haven	192
Minkin	12
Morriston	1,003
Mountain Ash	778
Mynyddbach	14
Nantymoel	56
Nantygio	307
Neath	1,295
Neath Abbey	71
Nelson	293
Newbridge	410
New Milford	300
New Quay	55
Newport	900
Newtown (N. Wales)	102
New Tredegar	301
Ogmore Vale	28
Pembrey and Pwll.	160
Pembroke	12
Pembroke Dock	20
Penarth	600
Penclawdd	193
Penderyn (Aberdare).	10
Penrhiwceiber	433
Pentre	1,362
Penycae (N. Wales).	130
Penygraig	406
Penywaun (Aberdare).	60
Peterstone	15
Pontardawe	212
Pontardulais	435
Pontlottyn	242
Pontnewydd	62
Pontrhydfendigaid	30
Pontrhydyfen	12
Pontrhydygroes	20
Pontyberem	108
Pontycŷmer and district	120
Pontycymmer	810
Pontygwaith	270
Pontypool	407
Pontypridd	1,645
Pontyrhyl	96
Porth	658
Porthcawl	49
Pyle	61
Resolven	661
Rheola	109
Rhuddlan	13
Rhydfelen	95
Rhyl (N. Wales)	45
Rhymney	770
Risca	630
Robertstown	82
Rogerstone	400
St. Asaph (N. Wales)	6
St. Bride's	21
St. Clears	66
St. David's	38
St. Fagan's	50
St. Mellon's	32
Saron (Pem.)	30
Senghenydd	487
Seven Sisters and Onllwyn	121
Skewen	461
Sutton (Pem.)	27
Swansea	500
Talbach and Margam	270
Taigarth and district	84
Talywain	74
Tongwynlais	135
Tonna and Aberdulais	102
Tonypandy	340
Tonyrefail	301
Trealaw	15
Trehanos	50
Trecynon	516
Tredegar	1,500
Treforest	56
Tregaron	60
Treharris	1,003
Treherbert, Blaenrhondda, and Blaenycwm	1,164
Treorky	1,488
Troodyrhiw	486
Tylorstown	650
Walton West (Pem.).	50
Watford (near Caerphilly)	
West Hook (Pem.).	47
Whitchurch	32
Ynyshir	176
Ynysybwl	792
Ystalyfera	392
Ystradgynlais	618
Total	**65,319**

I II III IV V VI VII VIII IX X

A truly religious revival?

The phenomenon of the 1904-5 revival proved to be as short lived as it was remarkable. It shone with such brilliance and with such intensity that those who experienced it thought it impossible that it could ever end. However, end it did after a little less than three years during which its leader Evan Roberts held his converts spellbound with his unconventional preaching, supported by Bible studies and prayer meetings. So successful was he that the Nonconformist establishment became alarmed, so much so that Roberts began to make enemies. Almost inevitably there were those who questioned the truth and Christian virtue of Roberts and the religious revival he created. Some unsavoury aspects of the revival and Roberts' way of doing things began to emerge and were quickly seized upon by an eager press. Perhaps the most damning piece to be written on the revival was published in 1909 which not only sounded the death-knell for Roberts' reputation but served as an epitaph to the revival he inspired.

> A Cwmavon minister who had not been allowed to preach for several Sundays approached a group of young men between the ages of 16 and 23: 'Am I to preach tonight' ... 'It depends upon what the Spirit tells us' ... The pastor as a representative of the normal type of religious experience was practically regarded as an alien ... The prevailing sentiment was expressed in the prayer   5
> of the man who thanked the Lord that He had shunted the ministers on the side line ... The same unsympathetic attitude was assumed by Evan Roberts towards aged Christians. In his presence young men deprecated the restraining influence of the old and actually prayed for their conversion and in some instances even for their removal by death. This side of the Revival was   5
> not noticed in the press reports. The insolence the young men were encouraged to cultivate towards the aged may be classed as one of the saddest features of the Revival of 1904-5.
> [J.V. Morgan, *The Welsh Religious Revival 1904-5*: A Retrospect and Criticism (1909)]

d) 'A Nation of Nonconformists'?

In 1891 the Liberal Prime Minister W.E. Gladstone uttered these words which he, as did those who heard them, truly believed to be the case. However, more recently, historians have powerfully challenged this 'Nonconformist myth'. In 1988 Tim Williams stated that 'religion, often conceived of as the opiate [drug] of the Welsh masses in this period [1880-

1914] ... was neither as neutralising nor as all-embracing as we might think'. He suggested that although 'it is clear that a large majority of practising Christians in Wales, perhaps 75 per cent, frequented Nonconformist places of worship', he poses the intriguing question 'But were the Welsh a nation of Nonconformists?'. His answer, 'in numerical terms', is that they were not. Indeed, by the end of the first decade of the twentieth century it is true to say that despite the revivals of the previous century and the one of 1904-5 only 750,000 people regularly attended a place of worship. Even if thousands of occasional 'hearers' are added, conservatively estimated at 150,000, the total amounts to 37.1% of the population of Wales as given in the 1911 Census. If Anglicans and the 65,000 Roman Catholics are extracted then Nonconformity could lay claim to around 22.6% of the total population. Dr. Williams argues that if this is taken into account then the influence of Nonconformity on the people of Wales must itself be reduced.

This is supported to some extent by the evidence gathered between 1906-10 by the Royal Commission appointed to inquire into the Church and other Religious Bodies in Wales. This found that though Nonconformity was still strong in rural Welsh-speaking areas it was declining in the Anglicised industrialised areas of the south and north east. In fact, it also points out that though the Nonconformist-inspired revivals had apparently run their course, there had been a religious revival of another sort – of the Anglican Church. As a result of reforms and a changed attitude, the Established Church was making something of a comeback, for example, between 1851 and 1910 over 340 new churches had been built in Wales and by 1911 its numbers had increased to 193,000. However, the Great War put paid to that. The bloodshed and suffering caused by the war had turned some against the idea of religion. The more practical issues of politics, work, wages and trade-unions became far more important in daily life. As the working classes became better educated they began to question their religion and even criticise some religious ideas and teaching. The world was changing but to many people the chapels and churches seemed slow to adapt, or incapable of adapting, to the new world. By the early 1920s the chapels were in decline.

I

II

III

IV

V

VI

VII

VIII

IX

X

I

II

III

IV

V

VI

VII

VIII

IX

X

Advice and Activities

(i) General

Suggested Further Reading

E.T. Davies, *Religion in the Industrial Revolution in South Wales* (Cardiff, 1965).

E.T. Davies, *Religion and Society in the Nineteenth Century* (Llandybie, 1981).

L.W. Evans, *Education in Industrial Wales, 1700-1900* (Cardiff, 1971).

G.E. Jones, *The Education of a Nation* (Cardiff, 1997).

P. Morgan (ed.), *Brad y Llyfrau Gleision* (Landysul, 1991).

G.T. Roberts, *The Language of the Blue Books* (Cardiff, 1998).

G. Williams, *Religion, Language and Nationality in Wales* (Cardiff, 1979).

Articles:

T. Parry, 'Literary Movements of the Nineteenth Century', in A.J. Roderick (ed.), *Wales through the Ages, vol. 2* (Llandybie, 1960).

C. Turner, 'The Nonconformist Response' in T. Herbert & G.E. Jones (eds.), *People and Protest: Wales 1815-1880* (Cardiff, 1988).

T. Williams, 'Language, Religion, Culture' in in T. Herbert & G.E. Jones (eds.), *People and Protest: Wales 1815-1880* (Cardiff, 1988).

Research

Look up the following figures i) Robert Owen ii) Henry Richard iii) Evan Roberts.

From what you have learnt, which of them deserves to be remembered if a book was to be written on 'Famous Welshmen'. Give reasons for your choice and opinion.

Issues for Debate

'A Nation of Nonconformists'? Argue a case **in favour** and **against** this statement about nineteenth-century Wales.

Points for Discussion

Education was nothing more than a political football played by the Anglicans and Nonconformists in a cynical attempt to capture the hearts and minds of an ignorant people. Discuss this controversial statement.

(ii) Examination Specific

Answering Source Questions

Read the sources on pages 207-209 and answer the following questions:

a) Compare sources C and D. How do the two sources contrast in their description of revivalist religious techniques? (8 marks)

b) Study sources A and E. How reliable are sources A and E to an historian as evidence of reactions to the Religious Revival? (16 marks)

c) How useful are the sources to an understanding of the Religious Revival in Wales between 1904-5?

Advice

a) Source C suggests that religious orthodoxy was an important part of the revivalist technique. Clearly, stress is placed on the emotional element, coupled with a sense of close friendship between members of the congregations.

Source D also describes a religious service but this time more emphasis is placed on the participation of the congregation – direct responses to the minister's questions – and the element of emotional hysteria. This is further underlined by the technique of naming a person who had not accepted their religious beliefs. This hightened still further the emotionally charged atmosphere.

b) Source A is an extract from a newspaper, presumably by a detached observer. No reason here to question the reliability of this account beyond considering the newspaper's motivation to sell copy and tell a good story. The reactions of the reporter are probably not untypical of many people in Wales. A rather superficial account.

I
II
III
IV
V
VI
VII
VIII
IX
X

Source E – a drawing done by a well-known cartoonist who supplied the *Western Mail* with much of his work. There is no indication of its date, its purpose or reason why it was drawn except perhaps to reflect the current fascination for the latest religious 'fad' or phenomenon. Clearly, religious services underground was news as was the fact of them being requested, presumably, by the workforce. No indication if this was common practice or just a 'one-off'. No reason to doubt the truth or sincerity of the cartoonist's work.

c) The sources give a good insight into the actual services and some of the methods used by the revivalists. At the same time, they give relatively little information about the extent of its influence, the nature of its support or the depth of its impact. Most of the sources tend to be rather superficial in their treatment of the revival. Again, there is no consideration of the impact on others or why, in some areas, there was a strong impact but not in others.

The limitations of the sources must be highlighted in so far as they shed little light on the popularity of the revival in a wider context. There are no sources offering a critical view of the revival.

I

II

III

IV

V

VI

VII

VIII

IX

X

Chapter VI

Culture, Language and The 'National Revival'

1. Language

■ **Key Issue:**
Why did the Welsh language survive?

a) From Monoglotism to Bilingualism:
The Industrial and Urban Dilemma

> The Native Gibberish is usually prattled throughout the whole Taphydome, except in their Market Towns, whose Inhabitants being a little rais'd, and (as it were) pufft up into Bubbles, above the ordinary Scum, do begin to despise it ... 'Tis usually cashier'd out of Gentlemen's Houses ... the Lingua will be English'd out of Wales.
>
> [William Richards, *Wallography* (1682)]

This savage condemnation of the Welsh language by an English satirist was as near as representative of the English view of the Welsh at the beginning of the nineteenth century, as it had been at the end of the seventeenth. When Richards penned 'his diabolical diatribe', the people of whom he wrote were almost entirely Welsh speaking. If, as has been estimated, as many as 90%, of the population were speakers of the 'native gibberish' it is believed that a high proportion of these were fluent only in Welsh and therefore ignorant of the English language. A little over a century later in 1801 it is estimated that around 90% of the people of Wales were Welsh speaking of whom between 65% and 70% were probably monoglot. The inescapable fact of the matter is that despite its lowly status, vilification by the English press and neglect bordering on suppression by the English establishment and governing classes (both English and Welsh), the Welsh language continued to flourish and dictate the rhythm of speech in every-

I

II

III

IV

V

VI

VII

VIII

IX

X

day life. Naturally some parts of Wales were more anglicised than others, mainly along the border and in areas long settled by English immigrants like south Pembrokeshire and Gower, but the rural heartland remained solidly Welsh in speech and thought. Yet within a century of the first census of 1801 Wales had been transformed, changing from a native-speaking largely monoglot country into a bilingual nation where English was increasingly gaining ground at the expense of Welsh.

(i) The Traditional Interpretation

The reasons for this apparent transformation are many and varied but the chief cause was once held to be the rapid industrialisation of the country. It was argued that as the iron, steel, tinplate and especially the labour-intensive coal industries grew in size, wealth and importance so did their insatiable demand for workers. Fed by immigration from without and emigration from within, this almost limitless appetite for industrial fodder led inexorably to rural depopulation matched by a corresponding expansion in urban development thus upsetting the linguistic, and in some of the new urban-industrialised communities, ethnic balance. For example, recalling his youth in Porth in the Rhondda during the 1890s *(Unfinished Journey, 1938)*, the novelist Jack Jones stated that

> The Welsh were in a minority .... they were mixed with English, Irish and Scotch people, whose fathers and grandfathers had been brought into Wales by the old Iron Kings. At first I knew only Welsh from my parents and grandparents, but as I went on playing with the Scott, Hartley, Ward and McGill children, I became more fluent than in my native language. Dad was annoyed when I started replying in English to what he had said in Welsh, but our mam said, in Welsh: 'Oh, let him alone. What odds, anyway?'

The counties to which much of this industry was attracted were Glamorgan and Monmouthshire the populations of which rose accordingly by 77% and 117% respectively between the census of 1801 and 1841. The hike in their respective populations between 1851 and 1911 was equally considerable particularly in Glamorgan which rose from 231,800 to 1,120,910, and in Monmouthshire rising from 157,400 to 395,719. To put it another way, in 1801 less than 25% of the people of Wales lived in these, as yet still largely rural counties, but by 1911 they accommodated around 65% of the nation's population, the majority of whom were concentrated in towns of ever increasing size and commercial significance. By 1911 a little over 60% of the population lived in towns and of the eighteen towns in Wales with a population in excess of 20,000 all bar one – Llanelli – were to be found in Glamorgan and Monmouthshire. Of these, two towns in particular saw a quite unprecedented growth in their size and populations, namely Cardiff and Swansea. Between 1801 and 1901 their populations grew, respectively, from 1,870 and 6,831 to 128,000 and 135,000. That they also served as ports is indicative of the huge increase in the volume of trade generated by Welsh industrial production. It was partly as a result of this commercial activity, in the ports as elsewhere such as in market towns, that Welsh gradually gave way to English, which was fast becoming the language of world trade. The massive increase in the import and export of goods was matched only by the volume of inward and outward migration which in turn had a detrimental effect on the Welsh language. As Cardiff's population rose the percentage number of Welsh speakers dropped from an estimated high of 80% in 1831 to a low of just 7% by 1911. It was a pattern repeated across Glamorgan, being much accelerated in the coastal lowlands which had become almost entirely monoglot English by 1891 but decreasing further up the upland valleys. The varying rates of decline in Welsh speakers in proportion to the increase in population can best be illustrated by the experience of Pontypridd. A modest town of some 7,600 people in 1875 of whom it is estimated around 75% spoke Welsh, by 1901 its population had grown rapidly to 32,316, but the numbers of those fluent in Welsh had halved to 38%.

A high proportion of those who crowded into towns like Pontypridd, Cardiff and Swansea came from the rural, Welsh-speaking heartland of Wales. The evidence for rural depopulation is most marked in the counties of Cardiganshire, Merionethshire and Montgomeryshire, each of which registered a net loss in population in each decade between 1871 (from 1881 in the case of Merionethshire) and 1911.

Table 18

	1871	1881	1891	1901	1911
Cardiganshire	73,400	70,300	62,600	61,100	59,900
Merionethshire	46,600	52,000	49,200	48,900	45,600
Montgomeryshire	67,600	65,700	58,000	54,900	53,100

I
II
III
IV
V
VI
VII
VIII
IX
X

217

The effect of this on the Welsh language was considered to be little short of catastrophic for as Geraint Jenkins pointed out, 'As a result of industrialisation, urbanisation and in-migration, the prevailing trend was for greater numbers of bilingual communities to develop, and even in the heartlands the fabric of the old monoglot Welsh communities had begun to unravel'. Rural migration, in many cases, cut across traditional ties of community, which had held firm for generations, and thus weakened the cultural and linguistic base of what the late E.G. Bowen, a human geographer, called 'inner Wales'. Technological improvements in communications and the construction of new roads and railways breached the protective insularity that came with geographical remoteness which served, ultimately, to erode still further the language and culture of rural Wales. The rural communities of Welsh-speaking Wales became vulnerable and found it harder still to resist the forces of tourism, commercialism and English linguistic imperialism.

(ii) The Early Revisionist or 'Brinley Thomas' Interpretation

Clearly, the argument is a cogent one in as much as it offers a credible set of reasons and a plausible sequence of events to explain the gradual erosion of the Welsh language. However, this traditionalist argument has been powerfully challenged not least by the late Brinley Thomas who, according to Geraint Jenkins,

> ... stood the conventional wisdom of the time on its head by declaring that the industrialisation of south Wales had enabled the surplus rural population to be absorbed internally, thereby sparing Wales from the kind of massive rural exodus which befell Ireland in the same period and thus also facillitating the retention of the Welsh language and culture.

Brinley Thomas argued that the flow of migrants from rural or 'inner' Wales reduced rather than depleted the numbers of native speakers but that moving south and east, as opposed to leaving the country altogether, had the effect of replenishing and reinforcing the language in the industrial valleys of 'outer' Wales. Unlike the Irish, far fewer Welsh were tempted to emigrate either to the United States or to England because the industrialisation of the country meant they did not need to, they were as likely to find alternative employment and better prospects within Wales as outside it. To support his case Thomas showed that although the rural areas suffered a net loss in population of some 388,000 between 1851 and 1911 this was more than balanced by the net gain of around 366,000 migrants into Glamorgan and Monmouthshire more than 80% of whom, at least until the beginning of the twentieth century, came from rural Wales. In the majority of the industrial districts of south-east Wales, particularly in Glamorgan and the upland valleys of west Monmouthshire, the native Welsh were able to assimilate the newcomers from across the border from England. Indeed, it is not until the first decade of the twentieth century that foreign, mainly English, immigration began to outstrip native migrants in such numbers that they could not be absorbed as easily as before.

To add weight to his case, Thomas used the experience of the Rhondda valley which had, in percentage terms, accommodated more migrants than any other part of south-east Wales, its population rising from 11,737 in 1861 to 127,980 by 1891. Describing the Rhondda in 1896 the *Report of the Welsh land Commission* stated: '... speaking broadly, the characteristics of Welsh life, its Nonconformist development, the habitual use of the Welsh language, and the prevalence of a Welsh type of character, are as marked as in the rural districts of Wales'. Apparently, the rural migrants who flocked into the coal-mining valley took with them their Welsh way of life and so helped perpetuate and develop the native culture and language in the heart of the industrial and urban communities of the south. As if to reinforce his point, it can be shown from the Census for 1911 that, numerically at least, there were three times more Welsh speakers in Glamorgan than in any one of the remaining twelve counties of Wales.

It was a controversial argument which was not without its critics but Brinley Thomas hit back stating that 'Instead of bemoaning the rural exodus, the Welsh patriot should sing the praises of industrial development which gave the Welsh language a new lease of life and Welsh Nonconformity a glorious high noon'.

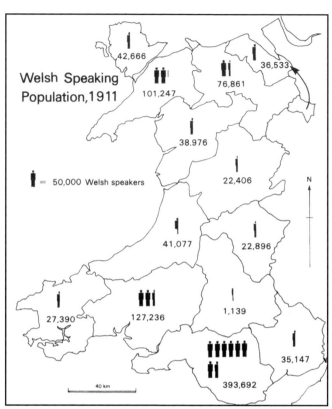

Map 12

Welsh-Speaking
Population, 1911

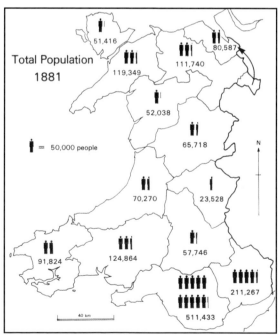

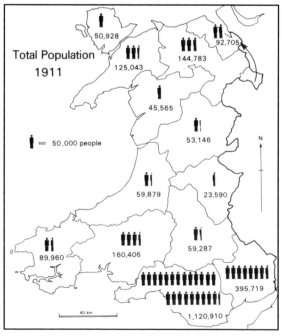

Map 13

Population of Wales (i) 1880 and (ii) 1911

(iii) The Later Revisionist Interpretation

Historians currently tend to take a more balanced view, they do not reject entirely the traditional interpretation but nor do they fully accept Brinley Thomas' persuasive arguments. Rather they highlight the complexities of the problem and suggest that Thomas' thesis falls short of conviction on several counts:

1) in underestimating the numbers of Welsh speakers who left Wales. It has been estimated that more than 77,000 Welsh-speakers had migrated to England by 1851 and that by 1911 their number exceeded 133,000 which makes them second only in size to those living in Glamorgan and a seventh of the estimated total in Britain.

2) that while the first generation of migrants did indeed take with them their 'Welsh way of life' the succeeding generations slowly but surely succumbed to English influence and speech. For example, in 1891 80% of Glamorgan's population of 1,120,910 were Welsh born but only 49.9% could speak the language. But by 1911 this had fallen to 38% of whom the majority were from the older generation and of these only some 34,000 were listed as monoglot Welsh. If anything, the linguistic shift in the industrial valleys moved first towards creating a bilingual rather than a purely Welsh-speaking society and once this had happened it was only a matter of time before English muscled Welsh out of all but the most homogeneous and determined of communities. That Welsh survived 'in a sea of Englishness' was pointed out by J.E. Southall, an Englishman but a passionate advocate of the Welsh language and culture, who praised the communities of the upper Rhymni valley for being an 'outlying fortress against the flood of English'.

His study of the 1901 census (*The Welsh Language Census of 1901* published in 1904) made depressing reading in that only 13% of the population of his adopted county of Monmouthshire were registered Welsh speakers. In despair he wrote, 'Where is the patriot who will arise to save Gwent ... from losing all sight of her Cymric kinship and of Cymric ideals and speech'. Indeed, historians have seized on the fact that the Welsh themselves seemed prone to be self-conscious about their language, especially in face of the patronising and disapproving attitude of the state. English was, after all, the language of an Empire spoken by over 60 million people worldwide and an inability to speak it was equated with social and cultural inferiority.

I

II

III

IV

V

VI

VII

VIII

IX

X

3) Thomas, it has been argued, underestimated the social and psychological pressures which tended to work in favour of English and against Welsh. It has been concluded that Thomas' arguments are valid up to c. 1870 but not thereafter since the march of Englishness was relentless and its effects on the populace was quite marked. In April 1902 a letter received and published by the *Glamorgan Free Press* highlights the reluctance or indifference of one generation to pass on Welsh to the next.

Sir, A good number of our Welsh parents cannot prevail upon their ownchildren to learn the Welsh language upon their own hearths and among their own family and I admit that it is a most difficult matter in many instances in a town like Pontypridd where the English tongue is so predominant among all classes. Even in the Welsh chapel after a Welsh service we find as soon as the service is over that most of the conversation takes place in English.

4) even in the Rhondda, which retained a strong Welsh-speaking population, the linguistic shift was most definitely towards the use of English. In 1909 the chairman of the Rhondda district of the Miners' Federation asked in a meeting 'Is there anyone here who wants the resolution in Welsh?' 'Everyone here understands English' came the reply.

b) Incline or Decline: The Statistical Paradox

It is true that there are more Welshmen speaking Welsh to-day than in any preceding period - there are more of them. It is equally true that more Welshmen speak English to-day, which is a far more important consideration.
[J. Vyrnwy Morgan, *A Study in Nationality* (1912)]

Published within a year of the census for 1911 the author was clearly unimpressed with the fact that the number of recorded Welsh speakers had reached an all time high of 977,366. Indeed, the numbers speaking Welsh had been steadily rising throughout the nineteenth century, increasing from an estimated near 600,000 in 1801 to close on 900,000 in 1891. Therefore, at the turn of the twentieth century more Welsh people than ever before were speaking the language which suggests that it was strong, vibrant and healthy. In view of this it might seem that Vyrnwy Morgan's apprehension about the fate of the language was at best misplaced, and at worst pessimistic. However, on closer inspection the decennial census data, beginning with that for 1891 which was the first to supply information on the language, showed that while the actual numbers of those speaking Welsh was rising their proportion of the population was falling. In crude percentage terms this meant that though an estimated 90% of the population could speak Welsh in 1801, this had fallen to 54% in 1891 followed by a further drop in numbers to 45% in 1911. To put it another way, the census for 1901 revealed that fully 84% of the population could speak English which shows that it was most definitely not a foreign language to the vast majority of Welsh people.

Historian John Davies sums up the linguistic fortunes of Wales for the period 1801 to 1911 in the following terms: 'there was a four-fold increase in the population of Wales, a two-fold increase in the number of Welsh speakers and a twelve-fold increase in the number of monoglot English speakers'. This highlights clearly the dilemma facing historians and sociolinguists for although the numbers speaking Welsh were increasing so were those speaking only English, by the same token those fluent only in Welsh were declining fast. In short, Welsh monoglotism was rapidly disappearing while English monoglotism was expanding at a phenomenal rate. The critical battleground as far as the fate of the language was concerned was with the bilingual masses since the majority of the increasing numbers of Welsh speakers were, or became after some schooling, bilingual. This fact, and its implications for the long-term future of the language, was quickly recognised by contemporaries such as the Revd. R.R. Williams of Tywyn who expressed his fears in an article published in *Y Goleuad* in December 1901.

> The three most Welsh counties of the North are Merioneth, Anglesey and Caernarfon - in that order. Of the inhabitants of those areas over three years old, only 6% in Merioneth, 8% in Anglesey and 10% in Caernarfon are English monoglots. But note: out of every hundred Merioneth Welsh 44 can speak the two languages; 44 also in Anglesey and 42 in Caernarfon. The situation therefore is that close to half the population of each of the most Welsh counties speak Welsh and English. In other words the three counties with fewest English inhabitants have already gone bilingual.

I

II

III

IV

V

VI

VII

VIII

IX

X

223

I

II

III

IV

V

Therefore, the rise in the numbers of Welsh-speakers throughout the nineteenth century did not necessarily bode well for the language, for the figures alone tell us nothing about the quality and daily use of that language. One method of gauging such matters is by surveying the reading materials available to Welsh-speakers and by investigating their popularity. There is a general consensus of opinion that after 1850 there was a veritable explosion of interest in and sale of Welsh language publications. In his *Letters on the Social and Political Condition of the Principality of Wales* published in 1866, Henry Richard claimed that five quarterlies, twenty-five monthlies and eight weeklies were published in Welsh with a combined total circulation of over 120,000. For example, in the late 1850s a certain Edward Jones of Cefnarthen was a regular subscriber to *Y Diwygiwr, Y Dysgedydd,* the *Evangelical Magazine* and the *Penny Encyclopaedia*. However, it is equally true that after 1890 the sale of Welsh language publications declined in proportion to the increase in the sale of English language papers such as the *Cambrian News*, *Western Mail* and *South Wales Daily News*. Clearly, these are generalisations and are not in themselves proof of anything, but they are indicative of certain trends.

VI

VII

VIII

IX

X

Statistics are a means to an end and not an end in themselves since it is in their interpretation that they are of most use to the historian. Herein lies the dilemma, for although statistics may be regarded as fixed points on a spectrum, interpretation is a random factor which can vary widely depending what case the historian wishes to make. In terms of the incline or decline of the Welsh language during the nineteenth century all the census data allows us to do, with relative certainty, is indicate likely trends. In this instance, the trend was for the gradual erosion of the language by means of increasing bilingualism. However, this assumes that the statistics generated by the census enumerators are reliable, and for the most part they are, but as a lesson to us all the following source suggests that as historians we cannot accept anything at face value.

> Two parishes, one in Caernarfonshire and one in Merionethshire, were selected by us for detailed examination. In these parishes there were 138 babies under one year of age, and 59 of these were returned as speaking Welsh. There were also 147 infants between one and two years of age, and 87 of these were registered as monoglot Welsh. Thus of 285 infants not yet two years of age, 146, or more than half, were represented as being able to speak Welsh and Welsh only. Children under two have been excluded by us from

5

the language tables; and, consequently, those strange statements as to their power of speech are not of much importance, excepting that they furnish good
10   grounds for regarding with much suspicion the trustworthiness of the statements as to persons of riper years. Thus in the same two parishes there were 1,587 children of from 5 to 15 years of age, children therefore, who must have had a more or less lengthy period of school attendance. In the schools of both of these parishes English has been taken as a class subject, not without
15   success; yet of these 1,587 children, 1,490 or 94% were returned as unable to speak English.

[General Report on the 1891 Census]

c) 'The curse of Wales': Attitudes to the Language

'The curse of Wales' proclaimed *The Times* newspaper (Sept. 1866) which regarded the Welsh language as an unfortunate anachronism in an increasingly English-speaking and English-dominated world where the twin pillars of modernism, progress and change, held sway. Nor was *The Times* alone in its criticism of what was perceived to be a backward and barbarous language calculated to inhibit the Welsh from enjoying the privileges that English civilisation and speech could bring. Certainly, this was the view expressed in the influential and highly controversial *Report into the State of Education in Wales* (1847) which bespoke the attitude of middle England and did much thereafter, to shape the opinions of Englishmen and the English establishment.

> The Welsh language is a vast drawback to Wales, and a manifold barrier to the moral progress and commercial prosperity of its people. It is not easy to over-estimate its evil effects. It is the language of the Cymri, and anterior to that of the ancient Britons. It dissevers the people from intercourse which would help advance their civilisation, and bars the access of improving knowledge to their minds. As proof of this, there is no Welsh literature worthy of the name.
>
> [Commissioner J.C. Symons, author of Volume Two of the Report (1847)]

Writing more than twenty years after *The Times*, the *Cambrian News* (July 1886) expressed its opinion that '... a rigid adherence to the Welsh language ... is the strongest chain that binds the poor farmers of the Principality to the soil ...'. The inference is clear, liberty is the ability to transcend one's environment and until the Welsh embraced the English tongue they would

I

II

III

IV

V

VI

VII

VIII

IX

X

I
II
III
IV
V
VI
VII
VIII
IX
X

remain forever bound to the primitive existence that was the lot of the rural population. One might expect an English newspaper like *The Times*, geared as it was towards the wealthy, the educated and the informed upper class of English society, to utter such biased and often unreliable 'truths' on matters pertaining to a nation and a people it knew little or nothing about and for whom it cared even less, but the *Cambrian News* was published in Aberystwyth. The popular press, be it Welsh or English and whether it be daily, weekly or monthly in circulation, is an important tool for historians wishing to properly gauge the attitudes of contemporaries to the Welsh language. Naturally, as with all sources of evidence left at the disposal of the historian, caution must be exercised, particularly so in the case of the press many of which were imprints of owner-publishers who voiced, opined or campaigned on issues of personal interest, taste and prejudice. Nevertheless, even taking account of their imperfections, newspapers remain the most vivid reflections of the attitudes of those people who purchased and read them.

Unsurprisingly perhaps, the *Cambrian News* was managed and edited from 1873 (and owned from 1880) by a Lancastrian Englishman, John Gibson who was, in the words of K.O. Morgan, 'outstandingly ignorant of the Welsh language even in so Welsh an area!'. With a regular weekly circulation on or near the 7,000 mark, the *Cambrian News* was one of the most influential newspapers in Wales. It was, therefore, in a strong position to influence and even shape the views of its Welsh readership many of whom would hardly have objected to his patronising view of the Welsh language. On the other hand, it is equally evident that newspapers and periodicals could themselves be influenced by their readership to the extent of overturning the founding principle and editorial policy of the particular paper. After seventeen years of life the Ystalyfera-based *Llais Llafur* announced in 1915 that it would henceforth publish as an English-language newspaper entitled *Labour Voice*. The paper's editor explained why:

> They [the readership] were more Welsh than English, and for that reason *Llais Llafur* was a Welsh newspaper. Meantime, a new generation has been growing, and they have acquired new tastes and new inclinations. Speaking generally it may be said that the majority of middle-aged and young persons prefer reading English. Welsh remains the language for ordinary speech and public worship, but as a literary medium it becomes increasingly unadaptable to newspaper exigencies. We regret the anglicising of the *Llais* as much as anybody, but sentiment does not alter facts.

It is generally agreed that the Welsh, even Welsh-speakers, were somewhat indifferent to the fate of the language and though the idea that this was due to a sense of inferiority has largely, though not entirely, been dismissed, there is no doubting the fact that the acquisition of and facility in English was seen as desirable, if not essential, by an increasing minority from the early to middle decades of the nineteenth century. Such was the perceived hostility to Welsh in some areas that newspapers sympathetic to the plight of the language signalled their fears for its future. In 1924 the editor of the *Amman Valley Chronicle* reported, regretfully, that

> I am afraid our children are being denied the opportunity to converse in the vernacular, simply for the reason that the parents deem it a greater honour to be able to converse more fluently in the Saxon tongue. In few of our homes nowadays do we hear the Welsh language spoken, in fact the parents seem to have forgotten it with disastrous results for the future generation.

Nor must it be thought that this was a phenomenon peculiar to south Wales during the early years of the twentieth century. Writing more than forty years earlier in the early 1880s, that arch-nationalist, radical and Cymric coloniser of south America, Michael D. Jones of Llanuwchllyn was scathing in his condemnation of his compatriots for their apparent apathetic attitude towards their native tongue:

> ... it is the Welsh themselves who let English in, and make strenuous efforts to cast Welsh out of their homes, and chapels, and businesses, and who spinelessly allow the English to banish it from our courts of law. Whether Welsh is to live or die depends on the will of the Welsh people, and if it is killed the blame will be theirs. Let every Welshman uphold his language in his own home, in his place of worship, and in his business life, and then it will live.

It was left to the native intelligentsia, men of intellect and learning that comprised the growing, and Welsh-speaking middle class, academics from the newly-founded universities of Aberystwyth (1872), Cardiff (1883) and Bangor (1884), and exiles, largely London and Liverpool-based, to attempt to rescue the language and change the indifferent attitudes of their labouring compatriots. Pro-Welsh language movements were established with the aim of promoting the teaching of Welsh in schools and the more

I
II
III
IV
V

VI

VII
VIII
IX
X

I

II

III

IV

V

VI

VII

VIII

IX

X

widespread use of the language in the community. In 1885 *The Society for Utilizing the Welsh Language* was set up and though its aim was to foster bilingualism (as expressed in the remainder of its rather unwieldy title – *for the Purpose of Serving a Better and More Intelligent Knowledge of English*), it attempted to do so by asserting that Welsh was as important and the equal of English. The task facing such groups and individuals was not only in persuading the people of Wales to believe this to be true but in convincing national and (the newly-founded local governments '1888'), and the educational establishment in particular. Evidence presented to the Education Commission during 1886-88 succeeded in ensuring that Welsh would be treated on an equal basis with other languages in the nation's elementary schools. Indeed, such was the success in securing wider recognition of Welsh as a subject of equal weight and validity on the school curriculum that it might be said to have changed the attitudes of the next, if not the current, generation. In this respect, the Welsh Intermediate Education Act of 1889, which established a state system of schools designed to bridge the gulf between the elementary and university sector, has been justly hailed as a landmark in the changing attitude of the establishment towards the Welsh language. That the Act was of much wider concern and influence has been pointed out by K.O. Morgan: 'Educationally, socially, and administratively, it was one of the most impressive memorials of the political awakening of Wales'.

That these acts were passed in Westminster suggests that by the last quarter of the nineteenth century the language, as well as the people who spoke it, was not so ungenerously thought of in the corridors of power as had been the case less than half a century earlier. The attendance of the English statesman and politician, William Gladstone, at two eisteddfodau, one as Prime Minister, at Mold in 1873 and at Wrexham in 1888 is indicative of this gradual change of attitude. His speeches upholding the language as a 'venerable relic of the past' and his unqualified praise of the 'ancient history, the ancient deeds and the ancient language of ... the principality of Wales' did much to soften the oft quoted scorn of the English press which responded by attacking Gladstone's misguided sentimentality. In fact, he went further by suggesting that the English political system had largely failed Wales and the Welsh and that some form of redress would perhaps be necessary.

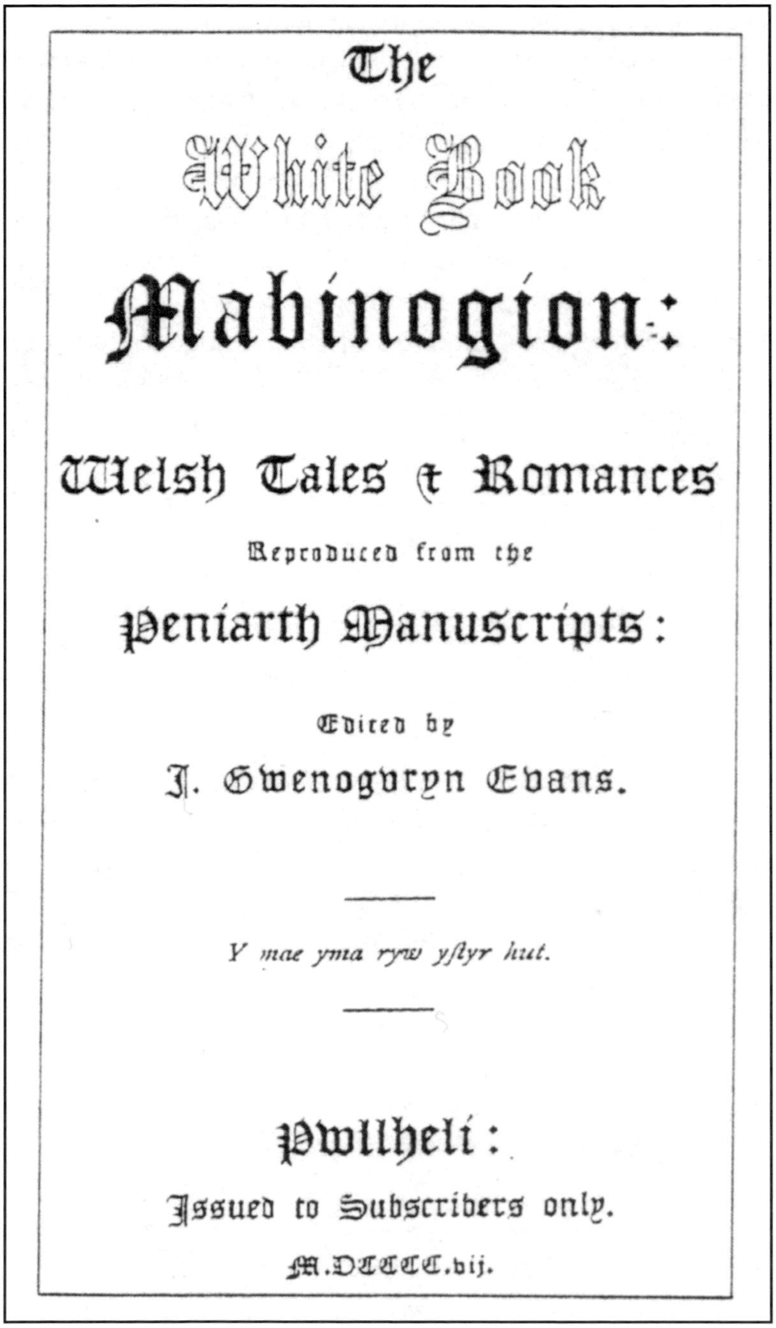

The
White Book
Mabinogion:
Welsh Tales & Romances
Reproduced from the
Peniarth Manuscripts:

Edited by
J. Gwenogvryn Evans.

———

Y mae yma ryw ystyr hut.

———

Pwllheli:
Issued to Subscribers only.
M.DCCCC.bij.

I II

III

IV V

VI

VII

VIII

IX

X

Fig. 35
Title-page of J. Gwenogvryn Evans' edition of *The White Book Mabinogion*
(1897). Evans' work was held up as a fine example of the quality and
pedigree of Welsh-language literature

I

II

III

IV

V

VI

VII

VIII

IX

X

If the likes of the *London Review*, the *Pall Mall Gazette*, the *Saturday Review* and even *Punch* had often indulged in ridiculing the Welsh, *The Times* turned its attention to criticising those, such as Gladstone, who stood out in defence of Welsh language and culture. Perhaps the clearest sign of an institutional change in the government's attitude came in 1907 with the establishment of a Welsh Department of the Board of Education. The Secretary of State for Education, Augustine Birrell, seems to have been persuaded to act in large part by the impassioned pleas of his fellow Liberals, Welshmen like Alfred Thomas who bore eloquent testimony to the concerns of his compatriots. In a letter (1906) to Birrell he set out his argument:

> Welsh ... is the medium through which the mass of the people can receive intellectual culture and give expression to their own genius. You will therefore we hope be inclined to agree with us that the language ought to be systematically taught in order that it may be the salutary factor that it ought to be in the national life.

Staffed by Welshmen sympathetic to and active in the cause of the language, the civil servants working in the Welsh Department were, according to Tim Williams, 'indefatigable in their attempts to give it a prominent position in school life, often leading them to be in advance of opinion in Wales on this question'. Writing in *Y Llenor* in 1931 the leading Welsh historian, J.E. Lloyd, surveyed the period between 1889 and 1907 and concluded that 'it is fair to say that there was no cause to complain after that of the lack of sympathy and support on the part of the authorities in London. None were better friends to the movement *[Cymdeithas yr Iaith Gymraeg]* than the Capital's education officials and their inspectors in Wales'. Changing the attitude of the Welsh people would prove far more challenging.

2. Truth or Treachery? The Blue Books Controversy, 1847

■ **Key Issue:**
Did the treachery of the Blue Books contribute to the growth of nationalism?

a) Background

On 10th March 1846 William Williams (1788-1865), Member of Parliament for Coventry, introduced a motion in the House of Commons for 'an inquiry to be made into the state of education in the Principality of Wales, especially into the means afforded to the labouring classes of acquiring a knowledge of the English language'. It was accepted, and within six months a commission had been set up to conduct the inquiry. Williams was a Welshman who hailed originally from Llanpumsaint In Carmarthenshire. He was a self-made man who had amassed a fortune through trade in London. His interest in the state of educational provision in Wales was doubtless motivated by a sincere desire to improve it but, unbeknown to him, he had set in motion a train of events the consequences of which would reverberate throughout the Principality for years to come. The subsequent investigation into education in Wales and the publication of its findings in three blue-coloured leather bound volumes has become part of the mythology as well as the fact of Welsh history. The problem confronting historians is in separating the mythical from the factual and arriving at a more sober judgement of the impact of the so-called 'Blue Books' on Wales and the Welsh. What perhaps might otherwise have amounted to no more than a footnote in history has been hailed by some as 'a landmark in the growth of Welsh national consciousness'. Consequently, much has been made of and claimed for the Blue Books by modern historians not least their perceived impact on the cultural, political and religious life of Wales quite apart from the sphere in which they were intended to be of greatest influence, education.

I
II
III
IV
V
VI
VII
VIII
IX
X

I

II

III

IV

V

VI

VII

VIII

IX

X

b) The Commissioners' Portrait of Wales and the Welsh

> You will also be enabled to form some estimate of the general state of intelligence and information of the poorer classes of Wales, and of the influence which an improved education might be expected to produce, on the general condition of society, and its moral and religious progress.

Such was the advice given to the Commissioners, Ralph Robert Wheeler Lingen, Jelinger Cookson Symons and Henry Vaughan Johnson, upon taking up their commission to investigate the state of education and educational provision in Wales. The implication of this additional advice is clear, it was meant to act as an aid to completing the report and as such was merely intended as a by-product. However, it seems the Commissioners took this part of their brief very seriously and in so doing they could not help but generate the kind of information which was subsequently to arouse the anger and passion of a nation which did not much like being socially, morally and religiously dissected. The main focus of these 'additional' inquiries concerned social and living conditions, cleanliness and morality particularly in respect of the fairer sex, religion and language. As a result of the Commissioners' investigations, which lasted the best part of a year between October 1846 and September 1847, and staggered submissions, Symons being the first to present his findings for Mid- and West Wales on 6 March 1847, the three volume report eventually comprised 1256 pages of detailed information. The wealth of detail lends itself very well to furnishing numerous examples of the Commissioners' findings particularly in respect of the prevailing social and living conditions.

According to Johnson the dire living conditions suffered by the people living in (and employed by) the slate quarrying and coal mining districts of North Wales was largely the fault of the people themselves. 'The condition of the quarrymen in the large quarries of Caernarfonshire is unequal. ... they remain in the state of degradation of the quarrymen in the parish of Llandwrog. But the lowest form of social degredation and moral depravity is met with in the mining districts, and is found to grow worse on approaching the English border' (Wrexham and Rhosllannerchrugog). His irritation with those who question his conclusions is clearly evident:

The existence of the evils mentioned above was less surprising than the remonstrances addressed to me by persons of high religious profession in the neighbourhood, representing the injustice of apprehending immoral results from habits of promiscuous intercourse. Nothing could more forcibly illustrate the imperfect nature of indigenous civilisation if isolated and unaided.

Nor did matters improve the further south Johnson travelled as the following description of cottages at Tal-y-Llyn in Merioneth suggests.

The cottages are formed of a few loose fragments of rock and shale, piled together without mortar or whitewash. The floors are of earth; the roofs are wattled, and many of these hovels have no window. They comprise one room, in which all the family sleeps. This is in some cases separated from the rest of the hut by wisps of straw, forming an imperfect screen. These squalid huts appear to be the deliberate choice of the people, who are not more poor than the peasantry in England.

Here at least the inhabitants did not share their homes with animals as was reported to be the case in Tregaron. Symons registers his disgust at witnessing 'a woman with a child in her arms' opening the door to her home and, on entering, being closely followed by 'a large sow'. This, he assures his readers, was not unknown in the rural districts of Wales since 'The pigs and poultry form the usual part of the family'.

The Commissioners had much to say about the cleanliness and morality, or lack of it!, of the Welsh people. According to Johnson's assistant John James. 'The state of civilisation in Newborough is very low ... [its inhabitants'] habits, morals and social conditions are degraded'. Of the colliers he met in Pembrokeshire Lingen had this to say, 'The average of life is very short – not above 33 years, as appears from the [parish] register. This may be accounted for by the personal dirtiness of the miners, who never wash their bodies'. What seems to have offended the Commissioners the most was the apparent 'lack of chastity', 'bestiality' and the general 'sinfulness' and 'vice in women'. In the opinion of Lingen, Welsh peasant girls were 'almost universally unchaste' and 'the wonder would be if they were otherwise'. Symons was appalled by what he was told regarding the old custom of *caru ar y gwely* – whereby courting couples were given leave by consenting parents to meet and talk together in their respective

I
II
III
IV
V
VI
VII
VIII
IX
X

233

bedrooms – exclaiming 'I heard the most revolting anecdotes of the gross and almost bestial indelicacy with which sexual intercourse takes place on these occasions'. In his opinion, 'the want of chastity results most frequently from the practice of "bundling", or courtship on beds, during the night – a practice still widely prevailing'. This custom was bad enough but the Commissioners were positively frothing at the mouth when they heard of a variation, or bastard form, of *caru ar y gwely* in which women were fertility-tested before marriage! The evidence gathered from the Begelly area of Pembrokeshire convinced Lingen that 'seduction [was] generally followed by marriage if the woman conceives: not otherwise', hence the local vicar's report that sixty-four out of seventy brides recently married were pregnant.

Nor was this 'vile practice' confined to south west Wales. As may be gathered by Johnson's comments this particular 'vice' was 'flagrant throughout North Wales and remains unchecked by any instrument of civilisation' but worse 'its existence has almost ceased to be considered as an evil; and the custom of Wales is said to justify the barbarous practice which precedes the rite of marriage'. Unsurprisingly, having found the miners of Rhosllannerchrugog not to his liking Johnson was equally dismissive of its womenfolk. Acting on information supplied by the local vicar, the Revd. Richards, Johnson had this to say:

> Mr. Richards tells me that although he spent some years as curate of Merthyr Tydfil, in the county of Glamorgan, which is usually considered the most depraved and uncivilised locality in Wales, yet he never met with so much poverty, so much social and moral degradation, as at Rhosllannerchrugog. He complained that throughout the district the women have no kind of knowledge of the duties of their sex, or of common household occupations and requirements; that till lately needlework was unknown among them.

Having established the primary evils affecting Welsh life, the Commissioners turned to uncovering their cause which, in their opinion, was two-fold: language and dissent. According to Lingen,

> My district exhibits the phenomenon of a peculiar language isolating the mass from the upper portion of society; ... his [the Welshman's] language keeps him under the hatches, being one in which he can neither acquire nor communicate the necessary information. It is a language of old-fashioned agriculture, of theology, and of simple rustic life, while all the world about him is English ...   5

I
II
III
IV
V

VI

VII
VIII
IX
X

He is left to live in an underworld of his own, and the march of society goes on so completely over his head, that he is never heard of excepting when the strange and abnormal features of a Revival, or a Rebecca or Chartist outbreak, call attention to a phase of society which could produce anything so contrary to all that we elsewhere experience.

The inference is clear, the language was equated with subversive activity and until it was expunged from Welsh life the prospects for peace, order and civility would remain bleak. Yet, having uttered these words, Lingen went on to acknowledge that, although Welsh was the natural medium, all classes had a mastery of their native tongue far beyond the ability of the corresponding classes in England in the English language. This was praise indeed and though his opinion was shared by Johnson, Symons preferred to remain aloof. His opinion was altogether less sanguine, preferring instead to link more directly the language with lawlessness and disorder:

> The evil of the Welsh language ... is obviously and fearfully great in courts of justice; ... it distorts the truth, favours fraud and abets perjury, which is frequently practised in courts ... This public exhibition of successful falsehood has a disastrous effect on public morals and regard for the truth. The mockery of an English trial of a Welsh criminal by a Welsh jury, addressed by counsel and judge in English, is too gross and shocking to need comment. It is nevertheless a mockery which must continue until the people are taught the English language ...

While acknowledging the power, influence and general popularity of religion in Wales, the Commissioners did not think this to be a force for good, since it was the religion of dissent, of nonconformity. It was therefore at variance with their own, they being communicants of the Anglican Church. Lingen, as ever, was to the fore in explaining his reasoning on the matter.

> Poetical and enthusiastic warmth of religious feeling, careful attendance upon religious services, zealous interest in religious knowledge, the comparative absence of crime, are found side by side with the most unreasoning prejudices or impulses; and utter want of method in thinking and acting; and (what is far worse) with a widespread disregard of temperance, whenever there are the means of excess, of chastity, of veracity, and of fair dealing.

I
II
III
IV
V
VI
VII
VIII
IX
X

235

Symons agreed, stating that the Nonconformists' use of the Welsh language was the primary cause of its survival and a means by which their 'religion' would continue to hold sway over an incredulous and ignorant people. His attack on the results of a century of Nonconformity was particularly scathing:

> Superstition prevails. Belief in charms, supernatural appearances, and even in witchcraft, sturdily survive all the civilisation and light which has long ago banished these remnants of the dark ages elsewhere. Little or none of such light has as yet penetrated the dense darkness which, harboured by their language, and undisturbed by availing efforts of enlightenment, enshrouds the minds of the people.

Focusing specifically on Methodism and its effects on the religiosity of the people, Symons took the town and environs of Tregaron as his example and concluded that 'Welsh Methodism sprung from this immediate neighbourhood, though its spread has been so extensive of late years that neither this place nor Llangeitho can be said to present any peculiar characteristics or results of Methodist instruction'. Johnson, on the other hand, had a grudging admiration for the mainstay of Nonconformist teaching, the Sunday School:

> However imperfect the results, it is impossible not to admire the vast number of schools which they [Dissenters] have established, the frequency of the attendance, the number, energy and devotion of the teachers, the regularity and decorum of the proceedings, and the permanent and striking effect which thay have produced upon society.

Unfortunately, when the report was published the instances of praise were overlooked and the overwhelming body of critical evidence was studied by an increasingly angry and disbelieving literate public. Indeed, the furore that followed publication caught the Commissioners by surprise and they were at a loss to explain it.

I
II
III
IV
V
VI
VII
VIII
IX
X

b) 'The Perfect Instrument of Empire':
The Language of the Blue Books

In the most recent (1998) critical study of the language in which the Blue Books was written Gwyneth Tyson Roberts has concluded that 'the Commissioners' claims of authority, objectivity and ability to discover the 'truth' about Wales, was consistently subverted by the language in which they are made'. The Commissioners, Englishmen all, were products of an educational and class system which operated within the defined boundaries of a world Empire which considered itself a civilising force. In the opinion of the one-time Liberal Prime Minister (1894-5) Lord Rosebery, the British Empire was 'the greatest secular agency for good that the world has ever seen'. It was this self-confidence, bordering on arrogance, which characterised the attitudes of many of those at the heart of that Empire, the Anglo-British middle and upper classes. Their sense of superiority was inflated by imperialist attitudes which were more than matched by their condescension to those, such as the ordinary Welsh, who seemed unable or unwilling to conform to the conventional image of patriotic Britishness. Although not in themselves unyieldingly hostile or unsympathetic to the Welsh people, the Commissioners' patronising view of Welsh life was, nevertheless, as much a threat to the native culture as had they been government agents acting on instructions to effect its total eradication. Taking their cue from the Report of the Commissioners, some English newspapers voiced their own prejudiced opinions of the 'ignorant' Welsh. *The Examiner* thought that 'their habits were those of animals and would not bear description', while the *Morning Chronicle* called for the extinction of the Welsh language and declared that those who persisted in speaking it were 'fast settling down into the most savage barbarism'. The tabloid publicity surrounding the publication of the reports served merely to exacerbate an already inflamed situation.

Ironically, careful consideration of the material contained in the reports suggest that much of what the Commissioners saw, experienced and had to say about mid-Victorian Wales was not far off the truth. There were massive social problems, poverty and ignorance was rife, where it existed educational provision did vary enormously and in the prevailing atmosphere of an English-dominated state, the Welsh language was a barrier to progress. Even some passionate critics of the report admitted as much, like

I
II
III
IV
V
VI
VII
VIII
IX
X

I

II

III

IV

V

VI

VII

VIII

IX

X

Lewis Edwards, Methodist minister, principal of Bala College and the influential editor of *Y Traethodydd*, who was troubled not so much by what was false as by what was true. Hugh Owen, one of the leading educational philanthropists in the Principality, agreed with many of the criticisms contained in the reports while Evan Jones ('Ieuan Gwynedd'), Independent minister, journalist and most vociferous critic of the perceived slur on Welsh womanhood, reacted by founding in 1850 *Y Gymraes* (The Welshwoman) a journal intended 'to purify the taste, enlarge the knowledge and improve the women of our country'. Clearly, it was not so much the critical air of the reports that was objected to but the manner and language in which it was written, and by whom it was written. Under the title *Facts, Figures and Statements in Illustration of the Dissent and Morality of Wales* (1849) Evan Jones published his response to the reports stating that of the three Commissioners Symons was, linguistically speaking, the least sensitive of the three, his overview being;

> ... the most incorrect in language, objectionable in style, reckless in assertion, abundant in fallacies, illogical in deduction, determined in purpose, and heedless in proof. Next to him must be ranged the chaotic, magniloquent, sneering and singularly incorrect production of Mr. Lingen. The Report of Mr. Vaughan Johnson is remarkably destitute in style, or happiness in diction. It is also alike destitute of ability and candour.

What roused most Welshmen to passionate indignation was the fact of having Englishmen pointing out and passing judgement on their deficiencies. In his *History of Brecknockshire*, published in 1805, Theophilous Jones felt constrained to explain the meaning and origin of the then common Welsh proverb, *Sais yw ef, Syn*! (He's a Saxon, Watch out); 'The treachery of the Saxons, whom the aboriginal Britons introduced into the island as friends and allies, and their cruelty in exterminating in cold blood the nobility of the ancient inhabitants ... still rankles in the bosoms of the indigenous sons of freedom'. It was a theme to which the Welsh would return more than forty years later in order to justify their anger and underpin their attack on the Blue Books.

c) A National Awakening?: Reactions in Wales

Ordinarily historians would shy away from ascribing motives and reactions to a large group of people, let alone a nation, since the variables are such as to warrant the resulting generalisation suspect. However, in this instance to say that the reaction in Wales to the Commissioners' report was one of anger and resentment is probably not wide of the mark. The popular outpouring of grief and outrage was remarkably uniform across the nation, taking little or no account of class, creed or religion. Nonconformists set aside their denominational rivalry and united in the face of the onslaught and, being joined by many Anglican clergy, they mounted a vigorous defence of themselves and their parishoners. From landowners and industrialists, the pillars of English imperialist authority, to schoolmasters, clerics and pamphleteers, representatives of a faceless, uneducated and largely voiceless mass, the cry of indignation was the same. Indeed, such was the level of hostility generated in Wales by 'this ego-trip of three arrogant and ignorant barristers' that within a few years of the publication of their reports it acquired the nickname *Brad y Llyfrau Gleision* or Treachery of the Blue Books. Intended as an historical pun on a Welsh legend of the Dark Ages known as *Brad y Cyllill Hirion* or The Treason of the Long Knives – which recounts the grisly fate of the chief representatives of Welsh nobility, led by Vortigern, who were slain while attending a banquet. Their throats were cut by their hosts the Saxon nobles, led by Hengist, and this in spite of his professions of peace and reconciliation. The choice of title is thought to have been inspired by a play of the same name published in Ruthin in 1853.

Penned by Edward Roberts ('Iorwerth Glan Aled') the theme of his play was taken up by a probable acquaintance, the Manchester exile Robert Jones ('Derfel'), whose derivative but satirical play, entitled *Brad y Llyfrau Gleision*, was published in 1854. Such was the effect of the reports on *Derfel*, a bardic name he later adopted as his surname, that, according to his own autobiography, he became obsessively nationalistic thereafter. The treachery referred to was not so much on the part of the Commissioners but that perpetrated by their Welsh assistants and those from whom they sought and received information. That co-operation was equated with collaboration is amply testified by the viciousness of the language adopted by those who wished to attack their less patriotic compatriots. The fact that many of them were Anglicans made matters worse.

I

II

III

IV

V

VI

VII

VIII

IX

X

239

In 1848 Owen Owen Roberts, physician and social reformer, publicly criticised the Commissioners, their findings and their 'biased' conclusions but his sternest words were reserved for the Anglican 'collaborators' whom he described as 'a cringing, sneaking, low-bred, mean, servile, back-biting set, who would make mischief between a cow and a haystack'! In fairness to the Anglicans the majority were as outraged as their Nonconformist compatriots by the contents of the reports, men like the Anglican cleric Thomas Price *('Carnhuanawc')* who, on being mocked by the Commissioners for what they believed was his misplaced sense of Welsh patriotism, called them 'libellous and mendacious foreigners' and quoted them the Book of Ecclesiasticus in that they should 'First understand, and then rebuke'.

There is sufficient evidence to suggest that the Blue Books touched more than simply a raw nerve in Wales but may also have fanned the flames or given some focus to latent nationalism. *Derfel* and *Carnhuanawc* aside there were others who came to express their anger over the reports in blatantly nationalistic terms.

As the following illustrations show expressions of Welsh nationalism took many forms

Fig. 36
Wales depicted as
Owain Glyndŵr
[undated]

240

Fig. 37
Postcard advertising the National Pageant of Wales (1909)

I

II

III

IV

V

VI

VII

VIII

IX

X

In an article published in *Y Traethodydd,* Evan Williams of Lledrod defined his vision of Christian nationalism in which he expressed his wish that not only should Welshmen alone be appointed to office in Wales but that Englishmen be actively discouraged from doing so.

Besides taking great delight in pointing out 'the faults in their style ... Their want of taste and natural incapacity for literary composition', the historian Jane Williams *('Ysgafell')* accused the Commissioners more seriously of aiming at 'the subversion of her nationality'.

The original proposer of the Commission, the hapless William Williams, was not spared the rod of criticism. Evan Jones *('Ieuan Gwynedd')* accused him of wanting 'to annihilate the Welsh language by means of English schools'. Even Sir Thomas Phillips, pillar of the establishment, who as mayor of Newport had opposed the Chartists, attacked the report for giving the lie that 'the Welsh element is never found at the top of the social scale', pointing out that he was a patriotic well-educated, Welsh-speaking Welshman.

The results of the Blue Books controversy were summed up by historian Gwyn A. Williams who believed that 'A form of Welsh nationalism, peculiarly Dissenter and Welsh-speaking, was stung into life'.

Fifty years before this historians were less direct but equally sure that the events inspired by the publication of the Commissioners' report did usher in a new era. In a study entitled *The Background to Modern Welsh Politics, 1789-1846* (published in 1936) Thomas Evans stated that 'The political value of education, the agitation for better education facilities for Wales, and the treason of the Blue Books, made the close of our period a turning point in Welsh history. The last of these was regarded as one of the greatest events of the nineteenth century'.

Advice and Activities

(i) General

Suggested Further Reading.

N. Coupland (ed.), *English in Wales: Diversity, Conflict and Change* (Clevedon, 1990).

E. Higgs, *Making Sense of the Census: The Manuscript Returns for England and Wales,* 1801-1901 (London, 1989).

G.H. Jenkins (ed.), *Language and Community in the Nineteenth Century* (Cardiff, 1998).

G.T. Roberts, *The Language of the Blue Books* (Cardiff, 1998).

G. Williams, *Religion, Language and Nationality in Wales* (Cardiff, 1979).

Issues for Debate

'Truth or Treachery'? State a case a) supporting and b) opposing the views expressed by the Blue Books' Commissioners about Wales and the Welsh.

Points for Discussion

1. Was the Welsh language in decline in the nineteenth-century?
2. Was there a 'national awakening' in Wales?

(ii) Examination Specific

Answering Essay Questions

The following example is an essay involving the consideration of an historical interpretation.

'Instead of bemoaning the rural exodus, the Welsh patriot should sing the praises of industrial development which gave the Welsh language a new lease of life'.

[B. Thomas, an academic historian specialising in the social and economic history of Wales].

I
II
III
IV
V
VI
VII
VIII
IX
X

243

Q. How valid is this interpretation of the effects of industrialisation on the fate of the Welsh language?

Advice

You need first to identify three key issues here – rural exodus/depopulation; industrialisation/urbanisation; the fate of the language which, it is suggested, was given a new lease of life. You need to evaluate the premise of the question, that where it was once thought that industrialisation harmed the language by drawing people away from the Welsh-speaking rural areas to multi-cultural English-speaking industrial towns this may not now be so. In fact, the statement raises the interesting issue of suggesting that the language was already in decline and that industrialisation helped it survive presumably by concentrating large numbers of Welsh speakers in urban communities whereas they had once been scattered between small, isolated rural communities. While this may be valid up to a point you will need to look at other factors that affected the Welsh language – the role of English-language newspapers, the school-curriculum, the attitudes of those in power both locally and nationally. You must set the effects of industrialisation against these other factors (including changes in the countryside which were not necessarily caused by industrialisation).

I
II
III
IV
V
VI
VII
VIII
IX
X

Chapter VII
Nationalism and Nationalist Movements

1. The Growth of Nationalism

■ Key Issue:
What were the key features of Welsh Nationalism? How and why did it grow in the nineteenth Century?

At the beginning of the nineteenth century Wales was overwhelmingly monoglot with upwards of 70% of her people fluent only in Welsh, but by its end the country had become largely bilingual. The implications of such an apparent sea-change in the linguistic fortunes of a small nation are massive, not least in terms of the effects on its culture and the medium in which that culture is transmitted and expressed. Language lies at the heart of a nation's culture which is itself central to a nation's identity, fluency in one and knowledge of the other may be said to fairly constitute a person's nationality. It is this, as yet, unresolved paradox, that so bedevills the modern Welsh, four-fifths of whom are no longer fluent in the language and probably three-fifths of whom have little knowledge of their culture. Consequently, it has been argued, the modern Welsh have a crisis of national identity. There is a need to find a shared and inclusive 'model of Welshness'. Thus far, attempts to define what it is to be Welsh have largely failed though notions of Welshness are as strong today, at the beginning of the twenty-first century, as at the beginning of the nineteenth. Ill-defined and unsatisfactory as it is, there is no disputing the fact that there existed a consciousness of Welshness that was shared by rich and poor and by the educated and uneducated. In order to make that consciousness of Welshness more meaningful and applicable to modern methods of study historians have identified three media through which it might be expressed; culture, religion and politics. It is by such means that historians hope to

I

II

III

IV

V

VI

VII

VIII

IX

X

resolve, at least in part, the difficulty they face in arriving at an all embracing (i.e. applicable to all or most Welsh people) definition of Welsh nationalism, a feat made possible perhaps when all three media coincide.

a) Cultural Nationalism

The almost peculiar brand of cultural nationalism that emerged in Wales during the nineteenth century has its roots in the cultural renaissance of the eighteenth. It was a century of enlightenment characterised by revival (religious as well as cultural), rediscovery and invention, all of which coalesced to create a cultural phenomenon where the line dividing myth from fact was very much blurred. Historian Prys Morgan explains the background:

> ... the cultural revival or renaissance ... was a crisis of modernisation, arising from the interaction between the disappearance of an ancient, traditional way of life and waves of interest in things Welsh coming from England. Revivalism was always balanced by innovation and adaptation to current needs, but by the late eighteenth century it was far outrun by wild romantic invention and uncontrolled patriotic enthusiasm.

The patriot is but a half step short of the nationalist and it was this 'patriotic enthusiasm' for things Welsh, be they literary, poetic, musical, religious or historical, which generated wider interest and provided a focus for people, irrespective of where in Wales they hailed from, to express their pride in being Welsh. The most visible, public and uniquely Welsh, demonstration of this cultural pride and enthusiasm was the eisteddfod. Revived, or created anew!, in the last decades of the eighteenth century, this festival gained in status and popularity and as it did so it took on the mantle (role) of being the symbolic representation of a national cultural organisation. In 1858 the first of the modern National Eisteddfodau was held in Llangollen to be followed by ever larger and better organised events. So impressive had they become that eminent English educationalists like Matthew Arnold, who attended the Chester Eisteddfod in 1866, said 'When I see the enthusiasm which these Eisteddfods [sic] awaken in your whole people ... I am filled with admiration'. To Arnold may be added the Liberal statesman and Prime Minister William Gladstone, the duke of Sussex (brother of King George IV) who attended the Denbigh eisteddfod of 1828 and Victoria future Queen of England who, with her mother the duchess of Kent, visited the Beumaris eisteddfod of

1832. In the opinion of John Davies 'The success of the eisteddfodau, large and small, offers ... proof of the mass appeal of Welsh-language culture, [that] the thousands who flocked to *Gwyl Gwalia* (the Festival of Wales) are proof that there was in Wales a hunger and thirst for Welshness'. The fact that much of this revived sense of Welshness was manufactured in the eighteenth century mattered not a jot to the ordinary people who delighted in their shared appreciation of things Welsh. It gave them a renewed sense confidence and pride in who and what they were and, significantly, it spoke for them all north and south of that imaginary line that deigned to divide the people of Wales.

The organisers and sponsors on the other hand, the motives of whom were often mixed, in so far as commercial considerations often outweighed cultural and linguistic concerns, were subject to 'the neuroses of a people ever conscious of the need to prove themselves to that great neighbour [England] ever ready to voice disapproval' (Hywel Teifi Edwards, *The Eisteddfod*, 1990). This concern was expressed in the Carmarthen eisteddfod of 1867 by John Griffiths, cleric and educationalist of Aberaeron, who responded to the critical attack on Welsh culture by *The Times* with a warning for his fellow eisteddfodwyr that '...we are aware that we shall have many eyes upon us, that we shall be scanned narrowly ... We are aware that there is an annual judgement passed upon us ...'. Oddly enough the burden of this sense of inspection tended to make more positive their self-consciousness by making them more self-aware, and it was pressure applied from outside Wales which often united and galvanised them into action. This can clearly be seen with the Blue Books controversy which did more to unite the Welsh in defence of their culture than any native institution or organisation founded specifically for the purpose had hitherto. The eisteddfod provided one, if not the perfect forum through which the indignant (unhappy) could respond and refute the scandalous allegations perpetrated by the Commissioners in their reports. For example, prose writers and poets such as John Ceiriog Hughes ('Ceiriog') reacted to the Blue Books' assault on Welsh womanhood by composing *Myfanwy Fychan*, a poem purporting to tell a fourteenth-century love story where the principal characters, the low-born bard Hywel and the high-born lady Myfanwy, conducted themselves with grace and dignity. Composed for the Llangollen eisteddfod of 1858, the composition was, of course, pure fiction but its sentiment and purpose is clear, – here was a story fit for the ears of middle-class Victorians.

I

II

III

IV

V

VI

VII

VIII

IX

X

Fig. 38
Railway poster advertising the Royal National Eisteddfod, Caernarfon 1906

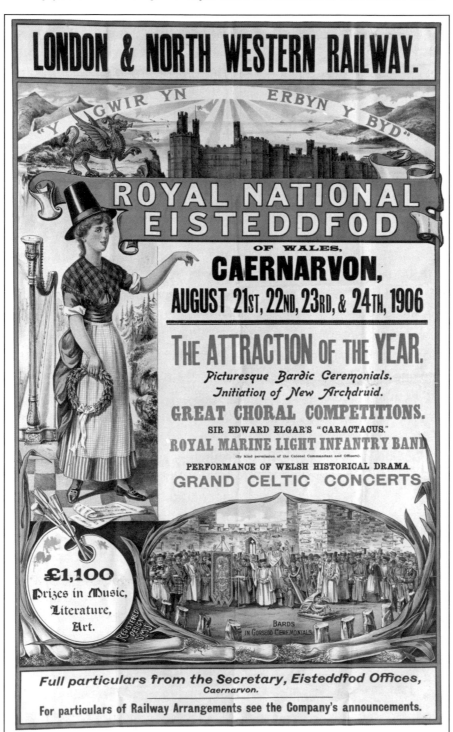

The popularity and regularity of the eisteddfodau provided a congenial (healthy) atmosphere in which 'Welsh' ideas and concerns could be expressed or discussed and even put into practice. Here was a public platform on which new proposals could be put forward such as happened at the Swansea eisteddfod of 1863 when a plan to found a national university for Wales, first put forward in London in 1854, was given greater credence. The 'cultural' publicity emanating from the eisteddfodic fields was more than matched by the explosion of interest in Welsh publishing from mid-century. Daily, weekly and monthly papers and periodicals served to support, defend, extend and even exaggerate aspects of the nation's culture and cultural history. Perhaps the most ambitious undertaking in the field of 'cultural' publishing was Thomas Gee's *Y Gwyddoniadur Cymreig*, a ten-volume Welsh-language encyclopaedia with contributions from 200 authors, which appeared between 1854 and 1879. Patriot that he was, Gee was also a hard-headed businessman and the fact that he spent £20,000 on the project suggests that there was a market out there. Fortunately for him he was right and he more than covered his costs. Perhaps the most active movements in support of Welsh culture were those which were founded and existed outside Wales, London-based societies like the Cymmrodorion and Gwyneddigion, to whom the nation owed early sponsorship of the eisteddfodau at home and the London Jubilee eisteddfod of 1887 an event which must, presumably, have aroused the curiosity of Londoners. Added to this was the increased pace and published output of scholarly activity which served to underpin the fact, as opposed to the myth, of the nation's past. Welsh culture was provided with academic credentials which could stand up to the scrutiny of a disbelieving English press and it was not long before the hallowed halls of English academe were resounding to the praises heaped on works of great scholarship penned by Welshmen.

Among the many who contributed to this new-found respectability was John Edward Lloyd a Liverpool-born Welshman and historian of immense talent whose *A History of Wales from Earliest Times to the Edwardian Conquest*, published in 1911, was a monumental work of historical scholarship. In the opinion of K.O. Morgan, it was a book in which the author successfully 'suffused arid academic detail with the passionate glow of patriotic devotion'. A patriot, certainly, but an objective scholar first is a description which best describes Lloyd and John Morris-Jones another whose contribution to the furtherance of Welsh culture is all but forgotten outside

I
II
III
IV
V
VI
VII
VIII
IX
X

academic circles. His part in the collective foundation of the Cymdeithas Dafydd ap Gwilym Society at Oxford University in 1886 did much to widen interest in Welsh literature and extend its appeal. A scholar, poet and critic, he was among the first to use that scholarship to attack, in 1896, the authenticity of the *gorsedd* of the bards which is perhaps a measure of how far the Welsh had come in that they had the confidence to question the basic structures and origins of their premier cultural festival. According to Prys Morgan 'It is no small irony that the eighteenth-century scholar-patriots, as they scurried about rescuing the last of the old traditions, actually created [new ones]'. By the same token it is no small irony that late nineteenth-century scholar-patriots, pledged as they were to conserving and nurturing native traditions, should be chiefly responsible for questioning their historical and cultural validity.

b) Religious Nationalism

A nation's culture is defined as much by what it believes as what it reads. The cultural renaissance of the eighteenth century was accompanied by a religious revival every bit as significant as that which touched the arts, language and literature. Without wishing to overstate the influence and power of the spread of religion as a result of this revival, there is no doubting the fact that a large proportion of the Welsh had taken to their hearts the teachings of these evangelical movements, the central plank of which concentrated on matters of morality and piety. According to Prys Morgan 'The number of the devout and pious was small, but they were often people of great consequence in the local community, their consequence out-weighing their small number, and they came with time to leaven the whole lump'. The growth of Nonconformity thereafter meant that by the middle decades of the nineteenth century patterns of adherence had been so firmly established that the main Nonconformist denominations – Baptists, Independents, Unitarians and especially the Methodists – could rightly proclaim that it was they and not the established Anglican Church which had a primary claim on the loyalty of the common people. This is significant for in the opinion of Ieuan Gwynedd Jones 'the massive growth of Nonconformity in Wales was itself the most characteristic protest movement of the time'. Clearly, the lines were being drawn between Nonconformity, which was becoming more closely identified with 'Welshness', and the Church of England which was seen increasingly as alien and un-typically Welsh. Added to this were the divisive issues of class and linguistic distinction since Nonconformity tended to champion the Welsh-speaking lower or labouring masses while the Anglican Church was perceived as the representative of the English-speaking middle and upper classes. Certainly, this seems to be what contemporaries believed, as may be instanced by a report of the Royal Commission on Land in Wales and Monmouth published in 1895.

5

> The immense majority of the tenant farmers in the country districts are Nonconformists ... On the most typical estates in Wales, the landlord and his family belong to the Established Church, while the bulk of the tenants belong to one or other of the Nonconformist organisations ... This remarkable fact had a powerful influence in creating a marked divergence between the opinions of the landowning class and the mass of the people, in enlarging the social difference between class and class which to some extent would have existed in any case, and in emphasizing the opposing interests of landlord and tenants.

Naturally matters are never quite as straightforward in real life as they may appear in the pages of a textbook and if J.E. Vincent's opinion counts for anything then we must take care in coming to a balanced judgement on the issue. Landowner, barrister and sometime correspondent for *The Times*, Vincent argued that the Church had changed to such an extent that it was now much a less a Church of the English as of the Welsh.

> I am far from saying that Denbighshire is at present free from clergymen who neglect their duties ... but on the whole, there can be very little doubt that improvements in the Church have been prodigious of late. Welsh services have been largely increased in number; mission halls and chapels have been erected … candidates for ordination are compelled to pass a stringent examination in Welsh ...
>
> > [Anon. *Letter from Wales*: a republication of a series of articles in *The Times* written on Welsh issues by Vincent (1889)]

Nevertheless, despite Vincent's impassioned plea and some blurring of the denominational divisions among the middle class and among the lower classes in the urban industrialised areas, the impression of 'Welsh' Nonconformity and 'English' Anglicanism continued to prevail. Indeed, it was brought into sharp relief during the so-called Tithe War which erupted in north-east Wales between 1886 and 1892. In his book *The Anti-Tithe*

I
II
III
IV
V
VI
VII
VIII
IX
X

251

I

II

III

IV

V

VI

VII

VIII

IX

X

Movement in Wales published in 1891, W. Thomas, a Nonconformist minister, drew attention not only to the unpopularity of the tithe but its injustice also, and he did so in blatantly racist terms: 'Is it not unjust to compel Independents, Methodists, Baptists, Wesleyans, Unitarians ... to contribute towards the support of the clergy of the Church of England ... Welsh tithes are taken out of the country to swell the revenues of English bishops, cathedral bodies and colleges'. Henry Richard certainly thought so when in 1866 he loudly proclaimed that 'The Nonconformists of Wales are the people of Wales'. This is more than simply a statement of statistical fact. It is, or seems to be, a declaration of an intensely nationalistic kind. True, it has been argued that Henry Richard was not so much a 'nationalist' as a 'Liberationist', that what motivated his election as Member of Parliament for Merthyr Tydfil was not so much the national claims of Wales but the class inequality of Nonconformists. While there is some truth in this, it is not entirely convincing in that it ignores the fact that during his election he campaigned as a Welsh-speaking Welshman who was at pains to remind voters of his Welsh nationality. His native pride and patriotism are not in doubt and though his sense of 'nationalism' was what might be described as 'primitive', it at least demonstrates an affinity with popular or ethnic nationalism, the trigger for which was invariably an injustice of some kind or other.

Independent minister, radical and member of the Peace Society, Henry Richard made much of the distinction between the two halves of Welsh society, only one of which he believed had the right to call itself truly Welsh. He gave vent to his thoughts in an article published in the *Aberdare Times* (14 Nov. 1868):

> The people who speak this language, who read this literature, who own this history, who inherit these traditions, who venerate these names, who created and sustain these marvellous religious organisations, the people forming three fourths of the people of Wales – have they not a right to say to this small properties class ... We are the Welsh people and not you? This country is ours and not yours ...

His argument that Nonconformity not only spoke for and represented the people but that it **was** the people is made credible on three counts:

- its increasingly close involvement with and latterly part sponsorship of the nation's cultural and folk festivals like the eisteddfodau
- its robust defence of the people, their language and culture in the wake of the Blue Books controversy
- its political triumph in the 1868 election.

Having once disapproved of the frivolity of folk festivals and customs, the Nonconformists (excepting the Methodists) had by the early 1830s, 'effected a sort of rapprochement with the eisteddfod and the higher culture it represented'. William Roberts ('Nefydd'), a Baptist minister, printer and author, believed 'that Welsh culture should now be supported because it had become respectable' (Prys Morgan, *The Eighteenth Century Renaissance*, 1981). An indication of this change in attitude is the fact that in 1831 Arthur Johnes, later a county court judge, was awarded an eisteddfodic prize sponsored by the Cymmrodorion Society for an essay entitled *The Causes which in Wales have produced Dissent from the Established Church.*

It took the publication of the Blue Books to stir up the Methodists on behalf of the Welsh language and culture but once roused, their support, representing as they did the majority of Welsh dissenters, helped ensure the close identification of Nonconformity with Welshness. Their energetic attack on the Blue Books contrasted with the apparent inertia of the Anglicans and anglicised gentry who were made to appear anti-Welsh. Although this was a totally false impression, it was a myth which quickly solidified into accepted fact. The Nonconformists reaped the benefits of this support when, in the 1860s, they turned to politics as a means of furthering their cause and the cause of the Welsh people. The 1868 election is said to have 'brought Welsh Nonconformity into the House of Commons' and so it did and among those elected was Henry Richard. As a result of the election of men like Richard, Welsh cultural and religious concerns which had been drawing ever closer were fused within a political framework which provided a focus for expression and action. Thus, in the words of Prys Morgan, 'The Nonconformists in the eighteen-fifties and 'sixties were conscious that their way of life, with its chapels and choirs, its magazines and Sunday Schools, and its radical politics, was now "The Welsh Way of Life"'.

Fig. 39
Owain Griffith's (Ywain Meirion) ballad commemorating the Chartist attack on Newport (1839) is an early example of Welsh nationalism being celebrated

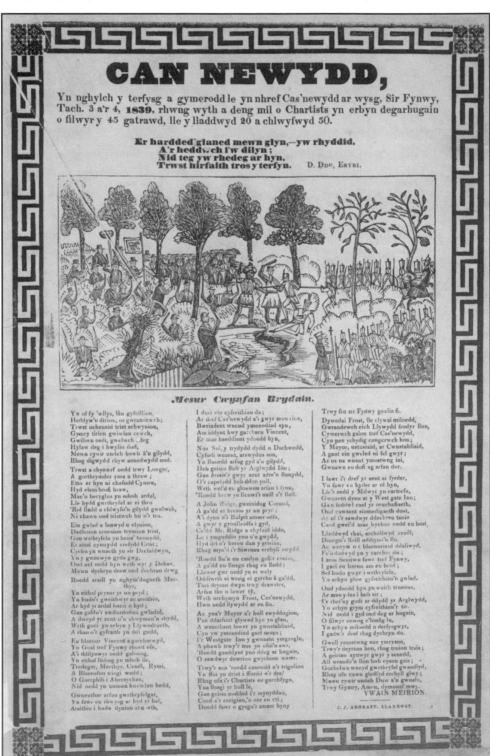

c) Political Nationalism

> A Welshman must be a Welshman, not merely by word and blood, but by principle and work. Nationality should not be blind and narrow.

Thus did Thomas Edward Ellis define Welsh nationalism at a public meeting held at Tywyn in 1885. At its core, he believed, was the Welsh language which he described, at another political meeting held in June 1886, as 'the anchor of Welsh nationality'. In a letter written to Thomas Jones in 1886, Ellis described the reaction of the people of Corris to the news that the prospective parliamentary candidate for Merioneth was Welsh-speaking: 'We were dragged from the station by a huge crowd. People delighted to get a man to speak Welsh – hence good reception'. Ellis was a keen promoter of the language and as part of his pledge to represent the people of his constituency he declared that he would, henceforth, conduct all his election meetings in Welsh. However, this did not meet with the approval of some newspapers, 'a silly proclamation' opined the *Cambrian News*, likely to alienate English residents in the county; 'Being made a Member of Parliament is not like being made a member of the Cymmrodorion Society!' it crowed. The influential *Cambrian News* warned Ellis and other culture-conscious Welshmen of the dangers of mixing patriotism and politics which might give rise to an aggressive form of nationalism, as had happened in Ireland.

That there were activists in Wales who bore comparison with their Irish counterparts, men like Thomas Davis and Michael Davitt founder of the Irish Land League, there is no doubt. Among the more prominent were Michael Daniel Jones and Robert Ambrose Jones ('Emrys ap Iwan'). Considered by many to be the father of modern Welsh nationalism, Michael D. Jones was, in the opinion of the Revd. Richard Griffith Owen, author of his biographical sketch in the *Dictionary of Welsh Biography* (1959), '... an out and out nationalist, the father of the nationalist renaissance in Wales [who] loathed the English-worshipping Welshman, and it has been said that "the credit should be given chiefly to him and to Emrys ap Iwan for transforming Welsh patriotism into a vigorous practical nationalism"'.

I
II
III
IV
V
VI
VII
VIII
IX
X

However, while Michael D. Jones' answer to the perceived injustices of the 'English' system was to cut and run to Patagonia, Emrys ap Iwan fought to change the system from within. A Methodist minister from Bryn Aber, near Abergele, Emrys ap Iwan was a prolific writer of letters whose 'pen was his sword', but he was also no mean pamphleteer who saw the value of such publications as a means of changing the attitudes of his fellow Welsh. His use of political propaganda was ahead of its time and in seeking to influence the electors of Anglesey he offered himself as a 'Welsh candidate' and 'outlined a specifically Welsh policy including home-rule, and a pledge to remain separate from all English parties. This was the first election address along these lines' (D.M. Lloyd, *Dictionary of Welsh Biography,1959*). Emrys ap Iwan was more nationalist than Nonconformist for as he himself said, when asked not to disagree with the opinions of his denomination, 'I am a Welshman as well as a Calvinistic Methodist, and I cannot promise anything as a Methodist which would deter me from speaking and feeling as a Welshman'.

Michael D. Jones and Emrys ap Iwan and others like them, most notably William Rees ('Gwilym Hiraethog') who made more familiar in Wales the sweep of nationalistic ideas in Europe and Ireland through his writings in the newspaper *Yr Amserau*, were a few steps further along the road to nationalism than men like Henry Richard whose nationalism was tempered by his strong religious convictions. Jones and Iwan represented a new breed of active and aggressive nationalists who prepared the ground for younger men to take up the cause and those that did took it all the way to Westminster. Foremost among the new generation of political nationalists, all of whom were Liberals, was Thomas Edward Ellis, a Methodist and son of a tenant farmer from Cynlas, Cefnddwysarn near Bala, whose election to Parliament in 1886 to represent Merioneth was hailed by some as a victory for the downtrodden Welsh-speaking, Nonconformist masses. Although he made much of his humble rustic origins he attempted always to appeal to a wider audience taking care to appreciate the divisions in Welsh society, his was a truly 'nationalistic' vision of an united Wales secure in the knowledge that it was mature enough to cope with the stresses and strains of home rule. He was instrumental in founding a movement dedicated to furthering the cause of Welsh statehood, Cymru Fydd, which was established in 1886 and as it grew in influence and prominence so did its political teeth. Where Liberal governments had in the past ignored or sidelined Welsh issues, the Liberal members of Cymru Fydd ensured that their voice would be heard.

Supported in Parliament by like-minded nationalists such as Lloyd George and D.A. Thomas and supported at home by powerful 'press barons' like Thomas Gee, publisher of *Baner ac Amserau Cymru*, Ellis succeeded in creating an atmosphere where Welsh nationalism could flourish. By the 1890s home rule for Wales was attracting as much attention in and outside Parliament as had home rule for Ireland. So closely identified with native nationalism had Ellis become and so persuasive was his influence in this respect that a young Lloyd George was moved to declare in a letter to D.R. Daniel: 'You know that I am a Welsh Nationalist of the Ellis type'. Although the political power of Welsh nationalism reached its apogee with the Cymru Fydd movement in the mid-1890s, a far more fundamental change had taken place in Welsh life. The Welsh had come of age as a nation, they may still have been deeply divided socially and linguistically, even culturally, but they were more aware of themselves as a people. Indeed, the last decade of the nineteenth century and the early years of the twentieth witnessed the founding and flowering of some of those essential features that distinguish a nation, − a city (Cardiff being regarded as an unofficial capital city), a National Museum, National Library and National University. Perhaps as a measure of how far the Welsh had come, J.V. Morgan, an historian of no mean repute, was able to discuss the fate of the Welsh language with reference to the tangible influence of native nationalism which, by the time he wrote his book, *The Welsh Mind in Evolution*, in 1925, was somewhere on the road to becoming more than simply a peripheral factor in Welsh political and social life.

> We cannot here discuss in detail all the .... factors that have contributed to this steady decline of the Welsh language, Welsh nationalists .... still persist in attributing it to the anti-Welsh policy of the Church, Parliament, and to the English system of education in Wales. It has not been due, they say, to any lack of [interest] among the native population, but to .... the efforts of the English and of English officials in Wales, to suppress it in order to crush the spirit of Welsh nationality.

I

II

III

IV

V

VI

VII

VIII

IX

X

I

II

III

IV

V

VI

VII

VIII

IX

X

2. Cymru Fydd

■ Key Issue:

'A movement doomed to failure'. Is this a fair or accurate description of Cymru Fydd?

a) Origin and Purpose

Cymru Fydd or 'Wales-to-be' was conceived in the minds of men who wished actively to participate in and promote the current and future well-being of the social, cultural and political life of their country. This they intended to do, in the words of historian John Davies, 'by developing a concept of nationality which connected history, literature, art, social values and political institutions in a single organic whole'. They were idealists, men of youth, ambition and enterprise who saw merit in fostering a sense of Welshness by giving the maturing but, hitherto directionless, ideas on Cymric nationalism greater shape and form. Paradoxically perhaps, these men were *emigres* with the result that the earliest meetings of a movement intended to further Welsh nationalist aspirations took place outside Wales. Admittedly, there was nothing novel in this as the patriotic London-Welsh Societies of the eighteenth century, the Cymmrodorion and Gwyneddigion founded in 1751 and 1770 respectively, have shown, but it was the harder-edged and broader-based 'political patriotism' of the Cymru Fydd faithful which set it apart from previous expatriate movements. Here was a movement which, though shortlived by comparison, lasting a mere decade, grew from small, vague and inauspicious beginnings into a sizeable organisation of some purpose and influence.

The first branch of Cymru Fydd was founded in London in 1886 closely followed by the opening of a second branch in Liverpool a year later. Wales had to wait four years before the movement established itself, in Barry in 1891, but thereafter it spread rapidly. Its foundation coincided with the election to Parliament as member for Merioneth of T.E. Ellis and it is to him, more than any other of the '"small company" in London who dreamt "many dreams about Wales"', that credit be given for originating the movement and, apparently, for suggesting its name. An indication, in part, of Ellis' motives for founding Cymru Fydd is provided in a letter written in February 1886 to his friend and fellow political activist D.R. Daniel:

> The social question and the future of Wales are in my thoughts from morn till night. I am unable to sit down steadfastly and apply myself continuously to any solid work, because a sort of feverish and mercurial emotion on these subjects quite distract me ... Wales, its members, its so-called leaders, and the masses seem to be drifting aimlessly, and spasmodically rousing themselves to activity and then settling down to greater apathy and servitude.

In its original conception and purpose Cymru Fydd differed little it seemed from its patriotic predecessors in so far as it, and they, were almost entirely given over to cultural and literary concerns. However, within four years of its foundation cultural nationalism had become heavily transfused with political patriotism with the result that the movement had, by championing disestablishment, home rule and land reform, taken on a distinctly radical appearance. Nor is this surprising given its infusion of new blood led by the likes of Lloyd George, D.A. Thomas and W. Llewelyn Williams all of whom, in imitation of 'Young Ireland' and 'Young Italy', espoused the cause of 'Young Wales'. Its gradual politicization tended towards the marginalisation of its cultural and intellectual élite, men of the calibre of John Viriamu Jones, John Edward Lloyd and Owen M. Edwards were eclipsed by the politicians who had taken control of the movement by 1894.

This is not to suggest that Cymru Fydd abandoned entirely its cultural and literary interests, it continued to promote things Welsh but did so within an overtly political framework believing that politics held the key to their protection and preservation. Such thinking was eloquently expressed by Ellis in a speech delivered to a packed house in Bala in September 1890 in which he outlined his vision of the future development of Wales:

> ... we shall work for a Legislature, elected by the manhood and womanhood of Wales, and to them responsible. It will be the symbol and cementer of our unity as a nation, our instrument in working out social ideals and industrial welfare, the pledge of our heritage ... the deliverer of our message and example to humanity, the rallying point of our nationality and fulfiller of our hopes.

Although for such men it was only a short step from cultural to political nationalism, it was realised by some if not by all, that to lose sight of the essential link between the two might sound the death-knell for a movement

I

II

III

IV

V

VI

VII

VIII

IX

X

I

II

III

IV

V

VI

VII

VIII

IX

X

which, it was thought, had come to exist to promote the one by means of the other. In the opinion of writer W.P. Wheldon (*Famous Welshmen*, 1944), T.E. Ellis was the living embodiment of this ideal: 'His speeches and writings, and his edition of Morgan Llwyd's works, show his literary qualities and indicate the close connection between the literary and political sides of the renaissance in Welsh life in the second half of the last century'.

Gradually, however, Ellis was supplanted by more radical visionaries who all but metamorphosised the movement into the would-be nationalist political organisation that strove to emerge after 1894. This 'new' movement was born in August 1894 at Llandrindod Wells where it was decided to draw up a constitution for a national Cymru Fydd League, aim at the amalgamation of all the various branches across Wales and employ the services of a salaried organiser. Consequently, 'its original objective of preserving the Welsh language and revitalising Welsh culture was', according to Kenneth Morgan, 'subordinated to the political aim of national self-government'. This did not meet with the approval of all its members and there were some dissenting voices. 'That is not the sort of "Nationalism" I should like to see in Wales – a Nationalism divorced from everything except politics', wrote Llewelyn Williams to J.E. Lloyd in September 1894. Williams was concerned that the League might evolve into a narrow nationalist political movement emulating the Irish Nationalist Party which had become, in his view, 'a sordid party ... compared with the Young Ireland party of the forties'. Nevertheless, the die was cast and the Cymru Fydd movement entered its final phase as an organisation determined to advance the cause of Home Rule by means of Welsh Liberalism and native Nonconformity.

b) Impact and Influence

... it became serious only when it went political in the 1890s ...

With his usual provocative style and characteristic bluntness the late Gwyn Williams, author of *When Was Wales?* (1985), opined that had Cymru Fydd not been politicised its impact and influence, indeed, its very importance, would have been far less than it actually was. That there is support for this opinion is suggested by John Davies' assertion that in its earliest form the movement, 'with its vague policies and the idealistic rhetoric of its leaders, was an amorphous (not united) body', lacking a clear focus and coherent programme for its activities. Had Cymru Fydd continued to drift, and it can justifiably be said to have done so in the first two or three years of its existence, it may have become but one in a long line of expatriate organisations which might have remained culturally active but politically inert. This did not happen, if anything, the movement's contribution to the cultural enrichment of Wales was negligible in comparison to its political achievements. Admittedly the movement did much to publicise Wales and Welsh issues and it did contribute to encouraging a pride and confidence in being Welsh but its greatest impact and influence lay in the political field, and this a strictly Liberal one.

Although not essentially political in origin there is no doubt that the movement owed allegiance to the Liberal Party whose membership suffused the organisation from its inception. Its principal founder T.E. Ellis was himself a politician and Liberal M.P. so that from the beginning there were political minds at work within the movement. It was perhaps only a matter of time before the movement evolved a political programme and when it did so it was unashamedly, and not unexpectedly, Liberal, Nonconformist and Nationalist in aim, content and deed. Consequently, the movement's impact was almost wholly political and its influence almost entirely Liberal which was no mean advantage in a country represented almost without exception by Liberals and given over almost completely to Liberalism. Working within the British Liberal Party framework the leaders of Cymru Fydd sought to influence party, and in consequence of it being in office, government policy in favour of disestablishment, land reform and, encouraged by the progress made by Irish home rule, their version of self-government. At first they met with little success but as their numbers swelled with recruits from among the parliamentary party representing Welsh constituencies (by 1892 more than half of the 31 Liberal M.P.s representing Welsh constituencies were members of Cymru Fydd) and as they became more militant in deed and nationalist in intent the Liberal leadership, if not always willing to act, took heed of their demands, .

It is likely that had the government not been forced to rely on the support of its 31 Welsh members as a result of its parliamentary majority falling to 40 in the 1892 election, political and other issues pertaining specifically to

I

II

III

IV

V

VI

VII

VIII

IX

X

I

II

III

IV

V

VI

VII

VIII

IX

X

Wales such as disestablishment, might well have been delayed or even ignored. As it was the Welsh parliamentary lobby, at the heart of which were the Cymru Fydd radicals Lloyd George and D.A. Thomas, had to struggle to persuade the government to introduce, let alone pass, a Welsh Disestablishment Bill and then only after the revolt, early in April 1894, of 'The Four'. The four M.P.s in question were Lloyd George (representing Caernarfon Boroughs), D.A. Thomas (Merthyr Tydfil), Frank Edwards (Radnorshire) and Herbert Lewis (Flint Boroughs), and their action in refusing to receive the Liberal Whip was intended to embarrass the government for its equivocation and its inept handling of Welsh Disestablishment. In a letter to the Chief Whip, T.E. Ellis whom he urged, unsuccessfully, to join and lead them, Herbert Lewis put the case on behalf of 'The Four': 'My recent talks with Ministers and Members have convinced me that Wales is simply being led on from step to step without any definitive goal in view, that we have nothing to gain by subservience to the Liberal Party, and that we shall never get the English to do us justice until we show our independence of them'. In search of support, and not a little publicity, 'The Four' toured North Wales where, justifying their 'revolt' on nationalist grounds, they were warmly received by most and even applauded enthusiastically by some. Certainly, the Welsh press, both English and Welsh, was encouraging in its support of their protest with headlines and editorials proclaiming 'The Four' as nothing short of national heroes.

Whether or not the government's introduction, by Herbert Asquith, of the Bill for Disestablishment in Parliament later in April 1894 was due to this so-called 'Welsh Revolt' is a matter of conjecture but what is beyond question is the significance of the event in terms of the political evolution of the Cymru Fydd movement. Gradually, its leadership, more especially Lloyd George who emerged to become the movement's chief inspiration, came to realise that only through a Welsh legislature could measures pertaining to Wales receive the priority they deserved and to this end he formed, in August 1894 at Llandrindod Wells, the Cymru Fydd League with which he hoped to merge the Liberal Federations of North and South Wales. In effect, he sought to forge a political identity on nationalist, though not completely independent, party lines in imitation of, but not entirely consistent with the Irish Party in Parliament. Although a 'Welsh Party' had long been in existence in the Commons it was party in name only possessing none of the ideology, organisation, discipline and financial independence that characterised true parliamentary party politics. All that its members, a third of whom were not even Welsh, had in common was the fact that they represented Welsh constituencies. There was little co-ordination of or central direction in policy or indeed in policy-making. This changed somewhat after the 1892 election when the 'Welsh Party' took on a more compact and homogenous appearance with the election to Parliament of more native-born, like-minded nonconformist politicians who tended towards the nationalist cause. This new spirit of camaraderie and self-awareness as a group was particularly marked among the newly-elected Welsh Liberals, men like Herbert Lewis who suggested that in order to demonstrate its solidarity on behalf of Welsh nationalism the Welsh Party should sit in a 'solid phalanx' in the Commons. This did not, and probably could not, happen, certainly not in Westminster where the pressures of party often obscured or cut across notions of nationality. It is probably fair to say that a significant proportion of the members of the so-called 'Welsh Party' were Liberals first and Welsh nationalists second. It was this basic conflict between Liberalism and nationalism, not yet apparent to all, which was to end, in large part, in the destruction and ruin of Cymru Fydd.

In fact, if anything, Cymru Fydd seemed to be going from strength to strength and it swept all before it in 1895, the year in which it reached its apogee. The year began with the launch in January of a new nationalist journal *Young Wales* under the editorship of a former Independent minister J.H. Edwards. *Young Wales* was certainly more effective in disseminating the movement's message than had been its less radical precursor *Cymru Fydd* which ceased publication after three years and three changes of editor – T.J. Hughes, R.H. Morgan and O.M. Edwards respectively – in 1891. Aware of the pressures of party and Westminster politics, Lloyd George pressed ahead with plans to form an organisational base outside its constraining framework and he scored a notable success in persuading the North Wales Liberal Federation to merge with Cymru Fydd. The merger took place in a meeting at Aberystwyth in April 1895, the overwhelming success of which was marred only by the absence of delegates from the South Wales Liberal Federation. The call by delegates at Aberystwyth to set up a unified 'Welsh National Federation' fell on deaf ears and failed to persuade the southerners to act. Nothing daunted, Lloyd George and his supporters launched themselves into a vigorous campaign to win over their fellow Liberals and 'nationalists' in South Wales. To judge from his private letters home to his wife it seems Lloyd George was more than satisfied with the reception his lecture tour of the South Wales valleys had received, even in 'semi-English districts' like Tredegar where the locals had 'sunk into a morbid footballism'. The response of Merthyr Tydfil and the Rhondda was especially welcome and gave Lloyd George cause for optimism in being able to win over South Wales.

> Last night's demonstration was simply immense – that is the word. Nothing like it in the Rhondda – not in the memory of the oldest inhabitant has anything to equal it been seen. Crowds from all parts of the Rhondda came down. Hundreds of D.A.Thomas' own colliers amongst them. Mabon looked blue. I talked Home Rule for Wales & and all the nationalist stuff which the Mabon crew so detest – but the people cheered to the echo. The Rhondda has been captured.
>
> [Lloyd George to his wife (21 November 1895)]

Within two months of this meeting Lloyd George's hopes and aspirations for Cymru Fydd, Welsh nationalism and a Welsh political party had evaporated after suffering a humiliating defeat at the hands of hostile delegates of the South Wales Liberal Federation. The infamous Newport meeting in January 1896 sounded the death-knell for a movement which had exercised considerable political influence in and outside Westminster between 1892 and 1895. The extent of its impact on local politics may be instanced by its success in forcing through the adoption of its member, William Jones, as prospective parliamentary candidate for the constituency of Arfon in direct contravention of the party's official nomination of D.P. Williams, for what was considered to be a safe Liberal seat. In the Commons also the nationalism of Cymru Fydd was a persuasive force in carrying through by 26 votes a motion for 'home rule all round'. On the other hand, it has been argued that beyond the ranks of Liberal party activists and local Liberal associations Cymru Fydd had little popular support. It was an organisation attuned more to the intellectual wavelength of the middle classes than the labouring masses, the majority of whom probably had neither the time nor the inclination to become involved in matters which impinged very little on their every-day working lives. For them nationalism was a luxury they could ill afford.

I
II
III
IV
V
VI
VII
VIII
IX
X

c) Decline and Demise

The climax of the Cymru Fydd movement came with a meeting of the South Wales Liberal Federation at Newport on 16 January 1896. Having successfully assimilated the North Wales Liberal Federation it only remained to convince their southern counterparts to follow suit and vote for merger with Cymru Fydd. Lloyd George was under no illusion as to the difficulty of the task that faced him, as early as February 1892 Llewelyn Williams had written to Ellis expressing his opinion that Cardiff was 'already lost to Welsh nationalism' while Swansea was described as 'a howling wilderness of Philistinism', yet Lloyd George remained hopeful, even optimistic, of success. A letter written to his wife the day before the crucial meeting suggests why: 'Heard from Rhondda that the Cymru Fyddites scored "a grand victory" there last night & that all the delegates are to vote for us tomorrow at Newport. That cripples Mabon's mischievousness'. Unfortunately, and despite Lloyd George's best efforts, the meeting descended into chaos and the proposal for merger was heavily defeated by 133 votes to 70. According to a correspondent of the *Western Mail* (17 January 1896) Lloyd George 'was howled down' while another eye-witness, Herbert Lewis, noted in his diary that his friend and colleague was simply 'shut up' unable to make himself heard above the din of opposition. Lloyd George explained the reason for his defeat to his wife: 'The meeting of the Federation was a packed one. Associations supposed to be favourable to us were refused representation and men not elected at all received tickets'. Of greater concern to Lloyd George than the mere fact of misrepresentation, only seven of the twenty South Wales constituencies were allowed delegates at the meeting, was that 'The majority present were Englishmen from the Newport district'. That he returned to this theme in a letter to Herbert Lewis, stating that the meeting 'was disgracefully packed with Newport Englishmen' and suggesting elsewhere, in a letter to his wife, that 'Welsh Wales is with us to the fore. We have simply got to stir it up', underlines the rampant nationalism that pervaded the movement. It was this, rightly or wrongly, which impressed itself and so frightened the Anglicised, commercialised and industrialised south. Robert Bird, an English-speaking businessman and Cardiff alderman, declared 'that Liberalism is more important than Welshness' and that the southeast would never submit 'to the domination of Welsh ideas'.

I

II

III

IV

V

VI

VII

VIII

IX

X

Suspicious of Lloyd George's motives and only lukewarm in their support of Cymru Fydd, the leadership of the South Wales Liberals were generally opposed to plans for a merger because they feared domination by Welsh-speaking Wales – and North Welsh-speaking at that! Even those Liberals like D.A. Thomas who had once been so active in promoting the movement – he had once proposed the setting up of an independent Welsh political party – spurned the opportunity to establish Cymru Fydd as a truly national organisation representative of the whole of Wales. Relationships, both personal and political, many of them of long-standing, foundered on the rocks of ambition. Men like D.A. Thomas envied the growing profile and popularity of his erstwhile companion Lloyd George but, more seriously, he feared being marginalised in his own backyard should a Lloyd George-dominated Cymru Fydd ever secure control of the south. Consequently, he used his position as president of the South Wales Liberal Federation to undermine Lloyd George and usurp the rights of those south Wales constituencies which showed the slightest inclination towards supporting a merger with Cymru Fydd. Others also were reluctant to allow Cymru Fydd to 'capture' the organisational base of Welsh Liberalism and thereby enabling them to found a Welsh Liberal Party as distinct from its counterpart in England. In the sceptical opinion of one Welsh Liberal, and a North Walian to boot!, Fred Llewellyn Jones 'The whole movement from the beginning on is a beautifully arranged attempt to boss Welsh people' and even the North Wales Liberal Federation 'was far from being in love with the Cymru Fydd movement'.

Far from being discouraged Lloyd George determined to turn the tide in south Wales, which plan he outlined in a letter to his wife: 'The next step is that we mean to summon a Conference of South Wales & and fight it out. I am in bellicose form & don't know when I can get home'. Herbert Lewis, friend and fellow Cymru Fydd faithful, was equally adamant that the struggle would continue; 'This will be the end of the negotiations with them and the W.N.F. (Welsh National Federation) will go ahead'. Their optimism, however, was gravely misplaced, Cymru Fydd quickly wilted and died and though a Welsh National Liberal Council was proposed – by Lloyd George – and set up in early 1898 it was far from the national, and nationalist, organisation envisaged by the Cymru Fyddites.

Few in the southeast mourned its passing but to blame entirely English-speaking Welshmen for the movement's ruin is to ignore other factors which came to bear heavily on the future of the League. Chief among them was the fact that after 1895, having lost the general election, the Liberals were no longer the party of government which weakened considerably the League's attractiveness and effectiveness. The Welsh Liberals no longer held the balance of power and their ability to influence events at a national level diminished accordingly. In fact the Liberals had been heavily defeated in 1895 and though their losses in Wales were less than those suffered elsewhere in the country, it inevitably damaged a Liberal-dominated or associated organisation. The bitterness that the contest engendered within Liberal ranks contributed to the movement's demise inasmuch as it paralysed the party's operations in Wales and for some time after 1896 suspicion, hostility and non-co-operation were the order of the day.

Perhaps the most decisive factor in the movement's slide into oblivion was Lloyd George himself. His complaint that the Newport meeting was unrepresentative of the S.W.L.F. was met with derision by his opponents who pointed out, fairly, that Cymru Fydd was no more than a tool for his ambition. His strident nationalism, forceful personality and obvious talent proved too much for those fearful of change, who were full of resentment and in need of careful and sensitive handling. After the heat generated by the debacle of January 1896 cooled off, Lloyd George was able to take a more sober and balanced view of this, the first rebuff of his career. He abandoned the movement, set aside his nationalistic tendencies and gave up on the struggle for Home Rule. His biographer, K.O. Morgan, sums up the reasons why:

> It dawned upon him that while Welsh Liberals were firm for Church disestablishment, land reform, education and temperance, and for national equality within the British Isles, they did not want separatism. The Welsh were just not like the Irish. They did not want to be cut off from England or from the imperial system. Welsh home rule was, in effect, struck off the political agenda, perhaps for ever, and Lloyd George recognised this fact. He would fight for a losing cause but not for a lost one.

I

II

III

IV

V

VI

VII

VIII

IX

X

267

Advice and Activities

(i) General

Suggested Further Reading

J. Davies, *Hanes Cymru/A History of Wales* (London, 1991/1993).

W. Jones, *Thomas Edward Ellis, 1859-1899* (Cardiff, 1986).

K.O. Morgan, *Rebirth of a Nation Wales, 1880-1980* (Cardiff, 1980).

K.O. Morgan (ed.), *Lloyd George Family Letters 1885-1936* (Cardiff, 1973).

Articles:

G.E. Jones, 'Wales 1880-1914', in T. Herbert & G.E. Jones (eds.), *Wales 1880-1914* (Cardiff, 1988).

K.O. Morgan, 'Radicalism and Nationalism' in A.J. Roderick (ed.), *Wales through the Ages, vol. 2* (Llandybie, 1960).

Research

As you read through his chapter you will need to have a dictionary to hand because it has been written in such a way as to provide you with an enhanced vocabulary. Get to know the meanings of the words you have had to look up and try and use them in your essays and assignments. You should certainly be looking up the meaning of the following words – culture, nationalism and renaissance.

Issues for Debate

'The contribution of Lloyd George to the development of Welsh Nationalism up to 1896 was far greater than that of Tom Ellis'.
State a case **for** and **against** this opinion.

Points for Discussion

1. Welsh nationalism was political in nature, cultural in character and religious in its fervour. Discuss the validity of this statement?
2. Discuss your definition of nationalism.
3. Why did the Cymru Fydd movement fail?
4. Was the Cymru Fydd movement at all significant for Wales?

(ii) Examination Specific

Answering Essay Questions

Q. How significant was the Cymru Fydd movement in the growth of Welsh National Consciousness by 1914?

Advice

This essay requires you to analyse and evaluate the development of Welsh National Consciousness up to and including 1914.

The key words around which the essay should be framed are 'significant' and 'growth'. But where do you begin if the essay does not provide a start date? This depends on the course and module you are studying, which is why it is essential that you become familiar with the syllabus. In this particular instance the question relates to Period Study 3 – Aspects of the History of Wales and England, c. 1815-1914 – module 4 which begins in 1868. Therefore, you must work within these dates.

You should pay particular attention to analysing the extent of the support enjoyed by the Cymru Fydd movement e.g. how far was it representative of the whole of Wales? You must look also at the relationship between Cymru Fydd and the Liberal Party e.g. was the success/popularity of Cymru Fydd determined by the success/popularity of the Liberals in Wales? The roles of Lloyd George and D.A. Thomas must be examined and evaluated – e.g. did one create while the other destroyed or is it more complex than that. You must point out that the movement was the focus of a small group and that their views may not have been shared by the mass of the population. The movement did make a significant contribution in its attempt to establish an

I

II

III

IV

V

VI

VII

VIII

IX

X

independent Welsh perspective on political life in Wales. However, you must note the fact that after 1896 the Cymru Fydd movement was effectively over. Therefore, you will need to analyse those factors /events / institutions which contributed towards the growth of national consciousness between 1896 and 1914. Evaluate the contribution of the Cymru Fydd movement against these other factors. You are likely to conclude that the Cymru Fydd movement was significant but only up to a point.

Chapter VIII
Politics and Political Issues

1. Nonconformity and Radical Politics, 1815-68

■ Key Issue:
What inspired the Welsh people towards radicalism and political agitation?

a) Radicalism and Nonconformity

In the period between 1815-1868, religion was very important to the development of Radicalism in Wales. In fact, it might be argued that Welsh Radicalism during this critical time (certainly up to the mid 1840s) should perhaps be seen, primarily, as an expression of religious tensions. The reason for this was summed up perfectly by Lewis Edwards, editor of *Y Traethodydd*, who believed that 'The great issue of this age is the union between Church and State', i.e. the alliance between Parliament, as the seat of government, and the Established Church, whose Bishops sat in the House of Lords. Nonconformists especially, and even some Anglicans, felt threatened by what they regarded as State interference in matters of religion and in the internal affairs of the Church. Certainly, by the early 1820s the growing dissatisfaction of Welsh Nonconformists with the privileged status and oppressive nature of the Established Anglican Church convinced many that political action was necessary to change matters. Another reason why radicalism and Nonconformity were so closely linked was due to the fact that outside of the narrow and privileged circle that made up the pre-Parliamentary reform electorate, the chapel provided the only means of collective political expression.

I

II

III

IV

V

VI

VII

VIII

IX

X

I

II

III

IV

V

VI

VII

VIII

IX

X

Another powerful factor in the growth of radical Nonconformity was the increasing influence of the denominational press which did so much to provide the people with a political education. For the majority of radical Nonconformists, politics was merely a means to an end and not an end in itself. They did not seek the vote or political power for its own sake but as a way of achieving their aims of religious toleration and freedom both from the State and Established Church. It was not until the late 1840s or early 1850s that Nonconformity began to enter the political mainstream and embrace more fully social, political and cultural issues, and only then because they could no longer be ignored. Consequently, the period from roughly 1859 to 1868 is regarded by many historians as one of considerable significance in the political history of Wales for it witnessed the rapid growth in the political consciousness of the Welsh.

However, not all Nonconformists were radicals and not all radicals were Nonconformists. The Methodists for example, were especially reluctant to enter the political arena and only did so largely as a result of the Blue Books controversy of 1847. Stung into action by the criticisms of Anglican Commissioners on various aspects of Welsh faith, life and education, Methodism joined the Nonconformist chorus calling for electoral reform and political power.

Welsh radicalism may have owed its origins to native Nonconformity, which was largely representative of the rural middle-class in Wales, but its development into a potent political force owed as much, if not more, to the working-class radicals of industrial towns and districts like Merthyr and Newport. It is here in 1831 and 1839 that radicalism, inspired to action by appalling living and working conditions and encouraged by English radicals, spilled over into violence. Although left frustrated and angry by the shortcomings of the 1832 Parliamentary Reform Act and the passing of the Tithe Commutation Act of 1836, radical Nonconformists were generally opposed to such violent outbursts and were reluctant to apply such pressure on governments for action on reform, preferring instead to lobby and preach for a cause they believed was right.

This is not to suggest that there were no links between working-class radicals and middle-class Nonconformist radicals, (a fair percentage of the working class in Wales were, after all, chapel-going worshippers), but their ever closer association at a political level was an evolutionary process which took some time to occur. As working class radicalism evolved into Chartism and trade unionism, radical Nonconformity not so much evolved as became closely associated with the Liberal Party and Liberal politics. Thus, from the 1860s, the mantle of Welsh radicalism was taken up by the reforming wing of the Liberal Party.

Fig. 40
Two cartoons by Cruikshank showing how frightened the government was by what it saw as the threat posed by radicalism (1819-1825)

I

II

III

IV

V

VI

VII

VIII

IX

X

b) Movements, Societies and Leagues

The nineteenth century witnessed the appearance of a number of movements and the formation of a variety of societies and leagues dedicated to reform of one sort or another. Many were motivated by the idea of a moral crusade to improve the lot of the poor and ignorant, some were inspired by such high ideals as religious toleration and freedom while others were concerned by the increasing militancy and lack of representation of the working classes. Yet all came to share the belief that, ultimately, it was only through politics, Parliament and political reform that lasting change in most spheres of daily life could be achieved.

(i) The Oxford Movement

The man credited with launching the Oxford Movement with his Assize Sermon of 1833 was John Keble (d. 1866). Keble was one of a number of clerical Oxford dons who founded the movement in an attempt to combat what they regarded as the excessive control of the Church of England by Parliament. Keble's sermon was prompted by the government's decision to reform the Church in Ireland which resulted in the halving of the number of Irish dioceses. Although Keble did not necessarily disagree with the idea of Church reform, he did object to the interference of Parliament in Church affairs. What worried Keble and others was the fact that a Parliament that was no longer truly Anglican (an increasing number of M.P.s came from Nonconformist backgrounds) had the power to control and reform the Church. Between 1833 and 1840 Parliament was successful in passing a series of bills to reform the Church:

- pluralism, the right of clerics to hold more than one parish to boost their often poor pay, was curbed;
- the tithe was no longer to be paid in kind, as in produce, but only in cash;
- responsibility for the registration of births, deaths and marriages was transferred from the Church to the state;
- the Church was ordered to hold its Sunday services in Welsh in those areas where it was the language of the majority of parishoners.

On the other hand, an attempt in 1836 to reduce the number of dioceses in Wales from four to two by uniting Bangor with St. Asaph and, more controversially, Llandaff with Bristol, failed in the face of intense opposition from Welsh Anglicans some of whom, like Issac Williams of Llangorwen near Aberystwyth, were members of the Oxford Movement. Although many of the reforms introduced into the Church actually benefited and improved it, the Oxford Movement continued its campaign

- to make the Church less political by separating it from Parliament;
- to give the Church the power to manage its own affairs by making it more independent of Parliament;
- to help the Church to become the divine and spiritual institution it had been by rediscovering its catholic roots;
- to support the case and boost the popularity of the Church by publishing a series of short pamphlets, known as *Tracts for the Times*, between 1833 and 1841.

Although the Movement had many opponents both within and outside the Anglican church, especially in Parliament where anglican bishops sitting in the House of Lords had to confront the ever increasing influence of Nonconformist MPs In the Commons, it continued its work to revitalise the Church which in Wales was led by the likes of Bishop Thirlwall of St. David's. Due in part to his leadership and to the inspiration provided by the Oxford Movement, it was, in the words of Gwyn A. Williams, the

> Anglicans above all who moved into the surging eisteddfod movement and the national revival, who proved to be the largest single group of subscribers to the new 'people's university' at Aberystwyth and who were some of the most committed to a Welsh nationality – a fact systematically eliminated from the over-powering history of modern Wales shortly to be composed by a triumphant Nonconformist populism.

(ii) The Peace Society

The Peace Society was never more than a movement of peripheral interest in Wales but one of its leading supporters was a man of immense character and influence on Welsh Nonconformist politics. The Tregaron-born (1812) and London-trained minister (Highbury Independent College, 1830-34), Henry Richard (d. 1888), early took an interest in the cause of international peace. In his capacity as minister of Marlborough Congregational Church, London (1835-50), he preached peace from the pulpit and urged the British and European governments to enter into a new spirit of international co-operation. In 1848 Richard was appointed secretary of the Peace Society,

I

II

III

IV

V

VI

VII

VIII

IX

X

a post which enabled him to attend the Peace Conferences held in Brussels, Paris and Frankfort between 1848 and 1850. Soon after he was appointed editor of the Society's monthly magazine, *Herald of Peace*. His experience at the conferences persuaded him to resign his ministry and take up the cause of peace full time. However, his interests soon widened beyond the cause of peace and over the next thirty years he took up other equally worthy causes such as the Land Question, religion and the State and education. He was persuaded that politics was the only way in which he could further his various causes and though at first he hesitated (he withdrew as Liberal candidate for Cardiganshire in 1865) he was duly elected the member for Merthyr in 1868. He used his Parliamentary position to good effect and was especially effective in a Commons speech of 1873 which supported a resolution calling for the setting up of a system of international arbitration. His advocacy of European and World peace earned for him the title the 'Apostle of Peace' which, in the minds of many, was thought to represent the attitude of the Welsh people as a whole.

(iii) The Liberation Society

The Liberation Society was to play an important part in the political education of Wales. It was founded in 1844 as The Anti-State-Church Association and its aim was two-fold; to separate Church and State and to promote Parliamentary reform. Although founded by English non-conformists led by Edward Miall of Leicester, who first proposed the establishment of such an organisation in his newspaper *The Nonconformist* (est. 1841), the Association's inaugural meeting in London was well attended by Welsh delegates.

Table 19

Welsh delegates at the inaugural meeting of The Anti-State-Church Association

County	No. of Delegates
Monmouthshire	8
Glamorgan	4
Montgomeryshire	4
Carmarthenshire	3
Denbighshire	2
Merionethshire	1
Total	22

Nevertheless, in spite of strong Welsh representation at the inaugural conference, membership of the Association was only slowly taken up in Wales. This is how it might have remained but for two events which together conspired to promote the movement in Wales:

- the appointment of a London Welshman, J.C. Williams, as secretary of the Association
- the publication in 1847 of the government report into the state of education in Wales (Blue Books).

Williams worked tirelessly to promote the Association and under his leadership cells were established in Wales. With the publication of the so-called Blue Books his work was given an enormous boost. The Blue Books enraged the various Nonconformist denominations. They set aside their accustomed rivalry and formed an alliance to counter what they regarded as a slander on the Welsh people and their faith. The counter attack was led by the normally isolationist Methodists who found their champion in the person and the pen of Lewis Edwards of Bala. In the spring quarterly edition of *Y Traethodydd* (The Essayist, est. 1845), Edwards, its editor, aimed to rouse his fellow Methodists to political action and hoped that 'principled Nonconformists would be elected to Parliament by every county and every borough in Wales'. His conclusion that 'The great issue of this age is the union between Church and State' suggests that until the Nonconformists had a clear voice in Parliament, the established Church would continue to slander, denigrate and marginalise them. The fact that Edwards was joined

I
II
III
IV
V
VI
VII
VIII
IX
X

I

II

III

IV

V

VI

VII

VIII

IX

X

by a host of other equally weighty Nonconformist writers and intellectuals, such as Henry Richard, Evan Jones (Ieuan Gwynedd) and R.J. Derfel, caused historian John Davies to conclude that 'it is possible to discern the seed of the notion that the chapel people were the only true Welsh and that Welshness was synonymous with Nonconformity'. More important still was the growing awareness of the power of Parliament and the persuasion of politics among Nonconformists. This was particularly true of the largest Nonconformist denomination in Wales, the Methodists, who had long shunned politics and political action believing it to be sinful.

In 1853 the Association changed its name to the Society for the Liberation of Religion from State Patronage and Control. It was in this guise that Welsh Nonconformists embraced a movement which many of them came increasingly to see as a means by which they might achieve their complete liberation, not only in religion but in social, political and cultural terms also. In England the Liberation Society became increasingly influential and every election after 1847 witnessed a growing professionalism in its organisation of Nonconformist opinion. After establishing a firm foothold in the border region and in parts of south-east Wales during the late 1840s and 1850s, the pace at which Liberation committees were set up across the country declined. Despite the growing enthusiasm for the work of the Society, its impact in west, mid and north Wales continued to be marginal and was nowhere near as great as in Glamorgan and Monmouthshire. This was due to a number of factors:

- lack of funds – subscription income from Wales was too small to sustain the Society's activities
- shortage of tracts and other written materials in Welsh – the cost of translating and publishing was too great
- the infrequency of tours in Wales by Society lecturers – the majority of lecturers were monoglot English speakers and there was not enough money to support them or to train sufficient Welsh speakers
- poor organisation meant that there were few local committees – there was a crippling lack of local activists with the time and energy to organise
- the reluctance of some Nonconformists to participate in direct action – only gradually did the Methodists come to see the benefits of political action.

In 1862 The Liberation Society turned its full attention and resources to Wales. Separate conferences were held and organising committees were established in north and south Wales. District and electoral agents were appointed with annual salaries of between £40 and £50, while the services of political experts and itinerant lecturers were regularly engaged at election times. In north Wales the number of Liberation committees contributing funds to the parent organisation increased from ten in 1863 to fifty-five in 1868. In south Wales too the rate of success in establishing local committees was equally as great, increasing from twenty-two to forty-five. There is little doubt that the Society owed much of its success in Wales to the Welsh press, particularly denominational magazines such as *Y Diwygiwr* and *Seren Gomer*, which came out in favour of its activities. The society's own publication *The Liberator* too undoubtedly contributed to its success.

Besides awakening Welsh Nonconformists to the power of political action, the Liberation Society's greatest contribution to Welsh political life was in its encouragement and organisation of voter registration. The passing of the 1867 Reform Act, in which the vote was extended to working-class urban electors based on household suffrage, prompted the Liberation Society to support the founding in Aberdare of the Welsh Representation Society which aimed to promote Nonconformist parliamentary representation, and in Carmarthen the following year of the South Wales Liberal Registration Society. Less than a year later the Society helped form a Welsh Reform Association, all of which political activity contributed to making the 1868 elections of special significance. Yet for all its hard work behind the scenes, the Liberation Society's only success in direct politicking in Wales occurred in the Merthyr election of 1868 when one of its members, Henry Richard, was elected after a very effective campaign. After 1868 the Society intensified its efforts to educate the Welsh in the ways and means of politics and in 1883 its organisational structure and aims in Wales were redefined in order to concentrate on specifically Welsh issues such as disestablishment. With the infusion of new blood in the 1890s in the shape of politicians like Lloyd George, who served on its executive, the Liberation Society was instrumental in persuading the government to draw up the ill-fated Welsh Disestablishment Bill of 1894.

I

II

III

IV

V

VI

VII

VIII

IX

X

(iv) The Reform League

It has been calculated that in 1866 only 62,000 people in Wales, out of a total population of 1.35 million, were entitled to vote. This shocking statistic convinced many, even some politically-inactive Nonconformists, that something had to be done. Sparked into life by the early Dissenters, awakened by the controversy of the Blue Books and organised by the Liberation Society, politically-active Nonconformists were ready to widen their horizons. They were helped to realise their ambition by a number of political pressure groups which had emerged in the late 1850s and early 1860s. Perhaps the two most important groups were the National Reform Union and the Reform League both of which were founded and based in England.

- The National Reform Union was established in 1864. It was a largely middle-class organisation which campaigned for household suffrage (i.e extending the vote to all householders). It was a Manchester-based society which was particularly popular with Nonconformists and it had its greatest impact on north Wales. By 1866 the society was working very closely with the Reform League which had taken the lead in matters of reform.
- The Reform League, founded in 1865, was a working-class society which, unlike the moderate National Reform Union, did not believe that property-ownership should decide a person's right to vote. The League, therefore, pressed for manhood suffrage and the ballot. Much of its support in Wales came from the industrial south.

The League formed over 400 branches across the country of which around 13 were established in Wales. However, with the possible exception of Merthyr Tydfil, long a hot-bed of political reform and working-class agitation, the response in Wales to the work of the League was lukewarm. Although large numbers of men turned up at meetings to listen to visiting lecturers, they were reluctant to join their local branches or to contribute to funding its activities. This apathy left activists like the Rev. John Jones of Llangollen, a Vice-President of the League in Wales, angry and frustrated. In his influential book on electoral affairs, *Llawlyfr Etholiadaeth Cymru* (Welsh Electoral Handbook), he attempted to educate his reluctant compatriots in the benefits of politics and in having the vote. In his opinion this apathy could be traced back to the reign of Henry VIII when, as a result of the Acts of

Union (1536-43), the Welsh were 'given a share of the privileges of the kingdom' and, as a consequence, 'the nation sat quietly at the feet of the victor; and from that day to this, the nation has let herself go into a lukewarm state and political indifference'.

On the other hand, it is equally evident that there were in Wales, in the words of the Rev. Jones 'glorious exceptions', individuals and groups willing to support the work of the League. For example, the setting up of the Cardiff and Merthyr branches of the society were inspired by the Trades' Council and Shoemakers' Union respectively. Indeed, had it not been for the work of such organisations as the Union and League, and others like the Liberation Society, the Welsh would have remained in 'ignorance about national issues'. Even Henry Richard, a past critic of his countrymen's apathy and ignorance, was able to write in 1866 that 'the Welsh people have begun to take an intelligent and earnest interest in politics'. This change was due, in no small measure, to the growing power and influence of the Welsh press which both informed and encouraged its readers to greater awareness and participation. The reward for those persistent in their desire to see and effect change in the British political system was the 1867 Parliamentary Reform Act which gave the vote to every householder in borough constituencies and to every householder in county constituencies whose premises were rated at £12 or more a year. As a direct result of the passing of the Act the number of electors in Wales almost doubled from 62,000 to 121,000 with Merthyr leading the way in the borough constituencies, witnessing a rise in the number of voters from 1,387 to 14,577. That Wales and the Welsh probably had little to do with the passing of the Reform Act must be accepted but it is a fact that historians are divided over whether popular pressure was the deciding factor in persuading the government to pass the 1867 Reform Act, the first since the Great Reform Act of 1832, or whether it was as a result of political manoeuvring between the rival parties in Parliament.

c) The Welsh Press

According to Gwyn A. Williams, 'The new political consciousness broke in along the railways and through the press'. The railways brought news but the press 'made' news and it was, arguably, the Welsh denominational press which became the single most important factor in the political

I

II

III

IV

V

VI

VII

VIII

IX

X

281

education of the people of Wales. The repeal of the so-called 'Taxes on Knowledge' (stamp duty) in 1854 followed by the abolition of paper duties in 1861 served to encourage the printing of indigenous periodicals and newspapers, the majority of which were in Welsh. This 'explosion into print' witnessed a clear shift in the attitude of the Welsh-language denominational press which had turned to giving greater attention to political issues. At a time when English newspapers had little circulation in Wales, these native newspapers and periodicals provided the political education of an increasingly literate and curious population. Among the large number of Nonconformist editors and writers, many of whom were well-known preachers and lecturers, two men stand above them all, William Rees (Gwilym Hiraethog) and Thomas Gee.

(i) William Rees (Gwilym Hiraethog) (1802-83)

Born in the parish of Llansannan, Denbighshire, of farming stock, Rees had had little formal education before he took up the ministry as an Independent. A powerful preacher and lecturer who spoke on matters as diverse as 'The 1848 Revolution', 'Garibaldi' and 'Williams Pantycelyn', he was among the first to realise the value of newspapers and the potential influence of 'preaching in print', and in 1843, soon after settling in Liverpool, he established *Yr Amserau*. It was the first critically and commercially successful Welsh-language newspaper and it dealt with such subjects as Corn Law Repeal, The Tithe, Elementary Education, Disestablishment and the Oxford Movement. Rees' series, 'The Letters of an Old Farmer' (*Llythyrau 'Rhen Ffarmwr*), proved especially popular, written as they were in the dialect of his native district of Hiraethog. He aroused in the Welsh an enthusiasm for political and religious liberty at home and a sympathy for the plight of those seeking the same abroad. He was a poet, a composer of hymns and a writer of novels whose works place him among the pioneers of the novel in Wales.

(ii) Thomas Gee (1815-98)

The son of an English printer who had settled in Denbigh, Gee became a staunch Radical and Nonconformist preacher who rejected his family's Anglicanism in favour of Calvinistic Methodism. Although Gee never took charge of a church he successfully combined his love of religion and preaching with his business interest as a printer and publisher. The movements with which Gee became closely associated were

- free, undenominational education for all
- the struggle against oppressive landlordism
- manhood suffrage and the secret ballot
- the reform of Parliament
- religious equality and the struggle for the Disestablishment of the Church in Wales.

He was able to lend powerful voice to these movements partly through his quarterly periodical *Y Traethodydd* (1845) but mainly through his weekly national newspapers, *Y Faner* (1857) and its successor *Baner ac Amersau Cymru* (1859). Under Gee's direction this paper, the result of a merger between his own paper and William Rees' *Yr Amserau*, came to exercise considerable influence on Welsh thought and public opinion in the latter half of the nineteenth century. In expressing the viewpoint of Radical and Nonconformist Wales it helped to shape and to enlighten opinion on important matters of the day. In fighting the cause of Welsh democracy in the field of education, politics and religion, and with a circulation of over 50,000, *Baner ac Amersau Cymru* made real the boast of an Aberdare periodical publisher – 'What we think today, Wales will think tomorrow'.

In the wake of Rees and Gee came a whole host of newspaper, pamphlet and periodical publications which flooded all over Wales. For example, in his volume entitled *The Provincial Newspaper Society*, 1836-1886, published in 1886, H. Whorlow estimated that there were some 83 newspapers in Wales as compared with 18 in 1856. Some Welsh towns – Abergavenny, Caernarfon, Cardiff, Carmarthen, Denbigh, Swansea and Merthyr chief among them – became centres of print with the power to influence their immediate hinterlands and, in newspaper terms, beyond with publications like *Yr Herald Cymraeg, Tarian y Gweithiwr, Y Genedl Gymreig, Cardiff Times, Carmarthen Times, Carnarvon and Denbigh Herald, The South Wales Daily News* and the *Merthyr Express*. The power of the press to influence politics in Wales is best summed up by Gwyn A. Williams, '... with the press, came the Liberation Society ... and after it, the Reform League, striking once more for a vote for the workers'. Politicians too came to appreciate the power of the Welsh press. Lloyd George was among those

I

II

III

IV

V

VI

VII

VIII

IX

X

who took to using, and abusing, the press in his quest for political promotion and publicity. After delivering a speech to a meeting of Cymru Fydd at Aberdare on 5 July 1894, Lloyd George wrote the following report to his wife:

> We had a magnificent meeting last night – about 4,000 people in all. *The South Wales Daily News* editor & and chief reporter were there & were very much impressed. They give my speech an exceedingly prominent position & type – dividing it into sections with flaming head-lines. They refer to it in the leading article as "the eloquent speech etc.".

Two days later Lloyd George wrote 'had two hours talk with the editor of *The South Wales Daily News* this morning'. Clearly, for him and for other budding politicians in Wales the press was becoming an indispensable aid to their ambitions for political power. Indeed, the period between the 1840s and the 1890s had witnessed a sea change in the nature and output of Welsh publishing. Where religion and religious issues had once dominated the printed page, politics and political issues now predominated. As evidence of this shift in attitude J.O. Jones' (Ap Ffarmwr) series of articles in the periodical *Young Wales* may be taken as an example of which the title of the December issue for 1895 is particularly revealing – 'The National Awakening in Wales. IV. In its Relations to the Press'. According to Jones, having been awakened to religion in the eighteenth century the Welsh, via the press, were as comprehensively awakened to politics in the nineteenth. Nor is this surprising given the observation of J.E. Vincent, the Welsh correspondent of *The Times*, in his *Letter from Wales* (published in 1889):

> The growth of journalism, and of vernacular journalism in particular, in the Principality has of late years been little short of phenomenal. My impression, indeed, is that Wales supports more journals in proportion to its population than any other part of the civilised world.

There is little doubt that due largely to the pioneering work of Nonconformists the press had, by the 1860s, become a political force in Wales. It was, gradually, able to rouse public interest in elections and to galvanise support for certain candidates usually of the pro-Liberal, Nonconformists persuasion.

The Merionethshire election of 1859 is testimony to the power of the press when it, led by the newly-merged *Baner ac Amserau Cymru*, used its influence to support the candidature of David Williams, a Liberal solicitor from Penrhyndeudraeth. He was put up against the local Tory landlord, W.W.E Wynne of Peniarth, who was the sitting M.P. In keeping with tradition, Wynne expected to be returned (for the third time in succession) unopposed but that he faced a contest which he only managed to win by 389 votes to 351 shows clearly the influence of the printed word. The 'Old Order', as represented by Wynne, of squire-landlord dominated rural constituencies, was shaken by the fact that their centuries-old hegemony had been challenged by their own tenants who dared to use their vote against them. Not surprisingly, evictions followed, as did the inevitable outcry in the pages of the Welsh press. Over the next decade the power of the press combined with the influence of the various reform leagues and societies contributed to a change in voter-attitudes and in traditional patterns of political support. The result was the memorable election of 1868 which, in one respect at least, may be said to mark the beginning of a shift in the trend of Welsh politics away from religious radicalism and towards secular nationalism. Of course, such a statement, if true, can only be made with the benefit of hindsight for though the iron-grip of Nonconformity on Welsh politics loosened its grasp it did so only gradually.

Having awakened the Welsh to politics Nonconformity had, in one sense, sown the seeds of its own destruction for though not apparent until the end of the opening decade of the twentieth century, an increasingly secularised population turned progressively away from the published papers and periodicals of the denominational press to embrace the pages of cheap, popular daily newspapers. In the anglicised, industrialised and heavily populated south-east especially, the political battles between Conservative and Liberal would henceforth be fought largely in the pages of the Tory *Western Mail* and the Liberal *South Wales Daily News*. Only in the Welsh-speaking rural heartlands of the west and north would Nonconformity continue to influence decisively its ever decreasing readership.

I

II

III

IV

V

VI

VII

VIII

IX

X

2. Political Awakening, 1868-1914

■ Key Issue:
What was the nature of the so-called 'political awakening' of Wales?

> The political subjugation of Wales was complete ... It had no voice in Parliament, no advocate in the Press, no valorous friend to do battle for its honour outside its borders, no one to meet enemies in the gate.
>
> [Tom Ellis, 'Wales and the Local Government Act, 1894', *Speeches and Addresses* (Wrexham, 1912)]

a) The 1868 Election

So much has been made of the general election of 1868 that, in the political history of Wales, the year looms large in the thinking of historians. In consequence of this, the year 1868 is claimed by some to have been an *Annus Mirabilis* (a remarkable year) in Welsh politics and its significance in the history of nineteenth-century Wales has reached almost mythic proportions. Is it possible then to distinguish between the myth and reality of the 1868 election in Wales? The answer, quite simply, is yes, provided we take care to distinguish between the history and historiography of the event.

Examining the evidence

• The History

In historical terms it is important to study the facts of what happened in order to seek out the truth. However, 'fact' and 'truth' are not necessarily the same thing which is why historians have to use their skill to interpret those facts. It is important to remember that facts do not change but their interpretation does. The key 'facts' surrounding the 1868 election are to be found in the sources printed below but they must be carefully sifted from the 'interpretations' of the writers of those sources.

• The Historiography

In historiographical terms it is important to remember that it is in the writing of such events after they have occurred that their significance can either be minimised or maximised, and where the facts of what happened can be distorted. The truth of what happened depends on the interpretation of the facts and on the opinion of the writer. Below are a number of extracts from the writings of modern historians. Each historian expresses his/her opinion on the significance and consequence of the election of 1868. Read the extracts carefully for though they might seem to be in agreement there are subtle differences of emphasis and interpretation.

A

> The memorable election in 1868 gave a new face to Welsh politics. In nearly two-thirds of the constituencies traditional leaders were overthrown by newcomers of Liberal and Nonconformist leanings; the political habits of two centuries had been thrown off . . . what was significant was the large number of evictions of tenants who dared to break loose politically from their landlords – as many as seventy in Cardigan and Carmarthen.
>
> [A.H. Dodd, *Life in Wales* (1972)]

B

> The great election of 1868 has always been regarded as one of the most important symbols of national awakening in Wales. It did indeed have great significance: the parliamentary returns provide testimony to the social and political changes that were taking place in the country. It was in 1868 that the seeds of change first bore fruit in Denbighshire; for the first time, proscription, influence and deference were effectively challenged at the polls.
>
> [Jane Morgan, 'Denbighshire's Annus Mirabilis: The Borough and County Elections of 1868', *The Welsh History Review* (1974)]

C

> The *annus mirabilis* of Welsh politics has always been seen as 1868, when the election of Henry Richard for Merthyr fused Liberalism and Nonconformity into a potent force. In fact specifically Welsh Nonconformist grievances were not at issue in 1868, and a number of Welsh M.P.'s were already both radical and Liberal. Members of Parliament had already campaigned over Nonconformist disabilities, particularly in education.
>
> [Gareth Jones, *Modern Wales* (1979)]

I
II
III
IV
V
VI
VII
VIII
IX
X

287

D

According to received tradition, it was the great expansion of the electorate in 1867 and the 'great election' of that *annus mirabilis*, 1868, which saw a decisive thrust away from [the] traditional pattern of political authority. Undoubtedly, the election results in 1868 were remarkable enough. There was the election of twenty-three Liberals as against only ten Conservatives in Wales. Most striking of all there was the return of three nonconformists including the famous radical pacifist, Henry Richard, 'the apostle of peace', in the highly democratic two-member constituency of Merthyr Tydfil ... But the transformation in 1868 was only a partial one. Twenty-four of the thirty-three Welsh MPs were still landowners; the bulk of the Welsh electorate, let alone the Welsh people, remained unrepresented. Nor did the new Welsh Liberal MPs have much to show for their efforts, as far as Wales was concerned, in the 1868-74 session of Parliament. The first motion on behalf of the disestablishment of the Church in Wales, moved by Watkin Williams, a barrister who sat for Denbigh District, failed ignominiously.

[Kenneth Morgan, *Rebirth of a Nation: Wales 1880-1980* (1981)]

E

With ... Nonconformist grievances central to the campaign of 1868, major change could be expected. The results were in fact sensational. In 1868 a new kind of Liberal was moving in, with new forces behind him. The election of 1868 was followed by a new wave of political evictions. A whole new roll-call of martyrs provoked a massive campaign which focused a Welsh hatred of the baron, the bishop and the brewer, the unholy trinity of Toryism.

[Gwyn Williams, *When was Wales* (1985)]

F

In the 1868 general election Wales returned twenty-three Liberals and ten Tories, as compared with eighteen Liberals and fourteen Tories in the previous election. The election results must not, however, be distorted. Only three Members of Parliament were Nonconformists, and the remaining thirty were Anglicans. Ten Tories were returned, and most of the twenty-three Liberals were Whig (wealthy landowners) in character. But some of the victories over the old order were dramatic, and the election did represent a cracking of the ice. The 1868 election signalled profound changes in Welsh political life.

[Gareth Evans, *A History of Wales* (1989)]

G

> That election [1868] was to have a central place in Welsh Liberal mythology. Forty years later, Lloyd George claimed that it had 'awakened the spirit of the mountains ... The political power of the landlords in Wales was shattered ... completely ...'. Lloyd George was guilty of some exaggeration. Most of the twenty-three Liberals were ... of the landed class, and every one of the ten Conservatives came from the ranks of the landowners. Nevertheless, the results from about a quarter of the Welsh constituencies showed the way in which the wind was blowing.
>
> [John Davies, *A History of Wales* (1990)]

Although it has become fashionable of late to argue that the significance of the election of 1868 in Wales has been exaggerated, clearly some historians are still loath to dismiss entirely the importance of the results. On the other hand, others would go so far as to suggest that the election of 1885 was far more important than that of 1868, particularly to the 'nonconformist middle-class' in Wales. Both followed Parliamentary Reform Acts which increased substantially the numbers of men eligible to vote and both witnessed electoral triumphs by the Liberals. For example, the 1867 Reform Act extended the vote to the working-class urban electorate on the basis of household suffrage. In British terms this added 938,000 voters to the existing electorate of 1,056,000. In Welsh terms this added 59,000 to the existing franchise of 62,000, which, in percentage terms of the entire population meant an increase from 4.5% to 9.1% of those eligible to vote. To illustrate the effects of this two borough constituencies, Denbigh Boroughs and Merthyr Tydfil, have been chosen. In Denbigh the number of voters increased from 934 to 2,785, but the greatest increase occurred in Merthyr with numbers rising from 1,387 to 14,577. Both returned Liberal members of Parliament, Watkin Williams and Henry Richard respectively, in what were hailed as remarkable victories. The biggest difference between the elections of 1868 and 1885 was in the character of those who were returned to Parliament in 1885 for, of the 34 elected

- only nine represented the landed gentry
- twenty were Welshmen of whom ten were Welsh-speaking
- around fourteen were Nonconformists.

In the opinion of K.O. Morgan 'Here, indeed, even more than 1868, was the *annus mirabilis* for Welsh Liberalism'.

I

II

III

IV

V

VI

VII

VIII

IX

X

289

b) Liberalism: ascendancy and decline

The growing link between Liberal Politics and Welsh Nonconformity ensured that in Wales it would be the Liberal Party rather than the Conservative Party that would command the respect and support of the Welsh people. This was due to a number of factors:

- Liberalism inherited the traditions of radicalism and the reforming nature of the radical wing of the Liberal Party appealed to the Welsh people.
- Liberalism became closely associated with Welsh Nonconformity which was the most popular form of worship in Wales and which had come to be associated with Welshness.
- Liberalism was in tune with the thoughts and feelings of the people and it invariably campaigned on issues which reflected popular opinion.
- The Liberal Party was well organised. The establishment of two Liberal Federations in north and south Wales during the 1880s reflected the growing number of local Liberal associations already established in towns and districts across Wales.
- The Liberals faced no real challenges to their authority in Wales. The Conservatives succeeded in winning some ground but it tended not to last. Only with the growth of the Labour movement was Liberalism challenged.
- Welsh Liberals were well represented and well led by dynamic leaders like Tom Ellis and Lloyd George.
- The Welsh press tended to support the Liberal Party which gave Liberalism in Wales a distinct advantage in terms of publicity and popularity.

As the following table of Liberal general election results in Wales (1880-1906) suggests the Liberals had little to fear from the Conservatives or Labour at least up to 1906. The ascendancy of Liberalism in Wales seemed complete and unassailable.

I
II
III
IV
V
VI
VII
VIII
IX
X

Table 20

Parliamentary Seats won by the Liberal Party in Wales, 1865-1906

Election Date	Parliamentary seats.
1865	18 out of 33
1868	23 out of 33
1874	19 out of 33
1880	29 out of 33
1885	30 out of 34
1886	25 out of 34
1892	31 out of 34
1895	25 out of 34
1900	28 out of 34
1906	33 out of 34

However, the impregnability of Liberalism in Wales was shown to be more apparent than real for by the early years of the twentieth century years of complacency had weakened the structure of the Local Liberal Associations and the party gradually lost support. Moreover, it seemed incapable of changing with the times and some of its policies seemed rooted in late nineteenth-century ideas. Perhaps the most important factor in the decline of the Liberal Party was the growth of the Labour movement. The Parliamentary Reform Acts of the nineteenth century gradually gave the working classes the opportunity to voice their concerns about issues which directly affected them such as poverty, unemployment, ill-health and poor housing. This brought about a change in the attitude of the Liberals and Conservatives towards the working classes since they realised that soon their votes would be crucial in winning future elections. The radicals within the Liberal party encouraged the working class to vote for them in return for representation in Parliament. In some local areas where the working class vote was at its strongest, the Liberals agreed to support the election of working men to Parliament. These working class M.P.s came to be called Lib-Labs and by 1906 their number had risen to 24.

However, some working-class radicals had for some time been growing impatient with the Liberals.The first signs of militant unionism, preparing to challenge middle-class and Nonconformist-dominated local Liberal associations, occurred in Merthyr and Caernarfonshire as early as the

I

II

III

IV

V

VI

VII

VIII

IX

X

elections of 1880. They believed that the only way for the poor and working class to improve themselves was by electing their own representatives to Parliament. Many of the working classes felt that the Lib-Labs did not represent their views so they decided to form their own party. This proved difficult since they had neither the money nor the support of powerful trade unions. Despite these problems they began to organise themselves into local socialist societies which by 1893 had come together to form the Independent Labour Party or ILP.

The ILP was founded and led by Keir Hardie. He realised that the new party was too weak to have much effect in Parliament so he aimed to strengthen its position in local government. Between 1895 and 1916 the number of Labour councillors increased significantly and it was clear that at a local level the labour movement was growing stronger. Hardie hoped that Labour's growing power in Britain's towns and cities would put pressure on the older political parties to act in the cause of social reform. Yet despite the fact that the valleys of south-east Wales, and Merthyr in particular, had been industrialised and urbanised for some considerable time the labour movement did not do well to begin with. The attitude of the Welsh working-class varied from apathy and indifference to outright hostility with the result that recruitment to the labour movement was slow. For much of the nineteenth century Wales was almost solidly Liberal and between 1890 and 1914 Welsh Liberal M.P.s were so many and so strong that they could influence government policy. The average Welsh voter seemed reluctant to support a party (Labour) and an idea (Socialism) that appeared foreign and English.

However, attitudes in Wales gradually began to change. Before 1906 few working Welshmen were members of unions, for example out of a workforce of 150,000 miners less than 45,000 were organised in trade unions. After 1906 this number rose substantially and as it did so support for the Liberal Party gradually faded away. What had seemed radical and reforming in the 1870s, 80s and 90s was no longer so well regarded but was considered weak and out of touch. While the Liberals fought for Home Rule and Disestablishment and sought religious and political independence, Labour fought for secure employment and decent wages and sought social justice. In truth, the Liberal party was simply not pursuing policies with which the newly-enfranchised working class could identify. In Wales at least, the writing was on the wall for the Liberal Party.

Fig. 41
Contemporary cartoon entitled 'Forced Fellowship' (1909). It shows the uneasy relationship between Labour and the Liberals. The caption reads: Suspicious Looking Party: 'Any objection to my company guv'nor? I'm going your way' – 'and further!'

FORCED FELLOWSHIP.

SUSPICIOUS-LOOKING PARTY. "ANY OBJECTION TO MY COMPANY, GUV'NOR? I'M AGOIN' YOUR WAY"—(aside) "AND FURTHER."

c) The Rise of Labour

While Churchmen and Nonconformists were locked in battle, a new industrial and political force, the labour movement, was emerging in Welsh society. Trade unionism, albeit in a slow and fragmentary manner, gathered strength and ventured uncertainly into the political arena, while the idea of independent working-class representation in Parliament and on local bodies took root.

Historian Ryland Wallace sums up perfectly well the rise of labour in Wales. It was a 'quiet revolution' which seemed to take the political parties and the Nonconformists by surprise.

What factors contributed to the rise of labour?

- **Trade Unions.** The origin of labour in economic and political terms can be traced back to early trade unionism and friendly societies of the 1820s and 30s. Although often poorly organised and short-lived, the fundamental idea of trade unionism, – to protect and further the rights of their members, remained to encourage and enthuse successive generations of workers. By the 1860s union membership and union activity had increased substantially, they had become better organised, better led and better funded. In 1861 The United Kingdom First Annual Trades Union Directory listed no less than 51 unions in Wales. Union leaders had come to realise that their workers' industrial and political interests could not easily be separated and that in order to advance the well-being of their members they must assume the role of political pressure groups. Their power had grown to such an extent that, in 1871, Gladstone's government passed the Trade Union Act. This act clarified the legality of trade unionism and provided for the proper regulation of their increasing funds. It was important because it was an indication of the growing electoral importance of workers. Although it took some considerable time for trade unionism to capture the hearts of Welsh workers, once persuaded that the only way to achieve decent wages and better working conditions was to support a party of workers to represent them in Parliament, the labour movement grew quickly in size and strength. Consequently, during the period 1880-1920 trade unionism became the main driving force behind the growth of the Labour Party in Wales.

I

II

III

IV

V

VI

VII

VIII

IX

X

- **Labour Representation League (LRL).** The founding of the Labour Representation League in 1869 followed hard on the heels of the short-lived Land and Labour League which was a militant organisation calling principally for the creation of a third political party. The LRL was a more moderate movement and its aim is best summed up by the title to its manifesto issued on its formation – 'An Association of Working Men and those Friendly to their Political and Social Advancement'. While the LRL did not advocate the creation of a Labour Political Party, it did aim to give the working man a political voice either by the election of its own candidates to Parliament or, by agreement with local associations of the Liberal Party, by the election of Liberals sympathetic to its cause. Gradually however, the LRL came to realise that its aims were not always compatible with those of local Liberals and that the only way forward was to assume a more independent line. Partly on account of internal arguments between pro and anti Liberal trade unionists and partly due to its disappointing showing in local and national elections, the LRL ceased to exist after 1879.

- **Parliamentary Reform Acts of 1867 and 1884.** These acts enfranchised more people than ever before adding, between them, some three million men to the British electoral register. The newly-enfranchised, the majority of whom after 1884 were unskilled agricultural workers, had a dramatic effect on the traditional pattern of British politics in that they gradually turned away from the party that had championed their cause, the Liberals, in favour of setting up their own organisation and supporting the aim of securing the election to Parliament of their own representatives. As a result of the 1884 Reform Act, the county vote (as opposed to the urban/borough vote) in Wales rose from 74,936 to 200,373. Here, Liberalism, in some strength, persisted a while longer but by the end of the first decade of the twentieth century the labour movement had made substantial headway.

- **Publicity and Propaganda.** The labour movement was well served by an ever expanding list of publications which generated a great deal of interest whilst spreading effective propaganda. As early as March 1855 the *People's Paper* declared 'To the miners of Wales, collectively, we say: 'Combine! Combine! to have your own representatives in Parliament, and then goodbye to coal-king tyranny for ever'. To further stir into action the industrial workers of Merthyr the newly-formed Merthyr Trades Council launched in early 1874 the *Workman's*

I

II

III

IV

V

VI

VII

VIII

IX

X

I

II

III

IV

V

VI

VII

VIII

IX

X

Advocate. Local magazines were supplemented by national publications like the *Labour Standard*, launched in May 1881, which acted as the mouthpiece for the Manhood Suffrage League founded in 1879. January 1884 saw the launch of *Justice*, a publication which represented the views of the Social Democratic Federation (SDF) which had been set up in 1881. In view of their close relationship with labour organisations these publications were able to exert a great deal of influence over their working-class readership. These publications, and others like them, were significant because the people had been given a voice which they used with dramatic effect to spread the word and thus organise themselves.

- **The decline of Liberalism.** The Liberal movement gradually lost its hold on the working class. Having represented their interests for much of the nineteenth century, the Liberal party failed to adapt to the growth of working-class radicalism which was altogether more militant in nature than either Liberal or Nonconformist radicalism. The fact that the Liberals attempted to harness the power of labour by establishing a political alliance known as Lib-Labism may, in one sense, be regarded as a sign of weakness rather than of strength. By the early to mid 1890s working men were, in the words of Ryland Wallace, 'becoming less acquiescent, not in terms of repudiation of the Liberal party – for years yet, labour leaders in Wales remained staunchly loyal to the traditional community values of Nonconformist Liberalism – but insofar as they wanted due emphasis on the labour side of the Lib-Lab alliance'. The writing was on the wall, change was inevitable, and it was not long in coming. As early as 1874 the pro-Liberal *South Wales Daily News* expressed its opinion that 'Surely there are many working class men in the Merthyr Boroughs ... who by character, education, and ability might worthily represent the Merthyr constituency'. By 1895 the Rhondda had done just that by rejecting the Liberal nominee in favour of one of their own. By 1908 Lib-Labism had ceased to exist, after its 24 M.P.s joined the newly-christened Labour Party.

- **The Independent Labour Party (ILP)** and the Labour Representation Committee (LRC). The Independent Labour Party was founded in 1893 in Bradford, consisting of 120 delegates drawn mainly from the industrial north and Scotland. Although there were no Welsh delegates at the Bradford conference, by 1906 at least four branches of the ILP had been established in Wales – at Cardiff, Merthyr Tydfil, Treharris and Wrexham. By 1898 a further 27 ILP branches had been set up in Wales more than a third of which owed their foundation to the miners' crushing defeat in the strike of that year. The ILP sought and was given, but only after a struggle, the support and financial backing of Trade Unions when in 1900 the Labour Representation Committee was set up. The Committee was given the task

(i)   of recruiting members to the labour movement;

(ii) of selecting candidates to represent the movement in Parliament;

(iii) of setting up a Parliamentary party strong enough to take on the Liberals and Conservatives.

On the eve of polling in the 1906 election the party changed from being the ILP to become the Labour Party and although they won only 29 of the 670 seats contested they could no longer be ignored. In 1908 the party's representation in Parliament nearly doubled when the Lib-Lab M.P.s threw in their lot with the Labour party.

- **Keir Hardie and Merthyr Tydfil.** Hardie's electoral triumph in Merthyr in 1900 was massively important in the history of the Labour movement in Wales. As the first Labour election victory in Wales it provided the inspiration and platform for the further development of the movement. Although he was returned with a small majority, it was undoubtedly a major political breakthrough which stunned the Liberals, particularly his opponent Pritchard Morgan. Hardie was a working-class socialist who had once been a mining union official in his native Scotland, his energy and enthusiasm combined with a certain charisma, appealed to the working class voters of Merthyr. Hardie thought the Welsh to be 'natural socialists' and he worked hard to promote the party in the country. By 1905, 25 local Labour Associations had been established across the country mainly in the industrial valleys of the south and east. Hardie recognised that the major task of the Labour Party in Wales was to win the workers from their Liberal allegiance, and, as a first step to achieving this, he secured the defection to Labour of the Lib-Lab M.P.s in 1908. In fact, in the opinion of many historians, 1908 was the turning point in the development of the Labour Party in Wales for though it was not until 1922 that Labour became the majority party in the Principality, it was clearly growing stronger from that time. Ironically, in view of Hardie's passionate pacifism, it was events during the First World War, 1914-18, which finally achieved the aim of firmly establishing Labour in Wales. That period witnessed the beginning of the break up of the alliance between the Chapels and the Liberals which heralded the death of Liberal Nonconformity.

I

II

III

IV

V

VI

VII

VIII

IX

X

297

Fig. 42
Keir Hardie's Election Poster

Table 21

British General Election Results, 1906-1924

Election Date	Liberals	Labour	Conservative
1906	377	29	157
1918	162	59	338
1922	117	142	347
1923	158	191	258
1924	40	151	419

d) Disestablishment

By the second half of the nineteenth century people began to question the right of the Anglican Church to be the established church. This was due to the fact that in Wales the Church represented only a minority, or roughly 20%, of Christians. This meant that the Nonconformist majority resented the legal requirement of having to maintain clergy with whom they did not sympathise and a church to which they did not belong. Irish nationalists had shown the way when, over time and in alliance with the Roman Catholic church, they brought pressure to bear in Parliament and succeeded finally in persuading the Liberal Prime Minister Gladstone to pass into law in 1869 the Disestablishment of the Church in Ireland. In Wales also, the growth of Welsh cultural and religious nationalism led to a similar campaign for disestablishment, the first sign of which showed itself in the outbreak of the so-called Tithe War in north-east Wales in 1886. The growth of the Liberal party and the widening of the franchise encouraged the campaign which became politicised as a result. After 1886, political propaganda and press publicity, conspired to ensure that disestablishment would assume a new importance in the legislative programme of Welsh Liberals who came to regard its passing into law as an issue of national pride.

Pressure from Welsh Liberals finally persuaded the Liberal leadership to adopt the cause and in 1891 the Liberal Party became formally committed to the Disestablishment of the Church in Wales. However, as the following letter written in January 1894 by Lloyd George to his wife shows, not all Liberals were in favour of disestablishment.

> Torr, the Liberal candidate for Horncastle is against Disestablishment or rather Disendowment & and I consider his victory would be a disaster for Wales. I have taken in hand the matter of either bringing him round or punishing him. I attended a meeting of the Liberation Society today and proposed that Fisher should be sent down to interview him and tell him that unless he voted for Welsh Disestb. [sic] the Liberationists in the constituency would be asked not to support him.

Acting independently and often with scant regard for party discipline, Welsh Liberal M.P.s pressed for legislation in Parliament. In fact, between 1870 and 1914 several attempts had been made either to pass motions or to

I

II

III

IV

V

VI

VII

VIII

IX

X

present Parliamentary bills on the subject of disestablishment but all but one, the last in 1914, were either withdrawn or defeated.

Table 22

Key Motions in Parliament for Disestablishment

1870	Watkin Williams, M.P. for Denbigh Boroughs
1886	Lewis Llewellyn Dillwyn, M.P. for Swansea
1889	Lewis Llewellyn Dillwyn, M.P. for Swansea
1891	Pritchard Morgan, M.P. for Merthyr Tydfil
1892	Samuel Smith, M.P. for Flintshire
1897	Samuel Smith, M.P. for Flintshire
1902	Wiliam Jones, M.P. for Arfon

Table 23

Parliamentary Bills on Disestablishment presented to Parliament

1892	Welsh Church Suspensory Bill (clarifying the assets of the church in Wales) – withdrawn
1894	Disestablishment Bill – withdrawn
1895	Disestablishment Bill – passed by 304 votes to 260 but delayed due to arguments over the 250 amendments proposed, 148 of which by Conservatives, before becoming law.
1909	Disestablishment Bill – withdrawn
1912-14	Disestablishment Bill – Passed in the Commons but defeated in the Lords. Returns to Commons where it is passed but its passage into law is delayed by the First World War.
1920	Welsh Church Act makes formal and legal the disestablishment of the Church in Wales.

This led to much bitterness and political in-fighting between Anglicans and Nonconformists, between Conservatives and Liberals and even among Liberals. A new breed of Welsh Liberal emerged during this period, men like Lloyd George and D.A. Thomas, who, on learning that the Disestablishment Bill was to be dropped from the legislative programme for 1894, took it upon themselves to lead a brief revolt against the party whip during April and May of that year. Some in the Liberal Party even blamed Lloyd George for the failure to secure disestablishment, for though he was passionately in favour of the cause he could hardly resist the temptation to add on other measures which would have widened considerably the scope of the act so as to include issues like education funding and control. It was in part his amendments to the bill, and Conservative opposition, that delayed its passing in the Commons and when it was ready to do so the Liberals lost the election. For ten years after 1895 the Conservative government, predictably, dropped the measure and disestablishment disappeared temporarily from the forefront of Parliamentary business.

Having stirred in the Welsh a greater sense of patriotism and national pride, the issue of Disestablishment became bound up in the developing sense of native nationalism that was sweeping the country. Due largely to the impassioned speeches of patriot politicians like Tom Ellis and Lloyd George and also as a result of the work of the Cymru Fydd movement, disestablishment and devolution moved ever closer on the Welsh Liberal party agenda. Unsurprisingly then, at the root of the Home Rule movement was the question of disestablishment and it was this issue more than any other, which inspired Welsh Liberal politicians to campaign for self-determination for only then they reasoned, would they achieve their aim. It is perhaps ironic that this campaign failed in respect of Home Rule but succeeded in that of Disestablishment. When Disestablishment was at last achieved it aroused little interest in the press which had relegated the issue to the back pages of its newspapers for it was no longer the newsworthy story it had been more than twenty years before.

e) Home Rule

Home Rule was a phenomenon not peculiar to Wales but was shared by Celtic nationalists in both Ireland and Scotland. The Irish were undoubtedly the most determined to seek Home Rule, if not outright independence. It was the struggle of the Irish nationalists, which stimulated and encouraged the much milder Welsh nationalists to plan a programme of their own. For much of the nineteenth century Welsh nationalism had simmered beneath the surface but it lacked drive and focus. Among the pioneers of Welsh separateness was the Independent minister from Llanuwchllyn Michael D. Jones who resented the oppression of 'Tory' landlords in Wales and came to detest the servility of his fellow-Welshmen. His vision of a self-governing

I
II
III
IV
V
VI
VII
VIII
IX
X

I

II

III

IV

V

VI

VII

VIII

IX

X

national entity where the Welsh could preserve and use their own language and traditions became the inspiration for later generations of well-educated and politically-powerful Welshmen. Indeed, the Welsh Colony of Patagonia, *Y Wladfa*, which he largely founded and financed in 1865, was regarded by many as the ideal blueprint for an independent Wales.

Inspired by radicalism and driven by the spirit of nationalism, patriotic, if largely political and Liberal, Welshmen had turned to seriously consider the merits of Home Rule for Wales. However, in truth few of them shared Michael D. Jones' vision of a politically-independent Wales free of all things English. Even fewer subscribed to his brand of aggressive nationalism. Welsh nationalism was nowhere near as extreme or as united as Irish nationalism and, for Liberal Welshmen at least, Home Rule was a means to an end and not an end in itself. Their concept of Home Rule was self-determination within an English imperial framework which, if achieved, would enable them to attain, in order of priority, Church disestablishment, land and education reform. The majority of Victorian Welshmen, it seems, did not want separatism, they did not want to be cut off from England but were seeking national equality within the British Isles. Yet when the first steps on the road to Home Rule were taken in 1886, with the formation of the Cymru Fydd movement, separatism was very much on the agenda.

Constitution and Rules of the 'Cymru Fydd Society' (1888)

1. That the main purpose of the 'Cymru Fydd Society' be to secure a National Legislature for Wales, dealing exclusively with Welsh affairs, while preserving the relations with the British Parliament upon all questions of Imperial interest.
2. That the Society shall assist in securing the return to the House of Commons of thoroughly representative men, who will in the meantime advocate Welsh reforms, in accordance with the National aspiration.
3. That the Society stimulate the Welsh Party to more united and energetic action with regard to Welsh reforms and the interests of Wales ...
4. That the Society shall exert its utmost efforts to establish like Societies within and without the Principality, and shall co-operate with other societies for the promotion of these objects.

Clearly, self-determination with a separate legislature for Wales were among the early aims of the movement but those on whose vision and idealism the success of Home Rule and Cymru Fydd relied soon waned.

Why did the movement fail?

- The exhausting experience of dealing with the daily realities of the complex British political system took their toll on the likes of Tom Ellis and Lloyd George. The wheels of government moved too slowly for those demanding action.
- The fundamental contradictions in the nature of Welsh nationalism took their toll on those whose vision and idealism were crucial for the success of the movement. The differences between urban/industrial English-speaking Wales and rural Welsh-speaking Wales were simply too great to bridge.
- There was no clear and consistently supported aim or vision. For some, Home Rule was an end in itself, for others it was merely a political device whereby issues such as Disestablishment or the Land Question could be resolved.
- There were violent disagreements between the leading sponsors of the Home Rule movement. The conflict between D.A. Thomas and Lloyd George all but killed the movement.
- The movement was too dependent on the Liberal party and on Liberal party politics. Welsh Liberals had to fight to keep Home Rule on the party agenda and only with the party in government could it have hoped to become a reality.
- There was little popular support for Home Rule in Wales, the people were simply not committed to it.
- The demise of Cymru Fydd denied the Home Rule movement an organisational base so when it died Home Rule died with it.

Although the Home Rule movement effectively came to an end after c. 1896 the idea for self-government did not completely die. Less than twenty years later a second Home Rule movement was begun by Edward Thomas John (d. 1933) who joined forces with the journalist and dramatist Beriah Gwynfe Evans (d. 1927) to promote the idea across Wales. However, the movement failed to rouse sufficient support either in Parliament or in Wales itself. Lloyd George offered little or no encouragement while John's fellow Welsh Liberals (he had been elected Liberal M.P. for East Denbighshire in 1910) were concerned that the Home Rule issue might divert attention away from their aim of securing a Parliamentary Bill on Disestablishment. John's sponsorship of a Home Rule Bill in 1914 failed miserably in the Commons and the issue of Welsh devolution was allowed to lapse.

Advice and Activities

(i) General

Suggested Further Reading

A.G. Jones, *Press, Politics and Society: A History of Journalism in Wales* (Cardiff, 1993).
K.O. Morgan, *Wales in British Politics 1868-1922* (3rd. edn., Cardiff, 1991).
C. Parry, *The Radical Tradition in Welsh Politics: A Study of Liberal and Labour Politics in Gwynedd, 1900-20* (Hull, 1970).

Articles:

T.I. Jeffreys-Jones, 'The Rise of Labour' in A.J. Roderick (ed.), *Wales through the Ages, vol. 2* (Llandybie, 1960).
I.G. Jones, 'Wales and Parliamentary Reform', in A.J. Roderick (ed.), *Wales through the Ages, vol. 2* (Llandybie, 1960).
G.O. Pierce, 'Nonconformity and Politics' in A.J. Roderick (ed.), *Wales through the Ages, vol. 2* (Llandybie, 1960).

Research

1. Look up the following key figures and write a short biographical sketch on each. Estimate the contribution each made to Welsh politics.
a) David Lloyd George
b) Thomas Edward Ellis
c) Keir Hardie
d) Thomas Gee

2. Look up the Parliamentary Reform Acts of 1832, 1867, 1884 and 1918. Assess how each contributed to widening the franchise and establishing greater democracy in England and Wales.

Issues for Debate

1. 'Nonconformity gave the impetus to all progressive movements in Wales during the 19th century.'

State a case **for** and **against** this statement.

Points for Discussion

1. Do you consider that the election of 1885 was far more important to the 'nonconformist middle-class' in Wales than that of 1868?
2. 'From radicalism to nationalism'. Is this an apt description of the trend of Welsh politics after 1868?
3. Could the Welsh Parliamentary Party in the 1880s and 1890s be justifiably called a 'national' party?

(ii) Examination Specific

Answering Structured Questions

Q.

a) **Explain briefly the rise of the Labour Party in Wales before 1915 (24 marks).**
b) **To what extent can Keir Hardie's victory in the Merthyr election of 1900 be attributed to the popularity of socialism? (36 marks).**

Advice

You need first to seek out and identify the key words. They are a) 'rise', and b) 'popularity' and 'socialism'. Once you have done this you should consider the following advice for each of the questions:

a) You should begin by outlining the rise of the Labour party from its foundation (as the ILP) in 1893 through to the death of Its leader Keir Hardie in 1915. You must show some awareness of the difference between the Labour movement (workers, trade unionism etc) and the Labour Parliamentary Party and be able to demonstrate how the one contributed to the development and rise to popularity of the other. Focus on the successive election victories of Keir Hardie in Merthyr after 1900 and detail the growth of grass roots support for the party – membership, location and number of branches – and the contribution industrial discontent made to the rise and popularity of Labour (especially the events of 1898).

b) Assess the nature of and support for socialism in Merthyr and explain why it contributed to Hardie's election victory – strong working class

ethic in Merthyr, centre of radicalism, trade unionism and industrial unrest – taking care to qualify your answer, noting that these need not indicate support for or belief in socialism – socialism was a new form of radicalism. You must deal with the key word 'popularity' – was this the only or most important factor? – NO. You must consider other factors such as the Liberal Party split – the hatred of the two Liberal candidates (D.A. Thomas and P. Morgan) for each other, the Boer War and its unpopularity with the electorate (Hardie anti-war/Morgan pro-war), the strong pacifist tradition of the area since Henry Richard's day, and Hardie's personal reputation.

Answering Synoptic Essay Questions

Look at the following example

Q.

'In 1815 only the privileged few had the vote but by 1918 almost the entire population of England and Wales had been enfranchised'. Had an electoral democracy been achieved in Wales and England by 1918?

Advice

The key words are 'electoral democracy' and 'achieved'. This question requires you to evaluate and analyse the electoral system between 1815 and 1918 before deciding whether an electoral 'democracy' had been achieved by 1918. Electoral democracy will need some explanation/definition. You should focus on the voting system (Ballot Act 1872), the extent of the franchise, the powers of the House of Lords, the regularity of general elections, the qualifications of and payments to MPs, the status of women and the effects of the Parliamentary Reform Acts of 1832, 1867, 1884 and 1918. You must try to avoid a list-like approach to your essay answer but treat each as a distinct issue within a structured format. You are likely to conclude that the political map of England and Wales had been quite radically changed by 1918 and that an electoral democracy had indeed been established.

Chapter IX

The Great Labour Unrest: Social and Industrial Discontent, 1895-1914

1. The Roots of Industrial Conflict

■ Key Issue:

What was the cause and nature of the social and industrial discontent in Wales in the period 1895-1914?

To the captains of industry, the employers and owners, the period before the Great War truly was a golden age of Welsh heavy industry. New technology, the availability of capital, the opening up of new world markets and the business expertise of men like Lord Penrhyn, the Slate Magnate and D.A. Thomas the Coal King, ensured that Welsh industry remained competitive and profitable. For the ordinary manual labourer the new century brought little change or relief from the generally low wages, poor and unhealthy working conditions and exploitation by their employers. For the mass of the workforce there was no golden age of Welsh heavy industry. Their hard work merely ensured that the *gold* remained in the hands of a select few. In his book *What We Want and Why*, published in 1922, Noah Ablett recalled his days before the war as a face worker in the mines.

> The hewer down in the mine away from the sunlight and fresh air, sometimes in a temperature up to 90 deg., every moment of the day inhaling coal and shale dust, perspiring so abnormally as few men in other industries can realise; head throbbing with the almost inhuman exertion [effort]; the roof perhaps 18 inches low, perhaps 20 feet high ..... breathing always noxious [unhealthy] smells due to the absence of any kind of sanitation .... liable

5

always to wounds and death from falls of roof and sides and over all the sickening dread of the awful explosion; such a man is entitled to our sympathy and our respect – but what he frequently gets – is abuse.

Whereas the majority of the working class had come to accept the social inequality, or so it seemed from their general apathy, even accepting their often harsh treatment at the hands of unsympathetic employers, they were becoming less prepared to suffer wage cuts and damaged livelihoods. This put pressure on men like William Abraham (Mabon) who represented a more traditional and conservative approach to industrial relations. He was a Liberal and a moderate miners' leader who believed in a policy of co-operation with owner-employers. However, by the last decade of the nineteenth century the industrial landscape was changing rapidly and the growth of the Labour movement was the result of the growth of the Trade Unions which in turn led to greater industrial militancy. Men like the Rhondda-born **Marxist** miners' leader Noah Ablett determined to seek better pay and working conditions and because of this he became a leading member of the South Wales Miners' Federation and soon a bitter opponent of D.A. Thomas. For the Trade Unions and their members the period before the Great War was anything but a golden age, it was rather an age of industrial unrest.

(i) What were the steps to industrial conflict?

The roots of that unrest may be traced to the last decade of the nineteenth century when industrial relations took a turn for the worse. Why?

- growth of combinations and cartels. For example, the founding of the Coalowners Association in 1873 and the amalgamation (joining) of several coal companies to form large combines – Powell Duffryn, Lewis Merthyr, the Ocean Company and and D.A. Thomas' Cambrian Combine – ensured that power in the south Wales coalfield would be concentrated in the hands of a few. These few became wealthy and more remote from their workers. They became less tolerant and understanding and their power meant that they could manipulate wages and prices almost at will.

- cost-conscious owners and employers. To increase profits employers cut costs which often led to cuts in the workforce and/or wages or even cuts in safety measures. The pit explosion at the Albion colliery in Cilfynydd in 1894 in which 250 miners were killed was blamed partly on the coalowners' refusal to cover the cost of expensive safety improvements.

- attempts by employers to rationalise the wage and price systems. To keep costs to a minimum the coal industry had operated (since 1875) a system called the sliding scale which linked wages to the selling price of coal. A change of 1s. (5p) in the price of coal would cause the average wage to change by up to 8%. Employers could control wages by over-producing or under-selling their coal.

- growth of trade unionism and working-class militancy. Workers were demanding stable and secure employment and the right to bargain with employers for a decent living wage. The unions were determined to secure a minimum wage and, in the coal industry, the end of the sliding scale.

- ideological and class differences between employers and employees. Wealthy employers like Lord Penrhyn refused to recognise his workers' trade union, let alone negotiate with it. As owner of slate quarries which lay on his land, he believed he had the right to dismiss men at will and cut their wages when the price of slate fell. Neither side could understand or fully appreciate the lifestyle or thinking of the other.

- international competition particularly from Germany and the USA. For example, the McKinley tariff of 1891, which imposed a high tax on all tinplate imports from Britain, led eventually to the collapse of the British tinplate industry. To remain competitive some plants were closed, wages were cut and some workers made redundant. By 1914 the coal, steel and slate industries were also suffering from intense foreign competition.

(ii) Was conflict inevitable?

Judge for yourself by reading carefully the following extracts which concentrate on attitudes and industrial relations in the pre-war coal industry.

Historian David Egan offers his opinion in his book *Coal Society* (1987).

> The public works of the Coalowners also involved them in acting as Justices of the Peace, Poor Law Guardians, Councillors and sometimes as M.P.'s ... The Coalowners were confident that they had the support and affection of their workers ... The story is told of how [Lewis Davies] gave money to one of his workmen who could no longer work because of illness. (Of) David   5
> Davies inviting 6,000 guests (to his son's 21st birthday) 3,400 of them were brought on four special trains from Davies' pits in the Upper Rhondda ...[yet] such a lavish use of their wealth was a fairly rare incident for the Coalowners ... Their lifestyle was becoming different to that of their workers. There was nothing unusual at the time in a strict dividing line between 'master' and   10
> 'workman'. But the Coalowners do seem to have been particularly hard employers ... Miners were treated almost as products than as human beings... They often blamed gas explosions on workers smoking their pipes. They always fought hard against paying compensation for deaths and injuries ...They were always ready to bring miners to court for breaches of contract   15
> and Colliery Rules ... For many years the 'discharge-note' was a powerful weapon used against trade unions as were large numbers of blacklegs to break a strike.

D.A. Thomas was a highly successful businessman and Liberal M.P. By the beginning of the Great War he was among the richest and most influential of the industrial 'kings' of Wales. Thomas wrote the following;

> I have provided men with the means to pay for the food and clothing of themselves and their families .... By increasing the means of the people I have contributed more to the material happiness and wellbeing of Welsh colliery workers and their families than have all the miners leaders combined .... Believe me, I am not out for the accumulation of wealth for its own sake....The only value of wealth is the influence and power it places in the hands of its possessor to do good.

W.F. Hay was a prominent socialist and militant miners' leader from the Rhondda. Hay expressed his views thus;

> The Welsh collier, defeated in many a bitter conflict to obtain human conditions; cheated in his work by unscrupulous managers speeded up by an iniquitious system of piece-work; ... thrown on the road and black-listed for demanding simple justice; ... murdered by the hundred and thousand through the neglect of elementary precautions; cheated by judge-made law from the scanty 'compensation' for the 'accidents' which greed of profit made inevitable; the victim of a thousand extortions and villainies – this grim slave of the lamp can hold this British Empre to ransom ...

(iii) The Miners' Strike of 1898. A turning point?

Between 1891 and 1899 wage rates for miners in the south Wales coalfield steadily declined. In 1896, 30,000 miners peacefully petitioned their employers to abolish the sliding scale. The coalowners refused. In January 1898 moderate miners' leaders Mabon (William Abraham) and William Brace tried to negotiate and reason with the coalowners who agreed to meet them for discussions but made no promises. As negotiations dragged on Mabon and Brace lost their credibility and more militant miners' leaders took the lead. The militants attempted to pressurise the coalowners into making concessions by demanding a basic wage, a 10% wage increase and an end to the sliding scale or else they would strike. The coalowners retaliated by suspending negotiations and locking-out their employees, the miners responded by carrying out their threat to strike. The strike lasted six months from March 1898 during which time the strikers and their families suffered great hardship. By the end of it a hungry, angry and dispirited workforce returned to the mines having won nothing, but determined never to forget. In October 1898 the South Wales Miners' Federation was formed in which all the local mining unions joined together to form one powerful organisation. In January 1899 the SWMF agreed to affiliate (join) the Miners' Federation of Great Britain and by 1908 over 144,000 south Wales miners (more than 70% of the total workforce) were members of the union.

I

II

III

IV

V

VI

VII

VIII

IX

X

2. The Taff Vale Railway Strike, 1900-01

■ **Key Issue:**
In what ways was the Taff Vale Dispute a landmark in industrial relations in Wales?

- When the directors of the Taff Vale Railway Company in south Wales refused to discuss the issues of long hours and unfair pay scales, the railwaymen's union the Amalgamated Society of Railway Servants (ASRS) called its members out on strike. Having won a similar strike back in 1890 the then newly-founded ASRS was confident of victory.
- The Taff Vale Company tried to keep the trains running by using **blackleg labour**. Violence broke out, damage was done to Company property and the dispute lasted some months. Through poverty and hunger the railwaymen were forced to submit and go back to work.
- The Company was determined to smash the union and it took the ASRS to court demanding damages for losses suffered during the strike.
- The Company won the court case but the union appealed against the decision and won. The Company then took the case to the highest court of law in the land, the House of Lords.
- Unfortunately for the union, the Lords found in favour of the employer and reversed the Court of Appeal's decision. Trade unionists throughout the country rose up and condemned what came to be called the Taff Vale Judgement. The union was forced to pay the Company the massive sum of £42,000 in compensation and legal costs.
- Despite the court's ruling, which put in jeopardy the very right to strike, the railwaymen were not dissuaded from further militant action, if anything it spurred them on, they and their fellow trade unionists, to fight what they believed was gross injustice.

The Taff Vale Dispute of 1901 was an event of enormous importance in the growth and development of both the Labour Party and the Trade Unions. It convinced many workers that some form of union protection from such greedy and untrustworthy employers was essential. It convinced the unions that they needed representation in Parliament in order to influence the passing or stopping of laws which might affect trade unionism and workers' rights. The Labour party took advantage of the bitterness caused by the

Taff Vale Judgement to press its claim to be the party to represent the workers in government. Its promise to do all it could to have the court's judgement reversed caused its membership to leap from 356,000 in 1901 to 861,000 by the end of 1902. In 1903 a worried Liberal party formed an alliance with the growing Labour party in order to fight the Conservatives at the next election. The price of Labour support in the election was the Trade Disputes Act of 1906. It said that in future no court cases could be brought against an union in the event of a damaging strike. This protected workers' right to strike and restored the industrial power of the unions. Unfortunately it did not signal an end to confrontation between unions and employers and management and workers. Socialism and socialist ideas had gained ground and increasingly moderate union leaders were being replaced by activists and militants.

3. The Penrhyn Lock-Out, 1900-03

■ **Key Issue:**
Why were the men locked out of the slate quarries of Lord Penrhyn in North Wales?

The slate industry dominated north-west Wales which was more rural than industrial in character. The largest, richest and most important of the Caernarfonshire slate quarries, Penrhyn in Bethesda, was owned by the Douglas-Pennants or Lords Penrhyn. The Penrhyn family were originally landowners who turned to exploiting the mineral rather than just the agricultural wealth of their vast estates (by 1890 the third largest in Wales) and in so doing became one of the most powerful industrialists in Wales. By 1898 the family's annual income from slate, £133,000, was more than double what they earned from their rents and from farming. However, all was not right in the quarries and between 1896 and 1903 there occurred two bitter and damaging strikes (September 1896 to August 1897 and November 1900 to November 1903) which fatally wounded and ultimately destroyed the north Wales slate industry. Why?

I

II

III

IV

V

VI

VII

VIII

IX

X

313

What caused the dispute and why was there so much bitterness?

Published within days of the outbreak of the strike an English local newspaper, the *Sheffield and Rotherham Independent* (29 November 1900), had no doubt what it thought had contributed to the dispute.

> [It is] a conflict between a man (Lord Penrhyn) who possesses absolutely feudal notions of his rights over his employees, and a number of men who resist him stubbornly but without method ... [The dispute] seems to be the kind that could be settled in a few hours by conference between reasonable employers and properly qualified Trade Union delegates.

The fact that a strike in a north Wales quarry was newsworthy enough to attract the attention of a Yorkshire-based newspaper suggests that this was no ordinary dispute. As soon as the strike vote was made known to him Lord Penrhyn did not wait for his employees to walk out he locked them out instead. Attempts by the quarrymen's union to meet and negotiate with Penrhyn failed. In a book on the dispute published in October 1901, entitled *The Penrhyn Lock-Out, 1900-01*, W.J. Parry outlined what he considered to be at the root of the strike and lock-out.

> The immediate cause of the outbreak ... was ... a system of big contracts, let to one man ... which in the opinion of the men, was a great injustice to a large class of workers. An inferior class of workmen took these contracts, and engaged a superior class of men to work under at reduced prices. In October last 14 men were engaged on a part of *Fridd Ponc*; two of the men were   5
> placed to do a certain job by the day; they were engaged on Thursday and Friday, and had not finished ... The men did not work on the Sunday, and the 14 were suspended for three days. In about a fortnight [they] were informed that they ... were to be distributed to various parts of the quarry, and in the meantime all their bargains were let in one contract to one of the big   10
> contractors, against whom there had been a growing enmity ... on the 18th of December, 1900 ... the deputation ... asked Mr. Young for the following concessions
> 1. The right freely to elect spokesmen ... to discuss grievances with the management ...   15
> 2. The right of the men during the dinner hour to discuss matters among themselves in the quarry.
> 3. The reinstatement of certain victimised leaders.
> 4. The establishment of a minimum wage.
> 5. The punishment of unjustifiable conduct on the part of foremen and   20
> officials towards the men.

6. The introduction, experimentally of a system of co-operative piece-work in place of work hitherto done under contract.
7. The humanising of the harsh rules of discipline, and the reduction of the punishments for breaches of them.
8. The reintroduction of the annual holiday on May 1st.
9. More democratic control of the Quarry Sick Club.

25

It was not long before anger and bitterness turned to violence. When Penrhyn attempted to re-open his quarry with casual or blackleg labour, his employees picketed the site. The scene was described in a report by E.A. Young, Senior Manager at the Penrhyn Quarry (6 March 1901).

> Eight days afterwards another contractor and his two sons were brutally attacked in the quarry by several hundred of the fellow-workmen. On the same day another mob of workmen hunted for several of the officials ... The same evening the workmen held a mass meeting, at which they passed a resolution to return to work again on the following morning ... although the majority of men had started work at the usual time ... they were prevented and intimidated from doing so, by numbers of men who gathered about in groups in various parts of the quarry.

5

Although some quarrymen men had returned to work the majority remained on strike. Penrhyn responded to their picketing and intimidation by sacking them all. Extra police were drafted in from Liverpool and at one stage armed troops were sent to break up rioting quarrymen. Being a wealthy man he could afford not to rely on the profits of his quarries and his determination to win was such that he was prepared to ruin the industry and see the end of quarrymaking in north Wales. His former employees did not have that luxury and for many of them the months without work and without pay pushed them ever deeper into poverty and despair. The fact that the strike and lock-out had occurred in the depths of winter made matters worse and by Christmas 1900 a committee for the relief of the unemployed quarrymen and their families was set up. By February 1901 the situation was becoming desperate and the following appeal for aid was made.

> We make an appeal on behalf of Old men, Widows, and Orphans who are already suffering great hardships in consequence of the Lock-Out. We who are on the spot, and are sufferers ourselves, know full well the justice of the men's cause, and the oppression they have suffered ever since the present

I

II

III

IV

V

VI

VII

VIII

IX

X

Lord Penrhyn came into possession. The good feeling that existed between his   5
late noble father and his workmen was destroyed at a stroke by the present
lord within three months of his coming into the property, and all his dealings
with them ever since have been tyrannical. He terminated at a month's notice
the conditions under which they worked with his noble father ... He did all
this without consulting the wishes of the men to whom it was of vital   10
importance. He has by his actions endeavoured to create ill-feeling in the
quarry between Unionist and Non-Unionist workmen.

On behalf of the Relief Committee,
W.J. Parry, Chairman
G. Roberts, JP, Vice-Chairman,
Daniel Lloyd, Treasurer
Rev. W.W. Lloyd, General Secretary (6 February, 1901).

'You can't face your creditors? Then walk backward' said an English under-
manager to a Penrhyn quarryman in distress. This hard-faced attitude and
the fact that Penrhyn and his management team were Englishmen turned
the majority of the local Welsh-speaking, chapel-going community against
him. Clerics, magistrates, shopkeepers, businessmen, even politicians,
were united in their support of the quarrymen. One of those who used his
legal and political expertise and connections to help them was the Liberal
M.P. for Caernarfon Boroughs, David Lloyd George. In a letter to his wife,
dated 22 March 1902, he wrote

I wish you would ask D.R. Daniel [secretary of the North Wales Quarrymen's
Union from 1896] to spend *y Pasg* and to discuss the Penrhyn business at
some time. What a vindictive speech Lord Penrhyn delivered the other day.
The strike must, so I am told, have cost him over £120,000 already. he took
his son to the quarry so as to warn them they would gain nothing by killing
him. It is one of the most desparate [*sic*] strikes on record.

After three long years the dispute finally ended in defeat for the quarrymen.
When the Penrhyn quarry re-opened less than two thirds of the strikers
were taken back. This was due partly to management's refusal to re-employ
'trouble makers' but mainly on account of the collapse in the market for
Welsh slate.

Examining the evidence: Lord Penrhyn – villain or victim?

The key figure in the dispute was undoubtedly the employer Lord Penrhyn. Much has been made about his arrogance and his refusal to recognise the Quarrymen's Union let alone discuss his worker's pay and conditions. On the other hand, he has been described as a kindly, thoughtful and concerned employer. Who is right? Here are some historians' opinions on 'Baron Penrhyn' and 'the dispute'. Read them and re-read the sources above and judge for yourselves.

> They [the quarrymen] formed an union in 1874. This met with persistent opposition from Lord Penrhyn, and when the workers at Bethesda submitted certain greviances to him ... he suspended their representatives from work. Three thousand quarrymen immediately came out on strike. They asked the Board of Trade to arbitrate (referee), but Lord Penrhyn insisted on impossible conditions before he would accept the intervention of government officials ...
> [David Williams, *A History of Modern Wales* (1950)]

> The resolutely respectable quarrymen of the north had a desperate struggle to get their union recognised at all by the politically neanderthal Baron Penrhyn and had to fight their way forward against ice-age opposition from a colonial mind.
>
> [Gwyn A. Williams, *When was Wales* (1982)]

> [Such] men were capitalists ... *par excellence*, owning the quarries, the land on which the houses of their workers were built and the means of communication. They wielded vast eceonomic power and clung to it ruthlessly, but they were also paternalists who maintained hospitals and controlled sickness benefit funds.
>
> [Gareth E. Jones, *Modern Wales* (1979)]

> Though one of the most generous landlords in the country, he [Lord Penrhyn] was in continual controversy with the quarrymen of Bethesda.
> [Thomas Richards, *Dictionary of Welsh Biography* (1959)]

> In [1886] the succession of a new Lord Penrhyn bent on smashing the quarrymen's union led to a stoppage of nearly a year in 1896-7, and in 1900 a second which, with help from outside sympathisers, was kept going for three years.
>
> [A.H. Dodd, *Life in Wales* (1972)]

I

II

III

IV

V

VI

VII

VIII

IX

X

317

The dispute arose ... from the way in which the second Baron Penrhyn interpreted his rights as an employer. The Penrhyn family, with its schools and its hospital, were paternalistic employers, but in return they expected obedience and submissiveness.

[John Davies, *A History of Wales* (1993)]

Fig. 43
Penrhyn Quarry Notice

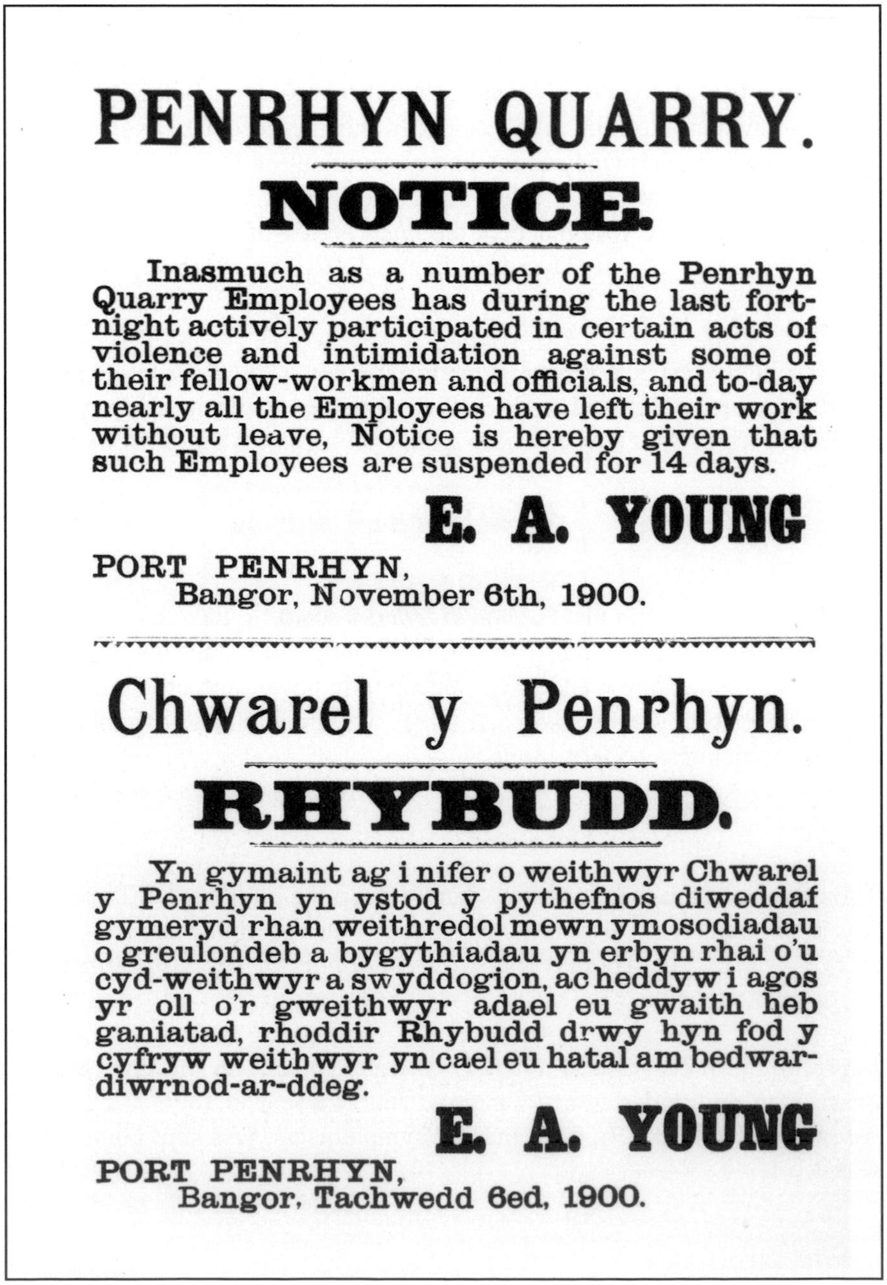

PENRHYN QUARRY.
NOTICE.

Inasmuch as a number of the Penrhyn Quarry Employees has during the last fort-night actively participated in certain acts of violence and intimidation against some of their fellow-workmen and officials, and to-day nearly all the Employees have left their work without leave, Notice is hereby given that such Employees are suspended for 14 days.

E. A. YOUNG

PORT PENRHYN,
Bangor, November 6th, 1900.

Chwarel y Penrhyn.
RHYBUDD.

Yn gymaint ag i nifer o weithwyr Chwarel y Penrhyn yn ystod y pythefnos diweddaf gymeryd rhan weithredol mewn ymosodiadau o greulondeb a bygythiadau yn erbyn rhai o'u cyd-weithwyr a swyddogion, ac heddyw i agos yr oll o'r gweithwyr adael eu gwaith heb ganiatad, rhoddir Rhybudd drwy hyn fod y cyfryw weithwyr yn cael eu hatal am bedwar-diwrnod-ar-ddeg.

E. A. YOUNG

PORT PENRHYN,
Bangor, Tachwedd 6ed, 1900.

4. Strikes and Riots

■ Key Issue:

Why were the strikes and riots of early twentieth-century Wales so violent and dangerous?

By 1910 industrial unrest was rife in Britain. The first area to be hit by strikes and stoppages was south Wales. During October and November 1910 nearly 30,000 Welsh miners went on strike in search of secure and safer employment and higher wages. Coal owners like D.A. Thomas attempted to break the strike by bringing in blackleg labour, this led to violence and the army was called in to restore order. The strike lasted eight months after which the defeated miners returned to work. Elsewhere in south Wales workers from other industries took to the streets either in sympathy with the miners or in protest at their own treatment at the hands of their employers. By 1911 the trade unions were directing much of their anger towards the government, which they accused of being repressive and anti-union, and, in particular, against Winston Churchill, the Home Secretary, whom they blamed for making matters worse by sending in troops.

a) The Tonypandy Riots

On 7 and 8 November 1910 the village of Tonypandy in the Rhondda was the scene of a riot by striking miners. Although there were riots elsewhere in south Wales during 1910-11, at Aberdare, Pontypridd and especially Llanelli where two striking railwaymen were shot dead by troops, it is the riot at Tonypandy that is best remembered today. The reasons why are many and varied. To socialists it became a legend in the history of the Labour movement in Wales, the spark that set the cause of industrial reform alight in the valleys. To others Tonypandy represents the tyranny of an English government who used British soldiers armed with rifles and bayonets against unarmed miners in search of decent wages and working conditions. Still more saw it as mob rule by greedy and unlawful thugs out to cause havoc. The truth of what happened at Tonypandy is still debated today.

Examining the evidence: The Tonypandy Riots

What caused the Tonypandy riots?

Read the views of two people who were there.

In 1948 Merthyr-born Arthur Horner, then a leading member of the miners' union but a seventeen year old youth new to the industry in 1910, was interviewed and asked to recall the cause of the so-called Tonypandy riots.

The Tonypandy incident followed the strike of 15,000 men employed in the Cambrian group of pits against the scandalous piece work rates imposed on the men at the coal face. The rate varied from district to district and even from mine to mine, but the biggest grievance arose because a man would find himself unable to get enough coal even to produce the miserable subsistence   5
wage. He might be assigned to a place where the seam wall was crushed into small coal, which in South Wales at that time was not paid for at all, he might have to put in exceptional timbering to prevent dangerous falls, and the management, knowing that he was not getting good coal, would not keep him supplied with enough trams to take away what he had hewed (cut) so that   10
whatever skill or hard work the man put in, he could still find himself with practically no earnings at all. In some of the pits the men used to cast lots for place. The men at that time were demanding a prescribed minimum of daily earnings for all piece workers, and with the resistance of the coal owners these flared up into disputes all over the Aberdare and Rhondda valleys   15

At the end of 1911 David Evans, a local journalist, published a book, *Labour Strife in the South Wales Coalfield 1910-11*, in which he explains what caused the riots.

The strikers had taken umbrage at the action of certain workmen in accepting employment at the pits of the Naval Company and marched in procession 3,000 strong... One of the leaders addressed the strikers. He complained that they had been refused permission to see the blacklegs, and had been advised to see Mr. Llywellyn [the mine manager]. But they had had enough of   5
deputations, and were determined to remain there and have an understanding with the blacklegs when they came out. By this time, a large proportion of the strikers had got completely out of hand ... stone throwing became general, and urgent messages were sent to the police headquarters at Tonypandy for reinforcements ... This force arrived at the Ely colliery soon after ... and   10
brought the total number of police to over a 100. Against between 3,000 and 4,000 desperate rioters spread out along the mountainside, well out of the reach of the police and employed in rolling down huge boulders in the direction of the colliery, the police force was hopelessly inadequate, and it became necessary to call in the aid of the military.   15

Why were the troops sent in to Tonypandy and who was responsible for deploying them?

One of the most controversial aspects of the Tonypandy riots was the use of troops in quelling the disturbances. Although troops had been used before by anxious British governments – Merthyr Tydfil in 1831, Newport in 1839 and south-west Wales between1839-44 – it was usually regarded as a last resort by reluctant ministers. This did not seem to be the case in 1910 and the question most frequently asked is why were they used at all? The following sources may help us to better understand the events surrounding the riots and the motives of those involved.

An extract from Arthur Horner's autobiography *Incorrigible Rebel* (1960).

> When I reached Tonypandy the rioting had been going on all through the night. All the shop fronts were smashed. It has begun after the owners had attempted..... to bring blackleg labour to man [the] colliery. I saw in action that day the vicious alliance of the government and the coal owners backed by police and armed troops, against miners who asked no more than a wage little over starvation level. I never forgot that lesson.

An extract from David Evans' book *Labour Strife in the South Wales Coalfield 1910-11* (1911)

> In their flight from Llwynypia, and under the impression that the victorious police were still at their heels, the rioters, desperate at the defeat of their plans to take the colliery, gave vent to their rage by smashing the windows of every shop that came within reach.

Interview with Metropolitan Police Officer W. Knipe (December 1910)

> Yes, ... they were trying ... to wreck the colliery premises. Well this went on for some hours, the same thing went on again the next day, in the afternoon and again in the night. Then on the third night it was really hell. We had a terrible job there, driving them back to the Square, well we only could get them as far as the Square. On that night ... they wrecked all the shops and buildings there. One shop in particular they skint out, that was Mr. T.P. Jenkins' shop, the draper's shop. And the whole of the time we could do nothing about it. They drove us back every time.

5

I
II
III
IV
V
VI
VII
VIII
IX
X

321

I

II

III

IV

V

VI

VII

VIII

IX

X

Mrs. Phillips, Draper, reported the following in an industry magazine *Draper's Record*, 19 November 1910)

> People were seen inside the counter handing goods out. They were afterwards walking in the Square wearing articles of clothing which had been stolen ... They were not a bit ashamed ... and the women were as bad as the men.

General Macready, officer commanding the troops in the Rhondda, recalls the riots in his book, *Annals of an Active Life* (1924)

> Investigations on the spot convinced me that the original reports regarding the attacks on the mines on November 8th had been exaggerated [by the police]. What were described as 'desperate attempts' to sack the [colliery] at Llwynypia proved to have been an attempt to force the gateway.... and a good deal of stone throwing.

Telegram from Mr. Lindsay, Chief Constable of Glamorgan, to Winston Churchill at the Home Office (10 a.m., 8 November 1910).

> All the Cambrian collieries menaced last night. The Llwynypia Colliery savagely attacked by a large crowd of strikers. Many casualties on both sides. Am expecting two companies of infantry and 200 cavalry today.... Position grave.

Telegram from Churchill to the Chief Constable, Mr. Lindsay (1.30 p.m., 8 November 1910)

> Your request for military. Infantry should not be used till all other means have failed. Following arrangements have therefore been made. 10 mounted constables and 200 foot constables of Metropolitan Police will come to Pontypridd by special train. Expect those forces sufficient, but as a further percautionary measure 200 cavalry will be moved into the district tonight. General Macready will command the military ... [who] .... will not however be available unless it is clear that the police reinforcements are unable to cope with the situation.

5

Telegram from Churchill to Gen. Macready (8.10 p.m., 8 November 1910).

As the situation appears to have become more serious you should, if the Chief Constable.... desires it, move all cavalry into the disturbed district without delay.

Telegram from Lleufer Thomas, Stipendiary magistrate to Winston Churchill at the Home Office (approx. 5.30 p.m. 8 November 1910).

Police cannot cope with the rioters at Llwynypia, Rhondda valley. Troops at Cardiff absolutely necessary for further protection. Will you order them to proceed forthwith.

Fig. 44
Scene at Tonypandy after the Riots. [Tonypandy] looked like a besieged area in wartime'. [Keir Hardie, MP for Merthyr]

I
II
III
IV
V
VI
VII
VIII
IX
X

DANGEROUS DISEASES NEED DRASTIC REMEDIES.

Fig. 45
Western Mail cartoon 'Dangerous diseases and drastic remedies'
(9 November 1910)

IN THE COMMONS AND OUT OF IT.

Fig. 46
Cartoons by J.M. Staniforth attacking
(i) Keir Hardie's defence of the
Tonypandy Rioters; (ii) the reputation
of the rioting miners (1910)

HIS OWN REPUTATION.

Winston Churchill speaking in Cardiff on a general election campaign tour (1950).

When I was Home Secretary in 1910, I had a great horror and fear of having to become responsible for the military firing on a crowd of rioters or strikers. I was always in sympathy with the miners and I think they are entitled to social dues ..... The Chief Constable of Glamorgan sent a request for the ....
5   military and troops... But here I .... stopped the ... troops and I sent instead 850 Metropolitan police with the sole object of preventing loss of life. The troops were kept in the background and all contact with the rioters was made by our trusted and unarmed London police who charged, not with rifles and bayonets, but with their rolled up mackintoshes. Thus all bloodshed ..... was
10   averted. That is the true story of Tonypandy and I hope it may replace in Welsh villages the cruel lie which they have been fed all these long years.

b) The Llanelli Riots

In 1911 the newly formed National Union of Railwaymen (NUR) called its members out on strike, troops were again called into action in south Wales and in one incident in the town of Llanelli two strikers were shot dead. Although some employers were prepared to give in to the demands of its workers to settle disputes, others, supported by the government, refused. The sources below provide an insight into the events surrounding the riots.

Examining the evidence

A

The first thing that struck me was the filthy roads, the unhealthy smoke and a tram pulled by a horse ... There was no escaping the smoke because all the steel, tinplate and other works were planted in the centre of the place and houses built disorderly around them. Oh such ugly disorder ...
    [A description of Llanelli from *Llais Llafur*, a radical socialist publication,
                                                                    September 1907]

B

Women joined with boys, men joined with both in this wholesale looting which continued for hours ... without interuption. Women seized on articles of clothing, and to ensure getting into their homes with their newly acquired finery, took off some of the clothes they were wearing and attired themselves in the new ones on the spot.
                                                [*South Wales Daily News*, 21 August 1911]

325

C

The Llanelly rioters, left to themselves, with no intrusion from the police and no assistance from the military for some hours, in a few streets of the town in the evening, wrought in their drunken frenzy more havoc to life and limb, shed more blood, produced more serious injury among themselves, than all the 50,000 soldiers who have been employed on strike duty all over the country during the last few days.

> [W.S. Churchill, Home Secretary, Parliamentary Debates (House of Commons), 22 August 1911]

D

The majority of the people of Llanelly are responsible members of society but that does not alter the fact that there is a large rowdy element which is a public danger ... It is undoubtedly a fact that there are enough hooligans in Llanelly to dominate the town.

There are women in Llanelly whose conduct bears a striking resemblance to that of the 'petroleuses' (women rioters) of the French Revolution ... If the Germans occupied Llanelly in the course of a war, then the town would not suffer as much at their hands, as it has done at the hands of the Llanelly people...

> [*Carmarthen Weekly Reporter*, 25 August 1911]

E

Myself and my wife were out shopping. When we were by the gates of the level crossing I found the ham close by the trucks and the boots as well which were lying there ...

> [From a Statement in his own defence by William Trimming, a rioter, Carmarthen Quarter Sessions Papers, August 1911]

F

Fig. 47 *Llanelli County Guardian*: smashed railway carriages at Llanelli station during the strike, 1911

G

Fig. 48   Workers' banner linking the 1911 disturbances and death to previous events (1911)

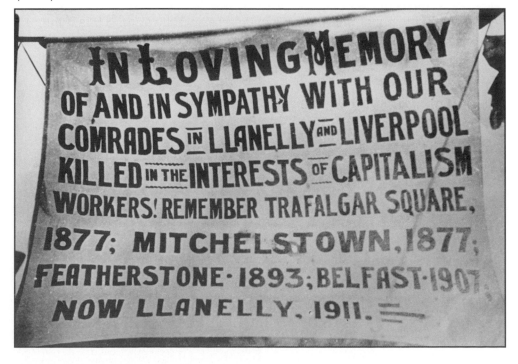

c) The Miners' Next Step and the Triple Alliance, 1912

The events at Tonypandy, Llanelli and elsewhere in south Wales convinced many in the Miners' Federation that the only solution to the plight of the workers was if the various trade unions combined to take on the might of the nations' employers, and the government if need be. More than that, radical unionists were preaching the doctrine known as **syndicalism** (taken from the French word 'syndic' or union) which called for profit sharing for workers, greater worker participation in decision-making and worker' control of industrial production. This was too revolutionary for the government and the country's employers who feared a workers' revolution. In 1912 the Syndicalist message was published by Noah Ablett in a pamphlet entitled *The Miners' Next Step* in which he outlined what his own union, the SWMF, and other unions should do to achieve their aim. Although the more radical proposals put forward by Ablett were never carried through, the pamphlet proved very influential and provided a blueprint for action and within a few months of its publication that is what happened. In 1912 the Miners' Federation organised the biggest strike in its history when over one million of its members came out in support of a minimum wage. Soon the dockers of the National Transport Workers Federation (NTWF) and railwaymen of the NUR followed suit and this *triple alliance* of powerful unions brought the country to a standstill. The strike ended when the government gave way and reluctantly agreed to a minimum wage.

Fig. 49
Title page of The Miners' next Step

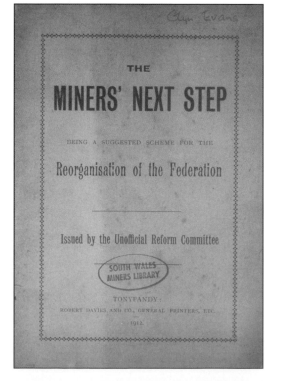

It has been said that had the Great War not happened when it did in 1914 the industrial unrest might have continued and become ever more bitter. Although during the war both government and unions worked well together, that spirit of friendliness soon disappeared with the war's end in 1918. However, there were exceptions. The miners of south Wales and the shipworkers of the Clyde in Scotland continued to strike periodically during the war. The British press called them traitors for betraying their country in its hour of need. They preferred to think of themselves as heroes fighting their own 'industrial' war for the rights of their workers. In 1918 the war for Britain's soldiers came to an end and they returned home victorious but, as the following strike bulletin issued by the NUR (12 April 1921) shows clearly, the 'war' for Britain's workers, temporarily suspended during hostilities, resumed with a vengeance.

> THE ISSUE – YOUR FELLOW WORKER'S FIGHT IS YOUR FIGHT.
> The Ruling Class have decided that now is the time to reduce the Working Class to conditions worse than pre-war. They have attacked the miners first believing that the miners hold the weakest sector of the working-class front ... defeat for the miners now means sure and certain defeat for ouserlves ... the whole forces of Capitalism are linked together in a desperate effort – let us hope a dying effort – to reduce the workers to a stage of industrial slavery.
> ... our Masters' voice – the Press of the country – has been running up and down the scales, improvising on the general theme, 'Wages must come down', or 'production must be increased'. Here and there, notably by the lock-out of the ship-joiners, we could discern the germ of future action. Press, pulpit, platform, theatre and cinema – every stage of Capital – has worked hard to swell the strain. Today we railwaymen have ceased work in order that we may line up with our fellow workers the miners, who have been brutally locked-out by the mine-owning section of the ruling-class.

I

II

III

IV

V

VI

VII

VIII

IX

X

Advice and Activities

(i) General

Suggested Further Reading.

G. Baber and L.J. Williams (eds.), Modern South Wales, *Essays in Economic History* (Cardiff, 1986).

E.W. Evans, *The Miners of South Wales* (Cardiff, 1961).

R.M. Jones, *The North Wales Quarrymen 1874-1922* (Cardiff, 1982).

J.H. Morris & L.J. Williams (eds.), *The South Wales Coal Industry, 1841-75* (Cardiff, 1958).

D. Smith and H. Francis, *The Fed* (Cardiff, 1997).

Articles:

G.M. Holmes, 'The South Wales Coal Industry, 1850-1914', *THSC* (1976).

D. Smith, 'From Riots to revolt: Tonypandy and the Miners' Next Step', in T. Herbert & G.E. Jones (eds.), *Wales 1880-1914* (Cardiff, 1988).

Research

Look up the following key figures and write a short biographical sketch on each. Concentrate on highlighting the part played by each in the industrial discontent of the pre-war period.

1. Noah Ablett
2. Winston Churchill
3. W.F. Hay
4. Arthur Horner
5. Mabon (William Abraham)
6. Lord Penrhyn
7. D.A. Thomas

I

II

III

IV

V

VI

VII

VIII

X

Issues for Debate

1. State a case a) **for** and b) **against** the view that conflict between employer and employee in pre-war Wales was inevitable.
2. State a case a) **supporting** and b) **opposing** Kenneth Morgan's opinion that '1898 was the 1868 of the coalfield' [K.O. Morgan, *Rebirth of a Nation: Wales, 1880-1980* (1980)].
   (Re-read chapter VIII, part 2 to help you)

(ii) Examination Specific

Answering Source Questions

1. Read the source by W.J. Parry on pages 312-313 and answer the following questions.
   a) Explain briefly what is meant by the phrase 'a system of co-operative piece work' (line 22) (4 marks).
   b) What information may be inferred from the source about the denial of basic democratic rights to workers at the Penrhyn Quarries? (8 marks).
   c) How useful is the source to an understanding of the issues at stake in the Penrhyn Lockout? (20 marks).

Advice

a) A group of quarrymen working together on a given task for an agreed sum of money.
b) The source lists a number of workers' demands – many of which could be seen as denials of basic democratic rights. e.g. 1. right to elect a spokesman 2. right to discuss matters etc. Note also the way management at the Quarry introduced changes without consulting the workers e.g. the loss of the annual May Day holiday, the 'system of big contracts'.
c) The source is particularly useful in giving an insight into the methods of management in the Penrhyn Quarries and the difficulties experienced by the workers in making representations to the employers. In addition, the source gives a great deal of information about the demands of the workers, most of which appear to be very reasonable. It is also useful for the way in which it informs the reader about working practices and the methods adopted for the awarding of contracts.

I

II

III

IV

V

VI

VII

VIII

IX

X

However, you must note the lack of perspective in that the source does not say anything about Lord Penrhyn or his attitude towards his employees.

2. Read the sources on the Llanelli riots on pages 323-325 and answer the following questions.
   a) **Compare sources B and C. How do these two sources contrast in their description of the Llanelli riots? (8 marks).**
   b) **Study sources A and D. How reliable are sources A and D to an historian as evidence of the causes of the Lanelli riots? (16 marks).**
   c) **How useful are the sources to an understanding of the Llanelli riots? (24 marks).**

Advice

a) Source B suggests that the riots were primarily concerned with stealing or looting and that both adults and children were involved. It also suggests that the looters were perfectly aware of what they were doing.

Source C suggests that the riots were far more violent in intent and that destruction and injury was the focus of the rioters' aims. There is also a suggestion that the rioters were acting under the influence of drink and may not have been fully aware of their actions.

b) Source A is reliable in so far as it was written before the riots and there is enough in the source to suggest that filth, poor health and living conditions were likely to contribute to some disturbance or unrest in the future. On the other hand, there is no reference or hint to the actual cause of the riots which was a strike by the railwaymen.

Source D is reliable in as much as it tries to offer its readership a balanced view of why the riots broke out in the town. On the other hand, its reference to a 'large rowdy element' is rather vague and it states as fact something that is really only an opinion i.e. 'that there are enough hooligans in Llanelly to dominate the town'. Note could be made of the fact that source D is a newspaper which is in the business of selling copy and sometimes prone to exaggerating events.

c) The sources give a reasonable insight into the nature of the riot and intent of the rioters together with some of the different reasons why they might have occurred. The sources offer a fair spread of opinion – mainly newspapers, a radical publication (if not immediately relevant), the views of a government minister and a trade union banner. However, apart from one source – which might be a rioter, an opportunist looter or an innocent man – there is no evidence from the rioters themselves. Their attitude, reasoning and motivation is entirely absent here, if anything, the evidence comes from third party reports, i.e. from people not directly involved but with sufficient knowledge of the events to express an opinion. Therefore, it might be argued that the sources present a somewhat superficial view of the riots. On the other hand, source G (supported by a passing reference in source C) does at least show the riot in its wider historical context pointing to a link with other similar events across the country over the past few years. Clearly, Llanelli was no isolated event.

Answering Synoptic Essay Questions

Look at the following example.

Study the two interpretations below and answer the question which follows.

Before 1914, the insatiable and unrelenting appetite of the rest of the world for smokeless, steam coals, created an economic infra-structure and attitudes of mind in the South Wales valleys which were far from healthy.

[T. Boyns & C. Barber, academic historians specialising in the social and economic history of Wales].

In many ways, this new industrial world of south Wales was a satisfied one, content with itself, happy with the new wealth that was enriching its community life as well as its pockets. It was not, in general, a world that questioned fundamentally the values that held it together.

[K.O. Morgan, an academic historian surveying generally the history of Wales].

I

II

III

IV

V

VI

VII

VIII

IX

X

333

Q. Analyse and evaluate the validity of these two interpretations of the nature of South Wales society in the period 1900-14.

Advice

In the first source, external factors, such as the demand overseas for Welsh steam coal, are suggested as being primarily responsible for creating the economic infra-structure of south Wales. Your answer should explore the validity of this assessment. While you are likely to agree with the assertion, you should note the controversial issue that the 'attitudes of mind were far from healthy'. This suggests that society was not at peace with itself which is an an issue very much open to debate.

In contrast, the second source suggests a different view of South Wales society – relatively prosperous and contented with itself. While its depiction of a vibrant, lively and culturally-rich society may be at odds with the first statement, you should note that these two views are not necessarily incompatible – society was being influenced/changed by the dynamics of a thriving economic life. On the other hand, this could and did create tension between employers and employees e.g. Taff Vale Dispute, Tonypandy and Llanelli.

It is important that you qualify what is meant by 'South Wales society' which was not uniform and homogeneous, there were local and regional differences e.g between the valleys of west Wales and the Rhondda and between the valley communities and the exporting-towns of the coastal belt i.e. Cardiff, Swansea and Newport.

I
II
III
IV
V
VI
VII
VIII
IX
X

Chapter X
War and The Impact of War, 1914 -18

1. War

■ Key Issue:
How did the Welsh people react to and cope with the experience of war and what impact did it have?

> I have frequently been astonished since I have been in this House to hear with what composure and how glibly Members talk of a European war .... A European war can only end in the ruin of the vanquished and the scarcely less fatal commercial dislocation and exhaustion of the conquerors.
>
> [Extract from a speech by *Winston Churchill* at the House of Commons (13 May 1901)]

On 4 August 1914, a little more than a month after the assassination of the Austrian Crown Prince Franz Ferdinand at Sarajevo (28 June 1914) by a Serbian-nationalist, Gavrilo Princip, Britain declared war on Germany. For the next four years Europe and the world was engulfed in a war that brought with it all the wonders and horrors of modern science and technology. The paradox is that while the governments of the European powers were ready for a war, few of them were prepared for this war, the first modern war and the first world war in history. War on land and sea was supplemented by war in the air which meant that no-one was safe from attack; there were to be no innocents in this war. Horses were gradually replaced by tanks and trucks, machine guns increased the rate of fire, planes fought duels in the air and ships were sunk by submarines. Mines, grenades and poisoned gas were used for the first time and the countryside was laid waste by literally millions of tons of high explosive shells fired by thousands of artillery guns.

I II III IV V VI VII VIII IX X

I

II

III

IV

V

VI

VII

VIII

IX

X

For the 12 million men on all sides who fought on the western, eastern and southern fronts, it was a living nightmare.

a) Attitudes to War

To assess the attitude of a person, let alone a people, to an event in which he or she is not directly involved, does not fully understand and is, consequently, largely ignorant of its significance for them, is fraught with difficulties. Historians approach the problem of resolving these 'difficulties' in different ways; some seek to use a dominant or respected figure, or figures, as a means of gauging the attitude of 'the people' while others tend to base their assumptions on general perceptions gained from surveying stores of archival material. Whatever method is used the historian must work within a disciplined framework which takes account of those issues, be they political, cultural, social, economic or religious in nature, that might unite or divide a people, shape their thinking and dictate their actions. In the following extract Professor Kenneth Morgan has opted to assess the attitudes of the Welsh people to war by taking Lloyd George as his subject, drawing on his thoughts and feelings and thereby making general assumptions on their behalf.

> 'I am moving through a nightmare world these days', wrote Lloyd George to his wife on 3 August 1914. All his prejudices were engaged against war with Germany, as they had been against war with the Boers in 1899. But, he concluded, if little Belgium were to be invaded, he would have no option but to endorse the Cabinet's decision .... to go to war. 'I must bear my share of the ghastly burden though it scorches my flesh to do so.' After 4 August, Lloyd George moved rapidly into a new mood of almost blithe adventure in meeting the challenges of total war.... As with Lloyd George, so with the vast majority of his fellow-countrymen. The overwhelming mass of the Welsh people cast aside their political and industrial divisions, and threw themselves into the war with gusto.
>
> [K.O. Morgan, *Rebirth of a Nation: Wales 1880-1980* (1981)]

How realistic his assessment of the mood of the Welsh public to the prospect of war depends on how representative Lloyd George was of his people. True, he was a Welsh-speaking Welshman from the rural heartland of the north-west, an area with which he still maintained links in terms of family and friends, and, as their Liberal M.P. for nigh on twenty-four years,

336

he could justly claim to represent and understand them, and they him. However, by 1914 less than 50% of the population spoke Welsh, more than 60% of Welsh people lived in the urban-industrialised areas of south-east Wales and an increasing number of them had turned to supporting the Labour Party. This might suggest that Lloyd George was out of touch with the views and attitudes of his fellow-countrymen. He had long ago left his humble Cymric roots for the bright lights of the capital city and there forged a new identity as a London-Welshman, politician and statesman *par excellence*. He was an exceptional Welshman who now led a life of privilege that few of his constituents could even imagine, let alone understand. Perhaps the greatest privilege of all was that he was fully informed of international events during the critical days and weeks after the assassination of Archduke Franz Ferdinand.

Unlike his Welsh contemporaries, Lloyd George had the luxury of time to reflect on the developing European crisis and the intellect to assess its likely impact on Britain. In this respect he may have been unrepresentative of the people of Wales, the vast majority of whom would have been denied such information. Lloyd George represented the attitude of the governing classes, the privileged, the wealthy and the well informed, the majority of whom supported the war and the government's policies. The attitudes of his fellow Welshmen and women to the war were conditioned by the information they read in the newspapers, that which was preached by way of the pulpit, was received by word of mouth or was fed by the government. The belief that they 'cast aside their political and industrial divisions, and threw themselves into the war with gusto' has been powerfully challenged by recent research which suggests that the Welsh people may not have responded with such enthusiasm.

> While some members of the public shared in the excitement induced by the first flush of patriotic fervour, most responded a good deal less vigorously than their leaders. 'When war broke out', wrote one novelist with reference to the ordinary people in the slate areas of Caernarfonshire, 'no-one knew what to make of it.' With the zeal of the recently-converted, Sir Henry Lewis expressed a harsher view that 'Bangor and Caernarvon people are stunned, mentally paralysed and need to be shaken up'. During these early weeks, however, the indignation of patriotic leaders could not dispel the public's perplexity and bewilderment. Ordinary people in Gwynedd, as elsewhere in Britain, were unaware of the reasons for the declaration of war, they knew nothing about the government's diplomatic policies and, conditioned by years

I

II

III

IV

V

VI

VII

VIII

IX

X

of peace, they experienced the greatest difficulty in perceiving the reality of war and assessing its implications for them.

[C. Parry, 'Gwynedd and the Great War, 1914-1918',
Welsh History Review (1988)]

At the heart of modern Gwynedd was the old county of Caernarfon which was the home of Lloyd George, so the 'bewildered' and 'perplexed' people who lived there were his people. Clearly, they did not share Lloyd George's 'mood of almost blithe adventure', but who were they? They were, in the main, the ordinary mass of the people who lived their lives by working on the land or in the slate quarries and in other occupations which required them to work by means of manual labour. Their experience of war had been confined to the Boer War (1899-1902), a remote conflict which hardly touched their lives. As the pre-war recruitment figures bear out, Gwynedd did not have a militarist tradition, few joined the army and those who did were regarded almost as social outcasts. The novelist Kate Roberts referred to those who 'belonged to the militia' as 'not ones to be proud of'.

Was Gwynedd representative of the attitude of the Welsh people towards the war? If the people of Glamorgan be taken as an example then the answer seems to be an emphatic no. The ordinary people from the industrial valleys of the south and east seemed less apathetic in their response to the war. The pre-war enlistment figures for Glamorgan, Monmouthshire and Breconshire tell a different story from that of Gwynedd for here was a region with a militaristic tradition. Almost as soon as war was declared thousands of potential recruits swamped the often hastily opened recruitment offices. The press report in the *Rhondda Leader* for 14th August 1914 (below) was typical of many to be found in local newspapers across south Wales.

The Call to the Colours
Thousands of Recruits
So spontaneous has been the response in Glamorgan to "the call to the colours" by the King through Lord Kitchener, the Secretary of State for War, that the machinery for receiving and enrolling the men has not been adequate All over South Wales young men have been calling at police stations to be enrolled, and these have been sent on to the Cardiff Barracks.

Their enthusiasm took even the government by surprise and they were thus ill-prepared to cope with the demand. Doubtless many were motivated by patriotism to serve and defend their country like Alf Jackson of Swansea who stated that 'It was the urge of the youngsters in those days to back Wales against the enemy. We didn't like the Kaiser and his way of doing things'. On the other hand, just as many shared Tredegar-born Private Oliver Powell's reason for joining the army within days of the declaration of war: 'Oh yes, a great patriot I was, bloody glad to get out of the pit. I thought we would have a good time, have a good adventure, it was supposed to be over by Christmas of 1914, what a joke'. Despite this mixed and often less than positive attitude to the war, Lloyd George was particularly encouraged by the recruitment figures coming out of south Wales. He declared in a speech given on 19th September 1914 that

> The world owes much to the little five-foot nations .... Wales must continue doing her duty. I should like to see a Welsh Army in the field. I should like to see the race that faced the Normans for hundreds of years in a struggle for freedom .... the race that fought for a generation under Glyndŵr against the greatest captain in Europe – I should like to see that race give a good taste of its quality in this struggle in Europe; and they are going to do it.

In expressing his pride in being a Welshman, Lloyd George was perhaps aiming to appeal to Welsh nationalists, men like Ifor Gruffydd of Anglesey who, writing later (in Welsh) of his attitude and experiences at the time, stated that 'soldiers and armies and all things military were distant and alien to us.... they belonged to the English and the making of war was England's work with us hearing of her achievements'. It has been demonstrated that proportionately fewer Welsh than English speakers enlisted in the army which may indicate that those most likely to be pro-Welsh nationalist were probably anti-war. Certainly, some Welsh language periodicals such as *Y Wawr*, edited by Ambrose Bebb, later a founder-member of the Welsh Nationalist Party and, from October 1916, *Y Deyrnas*, edited by the patriotic pacifist Thomas Rees, consistently opposed the war. On the other hand, Welsh-speaking Welshmen need not necessarily have been pro-Welsh Nationalist let alone anti-English. The fact that other equally influential Welsh language publications, such as the monthly *Y Beirniad* edited by the well known and highly respected scholar and poet Sir John Morris-Jones, hardly wavered in their support of the war, suggests that there was little to

I

II

III

IV

V

VI

VII

VIII

IX

X

I
II
III
IV
V
VI
VII
VIII
IX
X

separate the Welsh from their English-speaking compatriots in their respective attitudes to the war.

Hardly less enthusiastic in their response to the war were those whose attitudes were grounded in religion and the Christian tradition of peace. Particularly strong was the influence of nonconformist beliefs which placed a heavy emphasis on the principles of peace, which, if the criticism of the Anglican bishop of St. Asaph can be believed, were put above those of duty to king and country. Many ministers and their congregations, though not all, found it difficult to reconcile their religious beliefs with their patriotic duty. While they preached peace and restraint, others were preaching action in the cause of a just war. The most active in the latter respect was the celebrated Methodist minister the Rev. John Williams of Brynsiencyn, Anglesey, who caused a stir by preaching in the pulpit in full military uniform. Other like-minded ministers even volunteered their chapels to serve as temporary recruiting centres, an action which horrified the poet and University lecturer T. Gwynn Jones who subsequently walked out of his local chapel in Aberystwyth when the minister urged his congregation to pray for a British victory. On the other hand, in Harlech and the surrounding districts few, if any, responded to the call to serve their country, which, according to the English poet Robert Graves, who lived for much of the year in the area, was due almost entirely to the influence of the chapels. He wrote 'the chapels held soldiering to be sinful, and in Merioneth, the chapels had the last word'. In the opinion of one local newspaper, *The North Wales Observer and Express* (11 September 1914), Merioneth was without doubt 'the worst county in Wales for recruitment'.

The mixed response to the war was evident also in nonconformist publications such as the Methodist newspaper, *Y Goleuad*, which was passionately anti-war, while the Independent weekly newspaper, *Y Tyst*, was patriotic to the core. How far their respective editors, E. Morgan Humphreys and the Rev. Hugh M. Hughes represented the views of their readership is open to question. Humphreys was regularly criticised by a sizeable minority of his readership while Hughes often dissociated himself from the anti-war letters which he, nevertheless, continued to publish in the columns of *Y Tyst*. Like Hughes, Humphreys too discharged his duties as editor with remarkable equanimity which did not attempt the suppression or censorship of the views of his opponents. In the September edition of *Y*

Goleuad (1914) the pro-war recruiter and doyen of the Welsh cultural establishment Sir O.M. Edwards, was able to publish a damning letter addressed At *Ŵyr Meirionnydd* (To the men of Merioneth) in which he criticised their lack of patriotism stating that 'it [Merioneth] had done less so far than any other county in this crisis'. The Baptists too had their champions such as the Rev. E.K. Jones, a minister in Caernarfon, who regularly contributed to *Y Deyrnas* on the themes of press censorship, restrictions of free speech and the harsh treatment of conscientious objectors.

Pacifists too were to be found in Wales, people who had long preached against war and who believed that war itself was unjust and evil. Among the more famous and outspoken was the arch-socialist Keir Hardie, Labour M.P. for Merthyr Tydfil, who made plain his opposition to the war from the very beginning. On 6 August 1914, within two days of Britain's declaration of war, Hardie addressed a packed audience of his constituents at Aberdare the majority of whom he angered by attempting to lay the blame for war on Russian machinations rather than German ambitions. Swept along by a tide of patriotic fervour and sympathy for 'poor little Belgium', Hardie's largely-English speaking, working-class audience had, no doubt, been swayed in their attitude by the local press – the *Merthyr Express*, the *South Wales Daily News* and the *Aberdare Leader* – which proclaimed Britain's moral right to declare war on Germany. Paradoxically, another, and at that time, lesser known pacifist Emrys Hughes was of the firm opinion that the people of the Cynon and Rhondda valleys were anything but pro-war. According to him, 'The war feeling was not really so strong here as in the large cities. The miners were exempt and a young man of military age was still left unmolested and escaped the inconvenience and insult which were now the rule in most parts of the country'. A native of Abercynon and the son of a non-conformist minister, Hughes later declared that 'I was not misled by the outburst of rhetoric on the part of the politicians nor by the frenzied patriotism of the press ... Britain's entry into the war was neither justifiable nor justified ... the nation had been misled ... the people had been deceived'.

Gradually, as the war progressed through the autumn and winter months of 1914-15, attiudes began to change. Government propaganda had a part to play here in that stories of German atrocities in Belgium during the first few weeks of the conflict were used to justify Britain's involvement. So

I
II
III
IV
V
VI
VII
VIII
IX
X

I

II

III

IV

V

VI

VII

VIII

IX

X

successful was the government in this respect that before the year was out some nonconformist ministers had turned to preaching the creed 'praise the Lord and kill the Germans'. Government sponsored anti-German propaganda, some of it shamefully exaggerated and hysterical, began to mould public opinion. Those who had wrestled with their consciences were resolving them, however reluctantly in some cases, in favour of war. The once 'perplexed' and 'bewildered' were given a focus for their thoughts and feelings, they had something to fear, to hate and to overcome. Soon Wales too was suffering from 'Jingo fever' as the public gave way to their base instincts by venting their anger and frustration on innocent 'foreigners' like Professor Hermann Ethé of Aberystwyth. A distinguished linguist and teacher for many years at the University, Ethé was German by birth and by blood and it was the latter that the unruly mob of townsfolk who gathered outside his home on the sea-front wished to see splashed over the pavement. He was mercilessly persecuted, dismissed from his post and 'exiled' from 'the college by the sea'. Even in apparently apathetic Gwynedd, there were examples of 'jingo fever' such as the persecution in Pwllheli of the anti-war radical and blind Independent minister, Puleston Jones, by his own congregation. Perhaps the most visible display of 'patriotic fervour' was that witnessed at the Bangor eisteddfod in 1915 which was almost entirely given over to the pro-war lobby. Guest speakers were given the opportunity to peddle their particular brand of jingoism and the most effective of them was the recently-appointed Minister of Munitions, David Lloyd George, who delivered a warlike address which was greeted enthusiastically by the majority of the audience. Ironically, and as if to mirror the contrasting attitudes of the Welsh people to the war, both crown and chair were won at Bangor by the distinguished poet T. H. Parry-Williams, a noted pacifist and active anti-war crusader!

As the conflict entered its second year the grim reality of what war was about began to hit home. As casualty figures rose recruitment declined, conscription was introduced and jingoism subsided and the nation settled down to see out the conflict as best it could. No longer could the war be portrayed as an heroic adventure or even as a Christian crusade against evil, and despite the best efforts of the government to persuade the people to think otherwise, there was a growing despondency that saw the conflict in terms of an enterprise in utter futility and waste. By 1916 the Welsh nation had largely resolved its conflict of attitude to the war and, broadly speaking, you were either patriot or pacifist. This is not to suggest that all patriots were pro-war, the news of the carnage, death and destruction coming from the front had seen to that, but in a very real sense the people felt powerless to react one way or the other. In short, there was no alternative but to support the war until victory had been won. To do otherwise was to be disloyal, not so much to king and country, but to those fighting in the front line. Equally, to suggest that all pacifists were unpatriotic was patently untrue and although they consistently opposed the war they were hardly the pro-German traitors that both press and propaganda often made them out to be. Indeed, the majority of them claimed to be patriots yet they were attacked and persecuted by government, press and people alike.

If gauging the attitude of the people of Wales to war is fraught with complication then to attempt to quantify it is near impossible. Some historians have attempted to do this by using the recruitment figures as a basis for analysis. They point to the fact that in percentage terms more Welshmen were recruited to serve in the armed forces than were recruited from either England or Scotland, or indeed Ireland. In all, it has been estimated that some 280,000 Welshmen or 13.82% of the total population of Wales were recruited, a fact which has led one historian to declare that despite being 'a land with long traditions of radicalism and anti-militarism' Wales responded 'to the patriotic call with ... fervour'. However, to use such raw data is, in many respects, unhistorical for though it might suggest a people rampant with patriotic fervour for war, the truth is a little more sobering. For example, the figure includes those who volunteered, i.e. between August 1914 and December 1915, and those conscripted, i.e. after January 1916. It has been estimated that 122,985 men volunteered (approximately 43.9% of those who served in the armed forces) which suggests that more than half, 157,015 (approximately 56.1%) were conscripted. Although it may be argued that some, perhaps many, of those conscripted would have volunteered had they been given the choice, there is no disputing the fact that before the introduction of enforced military service the numbers enlisting voluntarily were in steep decline. For example, the Wrexham recruiting office which catered for the six counties of north Wales, recorded a total enlistment of 2,569 in August 1914 but this figure had fallen to 1,332 in January 1915 and it dropped still further to 634 in December 1915.

I
II
III
IV
V
VI
VII
VIII
IX
X

343

As the following tables show, statistical evidence must be used with caution for invariably they are based on estimates which may not be entirely accurate. Note, for example, the rounded figures in the third column of those who served in the armed forces, recent research has suggested that the figure for Wales should read 272,984 enlisted and conscripted between 1914-18. On the other hand, this does not include Welshmen who may have enlisted at military recruitment centres outside Wales, particularly Chester, Shrewsbury and Bristol, hence the rounded figure popularly used by the majority of historians. Again it must be pointed out that, proportionately speaking, Wales had a larger number of males of military age, i.e. 18-45, then either England or Scotland, a higher percentage of whom were exempt military service on account of their occupation as colliers.

Table 24

Estimates of numbers recruited into the armed forces, 1914-18

Country	Population in 1911 Census	Numbers served in the armed forces	Percentage of total population	Percentage of male population
England	34,045,294	4,530,000	13.31%	24.02%
Scotland	4,760,904	620,000	13.02%	23.71%
Wales	2,025,198	280,000	13.82%	21.52%
Ireland	4,930,198	170,000	3.87%	6.14%

Table 25

Estimates in percentages of those who volunteered August 1914-December 1915

Country	%
Scotland	6.18
England	5.5
Wales	4.8
Ireland	2.06

Estimates based on Statistics of the Military Effort of the British Empire during the Great War, 1914-1918 (The War Office, 1920).

By the same token, if historians were to use figures showing the numbers registered and imprisoned for being conscientious objectors or those involved in pacifist organisations, they would be no nearer to establishing a reliable and fool-proof guide to assessing the 'attitude' of the people to the war. Indeed, quantum methods of assessment require so much in the way of qualification as to render them almost useless. Therefore, the historical 'truth' in this instance must, by necessity, and however reluctantly, rely on generalisations, estimates and personal perceptions.

b) Lloyd George and the British War Effort

Once war had been declared the British government faced a possible crisis, it was simply unprepared for anything other than a short conflict lasting weeks rather than months. No survey of the country's economic resources had been made, there had been no attempt to accumulate essential raw materials or foodstuffs in the event of blockade and there had been no register of manpower. Recruitment centres were hastily set up and they were often disorganised and no account had been taken of the likely effects of mass enlistments on industrial and agricultural production. To make matters worse, the complacency of some senior politicians bordered on the negligent, like the Foreign Secretary Sir Edward Grey who declared, 'if we are engaged in war, we shall suffer but little more than we shall suffer if we stand aside'. A critical and clearly frustrated General Kitchener summed up his opinion of politicians like Grey, 'Did they consider when they went headlong into a war like this, that they were without an army, and without any preparation to equip one?' Fortunately there were politicians of considerable insight and ability who responded to the crisis in a positive and energetic way. Lloyd George was foremost among them. As subsequent events were to show, he alone of the Cabinet seemed to have the drive and the leadership necessary to win the war.

At the outbreak of war Lloyd George was one of the three most senior members of the government, after the Prime Minister Herbert Asquith. As Chancellor of the Exchequer he single-mindedly set about the task of ensuring Britain had the financial resources to meet the inevitably high costs of the conflict. His first war budget of November 1914 doubled the rate of income tax which yielded an additional revenue of a million pounds a week. Perhaps his greatest contribution to the war effort as Chancellor came in

I

II

III

IV

V

VI

VII

VIII

IX

X

I
II
III
IV
V
VI
VII
VIII
IX
X

March 1915 when he enlisted the support of the TUC in vastly increasing the size of the industrial workforce, particularly those employed in munitions and other related 'war' production. The influx of so many new workers, many of them women, posed a threat to the rigid distinction between the skilled and unskilled workers. As a result of the so-called 'Treasury Agreement', the TUC embraced Lloyd George's request that there be a 'dilution' of traditional skills for the duration of the war. Besides the significance of being consulted on matters of high policy for the first time, the TUC secured an assurance that in future they would be consulted, through local joint committees, on issues of strategic economic planning. Lloyd George hailed it as 'the great charter for labour'. History's verdict is equally praiseworthy, according to the historian A.J.P. Taylor, Lloyd George's 'Treasury Agreement revolutionized the position of the trade unions: where formerly they had opposed, they now participated'.

In May 1915 , Lloyd George was appointed the first Minister of Munitions in the newly-formed coalition government of Liberals and Unionists. Lloyd George's task was simple, to end the deplorable shortage of munitions at the front! To achieve this would, in the words of one contemporary, require 'nothing short of a miracle' or a man of genius with the vision and organisational ability to accomplish a massive increase in the production of shells, machine guns, mortars, artillery, and to ensure their delivery and continued supply. By sweeping aside traditional methods of administration in favour of a more radical approach which involved bypassing normal civil service and other bureaucratic channels, and by employing the services of businessmen, Lloyd George transformed the manufacture of war goods. For example, at the beginning of the war the army was in possession of 1,330 machine guns but by its end it had been supplied with 240,506. On the other hand, it took another two years for the ministry to satisfy the army's insatiable demand for artillery shells. Nevertheless, his efforts on behalf of the troops at the front did not go unappreciated as the following extract from the *Caernarvon and Denbigh Herald* newspaper (August 1915) shows. 'It was the new Lloyd George shells which gave us the heart to make the charge, after being so heavily hit. These new shells are magnificent and after our fellows got into the captured trenches they gave three cheers for Lloyd George.' The Welsh Wizard's success fell well short of a miracle but was brilliantly outstanding nonetheless.

In July 1916 , Lloyd George was appointed to succeed Kitchener, who had been lost at sea, as Minister of War. He immediately set about dealing with what he regarded as the shortcomings of the British General Staff. They in turn had difficulty in coming to terms with this new dynamic and imaginative approach to 'total war'. Lloyd George quarrelled with the commander of the British forces in France General Haig, whom he thought lacked imagination, for insisting that a new strategy be devised to deliver the 'knock-out blow' against the enemy. This, he insisted, could only be achieved either by pursuing an 'eastern strategy', the details of which remained vague, to relieve the pressure on the Western Front or through closer co-operation with France and their other allies. The British General Staff resisted the Minister of War at almost every turn but when he took office as Prime Minister they grudgingly co-operated. One of his better ideas was the formation of a War Cabinet which would consist of no more than a handful of ministers with the primary duty of directing the war. Asquith rejected the idea and on 5 December 1916 Lloyd George resigned. After much intrigue, involving the leader of the Unionists Bonar Law, Asquith too resigned in the mistaken belief that he was indispensible and that he would soon be asked back to lead the country. Unfortunately, he had seriously miscalculated and in his absence Bonar Law advised the king to call on Lloyd George to lead the country. Accepting the king's invitation to form a new government and with the support of the Unionists, Lloyd George became Prime Minister on 7 December 1916. Asquith felt betrayed and refused to serve in the government. In the words of A.J.P. Taylor 'Lloyd George's accession to power was a revolution, British style'.

As was his custom, he threw himself into his new role, he formed his War Cabinet and, within a short time, he had established new Ministries of Labour, Food, Shipping, Pensions and, in 1917, National Service. To increase the efficiency of administration these new ministries were linked through committees to his war cabinet which was served by a staff of energetic, mostly young and some Welsh, advisors nicknamed the 'Garden Suburb' on account of the huts in which they were housed. Perhaps his most controversial decision on taking office was the introduction of conscription which turned many in his own party against him. Under Asquith, the government had felt conscription was unnecessary and, aware of its unpopularity, they preferred voluntary enlistment. Those M.P.s in the party who disagreed with Asquith, among them prominent Welshmen like

Ellis Griffith and Sir Ivor Herbert, threw in their lot with Lloyd George and in January 1916 they founded the 'Liberal War Committee'. Other, equally prominent, Welsh Liberals – Llewelyn Williams, E.T. John and Caradog Rees – never wavered in their opposition to conscription and, as a consequence, in their enmity to Lloyd George.

c) Government Policy: DORA and its Consequences

By 1917 the whole nation had been mobilised for the war effort by a government determined to control every aspect of civilian life. Almost as soon as war was declared in August 1914, Parliament passed the Defence of the Realm Act (DORA) which gave it wide powers to ban, restrict or censor anything that it thought could harm the war effort. In short, the Prime Minister was invested with near dictatorial powers. Newspapers and periodicals were first to be affected by the new censorship laws especially those linked to political or pacifist organisations like the Socialist newspaper *Forward* which was suppressed for daring to publish the truth of Lloyd George's stormy meeting with militant Clydeside workers in December 1915. The major Welsh newspapers – *Yr Herald Cymraeg, Y Genedl Gymreig, Y Cymro* and *Baner ac Amserau Cymru* – loyally supported the government thus precluding the need for serious censorship. However, those periodicals known to be hostile to the war in general and government policy in particular were closely monitored and, if necessary, closed down. As a result of pressure applied by the authorities the Aberystwyth-based anti-war periodical *Y Wawr* ceased publication in late 1917. J.H. Jones, editor of the Liverpool-based Welsh newspaper *Y Brython*, was successfully prosecuted for being in breach of DORA. Occasionally the authorities were foiled in their attempts to suppress or intimidate their critics as in the case of the Independent minister, the Rev. T.E. Nicholas editor of the Socialist paper the *Merthyr Pioneer*. The pre-war, strike-busting Chief Constable of Glamorgan, Lionel Lindsay attempted several times to have the pro-marxist and sympathetic socialist clergyman prosecuted, but without success.

DORA enabled the state to control shipping and shipbuilding, engineering, agriculture, railways and the mines. Under the newly created Ministry of Munitions the government took charge of industrial production and supply which enabled it to control prices and profits. By passing the Munitions of War Act the government sought to control those workers directly involved in war work and one of its least popular provisions was in making it illegal to strike. Total war came to mean total state control. Inevitably there was criticism of the government which was accused by some of eroding civil liberties and of open dictatorship. The most vociferous and, in the government's view, dangerous opposition came from the pro-Socialist and anti-militarist unions the most militant of whom resisted attempts to control them. In spite of their generally held socialist-pacifist beliefs the majority of Welsh workers and their unions responded positively to the call to arms in 1914. They backed the government and took seriously their contribution to the war effort. Even the Welsh South Wales Miners Federation (SWMF), hardly a friend of the Liberal government, came out in support of the war though a number of its representatives like Noah Ablett, Will Hay and Arthur Horner remained true to their pacifist principles. The uneasy alliance lasted barely a year when in July 1915 the miners came out on strike thus paralysing the South Wales coalfield and interrupting the supply of much needed coal for the boilers of the Royal Navy's warships. With hardly a pause for breath the press rounded on the miners – 'Germay's Allles In Wales' was the headline carried by the *London Evening Standard* – and accused them variously, of treason, cowardice and of collaborating with German spies who were supposed to have bribed them with £60,000.

The truth was not nearly so sensational since the basis of their complaint had little to do with the war but turned on the fact that while the price of coal had risen by 50% their wages had failed to keep pace. Coal owners were enjoying huge profits, their shareholders benefited from higher dividends but the miners were finding it increasingly difficult to cope with the rising cost of living, particularly evident in the escalating price of food. All attempts at negotiating a new wage structure failed in the face of employers' reluctance to come to terms. As the crisis deepened the government became involved, Bonar Law advocated the use of the army to suppress what he considered was nothing short of a rebellion: 'It would be better to shoot a hundred men in suppressing a strike than to lose thousands on the field as a consequence'. Lloyd George took it upon himself to negotiate an end to the strife and he and two fellow ministers took a train to Cardiff to confront the leaders of the 'Fed'. A deal was worked out whereby the miners achieved all their wage demands in return for an assurance that they would do all in their power to avoid strike action for the duration of the war. Having achieved more in a few days than in the previous ten years solely on

I

II

III

IV

V

VI

VII

VIII

IX

X

account of the war, the miners were eager to test both employers and government again. Consequently, the 'deal' lasted little more than six months when the SWMF, against the wishes of the Miners' Federation of Great Britain, voted by a two thirds majority to strike if conscription was pushed through parliament. In the event, they refrained from strike action but the situation remained tense.

Nor did nationalisation ease the tension between government and miners, a policy welcomed by the Miners' Federation of Great Britain but greeted with undisguised scepticism by the SWMF. Fuelled by news of the 'workers' revolution in Russia – greeted by the miners of the Amman Valley in song – the unrest continued to mount. In May 1917 the tension boiled over leading to a series of strikes in which the miners were joined by other industrial workers from across the country. Lloyd George's response was a commission of inquiry to uncover the root cause of the industrial unrest in South Wales as well as in other areas across Britain. The findings of the commissioners were a damning indictment of the failure of past governments to remedy the grave social and economic problems that greatly affected the socially deprived, poverty ridden South Wales valleys. True to the spirit of his Liberal principles Lloyd George was as determined as ever to continue 'to wage implacable warfare against poverty' as he was in waging war against the enemy on the battlefield.

d) Warfare, Welfare and 'War Socialism'

In spite of the authoritarian nature of wartime government and the belligerent attitude of some unions there were benefits for the British people. Lloyd George believed that warfare and welfare went hand in hand and when he became Prime Minister in 1916 he set about improving the lot of the ordinary citizen. The government began to fund organisations like the Burry Port Garden Suburb Company which built homes with cheap rents for workers at the Pembrey munitions factory near Llanelli. State education, health and hospital care steadily improved, though this came too late to solve the looming recruitment crisis caused mainly by the fact that proportionately large numbers of recruits and conscripts were suffering from ill-health and were thus deemed unfit for military service. The introduction of stricter medicals after conscription in 1916 exacerbated the problem and of the 2.4 million men called up for war service in 1917-18 nearly a million or 40% of them were declared unfit for frontline duty. The

I

II

III

IV

V

VI

VII

VIII

IX

health and social problems of Edwardian Britain had come back to haunt the politicians who responded by creating a new Ministry of Health in 1919.

Working conditions improved, canteen services were introduced and wages for industrial and agricultural workers went up but only in return for no-strike deals. The most spectacular wage increase was won by male agricultural workers who saw their earnings rise by 200% between 1914 and 1919. After the 1915 strike the miners too enjoyed a period of unparalleled prosperity and job security. Unemployment in the country generally was at its lowest for more than a quarter of a century and in South Wales, the hub of industrial Britain, it was negligible. The same, unfortunately, cannot be said for North Wales particularly in those areas in the west where the slate industry predominated. Fewer houses were built and, as a direct result of the war, the export trade all but collapsed which led to a corresponding decline in the demand for slate. In stark contrast to the mining industry of South and North-East Wales, slate-quarrying was declared a non-essential industry deserving little in the way of government aid or protection. As the slate quarries closed their former employees either enlisted or moved to work elsewhere. Unlike mining and agriculture, the slate industry derived no benefit from state intervention.

At first life at home did not change that much but as the war continued its effects became harder to ignore. Housewives were among the first to notice the massive price rises and shortages of some basic foodstuffs in the shops. This was due in part to inflation but also to German submarines or U-Boats which were sinking hundreds of merchant ships, one in four by early 1917, bringing food and raw materials to Britain. The government used its powers under DORA to make waste illegal which, in one instance, led to a Welsh housewife being fined £20 for feeding meat to her dog. The situation had become so serious that in January 1918 rationing for essential foodstuffs was introduced. The man responsible for originating and implementing the plan for food rationing was a Welshman and former Liberal M.P., D.A. Thomas, Viscount Rhondda. Appointed Food Controller in June 1917 Lord Rhondda proved an outstanding success in framing a system which took no account of class or wealth but treated everyone equally. This, together with the nationalisation of key industries like coal and the regulation of agriculture, has been hailed by some as one of the key features of so-called 'War Socialism'.

I

II

III

IV

V

VI

VII

VIII

IX

X

Inevitably there was a downside and in spite of large wage increases, the government made ever greater demands on taxation. In 1915 the government was spending over one million pounds a day on the war so to avoid going bankrupt it doubled the basic rate of income tax from 1s. 3d. to 2s. 6d. (roughly 6p to 12p in the £). By late 1917 government spending had risen to £5.5 million a day which saw a corresponding increase in the basic rate of income tax, which by 1918, was roughly 6s. in the £ (30p). The demands of the public purse was insatiable and the people were encouraged to spend less and save more and to use these savings to buy war bonds from the government to help pay for the war. In return the government promised to pay the money back, with interest, once the war was over. The huge national debt at the end of the war made such promises difficult to fulfil.

2. The Impact of War

The Great War had a profound impact on all who experienced it, especially those in the front line who survived it or who learned of it second hand. Its legacy is still with us today, in the Balkans, where Bosnians, Croatians and Serbians attempt to undo the mistakes of the past that saw them thrown together against their will and, closer to home, where relatives of those British soldiers shot for alleged cowardice attempt to clear their names and, in so doing, right a terrible wrong. The cemeteries and memorials in France and Belgium like Hill 62, Thiepval and the Menin Gate, and those memorials that grace almost every town and village in Wales serve to remind us of the carnage, material devastation and terrible cost, in human terms, of the tragedy of war. Inevitably, it was once commonly assumed that war damaged a nation's society and ruined its economy, that the losses incurred, both physical and material, were such as to render the very notion of war repugnant. However, it is now widely recognised that 'total' war, involving the mass mobilisation of populations and economic resources, need not be regarded simply as a force for destruction but can be a vehicle for fundamental change. Historians are agreed that the impact of the Great War on the society and economy of Wales was massive, yet there is little consensus on its precise nature and significance. Some historians have gone as far as to say that the war caused a second industrial and agricultural revolution which witnessed changes on a scale equal to that which occurred in the whole of the previous century. Others have argued for a social and political revolution which saw the emancipation of women, the eclipse of the Liberal party and the rise of Labour. What is not in doubt is that post-war Wales was, in many respects, significantly different to that of its pre-war precursor.

a) Social and Economic Change

The post-war decline in Welsh industry and the stagnation of the Welsh economy has often been attributed to the disruption caused by the war. The heavy losses in manpower, destruction of material assets and the loss of overseas markets have been cited as reasons for Wales and Britain's declining position in international trade. However, historians now take a more pragmatic view of the changes that affected the Welsh economy during this period. They point to the fact that, with the possible exception of coal, exports were already declining before the war and that, in any event, Welsh industry was faced with the prospect of having to initiate changes. Therefore, the war did not initiate change but merely accelerated a process that was already occurring. The reasons why historians may have been misled in the past is because during the war the Welsh economy experienced a boom, the slate quarries of North Wales excepted, where full employment, job security and ever rising wages became the norm. In the words of W.J. Edwards, a writer from Aberdare, the Welsh miners 'had never had it so good'. Iron, coal and steel benefited greatly from war-time demand – Welsh steel was used to build the first tanks – productivity increased substantially and there was better and more efficient management. These, and other industries, were temporarily nationalised and taken into state ownership, the railways especially benefited from government control, where their potential was exploited to the full by a government more receptive to the unions and more amenable to the workers. However, these same industries suffered from a collapse in foreign and domestic demand in the post-war era and from de-nationalisation leaving them without the same level of state support and protection.

There was change too in the temper of industrial relations between unions and employers. The crisis of war drew both sides together in a temporary

I

II

III

IV

V

VI

VII

VIII

IX

X

and uneasy relationship which, as the miners' strike of 1915 showed, was volatile and fragile. Having won more concessions from both the employers and the government in the four years of war than they had achieved in the past 25 years, the unions were determined that the advent of peace would not alter their resolve to make more demands on behalf of their members. The increasing militancy of unions and their membership, particularly the SWMF, went hand in hand with the rise of the class-conscious socialism that was rife in the valleys of South Wales. Liberal values, as well as the Liberal party, were already in decline before the war but the move towards supporting Labour became a torrent during it. This sea change in the political affiliations of both unions and workers and the changed voting patterns of the population at large was due, in part, to the passing of The Representation of the People Act which witnessed a dramatic rise in the number of electors in Wales from roughly 430,000 in 1911 to 1,172,000 in 1918. A substantial proportion of these 'new' electors were women but most were ex-servicemen to whom the franchise was extended in recognition of their service on behalf of their country.

For the tenant farmers of Wales the war brought change and prosperity. The demand for milk and other dairy products, livestock and corn increased substantially. It has been estimated that agricultural prices rose by as much as 300% between 1914 and 1918. Farmers were helped to improve their farming methods by bodies such as the Welsh Council of Agriculture and the 130 or so branches of the Agricultural Organisation Society which offered advice and technical assistance. Allotment Societies too were established to support small-scale farming concerns and help maximise their efficiency. Until 1916 the government had been content to leave the agricultural industry to regulate itself but partly as a result of bad harvests in both Britain and America and on account of losses sustained at sea through the action of enemy submarines, it felt compelled to act 'by legislative and administrative action' to ensure the continued supply of essential foods. County War Agricultural Committees were established which were intended to work closely with the Food Production Department. In passing the Corn Production Act of 1917 the government encouraged greater efficiency in the production of important foodstuffs like potatoes, oats and wheat by guaranteeing farmers a fixed price. Even agricultural labourers were guaranteed a minimum wage which brought them economic security for the first time.

Despite the unprecedented scale of government intervention the response of the rural community was positive which, according to a contemporary report, was due to 'the general desire of farmers to contribute to the national effort and the feeling of confidence in the prospect of higher prices'. However, not everyone benefited, the landowning gentry saw the value of their large estates decline as increased taxation and inflation reduced their income from rents. Increasingly after 1917 estates which had been in existence for centuries were broken up and sold off mainly to 'land hungry' former tenants. The Talbot estate of Margam, the Hanbury estate of Pontypool Park in South Wales and the Glynllifon and Bodelwyddan estates in the north were among the first to be put up for auction. The change in the pattern of land-ownership was such as to earn for this momentous period in the agricultural history of Wales the title the 'green revolution'.

b) The Changing Role of Women

The effect of the war on the role and status of women has received much attention. It has been argued that women benefited enormously from the conflict because they were given the opportunity to participate in areas of work that had hitherto been closed to them. The crisis of war, the shortage of adult male workers and a lessening of gender discrimination in the labour market combined to liberate women and set them on the path to social equality and political emancipation.

As Minister of Munitions Lloyd George was the first to realise the impact that war would have on the economy in general and manpower in particular. With thousands of men volunteering, and after 1916 being conscripted, to fight at the front who would fill the vacancies in munitions factories and in other essential industries? Lloyd George's suggestion that women might fill the void was greeted with derision in some quarters and not least in the unions who viewed such moves with grave suspicion. In spite of determined opposition he persisted with the idea of mobilising women for the war effort arguing that an additional 1.25 million workers would add considerably to the productivity of industry.

Fig. 50

'Women's Fight for Rights'. Episodes from the Suffragette Movement's fight for Rights (1900-1914)

DEFIANCE: SUFFRAGETTES CHAINED TO DOWNING STREET RAILINGS BY THEMSELVES.

DEFIANCE: REMOVING A GRILLE AND THE SUFFRAGETTE CHAINED TO IT, IN THE HOUSE OF COMMONS.

THE HORSEWHIP: A MILITANT AT WORK AT A MEETING IN THE ALBERT HALL.

THE HAMMER: BREAKING WINDOWS IN OXFORD STREET.

THE HAMMER—AND ACIDS: BROKEN WINDOWS AT REGENT STREET POST-OFFICE—AND A DAMAGED LETTER.

ASSAULT: A BAG OF FLOUR THROWN AT MR. ASQUITH'S MOTOR-CAR.

Partly in response to Lloyd George's efforts on their behalf but more as a consequence of their anger over the failure of government to make use of them, the Suffragette leader Christabel Pankhurst led a march of 30,000 women through London in July 1915, demanding the 'Right to Serve'. The government took advantage of the publicity to support her. The crisis of war convinced even the Suffragette leader Mrs. Pankhurst, hardly a friend of the Liberal government, that a new approach had to be adopted by the movement. 'We want to help Britain even though it is governed by Mr.

Asquith and his Liberals. We should rally to the country, not the government. It is a thousand times more the duty of suffragettes to fight the Kaiser for the sake of liberty than it is to fight anti-suffrage governments.' Soon Lloyd George was employing increasing numbers of women in the munitions factories and between July 1915 and July 1918 their numbers rose from 255,000 to 948,000. This was dirty, dangerous work, the hours were long and the pay poor but the 'munitionettes' as they were called, worked hard to increase the production of bullets and shells. They were inspired by the propaganda posters which said 'Women's battle cry is work, work, work' and 'Shells made by women may save their husbands' lives'.

Unfortunately, not everything changed, for in spite of Lloyd George's promises of a fair minimum wage, the unions were instrumental in ensuring that women factory workers were paid about half that received by men. Nevertheless, they responded to the government's 'call to arms' with as much enthusiasm as had been shown by their menfolk in the early weeks and months of the war. By 1918 women were employed in a variety of jobs: train station porters, railway ticket collectors, bus-conductors, policewomen, postwomen, drivers and even grave-diggers.

Table 26

The distribution and estimated numbers of the female workforce across Britain

Area of work	Numbers employed
Civil Service/Government Depts.	200,000
Clerical/Office Work	500,000
Agriculture	250,000
Munitions/Engineering	900,000
Public Service/trams, buses etc	150,000
Auxiliary Services of the Armed Forces	100,000
Nurses	120,000
YMCA	30,000

[Quoted from N.B. Dearle, *The Labour Cost of the Great War* (1928)]

I

II

III

IV

V

VI

VII

VIII

IX

X

In all, some 2.25 million women were mobilised, far more than even Lloyd George had expected possible. Women had proved themselves, according to Herbert Asquith, 'as active and as efficient as men'. As a reward for loyal service Asquith's successor as Prime Minister, Lloyd George, supported the passing of The Representation of the People Act (1918) enfranchising women over 30 years of age (those under 30 were considered politically 'immature') and enabling them to stand for election to the House of Commons. The clause in the Act relating specifically to women's suffrage was passed in Parliamentary Committee stage by 385 to 55. What the Women's Suffrage Movement had failed to achieve in 50 years was largely achieved in four years of war. Yet in spite of the advances made by women during the war, once demobilisation was complete, they reverted to the pre-war pattern of employment. It took another world war to accelerate the process of change.

I

II

III

IV

V

VI

VII

VIII

IX

X

Advice and Activities

(i) General

Suggested Further Reading

M. Beloff, *Wars and Welfare: Britain 1914-45* (London, 1983).

J.C. Dunn, *The War the Infantry Knew, 1914-19* (London, 1989).

P.J. Haythornthwaite, *The World War One Source Book* (Oxford, 1992).

C. Hughes, Mametz: *Lloyd George's Army at the Battle of the Somme* (Norwich, 1990).

K.O. Morgan, *Lloyd George* (London, 1974).

J. Richard (ed.), *Wales and the Western Front* (Cardiff, 1994).

P. Simkins, *Kitchener's Army: The Raising of the New Armies, 1914-16* (Manchester, 1988).

K. Strange, *Wales and the First World War* (Mid-Glamorgan County Council Education Department, n.d.).

A. Thorpe, *The Longman Companion to Britain in the Ear of the World Wars, 1914-45* (London, 1994).

R. Turvey, *Wales and Britain, 1906-51* (London, 1997).

Research

Using the books above

a) Outline the main features of warfare on the western front.

b) Study the contribution (i) Welsh soldiers (regiments); (ii) Lloyd George made to the war effort.

I

II

III

IV

V

VI

VII

VIII

IX

X

(ii) Examination Specific

Answering Structured Questions

Q.

a) Explain briefly the main features of warfare on the Western Front (24 marks).

b) To what extent did Lloyd George contribute to the winning of the First World War? (36 marks).

Advice

You need first to seek out and identify the key words. They are a) 'warfare', and b) 'contribute' and 'winning'. Once you have done this you should consider the following advice for each of the questions.

a) You must deal with the key word 'warfare' by discussing such issues as tactics, strategy, weaponry, combat and life in the trenches.

b) You will be expected to trace the contribution of Lloyd George to the war effort starting with his economic reforms as Chancellor of the Exchequer through to his work at the Ministry of Munitions and at the War Office (1914-16). The main focus of your answer should be on his time as Prime Minister (1916-18) and his attempts to run the war effort. Concentrate especially on his leadership qualities and organisational skills. There should also be some assessment on how well Lloyd George performed by comparing the way he handled difficult military problems with his successful handling of the home front. Note also the contribution of others, and other factors, to winning the war and set Lloyd George's contribution alongside these. A judgement will be required here.

Answering Essay Questions

The following example is an essay involving the consideration of an historical interpretation.

'The First World War, above all else, changed the attitude of people towards women and ensured the success of the campaign of the Suffragette Movement?

[L.D. Owens, an historian, writing on aspects of twentieth century history].

Q. How valid is this interpretation of the importance of the First World War as a factor contributing to the success of the campaign for the vote for women?

Advice

The key words here are 'valid', 'importance', 'contributing' and 'success'.

(i) valid – is this a worthy interpretation and do you agree with it?
(ii) importance – how important was the First World War? You will have to evaluate this – was it very important or less important when set alongside other factors.
(iii) contributing – this tells you that the war did contribute something to the votes for women campaign. You will have to work out and evaluate its contribution.
(iv) success – this tells you that the campaign for the vote for women was successful. What part did the war play in this success?

There is some overlap here so your plan will be crucial to the success of your essay – avoid repetition, structure your essay in such a way that the points are clearly distinguished and supported but that they also support each other.

You must not be content simply to stress the role of women during the war for although this is important you need also to say how it was responsible for the success of the Suffragette Movement e.g. reward for their contribution to the war effort (this must be described and evaluated). You may qualify your answer by pointing out that these rewards went to a select group of women and not to all (the 1918 reform act was aimed at women over 30 etc). Better answers will take a broader view of the issue by highlighting political, social, economic and technological factors/changes which contributed to the work of the Suffragists.

I
II
III
IV
V
VI
VII
VIII
IX
X

361

INDEX

I

II

III

IV

V

VI

VII

VIII

IX

X

I
II
III
IV
V
VI
VII
VIII
IX
X

I

II

III

IV

V.

VI

VII

VIII

IX

X

I

II

III

IV

V

VI

VII

VIII

IX

X

I

II

III

IV

V

VI

VII

VIII

IX

X